Shepherding God's Flock

A PREACHER'S HANDBOOK ON PASTORAL MINISTRY, COUNSELING, AND LEADERSHIP

3 BOOKS IN ONE

THE PASTORAL LIFE
PASTORAL COUNSELING
PASTORAL LEADERSHIP

JAY E. ADAMS

**PRESBYTERIAN AND
REFORMED PUBLISHING COMPANY**
Box 817
Phillipsburg, New Jersey 08865

Originally published in three separate volumes:
Volume 1, Copyright 1974 by Jay E. Adams
Volume 2, Copyright 1975 by Jay E. Adams
Volume 3, Copyright 1975 by Jay E. Adams

Combination volume issued 1980
by Presbyterian and Reformed Publishing Company
ISBN: 0-87552-058-8

First printing, April 1979
Second printing, February 1980
Third printing, June 1981
Fourth printing, July 1983

PHOTOLITHOPRINTED BY CUSHING - MALLOY, INC.
ANN ARBOR, MICHIGAN, UNITED STATES OF AMERICA

PREFACE

Shepherding God's Flock is an attempt to provide a clearly written textbook that will cover various areas of practical theology (other than preaching) in an exegetically and theologically sound manner. It is my aim to provide practical applications of biblical truth as well. Written in simple English, the series is intended also to help elders and deacons in their endeavors.

Originally I had planned to issue several additional titles in this series and then release them all in a combined volume along with an index. Unfortunately other writing obligations have interfered, causing me to postpone these plans.

The proposal to combine the three existing books in the series into one volume is a happy solution, one that will make the material readily available to interested students, pastors, and laymen.

It is my prayer that the new edition of *Shepherding God's Flock* will be a blessing to many throughout the Great Shepherd's Church.

Jay E. Adams, 1978
Dean of the Institute of Pastoral Studies
Christian Counseling & Educational Center

CONTENTS

PART 1   Pastoral Life

PART 2   Pastoral Counseling

PART 3 Pastoral Leadership

1
THE PASTORAL LIFE

CHAPTER I
THEOLOGY AND PASTORAL WORK

There has been revival of interest in the theology of pastoral activity, particularly among liberal and neo-orthodox writers.[1] While the interest must be welcomed, one cannot refrain from observing that the conclusions reached by beginning with unscriptural views of God and man have been universally unsatisfactory. On the other hand, many conservative writers have all but failed to recognize the implications of theology in writing about pastoral care. Often unwittingly, they have applied themselves to the task with fuzzy or erroneous theological thinking that ends in similarly unacceptable results. Others, attempting to bypass theological and exegetical questions while concentrating upon practical matters, have not fared much better.

The fact of the matter is that it is irresponsible and dangerous to attempt to do practical work apart from a sound theological base. The only proper basis for Christian living and pastoral ministry is biblical and theological. It is incorrect to view any of the theological disciplines totally by itself in an isolated manner; such compartmental thinking often has had very damaging effects upon the church. Ivory towerism on one end of the continuum and activism on the other are equally dangerous. While theological thought must never divorce itself from the questions asked in contemporary society, neither may the practical theologians ignore the biblical and theological answers hammered out by careful exegesis and debate over the centuries.

Because theology and pastoral concerns are frequently indistinguishable in the Scriptures, practical theologians in all that they do must be conscious of the integral relationships between the two.

---

[1]Cf. William Oglesby (ed.), *The New Shape of Pastoral Theology* (Abingdon Press, Nashville and New York: 1969); Josef Goldbrunner, *Realization Anthropology of Pastoral Care* (University of Notre Dame Press, Notre Dame: 1966); Stewart Lawton, *Pastoral Implications of Biblical Theology* (The Seabury Press, New York: 1968); Edward Thurneysen, *A Theology of Pastoral Care* (John Knox Press, Richmond: 1962); Seward Hiltner, *Theological Dynamics.*

Where the Scriptures make a distinguishable demarcation (not separation) between theology and practical living (e.g., Ephesians 1-3/4-6), the biblical emphasis clearly shows that the practical is based upon, grows out of and everywhere is conditioned by the theological (cf. the pivotal "therefore" in Ephesians 4:1).[2]

Practical ministry can never be anything less than the ministry of the *Word*. That Word, understood exegetically and systematically, must permeate and motivate all practical work. The directions that one's practical activities take, the norms by which he operates and the motivation behind what he does must emerge from a biblical theological study of the Scriptures.[3] The pursuit of Practical Theology, therefore, must be seen as the study and application of the biblical means of expressing one's theology.

It is important for the reader to understand my viewpoint and stance concerning this matter, since all of the material that is contained in this book is self-consciously predicated upon the assumption that the Reformation (or Reformed) theology is a correct interpretation of the Word of God. Believing that all doctrine has implications in ministry and life, I would consider the doctrine of the perseverance of the saints (for example) vital to mature Christian living and witness. One's view of the marks and purity of the church will influence the level of relationship that he sustains to ministers in liberal denominations. His understanding of the biblical data on church discipline will control his counseling of persons struggling with problems of divorce. Ministry and life, then, are inseparably intertwined with theology. The pastoral worker, therefore, cannot escape either the need for a theology of pastoral work (ministry) or the implications of theology in all that he does. If the pastor finds that he fails in his everyday dealings with men and women, he should recognize that the source of his problem may not be lack of experience, strategy or skills; in more instances than he may wish to admit, his failures may stem from shoddy or erroneous biblical understanding or theological thinking. Ineffective and harmful approaches to the members of one's congregation and to the community may be quite simply the result of faulty conceptions of both men and God.

---

[2]For a very helpful discussion of the relation that systematic theology bears to practical work, see Benjamin B. Warfield, *The Savior of the World* (Mack Publishing Company, Cherry Hill: 1972), pp. 221-230. Here Warfield is considering "The Indispensableness of Systematic Theology to the Preacher," but the concepts clearly are transferable to pastoral work.

[3]Warfield defines Systematic Theology as "nothing other than the saving truth of God presented in systematic form." *Ibid.,* p. 222.

While in pastoral work one synthesizes and applies the truth acquired by exegesis and theology, set into perspective by church history, he also must acquire that wisdom and those skills which are requisite to the ministry of this truth to men.

Knowledge of the truth is the starting point, but these additional qualities, so essential to pastoral work, can be acquired only by careful guidance in the discovery, development and exercise of one's gifts. This book serves mainly as an aid in pointing the student and the pastor to some of the ways and means by which to make such acquisitions.[4] The art of pastoral work, therefore, involves dedicated ministry to believers in which theologically correct concepts are applied to the conduct of congregational and individual living. One of John's striking phrases that captures this concept in a memorable manner is "walking in the truth" (II John 4; III John 3).

EXERCISES

For the Student

1. Make a biblical study of the relationship of truth to pastoral ministry. Limit your study to the Pastoral Epistles. Submit a two-page paper on any one aspect of the question that intrigues you.

2. Interview four or five pastors of differing theological persuasions, asking each one to tell you how his theological belief concerning any two doctrines (of your own choosing) affects his pastoral activities. If he does not know, probe deeply enough to discover. Perhaps his professed beliefs and his practice are inconsistent. Report to the class on the results of your study.

For the Pastor

1. Examine two or three of your present pastoral practices to see if you could articulate a clear relationship between these and your Scriptural and theological understanding.

---

[4]Much (if not all) of the work in this area must be accompanied by observation and participation. Exercises aimed at facilitating both have been included at points to help both pastors and students. For the latter, there are exercises to be assigned in class. For the former, there are others in which he can engage on his own.

2. Answer specifically: What influence does one's doctrine of the church exert upon his everyday ministerial activities? List the implications of your own beliefs.

CHAPTER II
PASTORAL THEOLOGY

The name "pastoral" is a uniquely Christian term that expresses a fundamental concept that is deeply embedded in every biblical portrayal of Christian ministry. The term refers to a rich scriptural figure that finds its beginning and end in God. He, who is the "Shepherd of Israel" (Psalm 80:1), ultimately demonstrated the meaning of His covenantal love as the Great Shepherd of the sheep by giving His life for them (John 10:11).[1] The figure virtually bursts with significance, far more than didactic statements ever could express. Let us, therefore, try only to capture something of what it meant for David (as a former shepherd) to write:

"The Lord is my Shepherd; I shall not want" (Psalm 23:1),

for in that great declaration lies all that is meant by "Pastoral Work." To help to understand this, reread the sentence this way:

"The Lord is my Pastor; I shall not want" (Psalm 23:1).

The shepherd is the one who provides full and complete care for all of his sheep. Sheep are helpless (Isaiah 53:7), are followers (John 10:3-5), are likely to wander and stray (Isaiah 53:6), but under his care they do not lack.

Psalm 23:1 is what the Greeks have called an enthymeme. An enthymeme is a loose syllogism in which one of the three terms is missing. When David brings the two ideas of God as Shepherd and His sheep not lacking ("wanting") into close juxtaposition, he intends to say that the second fact necessarily follows and flows from the first as a consequence thereof. Stated syllogistically, it would read something like this:

---

[1]Jesus never called Himself bishop, elder or preacher, but He did refer to Himself as Shepherd. The covenantal connection is seen clearly in such passages as Ezekiel 34:31: "You are my flock, the sheep of my pasture, and I am your God." The normal covenantal slogan contains the two elements: "Your God . . . my people." Here, the former is retained while the phrases "my flock" and "the sheep of my pasture" are substituted for the latter. The ideas of the People and the Flock are closely connected in the Scriptures.

The Lord is my Shepherd.
Shepherds meet all of the needs of their flocks.
Therefore: The Lord will meet all of my needs.

But poetry and syllogisms clash. Most beautifully (and cogently) David, the shepherd, says to readers who knew all about the ways of shepherds and sheep:
"The Lord is my Shepherd; [therefore] I shall not lack." The rest of this remarkable Psalm shows something of the ways in which the heavenly Shepherd cares for the needs of His sheep. We may note some of these in passing, for they correspond to the work of the undershepherd in his pastoral ministry.
The Twenty-third Psalm speaks of:

1. *Concern for each individual sheep:* "The Lord is *my* Shepherd." The Good Shepherd "calls them *by name*" (John 10:3), He "knows them" (10:27), and goes out to seek the *"one"* which is lost" (Luke 15:4).

2. *Rest:* "he makes me to lie down." He knows our frame, how much we can handle and what is too much for us and treats us accordingly.

3. *Provision for daily sustenance:* "green pastures . . . still waters" (food and drink).

4. *Refreshment and encouragement* when tired, worn or discouraged: "he restores my soul [poetic for 'me']."

5. *Guidance and leadership:* "he leads [not *drives*] me." Cf. John 10:3, 4: "he . . . leads them out . . . he goes before them." Cf. also Revelation 7:17, and further back, Psalm 80:1, "Shepherd of Israel... who leads Joseph as a flock."

6. *Instruction, training and discipline:* " . . . leads in the paths of righteousness." Cf. II Timothy 3:16: "for training in righteousness."

7. *Provision for goals and motivation:* "for his Name's sake."

8. *Security and protection;* "I will fear no evil . . . your rod and staff protect me." Protection from falling, from attack by wolves without and within. Cf. I Peter 2:25: "The Shepherd and Guardian of your souls," Hebrews 13:17: "your leaders . . . watch over your souls," Acts 20:28-30: "Be on guard . . . for all the flock . . . to shepherd the church of God . . . after my departure savage wolves will come in among you, not

sparing the flock, and from among your own selves," and John 10:11, when the wolf comes, he "lays down his life for the sheep."

9. *Personal fellowship and loving friendship:* "you are with me." Cf. John 10:14, 15: "... I know my own, and my own know me even as the Father knows me and I know the Father." The loving care and concern of the shepherd/sheep relationship reaches its epitome, perhaps in Revelation 7:17, where in comforting words of reassurance God says of potential martyrs that "the Lamb [note how the shepherd and the redemptive covenantal themes here merge to form the otherwise strange concept of a lamb as Shepherd] ... shall be their shepherd and shall guide them to springs of the water of life."

From the wealth of this biblical ore, and much more, the Christian minister defines his work as a pastor. It is his task, in following the Chief and Great Shepherd of the sheep (I Peter 5:4; Hebrews 13:20), to shepherd God's flock so that they do not lack. That is to say, he must meet their every need.[2]

The important list of church office bearers in Ephesians 4:11 describes the Christian minister as a "pastor and teacher" (or perhaps, to convey the Greek text most clearly, a "pastor-teacher").[3]

In this verse the minister's *teaching* is viewed as distinct (but not separate) from his *pastoral* duties. That is to say, the two works are distinguished by the use of two terms but not in such a way that two offices composed of different personnel are in view. Rather they are viewed as two distinct but inseparable functions of one man who occupies one office. Elsewhere the two functions appear as distinguishable works that together constitute the complete task of one man:

Him we proclaim, nouthetically confronting every man (pastoral work) and teaching every man . . . (Colossians 1:28).[4]

Because the work of teaching (a word that is not sharply differentiated from preaching in the New Testament) is distinguishable (although not

---

[2]This means (of course) meeting *needs,* not every *wish or desire.* The Word of God has been given to provide all things necessary to do so. (Cf. II Timothy 3:15-17; Hebrews 13:20-21.) See Jay Adams, *The Christian Counselor's Manual,* pp. 93-95.

[3]There are four occurrences of *tous,* not five: "*Some* apostles, *some* prophets, *some* evangelists and *some* pastors and teachers." If Paul had conceived of the pastor and teacher as separate, he would have distinguished the two by a fifth: "*some* pastors and *some* teachers."

[4]Cf. also I Thessalonians 5:12, 13.

separable) from pastoral work, it is proper to study pastoral work as a distinct discipline, though not in isolation. While always remembering the important relationships that pastoral work and preaching sustain to one another, in this book the former has been given full consideration, while the latter has not. Preaching and teaching, to be sure, constitute a part of the feeding, training and leading ministry of the shepherd and, therefore, in one sense may be viewed as a vital part of *pastoral* activity. Yet, even Paul sees some distinction between ministry as a pastor and ministry as a teacher. Following his lead, therefore, for purposes of study we have distinguished, though not separated, the two.

The Scriptures disclose that in the thinking of the apostles there was the closest possible relationship between the words *poimaino* (to shepherd), *poimen* (a shepherd), *presbuteros* (an elder), *episkopos* (an overseer [bishop]) and *episkopeo* (to oversee).[5] To carry on the work of an overseer *(episkopos,* "bishop") does not mean to do the work of any sort of overseer in general, but in the New Testament it always carries the idea of overseeing *as a shepherd.* It involves the all-embracing oversight required by the descriptions of such work in Psalm 23, John 10 and elsewhere.[6] According to Acts 20:28, the Holy Spirit placed *("etheto,"* i.e., "set," "appointed" or "ordained") the elders (v. 17) to be "overseers" *(episkopous)* "among" (or "in"; Greek *en*) "the flock" (v. 28). As overseers, their function and duty was "to shepherd" *(poimainein)* the church of God. That *poimaino* here does not refer to the more restricted idea of "feeding" alone, but rather to the complete care of the congregation (including feeding), is plain from the duties delineated, one of which is shepherdly protection from false teachers (cf. vv. 29, 30).

Peter, whose ministry was restored in shepherding terms (John 21:15-19) never forgot those words, as his writings indicate. In I Peter 2:25, he refers to the Lord Jesus as "the Shepherd *(poimena)* and Overseer *(episkopon)* of our souls." Here the *kai* ("and") may be epexegetical, making the latter phrase explanatory of the first: "the Shepherd, even the Overseer of our souls." At any rate, the closeness of the concepts of shepherding and

---

[5]Titus 1:5, 7 and Acts 20:17, 28 indicate that the words *episkopos* and *presbuteros* are used almost interchangeably to refer to the same man. Clearly they do not constitute two separate offices. The same man when viewed as to his character and qualifications is called *presbuteros* ("elder" or "mature"), but with reference to his work *episkopos* ("overseer").

[6]It is most interesting to note that in the Old Testament theocracy, kings were called shepherds (Zechariah 10:2,3; 11:15-17; Ezekiel 34; Isaiah 63:11, 12; Psalm 78:70-72. Cyrus too is called God's shepherd: Isaiah 44:28, since God in His providence raised him up to a work of caring for His people). Rule that involves loving care in its oversight was required of the monarch.

overseeing in Peter seems to indicate a generally apostolic, not merely Pauline connection.[7]

Peter similarly links shepherding and oversight in another place (I Peter 5:1-2). He exhorts his fellow presbyters (calling himself a *sumpresbuteros)* to "shepherd *(poimanate)* the flock of God among you, overseeing *(episkopountes)* not by constraint. . . ."

Thus it seems that the overseeing of the flock, as flock (congregation) and as individual sheep, is the fundamental notion in *pastoral* work as distinguished from *teaching.* It is that oversight of congregation and member to which we shall address ourselves in this book. The work to which the Christian minister is called therefore is essentially *pastoral.* [8] To some consideration of that all-embracing task we shall now turn.

EXERCISES

For the Student

1. Make a thorough study of the scriptural idea of shepherding, using those passages that have been mentioned in this chapter as a foundation.

2. Choose one facet of shepherding (e.g., protection of the flock from wolves) and develop a biblical study of the concept. Be prepared to report your findings to the class.

For the Pastor

Consider the needs of your flock. Using the elements of shepherding distinguished in this chapter:

1. Determine the three greatest needs in your congregation (list).

_____

_____

_____

---

[7]Cf. also Hebrews 13:17, 20.

[8]Historically, Zwingli's book, *The Shepherd,* had much to do with the emergence of the modern usage of the word pastor in Protestant circles. In the 1700's the word *poimenics* began to appear as a term used to refer to the study of shepherding.

2. Analyze what you are doing to meet them.

_____

_____

_____

_____

_____

_____

_____

3. Lay out a program of pastoral activity and preaching for the next year calculated to help to bring about the desired effects. Make a special effort to fill in any apparent gaps.

_____

_____

_____

_____

_____

_____

_____

_____

_____

_____

_____

_____

SECTION ONE

THE SHEPHERD LIFE

CHAPTER III
COUNTING THE COST

When Jesus spoke of ministering discipleship, He warned against failure to count the cost (Luke 14:25-33). It has become far too fashionable for men to move in and out of the ministry at will with (it would seem) little or no consideration for this matter. While those who discover that they wrongly have sought ordination to the gospel ministry clearly do the right thing when they publicly declare this to be so and demit the ministry, there are many who long continue in a kind of ecclesiastical no-man's land. Many ministers may find it necessary to make tents for a while—that is not what is in mind; indeed, the tent-making periods may be part of the cost. What is in view is that (increasingly?) there are large numbers of men who, without demitting the ministry, do not exercise the gifts and calling of the pastoral ministry, sometimes for years. There is every reason to believe that many of these men should fish or cut bait!

Moreover, among those who continue in the work of the pastorate, often there is too much looking back after having placed the hand on the plow. No wonder that the furrows in many congregations look so erratic.

At the outset, preferably before or at least during his seminary days, the potential minister of the gospel should reach some solid decisions based at least in part upon a counting of the cost. Part of the present problem, doubtless, stems from idealistic or anachronistic notions of what shepherding (or pastoral ministry) is like. As the biblical data plainly show, the task never was easy. But if ever the compounding of normal and cultural difficulties were at a peak, that time is now. At no other time in American history has popular respect for the church and its leadership dropped to such a low point. On the other hand, perhaps at no previous period have the demands that are made upon ministers been greater. This combination of factors does not make the pastoral ministry either an easy or inviting life calling. It takes more than the work itself to attract and hold men. And when you couple to these considerations the facts of meager pay,[1] lack of

---

[1]Chester Veldstra reveals some of the hardships in a pointed letter printed in *The Banner*, July 4, 1969, pp. 20, 21.

appreciation and an abundance of thoughtless criticism, the sum total of all is an unappealing picture.

Truly any man entering the ministry today must sweep aside all idealistic or romantic notions. That necessity, however, can be an advantage. It forces one to face the realities and to count the cost. Throughout this book, I have made a conscious attempt to use the camera and the tape recorder rather than to paint impressionistically. That means that there has been no desire to mask the many occasions for disappointment and discouragement that arise. Indeed, I have tried to assess honestly the injustices, the financial hardships, the gossip, the frustrations, and the risks that many men have allowed to drive them away from the pastorate. It was not without cause that the apostle realistically invited young Timothy to "suffer hardship with him" in the work of the ministry (II Timothy 2:3). Yet at the same time I have always tried to suggest biblical ways and means of overcoming each of these. Every man entering the pastoral ministry should become apprised of the hard facts. In no other way can he count the cost, meet the problems for what they are and (hopefully) leave matters for the next man in a new and better shape.

By no means should a grimly realistic picture turn aside good men—men truly called by the Spirit of God (at least Paul did not seem to think so in writing to Timothy). Such men recognize in the difficulties themselves the essence of the pastoral challenge. They see the pastorate as a vital place to use their God-given gifts to serve the living Christ precisely *because* of its needs and opportunities.

When Jesus spoke of the gospel ministry, he too spoke both in terms of its liabilities and its assets. His words were:

> Truly I say to you, there is no one who has left house or wife or brothers or parents or children, for the sake of the kingdom of God, who shall not receive many times as much at this time, and in the age to come, eternal life (Luke 18:29-30).

Mark adds a note or two:

> . . . for My sake and for the gospel's sake, but that he shall receive a hundred times as much now in the present age houses and brothers and sisters and mothers and children and farms, along with persecutions (Mark 10:29, 30).

Those are realistic words; they face the facts squarely. There will be separation from loved ones and from property. And there will be persecution too. Yet, in the midst of the loss and trials, God in His own time and way promises to provide not only the rewards of the age to come, but *now* ("in this present age") many times over (or, with Mark, a hundred times as much) new brothers and sisters and family in Christ; and farms and houses as well.[2]

Usually the ministry involves separation from loved ones in time and space. Even when one's family lives within easy commuting distance, it is difficult to maintain contact. In most other professions, weekends are free and allow for visits and travel. When the pastor's children reach school age, he finds that weekday visitation is curtailed and weekends, of course, are tied up because of his usual regular weekend obligations at the church. The pastoral candidate, therefore, in counting the cost must reckon with the likelihood of meeting this problem.

It is not always easy to be faithful to one's call, particularly when he finds on the one hand more than enough occasions for discouragement and on the other, the normal pulls of relatives who (perhaps not understanding his problem, his motives or the heartaches involved) think that his failure to spend more time with them stems from willful neglect, lack of concern or selfishness. To maintain good family relationships, while remaining faithful to God and His work, can be extremely difficult. Add to this the sorts of problems that can grow from thoughtless or malicious accusations against a pastor's wife as the supposed cause of separation from relatives; and the subsequent strains upon relationships that possibly might grow out of these, and you have in one kettle all of the ingredients for a rather nasty stew. Yet often it is through learning how to please God in such thorny situations as these which lie at the heart of his own family situation that the faithful pastor who does not succumb to the temptation to throw it all overboard is stretched to fit the role of shepherd. It is often at this level that he discovers that God, in His providence, is at work in his life to "comfort (or as the word probably means, "counsel") him" in all his affliction so that he "may be able to counsel those who are in any affliction" with the same counsel (II Corinthians 1:4).

Observation of fledgling ministers during a ten-year period of teaching at Westminster Theological Seminary confirms the double fact that: (1) many of the finest men who go into the ministry have been matured beyond their

---

[2]Throughout my experience in several pastorates, I can testify to the faithfulness of God to fulfil this promise by providing for my needs and those of my wife and family. When time and space removed us from the close ties of blood relationships, God always provided the needed love, counsel and friendships in others who took their place. Incidentally, He provided also (in the other direction) sons and daughters for the parents left behind.

years by personal difficulty, struggle, loss and sorrow. Such struggles often take place in pre-seminary or seminary years; but perhaps equally as many men experience them during their first pastorate; (2) the men who prove to be most useful and successful in ministering the Word of God to others usually are those who have been through personal trials. There are exceptions, of course; God is not subject to our generalizations. But by and large what Paul found to be true, men preparing for the work of the pastorate today will discover, holds true for them as well. And one of the areas in which they often first will feel the impact of the unconditional call of Christ upon their lives will be in the severance of personal ties and the loss of private advantage. At times they may find themselves repeating Peter's words: "We have left our own things and followed You" (Luke 18:28). At such moments they will be sustained by recalling the promise that Christ graciously made in reply.

It is tragic to see and hear of young ministers who, having run afoul of this or some other trying situation by which they more fully could become prepared to minister meaningfully to the needs of others (James 1:3, 4), instead desert the ministry. Often before God allows a man to preach from a text like I Corinthians 10:13, he enables him to learn its meaning not only from the Greek text, not merely from the *New International Commentary,* but also from the textbook of personal experience.

Counting the cost requires a full recognition of the personal disadvantages (and assets), but it also involves taking stock of the heavy responsibilities involved in pastoral work. Such passages as the following, while stressing various aspects of the responsibility, all point in the same direction.

(1) I Thessalonians 5:12,13: "Appreciate those who diligently labor among you, and have charge over you in the Lord and nouthetically confront (counsel) you, and esteem them very highly in love because of their work."

(2) Hebrews 13:7: "Remember those who led you, who spoke the word of God to you; and considering the outcome of their way of life, imitate their faith."

(3) Hebrews 13:17: "Obey your leaders and submit to them; for they keep watch over your souls, as those who will give an account."

(4) James 3:1: "Let not many of you become teachers, my brethren, knowing that as such we shall incur a stricter judgment."

Solemnity, as well as warning, is conveyed by these verses. The work of caring for God's flock may not be undertaken "under compulsion, but voluntarily, according to the will of God . . . with eagerness [and only by those who prove] to be examples to the flock" (I Peter 5:2, 3). Yet, if God has given the gifts and called the man, He expects nothing less than the humble eagerness that alone can strike the proper balance needed to carry one through the stresses and strains of the work. One must place confidence not in himself, but in God. Yet he must not allow anyone to despise his youth (I Timothy 4:12); he must not be timid, but must exercise power, love and discipline through the Spirit (II Timothy 1:7), and must be able to correct those who oppose the truth without becoming quarrelsome (II Timothy 2:25; Titus 1:9, 10).

Aware of the problems, properly chastened by the Word and God's providence, a man must examine his call to the ministry soberly and then enthusiastically enter into the work with willingness and caution.

I do not propose to discuss the call to the ministry. Edmund P. Clowney, president of Westminster Theological Seminary, in *Called to the Ministry,* which is a very helpful discussion of this subject, has correlated all relevant scriptural passages and presented forthrightly to anyone who wishes to do so how he may test his gifts and call.[3] All that I propose to do at this place is to issue the invitation to good men, blessed with outstanding gifts from God, to consider whether they may not be called by God to this fearful and exacting work which at once affords both the least and the most rewards.

In the Scriptures, the biblical qualifications for an elder are set forth explicitly in two places:

(1) I Timothy 3:1-7: "It is a trustworthy statement; if any man aspires to the office of overseer, it is a fine work he desires to do. An overseer, then, must be above reproach, the husband of one wife, temperate, prudent, respectable, hospitable, able to teach, not addicted to wine or pugnacious, but gentle, uncontentious, free from the love of money. He must be one who manages his own household well, keeping his children under control with all dignity (but if a man does not know how to manage his own household, how will he take care of the church of God?); and not a new convert, lest he become conceited and fall into the condemnation incurred by the devil. And he must have a good reputation with those outside the church, so that he may not fall into reproach and the snare of the devil."

---

[3]Edmund P. Clowney, *Called to the Ministry* (Philadelphia, Westminster Theological Seminary: 1964).

(2) Titus 1:5-9: "For this reason I left you in Crete, that you might set in order what remains, and appoint elders in every city as I directed you, namely, if any man be above reproach, the husband of one wife, having children who believe, not accused of dissipation or rebellion. For the overseer must be above reproach as God's steward, not self-willed, not quick-tempered, not addicted to wine, not pugnacious, not fond of sordid gain, but hospitable, loving what is good, sensible, just, devout, self-controlled, holding fast the faithful word which is in accordance with the teaching, that he may be able both to exhort in sound doctrine and to refute those who contradict."

Men who qualify for the work of ministry are men who can keep the gospel torch burning brightly, so that they are able to pass it on (undimmed) to those who follow (II Timothy 1:12, 14; 2:2). In the last passage mentioned, Paul says that the gospel deposit[4] must be placed in the hands of

(1) "faithful men," i.e., men of faith who will be faithful to the charge committed to them;

(2) men "who will be able to teach others also."

The word *hikanos* ("able") in II Timothy 2:2 means "sufficient for a task" or "able to do a job." The people that Paul has in mind are men who "have what it takes" (from God) to do the work of the ministry. They are men with the gifts who have learned to use them skillfully in the work of shepherding (cf. Psalm 78:72, Berkeley). While every such man with Paul will exclaim, "Who is adequate for these things?" (II Corinthians 2:16), he must be one who is able to declare with equal honesty and conviction, "Our adequacy is from God, who also made us adequate"[5] (3:5, 6).

Let us turn, then, to some of the abilities and skills that help a man under God to accomplish the work of the pastoral ministry himself and that enable him to pass on what he has learned to others who will follow.

---

[4]Verse 12b reads literally, "I am convinced that he is able to guard *my deposit* until that day" [emphasis mine]. The "deposit" may mean (grammatically) "what *I* have deposited with Him" or "what *He* has deposited with me," but in the light of v. 14 and chapter 2:2, which form the immediate context, doubtless it is the latter that Paul had in mind. What God deposited with Paul was transmitted to Timothy, who in turn was to deposit it with faithful men who would be able to pass the deposit on to others also.

[5]In II Corinthians 2:16; 3:5, 6, the word translated "adequate" is also *hikanos* .

EXERCISES

For the Student

1. What are my motives before God in preparing for pastoral ministry?

2. How do I evaluate the cost in my life? (personalize your response)

Assets	Liabilities

For the Pastor

1. Am I growing weary in well-doing? If so, what may be the cause?

2. What does God expect me to do if my youthful high ideals have changed?

   a. To evaluate this, use the student's exercise above and answer it as you think you would have when you were preparing for the ministry.

   b. Then reflect upon these answers to see if they still hold true to-day.

   c. Ask, how have my ideas of the ministry changed?

   Are these changes more mature, more realistic, more biblical or not?

CHAPTER IV
AREAS OF ADEQUACY

Educational and Intellectual

I shall not begin with the minister's personal relationship to Christ simply because in what has been said already that emphasis has been uppermost. More must be said about particular aspects of this at later points. Moreover, the divisions of thought now to be considered are, in a final sense, artificial. One's intellectual and educational stance cannot be divorced from his physical, let us say. Moreover, the educational side and the physical side are both aspects of his relationship to Christ. Not some, but *all* matters are spiritual. While there may be a part of one's life and work that can be called "most holy," *all* of life for the Christian, to the very last item, is to be holy to the Lord. Physical exercise, diet and the general concerns of the body must not be considered to be secular concerns. The use and care of the body is a moral matter; by abusing his body, a Christian abuses nothing less than the temple of the Holy Spirit (1 Corinthians 6:19). The issue is momentous: desecration of the house of the living God! As Paul put it, "The body is . . . for the Lord, and the Lord for the body" (1 Corinthians 6:13).

Since the office of pastor/teacher requires teaching (formal and informal), wise understanding and application of God's truth and ability to communicate the same, the educational and intellectual side of ministerial training in most instances is vital. While it is true that God loves to use weak vessels powerfully to show that the power is of Him, nevertheless He never discourages intellectual preparation so long as it is dedicated in submissive fervor to Him. The Bible is not an anti-intellectual Book.[1]

---

[1] To begin with, Christianity, like Old Testament Judaism, is a religion of a Book. Wherever Christianity has spread, therefore, it has furthered literacy in order to enable men to read and assimilate God's truth. Most of the writers of the Bible were literary experts. Psalm 23, 1 Corinthians 13, the poetry of the prophets, the beauty of expression in all of Luke's writings, the acrostic patterns, the parables, etc., are just a few reminders of the excellence of literary *form* in which God's revelation has been given. There is no anti-intellectualism in any of this. There is an artful simplicity and clarity in it all; but surely no one can fail to see the *art*. The writers were not sloppy; the book of Revelation, for example, was carefully constructed according to

In a day in which college preparation is becoming the norm and good speech on television and radio is commonplace, a minister cannot afford to be careless in his intellectual preparation. Always, in days past, God's servants—even if not *formally* trained (as Moses, Daniel, Paul, Luke and others were)—attained heights of verbal and written expression matching or normally surpassing the standards of the day. God's servants, who proclaim the matchless message of saving grace in Christ, can do no less today.[2] The message must be neither distorted nor obscured by the vehicle in which it is conveyed. While the New Testament was written in *koine* ("common" or fishmarket) Greek, the content raised the level of expression to what might be called a heightened *koine*.[3] Language, knowledge, approach and the general demeanor of the minister of Jesus Christ must always at least approximate the *koine* level of his day and then rise to a level beyond to which Christian content and activity should push it. Plainly, the educational and intellectual side of the minister (at minimum, therefore) in almost every case ought to be a cut above the modern *koine* .

The qualifications in I Timothy 3 and Titus 1 contain intellectual and educational elements: "able to teach (cf. II Timothy 2:24), holding fast the faithful word which is in accordance with the teaching, able both to exhort in sound doctrine and to refute those who contradict." He must be able to "speak and exhort and reprove with all authority" (Titus 2:15; cf. II Timothy 3:16; 4:2). As a "good servant of Christ Jesus," he must be "nourished on the words of faith and of sound doctrine" (I Timothy 4:6).

---

an outline divinely given (1:19). This was fleshed out in splendid forms built around the number seven. Surely the book was not the product of one who cared only for content and thought nothing of form. In a day of limited literacy, God's servants not only were literate men, but capable (for the most part) of speaking and writing in striking and memorable ways. Wherever Christianity went, it brought a concern for literacy and education precisely because it was a religion of a written revelation. It is evident that God puts no premium upon ignorance, carelessness or lack of form.

[2]This discussion is not a plea for a return to artificial forms of oratory replete with declamation and ministerial drones and tunes—precisely not that. Rather, the call is for the intellectual effort and acquisition of skills capable of presenting the message of Christ without obscurity in a vehicle that will not call attention to itself either by its awkwardness or inappropriateness, and thus divert attention from the truth that one seeks to proclaim. Cf. Jay Adams, *Pulpit Speech* (Presbyterian and Reformed Publishing Company, Nutley: 1971), pp.65ff., for a discussion of I Corinthians 2 in regard to this matter. Note also pp. 119ff. Moses was trained in all the learning of Egypt, Daniel at Babylon, Paul studied under Gamaliel and possibly in the world's second or third greatest university at Tarsus.(He quotes Cleanthes and Aratus; Lightfoot was convinced that he knew the writings of Seneca. Cf. also Acts 26:24.)

[3]To this fact must be added the consideration that the American educational *koine* today far surpasses the *koine* of previous generations. The educational preparation of the past, therefore, will not suffice but must be exceeded in our day.

He is to "take pains" with and to be "absorbed in" the things listed in that chapter, including "exhortation and teaching." He is to grow evidently in these skills and in this knowledge so that his "progress may be evident to all." While all of this intellectual activity is clearly set forth in the pastoral epistles in pastoral terms (education on fire and used in ministry) it is, nonetheless, intellectual activity involving much time, care and energy in intellectual (not intellectualizing[4]) pursuits. The minister of Christ, according to such passages, must be capable intellectually (as well as experientially) to assimilate and communicate God's truth effectively.

Physical

While physical skills and abilities are not essential for the work of the ministry, a body capable of withstanding the rigors of the work most certainly is. Sleepless nights, long hard days, emotionally tense and draining sessions all soon take their toll. To sustain such a vigorous and exhaustive pace as the ministry requires, one must develop both the concern and ability to care for his physical welfare and a body that has been disciplined and trained to meet the demands. Health helps in the ministry. It is true that, as Schmidt says, John Calvin did not enjoy good health:

> His circulation was out of order. He suffered from hemorrhoids complicated by ulcers. His toes were swollen by gout. Chronic rheumatism forced him to hobble about dragging his right leg. He became at times transfixed by piercing pains due to stones in the kidneys. He had difficulty in breathing. He spat blood. He was regularly shaken by spasms of fever. But he would not tolerate any interruption to the work of his ministry.[5]

But three facts must be noted about Calvin. (1) He must have had an extraordinarily tough constitution to be able to press on toward his many achievements under such formidable organic disabilities; (2) he had help—assistants, secretaries, etc.; (3) he cared for his body and took measures to preserve what physical abilities he possessed.

While God can use anyone with any sort of body to achieve His purposes, ordinarily for the sustained steady labor of the pastorate, the work to which He calls His servant requires a strong, healthy, well-disciplined body.[6] At the very least, one must agree that the minister, who is to be an

---

[4]I.e., entering into intellectual pursuits for their own sake.

[5]Schmidt, Albert-Marie, *Calvin and the Calvinistic Tradition* (Harper and Brothers, N. Y.: 1960), pp. 71-72.

[6]Cf. I Corinthians 9:27: "But I discipline my body and make it serve me, so that, while I am preaching to others, I myself may not be disqualified" (Berkeley).

example in all things, must lead his flock in demonstrating how to care for the temple of the Holy Spirit. Whatever his body's condition, with all its limitations, his task is to hone it to its sharpest edge, making it capable of becoming as effective an instrument in the hand of God as that body can be.

Among other things, good eating and sleeping habits as well as other health concerns should play controlling roles in both the planning and execution of scheduling and routine activities. Adequate (not excessive) sleep is essential. Significant sleep loss can cause irritability, suspicion and, when excessive, even every effect of LSD. Nothing should need to be said of the importance of maintaining an unoffending bodily and physical appearance. Yet there are ministers who reek of B.O.; others have such foul breath that one could not speak with them for five minutes straight. Some look so shoddy or unkempt most of the time that members of the congregation are ashamed to introduce them to a friend.

In short, since a man is a *whole* man (you accidentally hit your thumb with a hammer and it affects all that you do; even a slight fever can change one's entire outlook), the pastor must not neglect the body,[7] but rather will recognize that it is in the flesh and through the body that he has been called to carry out the work of the ministry. Worn, unalert bodies hinder ministers in their preaching and ministerial duties. Since the man is a whole man, it could not be otherwise. Of course, the psychosomatic factor cuts both ways. To care for the body means also to refrain from worry, bitterness, resentment, fear and whatever sinfully-expressed bodily emotions may harm the body by causing ulcers, colitis, depression, paralysis, and a host of other maladies. The process is reciprocal: worry leads to ulcers, ulcers may become the occasion for more worry or fear, which leads to more ulcers, *ad infinitum*.

On the other hand, the seminarian or young minister must not be surprised if the share of physical suffering, heartaches and temptation that he experiences seems disproportionate to that of others. God often subjects His choice servants to trials to ripen, sweeten and thus better prepare them for ministry (remember II Corinthians 1:14). The road to ministry runs through the valleys of trial and affliction. It is not an easy way; Christ has not promised anything more than tribulation and persecution from without. But from within, He has promised happiness, peace and comfort with "all joy." Not all bodily affliction can be averted (as the book of Job and John 9:1-3 make clear), but to the extent to which he is responsible for its physical welfare, the pastor must care for his body.

---

[7]Christianity uniquely teaches the redemption and resurrection of the body. Unlike Greek thought, Christians respect the body. This position demands bodily care and concern.

EXERCISES

For the Student

1. What, intellectually and physically, are your present capabilities?

2. Are they adequate for the work of pastoral ministry?

3. What does God want you to do to become better suited for His work?

For the Pastor

1. Have you continued to assess your capabilities?

   a. How have you grown?

   b. In what areas?

   c. Where is growth most needed?

2. Are you injuring your body in any way? If so, what does God want you to do about the problem?

3. Are you as capable in communication as the local T.V. announcer? Can you be? How?

CHAPTER V
FIVE VITAL FACTORS

Personal Relationship To God

While fixing the shoes of others, the shoemaker's own soles may wear through. Physician heal yourself! It is so easy for the minister, in spite of Paul's warning (I Timothy 4:14-16), in becoming a servant to the flock, to neglect himself. This may be remedied by continually remembering that he must glorify God and by recognizing that there is a proper self-concern that ultimately is for the benefit of the whole congregation. At the bottom of all problems of preaching and pastoral effort, there is always one basic deficiency: the deficiencies of the pastor/teacher himself. Our churches will hear better preaching only when it is done by better preachers; the congregation will receive better shepherding only when it is done by better shepherds. How vital it is not only for his own sake, but for everyone else as well, for a pastor to cultivate and sustain a vital relationship with God.

One great temptation, for instance, is for the minister to read the Scriptures only in terms of sermons and ministry. Since he must preach to others, counsel with others, and in a dozen different ways minister from the Book to someone else, it is not hard for the minister to neglect the sort of reading that is calculated to penetrate his own heart and affect his life. Couple with that the problem that the seminary graduate faces every time that he studies a passage of Scripture: how can he read the English Bible "devotionally" when he wonders what the Greek or Hebrew and the commentaries have to say about the passage? If he does not reach for his study aids, he is troubled; if he does, he has ceased to worship. What is the way out of the dilemma?

One answer that has commended itself to many men is to stop divorcing personal "devotions" (as they are usually called) from study. Instead, the minister must develop the new practice of *studying devotionally.* When he studies for his sermons, in his general reading, or whatever the occasion may be, he will study *first* with the aim of personal application leading to personal worship and prayer. Thus, the meaning of a Greek verb tense understood for the first time may lead to praise and thanksgiving or perhaps conviction of sin and confession. The recognition of the core thought and purpose of a parable that heretofore remained a mystery may occasion a burst of song. Such study, that snags the life of the man as he works, that buffets and refines and shapes the student, eventuates in a different sort of preaching and teaching of the Scriptures. The man who studies first with his own relationship to God in view is a man who will preach more vitally to the lives of others. A scholarship on fire will release one from the perplexing burden of trying to balance items on two ends of a continuum that never should have been spun apart in the first place. It will wash out the coldly academic and yet as assiduously avoid the shallow contentless experiential.

To make the change and acquire the new habits may take a while. Nevertheless, the pastor who perseveres will be glad that he did.

Evangelism

"Do the work of an evangelist" (II Timothy 4:5), Paul wrote to young Timothy. The pastoral ministry, as such, is not basically evangelistic in orientation. The man who as a life calling has been given the two enormous tasks of pastoring and teaching God's flock cannot, *as a life calling,* also do the work of an evangelist. This is so particularly in those situations where, because the congregation fails to exert its proper witness in the community, the pastor tries (hopelessly spreading himself too thin to do anything well) to do the work of evangelism that God has committed to his whole congregation. That is precisely not what Paul had in mind. The pastor/teacher *as such* is called to the work of shepherding and feeding the flock of God. As pastor/teacher, he is not called to evangelize.

It is not shepherds, but sheep that make more sheep. Shepherds care for them. It is the job of a pastor/teacher to equip, train and feed the flock. But *as one of the sheep* of God which he is too, he also must evangelize; and *as an example to the flock* he is to take the lead in evangelizing.[1] But he *cannot,* and *must* not attempt to, do the evangelistic work of the congregation for them. He, as one man limited in time, space and energy, cannot be where they are with all of the opportunities that are afforded to each one of them alone. Indeed, as he serves as a teaching model of the evangelist and as he concentrates on helping to equip all of the saints for their work of

---

[1]Cf. I Timothy 4:12; II Timothy 3:10, 11; Titus 2:7. How else can he train them properly in evangelism? Since biblical training is to be done by discipling (modeling, apprenticeship), he must be the prime model for his congregation. The James Kennedy method for "evangelism explosion" has demonstrated the modeling method, cf. *The Big Umbrella,* pp. 249-265. If God requires a minister to be a soul–winner personally and as an example, how can a presbytery (1) fail to inquire into whether God has used a ministerial candidate to win souls and (2) ordain him if he has not yet been so used?

ministry (Ephesians 4:11, 12) as God intended, ultimately more evangelistic activity will take place than he possibly could engage in on his own. In addition, the blessings of participation and personal growth for each member of the congregation that this will bring will be incalculable.

Yet, while we place a strong emphasis upon this important truth that the pastor/teacher is *called* not to the work of evangelism, but rather to pastoring and teaching in such a way that he encourages and equips the whole flock to participate in evangelism, an equally strong warning must be issued. It is altogether possible for a pastor to become so encased in the Christian bubble, spending virtually all of his waking hours either in the study or with Christian people, that he fails to evangelize at all. The only final answer to this, in some cases, is for him (1) *as an example* to commit himself to the task of taking others with him to train them in evangelistic approaches, and (2) *as an individual* prayerfully to build into his schedule time to witness and to seize occasions ripe for witnessing. Both extremes must be avoided. More must be said about evangelism in the local church at a later place.

Prayer

In this one word the simplest, yet probably the most difficult, part of pastoral work is identified. Prayer is not a problem to describe; there is no end to the books written on the subject. The real difficulty for the pastor, to put it simply, is to pray well. He must recognize that prayer is not merely a personal matter but is a part of the pastoral task to which he has been called (Acts 6:4). He must pray not only personally, but also with and for the members of his congregation. Prayer, then, is work, work that in order to do well he must take the *time* to do and for which he must develop the *self-discipline*. The control of time and self-discipline are crucial elements in effective pastoral work, and much more needs to be said about both later on. Scheduling must be conjoined as a means to accomplishing both objectives.

It takes time to pray. When the apostles recognized that other matters crowding in had begun to hamper them so that they did not have the time to pray as well as to engage in other essential aspects of the work to which God had called them, they took the matter into hand and *made time for prayer*. They assigned unessential matters to another group (deacons), whose office was created for this very purpose. They declared: "We will devote ourselves to the ministry of the Word and to prayer" (Acts 6:4). The point of this passage is twofold:

1.   Other matters must never be allowed to supersede the essentials.

2. To find time for the essentials, unessential aspects of the work must be delegated to others.

Apart from a strict adherence to these two vital principles, every minister soon will discover that not only his prayer life, but also his ministry as a whole will begin to slide downhill. Time for unhurried prayer and meditation about what one is doing in the light of the Scriptures, as well as prayer for the success of the ministry of the Word among the members of the flock, is nothing less than an *essential* for the pastor. He must find, reserve and zealously guard time for pastoral prayer; otherwise such time will slip away.

Cultivation of the Mind

In the daily work of the pastorate, it is easy for one to dry up, unless he works at keeping the mind green. There are men who have learned the ways and means of self-discipline so well that they are able to keep on top of what is happening on their own. Most pastors, however, even those who are well-disciplined in other ways, will find a program that goes beyond self-disciplined study stimulating and rewarding in many ways.[2] The following fourfold program suggests one way in which a number of successful pastors have discovered that they can keep growing.

1. *Set aside mornings for self-directed, self-disciplined study.*

The minister must be characterized as a man of the Book and of study in general. True to the image of a good student, the Apostle Paul (though recognizing that his death was imminent) requested Timothy to bring his books to him in prison (II Timothy 4:13). He kept his mind alive—by study—until the end.

The morning factor is an important consideration, although not an inflexible one. In emergency (e.g., crisis counseling) situations—those that cannot wait until a scheduled time—afternoon study might be substituted. Yet, as a rule, mornings and early afternoons are the best time for study since:

(a) Visitation (other than hospital visitation) cannot be carried on in the morning or early afternoon.

---

[2]Going beyond self-directed and self-disciplined study by no means excludes it. Indeed, it is only the man who is regularly involved in the former who can reap the real benefits from more formal work. Yet, even for the self-directed man, Proverbs points out the need to strike one's thoughts against those of another: Proverbs 27:17. This sharpens the otherwise dulling and rusting metal of one's mind.

(b) It is wise to fill the mind with considerations for the day about which one can meditate during activities (like driving) that do not preclude such thought during the rest of the day.

(c) Regular scheduling of study can be made known to the members of the congregation, thus enabling the pastor to pare to the minimum unnecessary telephone calls and other interruptions. If, after all else has been tried (unsuccessfully), one finds that there is no other way to secure the privacy of his study time, he may (1) refuse to answer the phone; (2) have all calls screened (good procedure when possible under any circumstances); or (3) study in a local seminary or college library every morning for a month or two (probably it is wise to spend at least one day each week in another library anyway if only to check out magazines and other periodicals and to gain knowledge of and access to the books on the new acquisition shelf).

(d) Most productive thought is possible during this period. Oswald writes: "First thing in the morning and late in the evening, you are less efficient than around midday. . . performance steadily improved as the middle of the day drew near, to decline again with the approach of evening."[3]

During the morning study hours, sermon preparation, general reading, necessary correspondence (it is wise to learn to answer all letters on one side of one page[4]), prayer, organizing tasks and other such activities can be carried on. By far, the amount of time spent in study, and in particular in the study of the Word, ought to outstrip the time devoted to anything else.

One cannot regulate the time he spends without a schedule. It is wise, therefore, to schedule how much of the morning (mornings last at least until one o'clock lunch!) he will devote to what and to adhere to this assiduously.[5] It is only by such well-disciplined procedures that one can accomplish *all* of the necessary tasks that the pastorate requires.

2. *Take formal courses of study regularly.*

There is no better way in which to force oneself to disciplined study and

---

[3]Ian Oswald, *Sleep* (Penguin Books, Middlesex: 1972), pp. 12, 13.

[4]If Oswald is correct (see previous footnote), it is probably wise to devote the opening of the day's activity to routine correspondence. In this way the more valuable later hours can be devoted exclusively to study. Getting the correspondence attended to also frees the mind for study. Perhaps it helps to get it moving for such work as well.

[5]If necessary, set an alarm clock to denote beginning and end of allotted periods of time.

thought of material beyond the scope of one's own narrow interests and limitations. If a pastor takes at least one college or seminary course or its equivalent each year, he will quickly discover the values of doing so. A refresher course in Hebrew or Greek may be just what he needs to challenge and encourage him to interpret the Scriptures more faithfully. A course in English literature or the history of ideas or in philosophy may push him to analyze afresh the culture and milieu within which he ministers the Word. Whatever resources lie at hand always ought to be exploited. If there is no seminary or university nearby, a local friendly physician may alert him to and acquire access for him to attend medical lectures offered in the area. Some of these can be stimulating and valuable to him in his work of counseling.[6]

To attend the lectures of a man with whom one differs, or whose subject area is far removed from the scope of one's regular study interests, provides intellectual stimulation of a sort that might not occur otherwise. Such study ought to drive the pastor back to the Scriptures to grapple biblically with the fresh ideas and errors that he has confronted. In doing so, he himself will stay alive intellectually, his mind will not atrophy, and ultimately he will become a more thorough student of the Word. The *last* thing that he must do, however, is to incorporate into his thought and his sermons such information either by adopting or adapting it in an uncritical and eclectic fashion. Everything must be evaluated from a biblical stance. Therein lies the true value of such continued personal other-directed study.

3. *Teach something somewhere regularly.*

Whether it is in a Bible class, prayer meeting, a local Bible institute or a night adult course at the high school, teach! The discipline of organizing lectures, seminars and other classroom presentations is necessary and invaluable. Too much of the modern minister's thought (and consequently, preaching) is fragmented and piecemeal. The work of preparing a course (with its goals, scope, number of class periods, subjects to be treated, in what order, etc.) compels the teacher to think in systematic terms of the relationships of parts to the whole. It forces him to make essential generalizations, to spot themes, and to place emphases where they are

---

[6]Incidentally, the medical library of the local hospital contains a wealth of information useful to pastors that is sometimes not readily available elsewhere. It is frequently surprising what can be found in local lending libraries. One of the first assignments that a minister arriving in a new community should give himself is to discover where all of the local library resources may be found and what is the character of each. By the way, other ministers' libraries may contain valuable resources. Diligence in returning books on time will make many more available.

needed. The classroom drives the teacher to research and orderly composition. The give-and-take atmosphere of the class hour refines and often helps to correct concepts and (once again) sends him back to the Scriptures to study more deeply. The problems of teaching raise issues of how to gather materials, the need for writing syllabi (an activity in which almost every minister ought to engage from time to time) and other valuable activities from which his congregation is bound to profit. From his teaching, special lectures, magazine articles and even books will emerge. The time taken for each of these is worth the while.[7]

4. *Keep in touch with what is happening in God's world all around you.*

Take time to discover the best in all areas (cf. Philippians 4:8); keep in touch with everything. *Time* magazine and the daily newspaper are one way to stay in touch, but another way is to keep the car radio tuned in to the daily news programs, thus keeping up on what is happening while driving.

Most of what a minister does should have multiple effects. Driving thus can be combined with news gathering, saving hours of valuable time each year. Ministers should be conversant with important books, poetry, plays, music, art. The most surprising fact uncovered in a visit to Spurgeon's library[8] was that a very large portion (which appeared to be fully one-half of the library) was composed of non-theological titles. The latest books on every subject were bought and (obviously) read (sometimes marked). One reason why Spurgeon was able to preach so effectively to men and women of all walks of life, in his culture, and with examples and illustrations that rang true, was his wide acquaintance with everything that was going on around him.

Poise and Manners

The offense of the cross is one thing and cannot (must not) be avoided; the offense of the pastor is another. The pastor must develop a manner of humble confidence that grows genuinely out of his walk before God and men (Acts 24:16). But it is not always the matters of great moment to him that cause difficulty. Sometimes it is the small things in which he offends and thus loses the opportunity to minister. Offensive habits of picking the nose or head, jingling keys in the pocket, etc., can distract and drive off men (and especially women) from the truth and help that he may have for them. Good habits of general demeanor, therefore, should be cultivated. He

---

[7]In balance with other obligations, of course.
[8]Now housed at William Jewell College in Liberty, Missouri.

should learn to stand when women enter the room,[9] and help them with doors, chairs and coats. He should show courtesy, not affectation, in doing these things. They simply should be done and no attention called to the fact. Since he will be so frequently engaged in the activity, he should learn how to introduce one person to another. The "new" person (or inferior, e.g., a young child) is introduced to the old (or superior). If he forgets a name, he simply should admit it, ask for the name, and go on from there. However, some effort at learning to retain names is necessary (remember John 10:3!).

Eating manners are important to the pastor, since, like his Lord,[10] he will find that the dinner table is one good place to carry on his work of ministry. Because he will entertain and be entertained frequently, at least minimal attention should be given to this matter. If general work-a-day manners are unknown, the minister should assign his wife the task of teaching him. If she is unfamiliar with them too, she may do some research in Amy Vanderbilt's books or elsewhere and report back as soon as possible. Practice at home by the entire family until good manners become an every-day affair is the best way to learn. The minister should cultivate a taste for everything gastronomical. If his wife is an adventuresome cook, this will help. He should learn from Proverbs to eat neither too much nor too little.[11] Both extremes trouble hosts. Keep elbows off the table; wait until all are served before eating. And—this seems to be a minister's problem in particular—don't drag out books, papers, etc., during the meal! Bread-and-butter notes following a visit often are important. However, this custom seems to be disappearing. When in doubt, write. Visiting manners, including such concerns as leaving washbowls clean, making one's bed and normally writing thank–you letters merit every pastor's consideration.

I have hurried through these matters suggestively (not exhaustively) not because of their lack of importance (an entire ministry can be destroyed over bad breath), but because if more than suggestive reminders do not activate the minister to make the necessary evaluations and adjustments, all I could say in detail would be to no avail anyway.

---

[9]Yes, even in this day of Women's Lib!
[10]Cf. Matthew 9:10ff; 11:19; Mark 3:20, Luke 14:1, 7, 12, 13, etc.
[11]Cf. Proverbs 23:1, 6-8 (note especially the correct contextual rendering of 23:7 as, for instance, translated by the Berkeley version). What is true of rulers (v. 1) is often true of other hosts as well.

EXERCISES

For the Student

1. Draw up a Study Schedule for the next year including:

   a. Regular reading for courses.

   b. Auxiliary reading.

   c. Other study.

2. Schedule time for regular prayer and for evangelism.

3. Interview three pastors' wives and discover what they think are essential elements in pastoral poise and manners.

For the Pastor

1. Read over the section on Poise and Manners to your wife.

   a. Ask her to evaluate you.

   b. Ask her to add any additional suggestions that you may need to hear.

   c. Be sure you sincerely thank her; do not defend yourself, make excuses or get angry.

2. Ask yourself:

   a. What have I read in the last six months? Was it enough? Varied? Substantive?

   b. When did I last study formally? Teach a course? Write an article?

   c. What are my study habits?

   d. Do I regularly pray for myself? My family? My flock? For God's honor in all?

   e. When did I last lead someone to faith in Christ? When was the last attempt? Am I evangelizing adequately? Am I too tightly enclosed in the Christian bubble?

   f. In general, what is my relationship to God? What does it lack? What must be done about it?

CHAPTER VI
FAMILY AND SOCIAL LIFE

Family Life

No more critical matter can be considered since it is probably in this area that more pastors and more families suffer than in any other. Nothing can make a man more ineffective than bearing the weight of concern that comes from a bad marital relationship. When he also carries about guilt arising from failure as a parent, the load can become backbreaking. Moreover, too many pastors are plagued day by day with family difficulties occasioned by small salaries, high demands upon time and for quality performance, tensions between allegiance to the job and to the home, the tugs of large opportunities and the need to meet regular obligations, and dozens of similar considerations. Unless he can resolve these matters by getting control of his time and energies, the pastor will be doomed to a life of unnecessary struggle, confusion and despair, centering itself in the family and causing frequent upheavals and heartache. In no area is it easier for a minister to become discouraged and leave the ministry.[1] Yet, in no area can he have so healthy, meaningful and fruitful a ministry as in becoming an example for his flock of a Christian husband and father. How can he begin to achieve this high calling?

At the outset, the pastor must recognize that he is a husband first, a father second and a pastor third.[2] Only by adopting and firmly adhering to the biblical priorities can the pastor develop the sort of disciplined life necessary to carry on all three of these vital tasks to which he is called.

---

[1]Cf. some of the difficulties discussed in a survey of Evangelical ministers conducted by John and Letha Scanzoni, "The Minister and His Family," *Eternity* magazine, May 1967, pp. 14-16.

[2]Cf. *Christian Living in the Home,* p. 26, for comment on the biblical support for this generalization. I am not discussing the basic principles of marriage and family life nor the respective roles of husbands and wives here, since I have gone into some of these matters in *Christian Living in the Home.* Suffice it to say here that all that is true of the Christian husband (father) or wife (mother) is true *par excellence* of the pastor as an example.

To begin with, pastors (and through them congregations) must be brought to the realization that a good home life is fundamental to a successful pastorate. This is so crucial that the Scriptures not only explicitly say so, but also require it for ordination:

> He must be one who manages his own household well, keeping his children under control with all dignity (but if a man does not know how to manage his own household, how will he take care of the church of God?).[3]

Surely by the use of the key word *proistemi* ("manage"), Paul has placed a needed emphasis upon the importance of management. The problems of the management of the church are uppermost in his mind as he thinks of the larger tasks of management (planning, organization, enlistment, training and deployment of personnel, administration and discipline) to which the pastor (as such) is called; nevertheless, even the right to undertake these is predicated upon the ability of the would-be pastor to manage his own household well. For as Paul says, if he can't, surely he will not be able to manage the family of faith. There are at least five reasons why this is so:

1. The principles and skills of management are the same wherever they may be applied.

2. If he has failed with fewer persons, how can he succeed with the increased managerial burdens occasioned by managing a whole congregation?

3. If his own home is poorly managed, this will create intolerable burdens for him that, together with the regular tasks of the pastorate, will destroy his effectiveness as a pastor.

4. If he fails as a manager in his own home, there is no way that he can become the example that so many members of the flock so desperately need to show them concretely how to manage their homes (cf. 1 Timothy 4:12).

---

[3] 1 Timothy 3;4-5;12. See also Titus 1:6. Before ordination a minister's home life ought to be scrutinized at least as carefully as his doctrinal soundness. Indeed, the two are not disparate. More compromises involving fidelity to biblical doctrine have originated from poor home conditions than at first might be supposed.

5. If he is allowed to assume the pastorate under such circumstances, he is being encouraged to reverse God's priorities. Instead, he must be exhorted to put first things first. He is in no shape to take on the second task until he has displayed ability in performing well at the first.

The pastor's family is *his* family in several ways:

1. as the husband and father in the home;

2. as a pastoral example to the flock (including the way that he treats members of his own household);

3. as their shepherd (they too are a family of the congregation to whom he must minister).

There is, then, a triple reason for a pastor to spend much time in becoming the best husband and father that he can. He honors God, blesses his family and significantly helps his congregation thereby.

Social Life

Friendships

Friendships are essential; why do some pastors try to do without them? How desperately we need one another. When He wanted to show how closely He identified with us, Jesus said, "I have called you friends" (John 15:15). The friend, unlike the servant, has intimate knowledge of what one is doing. This, Jesus observed, is an essential and distinguishing characteristic of true friendship: "The servant does not know what his master is doing; but I have called you friends, for [note the explanatory and definitive nature of what follows] all that I heard from my Father I have made known to you" (v. 15). The true friend "sticks closer than a brother" (Proverbs 18:24),"loves at all times" (Proverbs 17:17), and "lays down his life for his friends" (John 15:13).

The need for such friendship in the ministry is great. There are discouraging, puzzling times; periods of indecision, opportunity (or even doubt) in which one's friends become all-important. Many pastors today would be more effective ministers if they had only cultivated friendships.

Friendships keep the pastor from becoming insular. They tend to give him perspective and balance. Friends, like iron, sharpen him (Proverbs 27:17). There is a tendency (which he must resist) for him to find his life becoming more and more circumscribed by committees, work and meetings, so that he may live ninety-nine per cent of his time within a small Christian bubble.[4] Isolation of this sort can hurt not only his own life, but inevitably will have a negative effect upon his ministry as well. Although Paul said that it would be impossible not to associate with unbelievers apart from leaving the world (I Corinthians 5:9-11), from observing the lives that some pastors lead one could only conclude that they are attempting to prove Paul wrong by accomplishing the impossible!

The fellowship of the saints will be proclaimed and promoted most effectively by those ministers who, themselves, are deeply involved in such fellowship. That the apostles both found strength and shared it with others through close involvement seems clear from the many personal references included in their letters (cf. esp. the epistles of Paul and John).

Entertaining in the Home

Pastors must take a leaf from the Savior's book and learn the importance of Christian fellowship at the table. It was from the context of the passover which He greatly "desired" to eat with the disciples that the Lord's supper emerged. It was at dinner parties that (sometimes even in the houses of Pharisees) the Lord gave some of His great speeches and that He witnessed to the lost. Christian ministers may discover the vast possibilities that the fellowship and closeness of the table provides (whether it be at a meal or when only eating a snack). More must be said later on about the ministry of entertaining others in the home. For now, perhaps, it is proper to discuss the matter only in its more general aspects.

What is important to understand is that every minister and his wife must be "given to hospitality" (Titus 1:8). Occasions, opportunities and needs all summon them to such activities. Hospitality in the Christian community is so important that two New Testament books were written to discuss the subject (II John, III John). Not only will hospitality afford opportunities for witness and for becoming better acquainted with the members of the

---

[4]The sad paradox is that while contacts become narrowed in this fashion and one would expect them to be deepened thereby, the contrary too often proves to be the case, since the pastor deliberately restrains the deepening process for fear of becoming too friendly to one or two and thus labeled with a charge of favoritism. The notion that a minister may not make friendships of differing sorts within the constituency to whom he ministers must be opposed. A clear gradation of friendships was maintained by the Lord Himself. First He chose the twelve; of these He singled out three (Peter, James, John) who, for example, accompanied Him to the mount of transfiguration (Mark 9:2) and into the garden (Mark 14:33); and of these three, one: John, the "disciple whom Jesus loved" (which can mean only one thing: on whom he set his special love). Pastors should be judicious about the choice and exercise of special friendships, must be careful about the nature of information revealed and what the friend does with information. Yet, such carefully cultivated friendships must be encouraged.

church, but often the pastor will find that he must take in travelling missionaries, entertain guest speakers, etc. Some ministers (and especially their children) have themselves received the greatest blessings thereby. The key thought here is that the pastor must learn to become a gracious host. This involves thoughtfulness and consideration in planning, as well as in entertaining itself. He must learn how to guide conversation, sense needs, etc.

To take but one example, let us consider the problem of the visiting speaker. Consideration will mean at least the following:

1. Someone will be there *on time* to pick up the guest at the airport.

2. He will be taken to his lodgings (in this case the pastor's home) *before* going to the meeting. Here he will be shown his room, allowed to freshen up and (when necessary) rest briefly before engaging in lengthy conversation or being taken to the church or meeting place. Travel can be rugged and quite fatiguing. Sometimes he may be hungry or thirsty. The pastor should make thoughtful inquiries about all such matters.

3. Plans should be made to entertain the guest in *one home,* not several. Packing and repacking of suitcases often is difficult.

4. Meals (except for perhaps a get-acquainted banquet or picnic with the church or elders of the congregation), *almost without exception,* should be served at one and the same home. Running about from one home to another for different meals is one of the most difficult burdens that can be imposed upon a speaker. First the running itself is exhausting. Moreover, the amount of conversation demanded is difficult. But most of all—whenever a housewife has a guest in for breakfast, noon or supper, she kills the fatted calf and insists that the guest have more and more and more. Three such meals several days in a row drives a speaker either to begin to reject food (which is somewhat impolite), or he himself becomes the fatted calf. And . . . enough of this sort of treatment can kill him too! Moreover, too much food, too much conversation and too many hours' activity without interruption (not to speak of late nights) dull the speaker's ability to preach well. The pastor who does not carefully insulate speakers, therefore, is unwise. Heavily overburdened schedules for such speakers are sinful. If the cost of all of the meals is too great, the pastor should ask the congregation for help.

5. If the speaker cannot be housed in a motel (usually this is the *best* arrangement), then he should be housed either in the home of someone that the pastor knows will be considerate or taken into the home of the pastor himself.

6. The pastor should provide for free time *alone* for the speaker. He needs time to study, write letters, pray and just generally to collect his thoughts. If the *speaker* is interested in doing so, the pastor may take him for a tour of the community. This will orient him and may give him material for illustrative use.

7. Above all things, the pastor should see to it that the speaker gets adequate sleep. Often, to do so, the pastor will have to restrain his own temptations to keep him up till all hours of the morning personally squeezing the juice from the lemon.

8. Checks for services rendered (strangely called honoraria) should be prepared beforehand and handed to the speaker before he leaves. The pastor should inquire about travel expenses (other than transportation expenses) and should see that reimbursements for these should be made as soon as possible. Transportation arrangements (plane tickets always should be forwarded, unless the speaker prefers to purchase them himself) should have been taken care of by mail long before the speaker's arrival. Long postponements of payment are especially odious. The speaker may have incurred a considerable amount of expense in coming (clothing laundered, travel expenses, etc.) and may be depending upon his check to meet it.

EXERCISES

For the Student

1. Are you (will you make) a good husband (father)? If so, why? If not, what must be done?

2. Are you now so regulating your life as a student that you spend adequate time with your family *even if grades at times must suffer?* Pressures will not lessen but will be even more demanding in the pastorate. Now is the time to develop habits that honor God and will bring blessing to your family. (Consider the next chapter for scheduling help.)

For the Pastor

1. Do your present family and social practices honor God and bring blessing to your friends and loved ones?

2. Talk this matter over with your wife and family to see . . .

   a. if some things must be changed.

   b. if they have suggestions about how to help you best make these changes.

3. In the space below, jot down whatever convictions you arrive at, each in one-sentence form, and refer to these daily as you enter the study.

   a. Pray daily about them.

   b. Revise them as you see need to do so.

   c. Place a check mark next to each one as it becomes a reality.

Convictions

_____

_____

_____

_____

_____

_____

_____

_____

_____

_____

CHAPTER VII
REPOSSESSING TIME

A Prime Pastoral Problem

In discussing the pastor's problems of management in his home, emphasis might be placed upon the management of his children. Yet more basic perhaps is the problem of time. Only when the pastor has gained control of his time can he begin to find the opportunities in freedom to live as a Christian husband and father should.

Universally, pastors complain about lack of time. In a pointed piece entitled, "Why Ministers Are Breaking Down," Wesley Shrader tells of a typical jam-packed day of one minister who "described simply and without a trace of self-pity a 13½-hour work day."[1] The Rev. Warren Carr of Durham, North Carolina, prepared a questionnaire asking his congregation to tell him how much time that they thought he should give to a list of specified tasks. The members of the congregation were shocked to discover that the average work week indicated by their answers was 82 hours. One answer proposed a schedule of 200 hours—32 more than there are in a week.[2] If this even approaches that which is typical of the demands that most congregations might make upon a minister, he must recognize that the solution to his problem is not likely to come from the congregation itself. Indeed, until properly instructed and wisely trained, the members of the congregation are more likely to present the major occasions for problems regarding time.[3] The minister who attempts to do all that his congregation expects will find that:

(1) the demands are unrealistic and cannot be met;

(2) the result will be guilt for having failed to measure up to an unrealistic standard;

---

[1] *Life Magazine,* August 20, 1956, p. 102.
[2] *Ibid.,* p. 98.
[3] Who else but the minister can instruct them? But if he does not observe the rubrics of personal discipline of life and time, he will not be able to do so. Undisciplined congregations, inconsiderately demanding the impossible, are the result of undisciplined ministers.

(3) all of this may lead to confusion and frustration over the lack of appreciation and judgmental words and actions of others.

Unless the minister recognizes that he is called to serve Christ, he will not serve his congregation well. Service to Christ means concern for others, willingness to hear their ideas and learn from their suggestions, and it means hard work; but it does not mean "external service" calculated to "please men."[4] The minister best serves his congregation when he serves Christ first. He therefore, as a good steward, must gain complete mastery over his time (which is not really his, but is Christ's time) in order to:

(1) be assured that *all* that he *must* do as a husband, father, Christian and pastor-teacher can be accomplished;

(2) be certain about his use of time so that he may say both "no" and "yes" to others without guilt, knowing that before God his answers are responsible;

(3) demonstrate to the congregation, which doubtless is composed of many others who are struggling with this important matter of time control, how a busy Christian can plan and utilize his time even in these hectic days in which we live;

(4) avoid the inevitable destructive feeling of depression that results from the failure to control the use of one's time and that leads to the accumulation of unfinished projects.

How, then, can the pastor overcome the problem? What can he do to take possession of (or, as in many cases, repossess) the time that Christ has given to him? There are two important answers to that question:

(1) He must recognize that he *does* have the time to do all that the Lord expects of him. Everyone has the same amount of time—24 hours a day. We all receive that same pie daily; the difference lies solely in how we slice it. God's expectations for any given day are reasonable. They may be hard,[5] but they are feasible. God never requires that which is impossible of His children. God's duties and priorities never conflict. God is not a God of confusion, but of order.[6] Conflicts of time always arise from confusing *human* desires and duties with God's. It should be a great relief to recognize these facts.

---

[4]Colossians 3:22-24; Ephesians 6:5-8. Cf. also I Thessalonians 2:4-6.
[5]The work of the ministry will never be easy; when four-day work weeks are adopted by others, faithful ministers will not be able to do so. Cf. I Thessalonians 2:9; 5:12; Colossians 4:17, etc.
[6]I Corinthians 14:33.

(2) The pastor may repossess his time for Christ by himself becoming an orderly rather than a confused person. It is not only for the worship service that the vital principle that *orderliness leads to peace* has implications. To those who are responsible to maintain order in His church He says: Let *all things* (including personal discipline) be done properly and in an orderly manner.[7] The confusion of a pastor's personal life will carry over into the whole work of the congregation. Disorderly lives lead to disorderly worship and service. A good steward of time is always an orderly person. This repossession of time can be achieved by planning and scheduling. To that all-important subject we must now turn our attention.

Planning and Scheduling

Sometimes it is wise for the pastor to begin by keeping a record of how he now spends his time. For a week, in a small notebook that can be carried in the pocket, he may note briefly the exact time and the activity (or nonactivity) every time that a change is made. He may discover with many others that hours are being nickled and dimed away in bits and pieces. Combined, a wasted 15 minutes here, 20 minutes there, and a half hour at a third point could provide significant blocks of additional time for important projects that are now being neglected. Moreover, study of the record may indicate foolish, wasteful patterns of activity in which, for example, travel (visitation perhaps) patterns show unnecessary duplications that might be eliminated at great savings of both gasoline and time.

But when it becomes clear that something must be done to change the situation, what should the pastor do? First, he must recognize the great importance of drawing up a schedule: God Himself works by a schedule.[8] Then, adjustments in present patterns must be made according to biblical priorities. Making a list as follows may help.

---

[7]I Corinthians 14:40 (see verse 33).
[8]Cf. Jay Adams, *The Christian Counselor's Manual,* Presbyterian & Reformed Publishing Co., Nutley: p. 173.

Worksheet for Scheduling

Unprofitable Activities to discontinue	Profitable Activities to continue or add	Items from Column Two in order of priority

In order to help pastors to determine how best to apportion their time and thus regain control of it in order to plan and schedule it, I offer the following outline. You would be wise to use a pencil with an eraser when filling it in; you will probably want to make changes as you go along. Pray about each matter. Remember, seek to discover God's priorities.

How many hours per week should you devote to:

I. *Study*
   A. The Study of God's Word
     1. For personal edification .... ____
     2. In preparation for sermons, Bible classes, etc. .... ____
     3. In actual preparation of sermons, etc. .... ____
   B. The Study of theology, languages, church history, pastoral counseling, homiletics, apologetics and other subjects relating directly to the work of the ministry
     1. Formally in graduate study .... ____
     2. Privately .... ____
       a. Books .... ____
       b. Journals, etc. .... ____
   C. The Study of problems facing the denomination, or delegated to committees to which you belong .... ____
   D. The Study of current affairs .... ____
   E. The Study of literature for personal cultivation, etc. .... ____
   F. Meditation .... ____
   G. Planning and preparing other aspects of worship .... ____
   H. Attending and traveling to meetings, conferences, workshops, etc. .... ____

                                      Total ____

II. *Prayer*
   A. For family and personal matters .... ____
   B. For the members of the congregation .... ____
   C. For the work of the congregation, denomination and the church in general .... ____
   D. Other works of confession, adoration, supplication, intercession and thanksgiving .... ____

                                        Total ____

III. *Personal and Family*
   A. Time spent with family .... ____
     1. Wife .... ____
     2. Children .... ____
     3. Whole family .... ____
     4. Relatives .... ____

                                      Subtotal ____

B. Time spent keeping manse attractive (cutting grass, shoveling snow, etc.) .... ____
C. Transacting personal business (banking, shopping, etc.) .... ____
D. Time spent in personal relaxation and recreation .... ____
E. Time spent with friends outside church .... ____

Total ____

IV. *Social*
  A. Socializing with members of congregation .... ____
  B. Socializing with other ministers .... ____
  C. Attending social functions .... ____
  D. Socializing with other friends .... ____
  E. Hospitality .... ____

Total ____

V. *Visitation*
  A. Of members in homes .... ____
  B. Catechizing .... ____
  C. Hospital visitation .... ____
  D. Visitation of shut-ins .... ____
  E. Time on road in travel for such work .... ____

Total ____

VI. *Counseling*
  A. In study .... ____
  B. Over the phone .... ____
  C. Marriage counseling .... ____
  D. Other specialized types of counseling .... ____

Total ____

VII. *Teaching and Evangelism*
  A. Communicants' classes .... ____
  B. Working with youth in S.S., D.V.B.S., youth programs, summer camps .... ____

C. Home Bible studies .... ——
D. Personal evangelism .... ——
E. Attending and traveling to meetings to teach or preach .... ——
F. Actual time involved in teaching, preaching and leading worship
.... ——
G. Conducting funerals and weddings .... ——

Total _____

VIII. *Administration*
A. Meeting with elders .... ——
B.1. Meeting with other groups regularly .... ——
C. Planning and attending special meetings .... ——
D. Publicity work .... ——
E. Preparation of items for bulletin (hymns, Scripture, notices,
    etc.) .... ——
F. Writing letters and other clerical matters .... ——
G. Using and answering the telephone .... ——

Total _____

IX. *Denominational*
A. Attending presbytery, General Assembly, committee meetings,
    installations, etc. .... ——
B. Writing articles for church publications .... ——
C. Travel as fraternal delegate, etc. .... ——

Total _____

X. *Community and Other Outside Relationships*
A. Attending local civic or educational functions .... ——
B. Addressing organizations (YMCA, Rotary Club, etc.) .... ——
C. Attending regional evangelical ministeriums .... ——
D. Attending professional meetings (Evangelical Theological
    Society meetings, etc.) .... ——

Total _____

XI. Unscheduled time for emergencies, opportunities, changes, etc. _____

XII. Other
    A. .... ____
    B. .... ____
    C. .... ____
    D. .... ____
    E. .... ____

Total _____

Grand Total _____

Remember, there are 168 hours in a week; 56 of these must be subtracted for sleeping, leaving 112. Figuring 3 hours a day (minimal) for eating, bathing, dressing, shaving and all other necessities, pares the figure to 91.

Sticking to the Schedule

Schedules should be considered servants, not masters. That means that, unlike the laws of the Medes and Persians, they must be made to allow for change and alteration. But this change should involve largely *shifts* in elements that already have been scheduled, or the use of time allotted for emergencies, opportunities, etc. Only rarely should change mean that good plans should be altered. If the original plans are good, proper in the sight of God, and the contemplated change cannot be brought about by the existing flexibility that the schedule provides, the pastor should question seriously whether the change ought to be made. Such changes, in the long run, are rarely opportunities. On the other hand, when the contemplated change *genuinely* seems to demand an alteration in the schedule, at least two things should happen: (1) The schedule should be reappraised to see if the change has not exposed flaws in the schedule that must be removed. There should follow a prayerful revision of the schedule leading toward improvement.[9] (2) If the contemplated change does not require permanent

---

[9]From time to time one's schedule should be reviewed; situations change. Health problems, for example, may demand alteration. If on review a pastor sees that he has taken on too much, he should not hesitate to cancel meetings, resign from committees or groups, or whatever is necessary to assume his proper obligations before God. Fatigue, strains and stresses at home, excessive tension, etc., all may be signs pointing toward the review of one's schedule. Some specific items, of course, will be filled in at the appropriate places each week; others each morning. Flexibility to alter one's schedule according to God's providence must always be maintained; scheduling must never violate the principles of James 4:13-17.

change, consideration must be given to *what* may be changed *when*. The pastor will find that there is an irreducible number of top priority items that cannot be changed.[10] These must be known and identified *before* the pressure to change occurs. Otherwise, it will be too easy to allow for wrong changes to be made.

If, for example, the pastor is invited to attend a meeting that may be of benefit to his work, yet is not an absolute necessity, and upon looking at his appointment book he notices that he has marked that hour off for time to spend with the children, unless he can find an equally good time to which he can move the family outing, he should decline the invitation, saying, "I'm sorry, I have an important obligation already scheduled for that time." That is not a lie; it is the truth. One's obligations to his family must be of the *utmost* importance to him and to his work. A minister who does not care for his family will have an unhappy home and, as a result, will be ineffective in his work. Moreover, his example to the flock as a husband and father will suffer.

The Unmade Call

When he knows how his time is allotted, the pastor will become invulnerable to inconsiderate and unthinking members of his congregation who otherwise will waste hours of time for him in numerous ways. Take, for instance, the burden of the unmade call that so many pastors carry around most of the time. The burden is unnecessary. How can it be relieved? Well, let's look at one example. Mrs. Smith is a well-meaning but frightfully thoughtless member of the congregation. She has become known to the pastor as the one who always provides "leads" for him to follow up. This might be good, but realistically speaking, the number of poor prospects that she provides (the last person said, "Mrs. Smith asked you to come? Who's she?") has made it all too clear that such suggestions must be put to an end. Yet, how to do so, that is the question. If the pastor has repossessed his time by careful planning and scheduling, he will be able to solve the problem. With a clear conscience, on the next occasion he will be able to respond honestly:

> Mrs. Smith, I am sorry, but by looking at my book I see that there is no time for me to make the visit until next month. If the opportunity is great, as you say, I don't think that it should be missed. Will *you* please make the visit this week or next since I can't, and then I'll follow through on your findings at a later point.

---

[10]Such as personal Bible Study and prayer, time with wife and children, etc.

One of two things may happen. He may thereby turn Mrs. Smith into a visitor or, as is more likely, he will put an end to her careless suggestion making.

Telephone Time

Consider another important matter: the use of the telephone. The telephone, at once, can be one of the pastor's greatest servants or enemies, depending upon how he controls his use of it. For one thing, he will find that unthinking members of his congregation will phone about the most trivial matters (e.g., to obtain a telephone number that they could have found in their mimeographed church directory or in the phone book). When they call, if they asked for the number and then hung up immediately, it would not be so bad; the call would have constituted only an interruption. But when they drone on, passing the time of day for fifteen to twenty minutes, and when there may be added to such a call four or five other fifteen to twenty-five-minute calls, one can see readily how much time can be consumed merely chatting on the phone. If a pastor is wise, he will *always* have calls screened for him. A secretary or his wife can easily sift out dozens of calls and save countless hours of precious time each week by giving the requested phone number to the inquirer, taking messages and telling the caller that the pastor cannot answer now.[11] Asking for a message is an important time saver. If the reply can be phoned back by the intermediary, the pastor again can avoid direct wasteful involvement. In short, the pastor must not think of the phone as his master, but rather as his servant.[12]

On the other hand if he considerately (e.g., determining ordinarily not to speak over five minutes on any call) uses the phone himself rather than make every visit personally, he can save hours of time and gallons of gasoline.

Each man will discover that the problems of telephone time management are unique to his situation and, therefore, must develop his own system, for handling them. But, if he fails to devise a system, the phone will plague him and by means of this powerful potential for good, he will waste hundreds of hours of time every year. When he recognizes that this time is God's time with which he has been entrusted as a stewardship, he will not lightly regard such matters as adopting a telephone time conservation system.

---

[11] Incidentally, a good secretary, whose services are properly used by a pastor, is worth five assistant pastors.

[12] It is vital for a pastor to be accessible to his congregation; someone must not always stand between. He and his screener must learn how to distinguish between matters that need his immediate personal attention and those that ought to be handled by a go-between.

EXERCISES

For the student and pastor

Keep a week-long schedule of the ways in which you currently are using your time and from an analysis and evaluation of it, using the following forms, draw up a weekly schedule that you believe represents the best God-honoring stewardship of your time.

WEEKLY SCHEDULE

	7 A.M. Morning	12 A.M. Afternoon	6 P.M. Evening	Special Notations
MONDAY				
TUESDAY				
WEDNESDAY				
THURSDAY				
FRIDAY				
SATURDAY				
SUNDAY				

WORKSHEET FOR SCHEDULING

Unprofitable Activities to discontinue	Profitable Activities to continue or add	Items from Column Two in order of priority

CHAPTER VIII
OTHER FACTORS TO CONSIDER

*Rest, Recreation, Hobbies
and Other Activities*

Since most of the normal everyday routine of the ministry (other than summer youth camps) involves much indoor activity, the wisest general rule for social or individual activities (and passivities—rest and relaxation have their place) is to *cultivate those which can be carried on outdoors.* Fishing, swimming, gardening, softball, golf, hiking, boating, camping, tennis, and a host of other such items might be listed. Some of these, in addition to their outdoor locale, involve strenuous physical activity. Some (like tennis and swimming) can be carried on all year round—outdoors when weather permits; indoors when it does not.

Not only the benefits of physical exercise should be sought, but the equally (perhaps even more) beneficial effects of their diversionary quality. The change of pace and change of mind that a vacation, an occasional fishing trip or a weekly tennis match affords may make all of the difference for a pastor deeply engrossed in the problems of his work. Returning refreshed, coming back to the work from a new perspective can change one's whole outlook. Sometimes pastors, because of the nature of their work, can become too closely attached to it. When their noses are always in the books, when their minds are always preoccupied with the burdens of counseling, they may lose perspective. Whenever the edge seems to be off one's work and he knows that it is not because of other sin, he should ask himself, "Have I been sinning against God by harming the temple of the Holy Spirit? Am I pushing my body beyond its limits, forgetting the admonition of Christ to the disciples when He said, 'Let us go off by ourselves to some place where we will be alone and you can rest a while'?"[1]

---

[1]Mark 6:31.

The pastor who takes time for rest and relaxation will do the work of the ministry better than he would otherwise, *provided* that he truly relaxes and rests. Some men for years have harnessed themselves to schedules that make no provision for diversion and find that whenever they attempt to take a needed rest, they do not rest, but become restless. They may suffer either from guilt (a problem to be settled only by honestly coming to grips with one's life schedule before God), bad habit, or *both*. But, as Jesus pointed out, the Christian worker needs (1) time by himself apart from those to whom he is ministering (2) rest from the work in which he busily is engaged. The problem of bad habit, therefore, must be dealt with, and dealt with biblically. Not to do so is sin. The minister before God (and as an example before his congregation) must learn to overcome sinful habit patterns and to develop a new biblical life style. While putting off the "former manner of life," he must become an example of the new life redeemed by Christ.

Jonathan Edwards wrote in the preface of David Brainerd's dairy:

> Another imperfection in Mr. Brainerd, which may be observed in the following account of his life, was his being excessive in his labors; not taking due care to proportion his fatigues to his strength.[2]

When the pastor glorifies God "in his body" (I Corinthians 6:20), he pleases God and better ministers to his flock. There is no necessary conflict between the *spiritual* and the *somatic,* as Romans 12:1-2 plainly indicates. To properly use one's body and *in God's service* is worship. All dualistic thinking that places the physical out of the realm of the spiritual misunderstands the fact of Christ's total lordship.

The Minister's Day Off

The Lord's Day is busy; its activities are taxing, but it is still the only day that the Lord has given as such to the pastor as well as to the flock. That does not preclude the possibility, and indeed necessity (as Christ made clear) of taking out other time, even in the *midst* of busy taxing activity, for *rest.* Many pastors have found that it is wise to set aside Monday as a day of rest and relaxation. Since there is no biblical directive governing the question, each man will find it necessary to evaluate his own situation, scheduling priorities, physical constitution, etc., and make the hard decisions that must be made about the matter. Doubtless, each pastor will work out his program differently. Young men, with no children in school, will find that

[2]Jonathan Edwards, *The Life and Diary of David Brainerd* (Moody Press, Chicago: n.d.), p. 232.

this situation affords its own opportunities and limitations. Others will discover that their schedules must be meshed with weekday school hours. At different times in his life, as such circumstances are altered, the pastor should revise his schedule to meet new situations.[3]

Saturday is an important day for every minister. Generally speaking, he should use it as every other man in his congregation properly does. When God gave six days to "labor and do all" one's work, that included Saturdays. All of one's work, however, does not mean merely remunerative work. It also constitutes his work around the house: fixing doorknobs, cutting the grass, caring for the family, planting flowers, etc. This, as for others, provides for a change of pace, happiness in the home and (a vital factor) the opportunity for all of the members of the family to *work together*. Saturday is wrongly used by some pastors as a day for visitation. Most members of the congregation simply don't want the pastor interfering in their day—the one day in the week that *they* also have for such family work and recreation.

Community Relationships

The pastor must be careful to maintain proper community relationships. According to I Timothy 3:7, he must "enjoy a favorable reputation among the outsiders, so that he may not fall into disgrace and into the trap of the devil." This important principle all too frequently has been forgotten and, as the result, neglected. Yet, the work of Christ has been hindered and the name of Christ has been slandered because of ministers who failed to pay bills, whose lawns were always the most unkempt on the block, etc.[4] It is not the reproach of Christ (Hebrews 13:12, 13) that the writer has in mind, but the unnecessary reproach that one may bring upon Christ by his own sinful failure.[5] Like those early Christian missionaries who "took nothing of the gentiles (heathen, unsaved persons to whom they were preaching the gospel) *for the sake of the name*" (III John 7), Christian pastors must be sure that their conduct in the community enhances rather than hinders their work for Christ.

The Christian minister lives *with* as well as *before* the community. He may make clear distinctions in his own mind between his personal life and

---

[3]Ministers will feel free to follow Christ's example in Mark 6, finding the right to take breaks from the work whenever the necessity to do so is laid upon them. Since this principle easily may be abused, they will need to be prayerfully earnest and conscientious about its application.

[4]Congregations often bear a responsibility for allowing a parsonage to become the community eyesore. Pastors may find it necessary to exhort their official boards about financial expenditures needed to enhance the condition of church property.

[5]Cf. rather Colossians 4:5, 6.

his work as an elder in the church, but the community will not. Everywhere that he goes and in everything that he does (like every Christian, but, as the unsaved community looks at it: *officially)* he represents Jesus Christ. That is why among the qualifications for an elder that are spelled out by Paul, he expressed concern about what the community thinks about him.

Beyond the physical condition of the property that he manages, the minister's own life as a man of the community, as a neighbor, as a husband and as a parent is of importance. He must be winsome and pleasant as a neighbor. He should be the *best* neighbor on the block. Becoming "all things to all men" that he might win some (I Corinthians 9:22), surely means in this context becoming a good neighbor and a worthy member of the community. He should mingle with and meet as many of the persons in his community as he can. He should become a good citizen who actively participates in everything that he can without neglect to his priorities, without compromise of his faith and without identifying Christ with causes championed by those who do not know Him.

He should be a *man* in his community. Many persons have strange ideas about ministers; they often view them as unmanly. The unsaved community doesn't see or hear a minister in his pulpit, only in his neighborhood. They, therefore, have no opportunity to learn of his fearless denunciations of sin or his courageous advocacy of unpopular views like predestination or limited atonement! They know him only in his dealings with them as a member of his community. Therefore, in such matters, he must be an example of Christian manhood.[6] What he is and what he does in neighborly relationships may be the only sermon that many in the community ever see or hear.

Should a minister be a joiner? Should he participate in clubs (e.g., Rotary, Lions), join the National Guard, take part in local school events, sports programs, etc.? Each situation will present unique opportunities and problems. In some communities, to associate one's self in any way with certain groups will by virtue of the act constitute compromise to the gospel. In others, the situation may be quite different. Always the three principles (here presented in the form of questions) enumerated below must govern:

---

[6]Cf. *Christian Living in the Home,* pp. 93-95, for a discussion of Christian manliness. The stereotyped ministerial type that turns off the men of the community is only reinforced by ministers who fail to show their manhood in the "ordinary" activities of life.

(1) Will the contemplated association in any way lead to compromise or confusion of the gospel of Christ?

(2) Will the contemplated association cut into my time too deeply to justify it? Will it square with my priorities before God?

(3) Will the contemplated association indicate to the community that Jesus Christ is to be identified with the program of this organization?

Often it is better to mix, mingle and meet than it is to join. Becoming part of an organization means taking upon one's self responsibilities for work and also means bearing responsibility for its pronouncements and programs. In economic, business, social and political activities in the community, the Christian minister must always walk circumspectly.

EXERCISES

For the Student

1. Have you begun to dry up physically? Spiritually? Check back through this chapter to see if there are any words you need to take to heart.

2. What are your present patterns of recreation, relaxation, etc.? Remember, you are (consciously or unconsciously) setting trends for your future ministry *now*. Examine your practices now; don't wait till you have already gotten into trouble in the pastorate.

3. What is your present relationship to a local church? Adequate? How? Inadequate? How? What does God want you to do to change?

For the Pastor

1. Examine your community relationships. In the chart below list the options (in pencil — you may want to do so again in another pastorate).

COMMUNITY RELATIONSHIPS

Present Relationships (to be continued or discontinued)	Additional Legitimate Relationships for Consideration	Relationships to Continue or to Add (in order of priority)

2. Discuss your Recreational Activities and Relaxation practices with the family (by now they are probably looking forward to your next conference) and together draw up a set of guidelines of policies to which you hope to adhere as God makes it possible to do so.

POLICIES AND GUIDELINES

_____

_____

_____

_____

_____

_____

_____

SECTION TWO

THE SHEPHERD'S CALL

CHAPTER IX
CANDIDATING

A minister's call to his work should acknowledge the recognition by the church of Christ of his gifts for ministry and their peculiar suitability for the tasks required to meet the needs of a particular congregation. The issuance and agreement to accept a call fundamentally should be based upon such considerations. A minister, therefore, should be *called to,* not merely be *leaving* a congregation.

Ordinarily, a process of mutual exploration of the suitability of the man to the task is conducted in which the minister (or minister-to-be) preaches for and visits with a congregation in order to evaluate a congregation and to be evaluated by its members. Such an official mutual evaluation is usually called candidating.

Often congregations wish to qualify potential candidates for evaluation before officially extending the invitation to candidate. Various approaches may be made to ascertain whether to explore the possibility further. While in some circumstances the informal approach may have beneficial advantages either for the congregation or for the minister or for both, informal *commitments* ought never to be expected and *rarely* should be made. There are obvious advantages, for instance, in pulpit committees visiting a church to hear him preach to his own congregation before qualifying a minister for candidacy, but if they restrict their decision to such informal procedures alone, never meeting with the minister to discuss his views and situation, they may wrongly disqualify a man on slim evidence (and on the basis of preaching alone). One sermon—fraught with all the possibilities for failure that impinge upon any single utterance—may quite misrepresent one's normal preaching. That is one reason why it is wise to urge congregations to act formally *from the outset* in considering every potential candidate. Meeting with men, hearing them preach (more than once), entertaining them in the homes of various members of the congregation and voting on them is the wisest course of all.

A very trying situation exists when some congregations pit various ministers over against one another as candidates. The arrangement in which each candidate is voted upon individually before moving on to another (assuming he is voted down or that he fails to accept the call) is far better both for ministers and for congregations. Occasions for possible divisions between the former or among the members of the latter or both, are thereby minimized. Any congregation that pits the names of three candidates against one another is *asking* for a three-way division of the congregation itself.

Ministers, therefore, for the sake of good relations with other ministers, and out of concern for congregations, must begin to make known whatever convictions they may have about such matters. These views ought to be expressed not only when the minister is about to leave, but also as he begins negotiations toward candidacy.[1] If more ministers were to make serious inquiries and requests about such matters, particularly stating under what conditions they would and would *not* allow themselves to be candidates, something significant might be able to be accomplished to abolish many of the harmful and abusive policies that so often are adopted by thoughtless pulpit committees and congregations. Many pastorates are begun with bad feelings that could have been avoided had the potential candidate taken the time and shown the courage to deal with what seemed to constitute possible inflammatory conditions. If ministers wish to avoid such unnecessary and complicating problems, they will examine carefully and often structure the circumstances under which they are being invited to candidate.

What to Preach

Let us assume that the congregation and the minister have reached agreement on the procedures of candidacy. The date has been set, and the minister must choose his sermon topics for the occasion. The ideal (not always achievable) would be for him to preach twice on Sunday, conduct a midweek meeting, visit around the congregation and meet with the elders during the week, and preach again the following Sunday. At the very least, he (and the congregation) should hold out for *more than Sunday*. Almost always the minimum of a weekend exposure is attainable.[2] Now, the

---

[1]Candidacy is at least a two-sided enterprise; why should the congregation alone dictate the structure for candidacy? Where a presbytery also intervenes, sometimes useful regulations governing candidacy can be determined at that level. While any true minister of the gospel and any congregation of the Lord Jesus Christ can, if motivated to work at it God's way, make a success of their relationship, it is wise to attempt to match the strengths of particular men to the weaknesses of specific congregations as much as is possible. That should be the goal of the two as they consider those matters that are involved in any possible future relationship between them.

[2]The exposure is, of course, a double exposure. Both congregation and the candidate must seek to learn all that they can about one another. It is always easier (and less painful) to avoid entering into an unfortunate relationship than it is to break one.

question arises, what should he preach? No one can answer that question for him. But some suggestions can be made. Assuming he will preach twice, he might be wise to do the following (and to let the pulpit committee know his intentions in advance):

1. *Morning:* Preach a pastoral sermon typical of the sort that the congregation might expect to receive on any Sunday were he to be called. He might stress the fact that he will take pains not to arouse any false expectations by preaching a one-of-its-kind, special, super hot-shot sermon on that occasion.

2. *Evening:* Preach a sermon from a passage that sets forth the work of the minister or that speaks of the relationship of a pastor to his people, etc. By this sermon (hopefully) he might indicate something of what the biblical goals for any future relationship might be as he sees them.

What to Look For

When the minister visits the church during his candidacy, he should seek to obtain as much information as possible so that any future decision may be based firmly upon factual data. That information should focus (at least) upon the following matters:

1. *The state of the congregation at present.* Is it small or large? Is it composed mainly of older or younger families (or is there balance in this)? Is it growing, stagnant or retrogressing (are there any obvious reasons for the latter two problems, if true)? Is the spirit of the whole good or bad; do the majority of the members seem committed to the work and anxious to see Christ honored in it? What sort of community does it serve? Are there divisions in the congregation? Are there serious doctrinal or moral issues that are unresolved? Does the youth work seem vital or apathetic? Do there seem to be peculiar practices or convictions present (e.g., tract racks stuffed with John Birch Society materials)? What do the scheduled events tell about it (request several old bulletins)? What seems to be the attitude toward a minister (e.g., how do they talk about former pastors)?

The reason for asking these questions (and many more like them) is not to disqualify the church if the answer to most of these questions happens to yield negative results; indeed some men do (and should) look for precisely that sort of congregation in which to minister. The purpose is to get as accurate a picture as possible so that any decision to accept a call to this congregation will be made deliberately in knowledge rather than in ignorance.

Not all men have the same measure of the same gifts. Not everyone can handle every sort of situation. Some men, for instance, are best at beginning new works; others best at maintaining established ones. Some can minister to both types of congregations equally as well. So, the prime reason for asking such questions is to determine as fully as possible whether the gifts that one has seem best suited to meet the needs of this particular congregation. But to make such a determination, he must discover what those needs are. Any pastor who chooses a congregation because it seems to lack problems not only does so for unworthy motives, but he is a fool as well, for there is no such congregation in this world of sin—only one which to the untrained eye may *seem* to. Ministers go to congregations to minister. That means to minister to needs. They must, therefore, not seek to avoid the confrontation of problems in choosing a congregation, but rather choose those congregations in which they see (from a sober appraisal of the facts) that God has given them the gifts to meet the needs (if He will graciously bless their use).

2. *The type of community in which the church is located.* Paul was able to minister to Jew or Greek, to bond or free, to educated or uneducated, to kings or countrymen. But not everyone called into the ministry is a Paul. Some men, by virtue of training and/or background, will be able to serve best in a rural or urban setting. Some will be better at meeting the challenge of changing neighborhoods than others, and some will best be able to reach affluent suburbanites. There is much room to rationalize about such matters. Each man, before God, must do all that he can to reach sober judgments about this question. Either way one may err. Someone raised in the city may find a country pastorate the most fruitful ministry for him. Another, out of fear or false humility, may (wrongly) shun the church in the more educated and affluent neighborhood. No one else can judge. Yet one ought to seek advice from respected brethren whenever in doubt. But the final decision must remain his own.

3. *The constituency and views of the elders.* There is no more important matter than the meeting of the candidate with the elders of the congregation. It is here that the most vital discussion will be held. Strangely, some congregations fail to arrange for such a meeting. If the meeting has not been arranged, it is essential for the candidate to request it. When the elders are not identical with the pulpit committee, the candidate should request that they be included in the meeting that he holds with the committee.

The meeting should be a two-sided encounter; it should by no means consist merely of an interrogation of the candidate. Rather, it should reflect clearly the twofold nature of the evaluation that is taking place. Indeed, sometimes the candidate may find it necessary to help the elders to carry out their part of the evaluation effectively by anticipating and offering responses to some of the basic questions that they ought to ask.[3]

Matters to Discuss

The outline that follows represents some matters that probably ought to be discussed during the meeting with the elders. If they do not themselves broach all of these questions, it would be wise for the candidate himself to raise them.

I. The Purpose and Role of the Minister

Stress might fall upon the calling and function of the pastor to tend sheep, not primarily to evangelize. Evangelism can be viewed as the work of the *whole* congregation. Ephesians 4:11, 12 would be of significance to this discussion. Mention might be made of the candidate's view of his relationship to the elders and how he would like to work together with them were the pastoral relationship consummated. Any special programs for which the candidate (or the elders) is particularly zealous that could be somewhat controversial might be mentioned.

II. Preaching

An affirmation that he believes that there can be no limitations upon preaching, that the "whole counsel of God" must be proclaimed, ought to be made.

III. Visitation and Counseling

If the candidate's views of the proper place and pursuit of these activities are likely to be new to the congregation in some respects, it might be well to broach the subject, at least *indicating* the sort of course of activities that he hopes to follow.[4] If he sees visitation by the elders as vital and also some visitation by others in the church, and recognizes that this would mean a change, he might mention his intention to teach and train toward these ends (not merely to *demand* them).

IV. The Diaconate

If, as is advocated in this textbook, the candidate sees the place of the diaconate in the church as more important than it has become in many congregations, he may note his concern to enlarge its functions to become a board of men dedicated to showing mercy in many ways and in relieving the elders of all tasks that would keep them from performing the distinctive functions of an elder.

---

[3]Frequently such help will be needed since the leadership of a pastor is lacking.
[4]Cf. ideas presented in Chapter 10.

V. Wife

If the pastor has clear convictions concerning the role and relationship of his wife to the congregation, he may wish to state these, especially if he discovers that there is a propensity on the part of members of the eldership to look on her as a sort of assistant to the pastor whose services can be elicited as a fringe benefit without pay. Watch out for questions like, "Does your wife play the organ?" or "Can your wife teach?" The candidate graciously should make it evident that his wife is not to be viewed as a P.W. (i.e., Pastor's Wife, with some sort of quasi official status), but rather as a p.w. (wife of the man who happens also to be called to be a pastor). He should explain that he considers her first task is to be his wife; secondly, to be the mother of his children; thirdly, to be a good member of the congregation. Beyond that, she should neither be expected to occupy nor should she expect[5] any special place in the congregation. As any other good member, she will use her gifts in the church as her duties as a wife and mother make that possible. The only real question of substance that the elders have a right to ask about the candidate's wife is whether in any way she might be a liability to his work and, hence, to the work of Christ.

VI. Delegation of Work

While in every new pastorate with meager trained personnel the minister will be willing to do more of the work of the congregation than is ideal, he must *from the outset* begin to *train others* to do those tasks that do not peculiarly belong to his role as a teaching elder and pastor of the flock. In well established churches, previous ministers may have set poor examples by not doing so. To begin well it would be wise to express the goal of discovering, developing and deploying all of the gifts of all of the members of the congregation.

VII. Church School

If the pastor sees the present Sunday school as an ineffective, inefficient instrument for teaching (in the upper levels particularly) and has a program for improving it by transforming it into a vital institution, complete with teacher training courses, textbooks, maps, examinations, reports, etc., teaching courses rather than classes (for example), he may be wise at least to hint at his intentions.

VIII. Prayer Meetings/Home Bible Studies

Likewise, if he has ideas, say, of splitting the prayer meeting into several

---

[5]Of course, the pastor and his wife will have to come to agreement on this matter themselves. Many wives relish the unbiblical role of P.W. In I Corinthians 9:5 Paul speaks of the minister's wife as "a sister (believing member of the congregation) who is a wife." No better description can be given.

regional Bible study-fellowship-prayer groups meeting in homes under elder leadership, he might do well to note the fact.

IX. *Finances, Housing, Vacation and Moving Expenses*

Because of arrangements that were vague rather than clear cut, heartaches, many problems and difficulties have arisen that never should have. Make sure that it is plain whether, for instance, when the call reads "one month's vacation" (that *might* include five Sundays) it means that or "four weeks." What allowances are offered for manse, utilities, car, books, telephone, etc.? Is there a *regular* increase of salary, or is this a matter for yearly congregational argument?[6] Such questions should be nailed down; candidates should not be hesitant to ask for explicit answers: "the laborer is worthy of his hire."

X. *Secretarial Help*

The matter should be raised. A good secretary can be one of the most valuable extensions to a pastor's work possible. Even if voluntary, even if only two days per week, secretarial services ought to be sought.

XI. *Formal Study*

If the pastor has intentions to take further study, these should be made known.

These are only some of many other questions that might be discussed. Obviously, all of them will not be raised by all candidates in all situations. Where one sees that the education of a congregation over a period of time will be needed to reach certain goals, he must be willing to be patient and not to raise too many matters too soon.

In general, however, it is always wise to mention, at least, ideas, practices or goals that are strongly held by the candidate and that might lead to con-

---

[6] It is not "unspiritual" for a candidate to discuss and even to negotiate the salary. Salaries offered by many congregations are scandalously inadequate. Often the congregation needs to face the challenge by hearing a candidate say, "I am sorry; I would come if the salary were more adequate, but in order to do the responsible thing for my wife and family I have no other choice than to turn down your offer." Better that the question be faced now than that it become an issue later. Better to begin rightly by *even at this point training the congregation about its Christian responsibility* than to allow it to continue in old questionable ways that cannot be supported biblically. Of course, it is important for any minister to be sure that he is not asking too much. But, in general, it may be said that it takes a salary equal to the average salary of the members to live and work adequately in any community. It does not take many families *who mean business* to provide this. Ten families giving one tenth of their income can do so. If a congregation offers the use of a church-owned automobile and/or gasoline payments, this can be better than salary. The automobile is perhaps the greatest of the pastor's occupational expenses. Whenever opting for a church-owned manse or a private dwelling is possible, the pastor should consider the latter. Congregations unrealistically think that a manse is equivalent to a great slice of salary, failing to realize that the widows of many pastors have ended their lives destitute—having built up no equity and having no place to live.

troversy later on. If they are discussed now, then there will be much less likelihood of later conflict.

Somewhere in the discussion, if such information is not forthcoming, the candidate should ask: "What will you expect of me?" Answers that are not explicit, as well as those that indicate possible conflicts of views, ought to be probed to determine the exact thinking of the *group* on the point. Do not take the ideas of one outspoken person for the consensus of the group. Determine, through discussion, whether there is, indeed, such a consensus.

While there is surely room for give-and-take on many views, programs and methods, the pastor should determine what (for him) is the irreducible minimum and should so probe the elders as to determine whether there would be agreement about these. Just as the pastor may not be ready or fully able to describe it, the elders may not be ready to commit themselves to a program at this point, but if they show a willingness to hear, explore and be convinced, this may be all that the candidate can ask for.

The *full* discussion that has been suggested here grows out of the conviction that if more were discussed more thoroughly beforehand, there would be less agony for all concerned later on. There have been too many church divisions (not to speak of the discouragement of pastors) occasioned by just such failure to discuss *possible* differences.

EXERCISES

For the Student

1. Draw up a list of

    a. Your own strengths and weaknesses;

    b. Possible improvements that will help you to overcome weaknesses (state specifically how you plan to overcome each). Pray regularly about these.

2. Describe the kind(s) of congregation(s) you are now

    a. best suited for;

    b. least suited for.

    Do not hesitate to discuss the matter with others who may know you well.

For the Pastor

1. Using the suggestions in the chapter as a starting point, in the space below make your own personal list of the issues that you would wish to discuss with the elders or pulpit committee of any congregation to which you might possibly be called. (It is better to be prepared ahead of time.)

2. In a brief paragraph, summarize the state of your congregation at present, listing unreached goals, rate of progress, problems intervening, etc.

CHAPTER X
GOING TO AND FRO

Receiving and Rejecting a Call

How does one decide? There are no easy answers to this question. The story of Calvin and Farel at Geneva is a classic in the annals of the problems of ministerial calling. The question has never been simple.

In general, prayer, the biblical principles that relate to the specific situation, a sober analysis of one's gifts and training, and the needs, challenges and opportunities of the contemplated field in God's providence will converge to bring about a decision. The call of the church itself, particularly when accompanied by an enthusiastic vote and presbyterial concurrence, should carry heavy weight, especially if it is pressed urgently upon the candidate. At times, the candidate will find it necessary in weighing all of the factors to list them on paper in columns.

If a call must be rejected, one should exercise great care about how he rejects. Word of the rejection should be sent *immediately* (and *first*) to the parties involved, together with some sort of explanation of why the rejection was forthcoming. The latter is important to cut down any unwarranted speculation, which can potentially be harmful to the church, the candidate (or both). The reason given does not necessarily have to be detailed, but honestly ought to speak to the real issue (or issues). Perhaps the problem lies in the candidate ("I do not assess my gifts to be adequate for the particular kind of work that seems to be necessary in your community," or: "After much prayer, thought and discussion with the elders here, I have concluded that the work at my present congregation is not at a point where I could justify leaving"). The problem may lie with the church ("I do not think that my wife and my five children can live on the salary offered," or "I cannot come to a church that restricts me from preaching the second coming as I understand that it is taught in the Scriptures," or "I could not labor freely under what seem to be the requirements and expectations that the elders have for a minister"). A clear explanation of this sort allows the congregation to take stock of the situation and to determine whether it might be wise to make certain changes and continue to press the call ("What would you consider to be a reasonable salary to meet your family's needs?").

It is especially vital first to inform the congregation whose call you are rejecting whenever there are more calls than one. The most distasteful way for members of a congregation to learn of the rejection of their call is to learn of the candidate's acceptance of another. The rule should be inflexible: always inform a church of a rejection (1) before telling anyone else; (2) before notifying another congregation of the acceptance of their call. The Christian world is exceedingly small. Members of one congregation in New Mexico may that very night telephone relatives who are members of the other congregation in Vermont. It is wise to make all rejections and acceptances by phone (and in that order). Where the presbytery presents a call, the formal acceptance or rejection takes place publicly. But the custom is for all parties concerned (apart from the final validation, or for that matter invalidation, of the call by the presbytery) to agree informally beforehand.

Leaving a Pastorate

Assuming that one has accepted a call to another congregation, what are his responsibilities in leaving? They are, generally speaking, to do all that he can to make the transition from his pastorate to the next one as smooth as possible.

Responsibilities to the Congregation

First, the minister should have let the elders (not the entire congregation) know that he was candidating *from the beginning.* If they know that serious candidating is going on, they have opportunity to pray about the matter and to discuss it with him. When he determines to leave, he should discuss the time of departure with the elders to try to ascertain what would be most advantageous both for him, the new congregation and the one that he is vacating. Time for transition matters should be allowed (some of the machinery for calling the next man, for conducting the work of the church in the interim, etc., may need his direction and help to set up) but a lame duck ministry of any substantial length is usually undesirable. Two (a maximum of three) months notice seems about right.

The departing minister should keep his hands off when it comes to the matter of who should be selected as his successor. However, if the elders or pulpit committee *seek* his advice on the subject, he should not refuse to give it. The best rule seems to be to offer only so much help of this sort as is *clearly* (specifically) requested.

Responsibilities to the Next Minister

1. Leave an accurate, up-to-date roll of the church members, with addresses and telephone numbers.

2. Leave accurate, up-to-date (but date it plainly since transitions from one pastor to another can be lengthy) prospect and contact lists.[1]

3. Compose and leave a notebook of helpful information about the area ("Joe's garage does excellent work at discount for preachers"), together with all the maps that might be helpful to a new pastor.

4. Leave a sealed statement (addressed to the next pastor) concerning the general state of the work, unfinished projects and goals yet unreached, problems yet to be overcome, opportunities on the horizon, etc.

5. Leave nothing prejudicial (for or against) *any* individual. If such matters are that *crucial,* they should be handled before leaving (at least brought to the attention of the elders, who, rather than the departing minister, can inform the next pastor if the situation continues). Nothing potentially slanderous may be left.

6. Future relationships ought to be confined to brief friendly visits, and especially growing relationships with the new pastor himself. Upon his departure from a congregation, a minister should burn his bridges. He is not competent to give advice from afar; situations have a way of changing. Moreover, when a new minister arrives, the work is now under his care (together with the elders), and advice asked by members (other than elders or the new pastor) who request it should be refused. Instead, the inquiring member should be directed to seek out the advice of the new minister. Even requests to conduct weddings and funerals should be accepted (and then reluctantly) only if they are encouraged by the new pastor. (To the member, along with thanks and other suitable comments, he writes: "I make it a policy usually not to return to do this, since I think that it is a transgression of the care and discipline of the new minister. Is there any special reason for the request beyond the great joy that it would give to both of us?" A copy is then sent to the new pastor with a handwritten note appended: "Joe, do you really think that there is any good reason beyond sentiment for me to return to conduct this wedding, or would you rather do it yourself?")

---

[1]A prospect—a lead that might bear fruit.

A contact—someone with whom work has been done and there seems to be at least the beginnings of a favorable response.

EXERCISES

For the Student

Interview at least five pastors, and, in the space below, summarize any additional advice that they may give you concerning the matters of receiving and rejecting of calls.

For the Pastor

1. If you have never done so, why not do the same as the student (using the space above). Your "interview" may not be spelled out as such; you might merely make it a point to bring up the matter with a half dozen other pastors.

2. To assume your responsibilities to those you leave behind when God removes you from your present pastorate, and toward the next pastor, your records must be intact, you may find it necessary to acquire certain materials, etc. When the decision to leave comes, you could easily become so pressed by other matters that all of your good intentions could fly away unfulfilled. Take inventory *now*. Begin to produce a packet of materials, etc., so that when the time comes it will be easy to meet your responsibilities. Indeed, such a packet would be of special value should the Lord suddenly take your life.

INVENTORY RECORD

Materials	Present Condition

SECTION THREE

THE SHEPHERD'S CARE OF THE FLOCK

CHAPTER XI
THE SHEPHERD VISITS

Biblical Visitation

Does the work of *visitation* fit the concept of *pastoral* work? Does not the conjunction of these two images (shepherding and visiting) seem contrived? Is there any internal congruity between them? Or, is pastoral visitation something that was devised by well-meaning pastoral theology professors?

Presumably there must be a legitimate biblical connection not immediately apparent to us perhaps, for in speaking of the worthless shepherd, Zechariah writes:

> Take again the equipment of a foolish shepherd, for I am raising up a shepherd in the land *who will not visit* the perishing, or seek the scattered, or heal the wounded; even the healthy he will not sustain. . . Woe to my worthless shepherd, who forsakes the flock! (Zechariah 11:15-17, Berkeley).

And Jeremiah, in similar tone, said:

> Therefore, thus says God concerning the shepherds who feed my people: 'you have scattered my flock and driven them away, and *have not visited them;* behold *I am about to visit you* for the evil of your deeds,' declares the Lord (Jeremiah 23:2).

A careful study of the use of the Hebrew word *paqad* ("visit") and *episkepto* (by which it is regularly translated in the LXX) shows that while the idea of visitation (as it is usually conceived) is not necessarily bound up with shepherding, there is a vital sense in which the two are peculiarly connected. In an earlier place we saw how the *episkopos* (bishop) oversees *as a shepherd* (cf. chapter two). The "visitation" in view in both the Old and New Testaments at its core is *oversight that shows concern for*. The concern which is at the core of biblical visitation is equivalent to a kind of remembering or *thinking about* another (cf. Psalm 8:4; 106:4, where the two words "visit" and "remember" are used in Hebrew parallelism) *that leads to action.* To visit is to *show concern for* in blessing[1] or in judgment.[2] It is to show concern that grows out of one's *oversight* and *inspection* (cf. the root of the English word "visit," which finds its meaning in the thought of "looking" after or "seeing"). The idea of God's oversight, interest in and active concern about the nations, His people, and individuals is paramount in the biblical use of the term. He, in contrast to all of the false gods, is so great that He *knows* and *cares* about men. He is *the God who cares enough to visit* (i.e., to look into and do something about their affairs).

Thus, the idea of taking measures to inspect and attend to whatever conditions one discovers, out of concern, is the main thrust of the word. The thought of God showing initiative in His relationships with men, at times also may be present. The image of knocking on doors and paying visits (as *the method* of showing concern), however, is not inherent in (or even a prominent thought related to) biblical visitation.[3]

Unfortunately, this biblical emphasis has been missed by many ministers of the church, who have equated visitation with *making house calls.* While it is true that the making of house visits is one way in which to show concern and to exercise one's oversight, it is *only one way.* Possibly the original idea of concern for another at the root of the term was closely connected with

---

[1]Cf. Genesis 50:24, 25; Exodus 4:31; Ruth 1:6—to "visit" here means "to turn favor toward again" (cf. Keil and Delitzsch); cf. also I Samuel 2:21; Psalm 65:9; 80:14; Isaiah 23:17; Luke 1:68, 78; 7:16. For a close parallel to Psalm 8:4, note Job 7:17, 18. It is possible that Psalm 8 has a secondary reference to God coming to and walking with Adam in the Garden. Christ, the Immanuel, is "God with us." He continues with us in the Holy Spirit until the consummation of the age. In Isaiah 26:16, the unusual thought of God's people visiting Him is introduced. There the thought seems to be that they visit God in prayer, i.e., they show concern for Him, a concern evidenced by their prayers.

[2]Cf. Exodus 20:5; 32:34; 34:7; Leviticus 18:25; Numbers 14:18; Deuteronomy 5:9; Job 35:15; Psalm 59:5; Isaiah 26:14; Proverbs 19:23, etc. In the New Testament the word mainly (if not exclusively) refers to God visiting in blessing.

[3]Although in the New Testament visitation may seem to take on this idea more pronouncedly (cf. James 1:27 and Matthew 25:36 where this idea incidentally *may* come into view), yet even here the dominant thought is not merely that of paying a call upon prisoners or orphans or widows, but rather of showing concern by *looking after* them, i.e., of taking care of them by meeting their needs. Cf. especially Matthew 25:36, where (with Berkeley) the verse should be translated: "sick and you looked after me (*epeskepsasthe*); in prison and you visited me (*elthate*,"coming")." Interestingly the writer distinguishes visiting (in the narrow sense) as *coming,* from visiting (in the larger sense) as *looking after* (the word regularly used for pastoral visitation).

In a quite different context, John promises to come in remembrance (III John 10). Here the idea of an actual visit is combined with the thoughts of remembrance and of apostolic discipline.

concern shown by paying just such a visit. But in biblical usage, there is a much fuller, richer meaning, certainly going far beyond the notion of making house calls. At its center is the idea of the Shepherd of Israel who watches over and meets every need of His flock.

Much time has been wasted by patterns of useless pastoral calling that developed from a misunderstanding of this term. House calls assuredly ought to be considered to be one means of exercising pastoral oversight, showing concern and dealing with people's problems, but just that—*one* means, and only one. The biblical data indicate that house calling may not be considered the only means, or necessarily the best means of discharging the pastoral function of visitation however. Indeed, in our day of sprawled-out cities, modern communication, rapid transportation, etc., making house calls is probably one of the most ineffective and inefficient methods of visitation available.

Since the word, and the passages in which it occurs, demands that *every* means for exercising oversight and showing concern be employed, *pastors will visit by making house calls.* But those who come to understand the depth of meaning in this word will not fall into the trap of believing that they have discharged their duty to visit-as-a-shepherd merely (or even principally) by making such calls. Nor will they place so large an emphasis upon house calls as traditionally some ministers have, through a faulty understanding of the biblical concept of shepherdly visitation.

Instead, they will see that visitation means the exercise of pastoral *care and discipline.* Thus *active concern* in meeting of needs, counseling with members, etc., will be seen to be of prime interest in *visitation.* To say that the shepherd "visits" is to say (with Zechariah and Jeremiah) that he *cares* for the flock by healing the wounded, tending them, gathering them together and the like. To "visit" is to carry on *all* of the shepherdly concerns bound up in the comprehensive care mentioned earlier. Modern translations (cf. NASV) have caught the true significance of the biblical (terms for) visitation when they translate them by such words as "tending," "attending to" or "care for."

A New View of Visitation

According to the older view, the pastor was to be in the home of his people constantly. He was to call regularly, along with the elders of the church. While there is no intention on my part to take anything away from the value of the contact and the work accomplished by means of such visitation, there is nevertheless need to see that the Scriptures lay a greater obligation upon the elders and the minister. Too often in the past, house calling was the sum and substance of pastoral visitation. No longer may the pastor be satisfied with simple calling, and the prayer and Bible reading exercises which often accompany it. The small talk, the superficial inquiries, the conversations that never got off the ground (not to speak of reaching their goals, because of interruptions by ringing telephones, pots boiling over, etc.) were all too often characteristic of the understanding of visitation-as-house-calling that prevailed.

For a time in the village context it may have been possible to settle for a slimline version of the biblical teaching without too many disastrous effects (not that there were none). But now that modern living patterns have changed so radically, the inadequacy of the method has become painfully apparent. People's lives are not being changed, their problems are not being solved, and their unsolved difficulties have grown alarmingly. Pastors too often are the last to learn of problems which, had they been aware of them earlier, they might have prevented from growing to larger proportions. Now so often people come for help only when the situation is all but hopeless. The present problem of the church thus virtually shrieks for a fresh examination and application of the scriptural concept of shepherdly visitation *as comprehensive care and discipline.*

Let us consider just one current difficulty. Not too long ago the members of each congregation lived close to one another. They were part of the same village or city block, etc. Persons on the same block knew one another, held block parties, had neighborhood baseball teams, etc. They were daily intertwined in each other's lives in a hundred ways. In the village any day in the week the pastor could walk down main street and, simply by doing so, see half of his congregation at the general store or along the way. Men went home for lunch. Everyone was home early at night. Very little of significance happened without everyone in town (including the pastor) soon becoming aware of it. Now, all of that has changed. The new mobility of society has destroyed much of what the word society used to mean. Members of a congregation may go months (or even years) on end without even seeing their pastor *or one another* except during the structured hours together each Sunday. They hardly know one another *as persons.*

Regular daily contact of church members in the past was built into the village or community living pattern. Today it is not. It was easy to have fellowship. No one had to think about the problem of contact; the problem rarely existed. Today, all sorts of pseudo-groups, in which people seek to meet the need for fellowship, have sprung up. This is clear evidence of the need. Discontent has been expressed with preaching and structured church services. Some of the discontent is valid, but, as is becoming quite apparent wherever it has been tried for any length of time, bulldozing down the walls of the church building, ripping apart the seams of the service and replacing sermons with slides fails to provide the answer. There are *two* needs to be met. While there may be temporary relief as a result, failing to meet one need in an effort to meet the other will never work. What the church most needs today is wise shepherding–shepherding that senses the true nature of the longings, the fears, the troubles and the acute needs of the flock. Creative shepherding will lead to guiding the flock into greener pastures and beside still waters.

By the two needs, I refer first to the need for fellowship, which has grown so great that desperate measures have been advocated in order to satisfy it. But secondly, there is also a need for orderly corporate worship, service and (especially) teaching. Overthrowing the structure of the latter[4] in order to gain the former in many cases already has proven to be counterproductive. The answer will never be found in either/or, but rather in both/and solutions. Both needs must be met in order to assure complete satisfaction.[5]

Therefore, whatever happens in any given case, the final solution (if biblical) will provide for an assembling together of members that allows for the fellowship of stimulating one another to love and good works (cf. Hebrews 10:24). Otherwise, the "habit" deplored in Hebrews 10:25 is likely to become all the more prevalent. When adequate fellowship is built into congregational activity (and today it must be *built in* consciously since it no longer comes naturally in these urbanized times in which we live), the members of the congregation will not complain about structure, nor will there be serious questions about preaching and teaching (provided that it is good).

Now, where do the pastor and pastoral visitation fit into this picture? In several ways.

1. Because pastors and elders recognize that visitation means meeting all of the needs of the sheep, they will read the signs of the times, which (for instance) will cause them to become deeply concerned about meeting the need for fellowship among the members of their congregation. They will recognize that throwing away the pews will not solve the problem, but also that making more pastoral calls will not do it either.

2. They will attempt to encourage both formal and informal fellowship among their members. Creatively they will think of ways in which to bring

[4]Reasonable changes that preserve order and that allow for more cooperative worship, etc., have proven beneficial. I am speaking of the reactionary extremes that too frequently have been bought out of desperation.

[5]The teachings of Christ and the apostles were social as well as individual and clearly presupposed a community. The gifts of the Spirit are given for mutual benefit; the *ecclesia* is a body of persons who must learn to function unitedly as the body of Christ.

members of the congregation together to get to know one another *as human beings,* not merely as the persons who sit across the room in meetings and always vote the other way. They will look, for instance, at the number of structured meetings per week and seek a better balance between structured and unstructured gatherings. They may ask, "Why should a midweek service be held (a) at the church (b) for all persons, (c) at which time the pastor speaks again?" They will come to see that many variations are possible instead that provide for better fellowship:

a. The midweek service could feature testimony and a hymn sing in addition to prayer (a minimal solution).

b. It could become a family night beginning early, with supper at church and closing early to allow children to get to bed.

c. It could be split into smaller groups, meeting in several homes over coffee and doughnuts for fellowship, Bible study and prayer.

The pastor is much too heavily overloaded to prepare a midweek talk; why should he? Instead, this time could be more unstructured, allowing for the people of God to meet together for Christian fellowship and the contributions of various others. Elders may learn to exert greater leadership through these meetings.

Why do churches feature Sunday evening *youth* groups only? Why can't there be a concomitant parents' hour for fellowship at least among those who have to come early to provide transportation for the young people anyway?

In many congregations, it is possible for members and friends of the congregation to have dinner together (it does not have to be elaborate) following the morning church service. This could be done regularly or monthly or quarterly. On this model, the evening service would be scuttled, a good bit of fellowship would be provided, and the day would be topped off by a late or mid-afternoon service. This format might be found very useful in communities in which it is dangerous to be on the streets after dark.

Again, in other places, on Sunday evenings the church could gather for a light supper early, hold a brief informal service at the conclusion and provide ample time for visitation among the members in each other's homes afterward.

Whatever plan is adopted (and these are only a few offered suggestively), one thing ought to be encouraged: members must learn the blessings of fellowship and hospitality once again. All of which leads to the next point.

3. The pastor will encourage hospitality by setting a good example himself. He will spend as much time (or more) fellowshipping over coffee or tea as in making routine house calls. Much of such fellowship will be in his own home (e.g., after the evening service for dessert). Often he will bring in two or three families who need to get to know one another. While he and his elders will probably get around to most of the homes once every year or so, he will certainly see to it that he makes other opportunities to get to know and to fellowship with every family and every member in the congregation. Out of these informal gatherings, where the conversation is allowed to drift, he will discover problems that may be handled best by setting up counseling appointments in the church study. In these more intensive, problem-oriented sessions, the work of healing the sheep most frequently will be carried on.

4. The pastor will not overestimate the importance of the house call by *equating* it with the biblical work of *visitation*.

Recognizing that visitation means complete care of the flock *as a whole* and of every member of the flock *individually*, he sees personal counsel, guidance, the meeting of congregational and individual needs (such as fellowship, the example we have just briefly explored), and even church discipline as functions of biblical visitation (caring concern). Therefore, he may wish to relate house calling to other aspects of visitation (congregational and personal care) in a manner similar to that which follows:

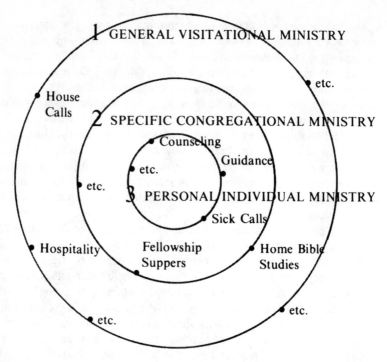

Figure #1
Visitation: Total Concern and Care

Circle #1 represents the most peripheral work of shepherdly visitation. House calling belongs to it. That does not make it less important. By faithfulness in the pursuit of activities like making house calls, offering hospitality, etc., much preventive work can be done and many problems can be uncovered before they grow more serious. But the work consists of regular, general activities designed to (1) discover problems, (2) show God's shepherdly concern by remembering members and their needs and (3) meet simple needs.

House calls, in particular, may be (a) formal or (b) informal. Formal calls are by appointment and made by the pastor or by an elder (or elders), or by both. Whenever elders visit in lieu of the pastor, they should be instructed to keep visitation records, which are inserted into the pastor's master file. Any important data about the visit should be conveyed to the pastor immediately. The three intentions of the formal call expressed above are the paramount objectives.

The making of appointments in house calling shows consideration, keeps the pastor from wasting time, allows the family to prepare (but families must be cautioned against overpreparation) and saves much gasoline.[6] Such house calls should always include Bible reading and prayer. Pastors should offer help in meeting any needs that the member(s) may care to mention, and without turning the visit into an inquisition should inquire after the state of the family in general.[7]

Informal calls are unplanned (occasional: "I happened to think of you as I was out going to . . . so I just stopped by") and have other purposes in view. Usually they are made without longstanding appointments. They can be the occasion for making important social visits in a member's home much like the gatherings that occur in the pastor's own home around dessert. At times there may be other means of contact. Some times of fellowship with the men of the congregation may include activities like golfing or fishing, or, perhaps, occasionally helping a member to paint his garage. The informal call or contact may include Bible reading and prayer (or may not) if the occasion affords opportunity.

EXERCISES

For the Student and Pastor

List as many ways as you can of discharging the biblical concern and care called visitation.

---

[6] It is preferable to have a secretary make most appointments. Too much time is wasted in telephone talk. People too often want to get quick solutions to problems over the telephone and will pressure the pastor to give them. So counseling appointments also should be made by another whenever possible. If he *must* make such appointments himself, he must learn to say clearly, "I cannot give you adequate answers before we have had time to discuss the problem thoroughly." Many still will persist. He must resist. Also, it is best not to have his wife make appointments for serious counseling matters. He must not allow others to think that he lets her know about counseling confidences.

[7] The Latin word *videre,* "to see" lies behind the English word *visit.* In whatever ways the pastor and the elders find most appropriate (so long as they are consistent with biblical norms), they must exercise their *oversight* (cf. esp. Hebrews 13:17).

For the Pastor

    1. List problems and needs in your congregation.

    2. From the Student-Pastor list above select the shepherdly ways and means of meeting these needs that seem most appropriate.

Needs	Ways & Means of Meeting Them

CHAPTER XII
HOUSE CALLING

How to Make House Calls

Before leaving the subject, it might be wise to discuss the matter of making house calls. Because much of this work has been and still must be carried on,[1] the subject has been studied thoroughly and much information has been gleaned about it.

I have already mentioned some problems connected with the making of appointments. Here, then, let us consider the actual visit itself.

The Entrance

Coming to the door after prayer for God's blessing upon the house call will help the pastor to be cheerful, relaxed (and thereby relaxing), confident and friendly. He should be sure that he comes from God's presence into the home. Everything in the call will be conditioned by this. Only then will the visit be the call of a "man of [from] God."

Unless the situation into which he enters is known to be grave and serious, the pastor should try to enter the home with a happy spirit. After an exchange of greetings, in which he attempts to size up the mood and situation (at least provisionally), the pastor should make an attempt to fit into or reshape the mood by his next responses. If the mood is casual or anticipatory (perhaps he even senses nervousness at his entrance), he might begin by commenting pleasantly about something that strikes his eye that might open a casual one- or two-minute exchange during which (1) he can

---

[1] It is of special importance for a minister entering into his duties as the newly-appointed pastor of a flock previously unknown to him to enter into an intensive campaign of house visitation. He would be wise to plan to call (with an elder) upon every home within a month or two following his arrival. Other efforts to know and become known also are important and should be coordinated with this campaign. It might be initiated (or climaxed) by a weekend retreat with the elders. Prior to arrival, especially if the period of waiting is at all extensive, the pastor-elect can request from the congregation to which he is going, a set of snapshots of all of the members of the congregation (together with their names), so that he and his family can begin to become acquainted with and pray for them. A wise pastor will ponder the meaning of Proverbs 24:27 with reference to his first weeks and months in a new pastorate.

further check up on his initial reading of the situation; (2) the householder can adapt to his presence and begin to relax. Often, an honest compliment will do well ("Your azaleas out front are lovely this year," or "Isn't that a new clock on your mantle?"). Such chit-chat ought not to be extended beyond a few sentences.

Sitting Down

Does this heading sound strange? Well, withhold judgment for a moment and consider the following brief, but pointed observation. It may save you a considerable amount of embarrassment. Here is an important don't: *Do not sit down until invited to do so.* Too many visits have been spoiled by the pastor thoughtlessly sitting down in a chair with a cracked leg that either (1) immediately gave way under him or (2) kept the householder's mind so preoccupied about whether it would that he (she) got nothing at all out of the call. The rule is: sit *where* directed *when* directed.

The Discussion

Giving suggestive opportunities to the householder to raise issues is one way for the pastor to begin if he knows of no special issue.[2] Mention the husband (or wife), the children, the marriage, school, work, the church, and—most important of all—the householder's own relationship to Christ. If nothing is forthcoming, a direct question is always in order ("Before I leave, is there any matter that you need to discuss with me?"). Sometimes in offering prayer a matter will surface ("I'm going to pray before I go; are there any particular matters that you'd like me to include in prayer?"). One minister finds it useful to send a note before every regular visit confirming the time and day and suggesting to the persons visited: "Be sure to jot down every question that you would like to discuss."[3] Another pastor, at the beginning of the visit, simply states: "I am here to be of as much help as I can be. What are the matters that you wish to take up?" Thus, together with the member, he sets up an agenda at the outset. At all costs, the pastor must make it clear that because God is interested in all of life, he, as God's shepherd, is willing to bring God's Word to bear upon any matter of concern. The discussion of problems probably should be reserved to those

---

[2] Cf. Theodore Cuyler, *How to Be a Pastor* (The Baker and Taylor Company, N.Y.: 1890), pp. 31ff: "Encourage them to talk about the Sabbath services; the truths preached; the difficulties raised or allayed; the light afforded, or the comforts given . . . of any special effects of the Word upon any of themselves. . . . Frown down all attempts against gossip, and seal your ears against malicious scandal. . . ."

[3] This note could contain a sentence with suggestive topics: "I shall be anxious to discuss any matters concerning the Church or recent sermons, or matters pertaining to your family or personal life."

problems that can be handled in one visit only. The discussion of problems taking longer ought to be scheduled for counseling in the study. By so scheduling further appointments, the pastor conveys interest and shows that he is interested in giving thorough rather than merely peripheral help. Most pastors will develop their own calling styles. Most find that style must be flexible and different approaches must be used with different people. The pastor who does not learn to adapt will fail to meet needs. Sometimes specific issues, growing out of past discussions, afford the best opportunities for giving assistance ("How has the problem with the discipline of the children worked out since we last talked?" . . . "Have you worked out the problem with Jonathan's mother yet?" . . . "Well, I am anxious to hear about how it went when you told the boss you were not going to put your job before your wife any longer!").Often a few minutes' thought beforehand, possibly coupled with a review of calling and counseling records, will provide the material for introducing such helpful openings.

Flexibility of approach is important. That means that rather than develop one standard approach to be used in all situations, the pastor who best exemplifies his Lord will learn how to deal with each *individually.* Jesus had no stereotype, but approached everyone differently (just notice the variety of approaches in the Gospel of John, for example). Yet, flexibility of approach, like all other true flexibility, grows out of cast iron structure. One can be flexible only when he is flexible in the use of something given. In this case he must be flexible in his use of clearly defined goals and objectives. It is not flexibility to allow the conversation to sail aimlessly across uncharted seas with no port in mind. There must be a destination in view, a captain in command, and a willingness to take any biblically legitimate course to reach that destination. Various factors may blockade the most direct route. Less direct yet more sure routes may need to be explored. In it all, the pastor must remain at the wheel and steer a course as direct as possible toward a known port in a charted manner. And, he must be careful not to allow contrary winds to blow him off course. The destination of the visit is twofold:

1. to uncover any special needs that ought to be met by the pastor;

2. to show God's loving concern for His sheep (a) by coming and (b) by offering any immediate assistance that might be required.

It should go without saying, but perhaps it is better to be clear and say it anyway, that the discussion—while centering upon the problems and needs of the householder(s)—will do so *in an importantly different context* than that which is developed, let us say, by a liberal or Unitarian visitor. From start to finish, the pastor comes as the representative of the Lord Jesus Christ. He is but an under-shepherd who works for and with the "Great Shepherd of the sheep" (Hebrews 13:20), who is the "Chief Shepherd" (I Peter 5:4) of the flock. As such, he mentions the will of the Shepherd, speaks always of His interests and continually represents Him as the one in whose *name* he has come. (Cf. esp. Matthew 10:40-42; Mark 9:41; Luke 24:47. In these passages Jesus plainly directed that ministry should not be carried out in one's own name, but in His.) This means that the pastor's conversation easily, and without either affectation or embarrassment, should turn from time to time to a discussion of the Lord and of His glory. His Word should be the basis for all advice and His help should be sought for all endeavors carried out in His name. Of all persons, the sheep should find it easiest and most comfortable to talk about the Shepherd with His undershepherds.

Length of the Call

Many pastoral calls are too lengthy. Within broad limits, *each call sets its own length.* Generally speaking the rule is: the more substantive the discussion, the longer the call. Chatty calls of an informal sort can be as brief as five minutes' duration; substantive calls might last hours. For the average call, a pastor might plan to spend from twenty minutes to one hour. When he finds that he still requires more time and that there is much yet to be accomplished, in many instances (probably most) it would be wise for him to terminate the present call and schedule a *series* of weekly counseling sessions in the study. While it is important to strike while the iron is hot, some pastors find that (especially in very tense discussions) they can get *only so much and no more* accomplished in one discussion. Ordinarily one hour of discussion under tension is about all that can be pursued fruitfully. It is better, usually, to nail down one or two initial steps in a solution that will help make progress toward the ultimate solution, and let these develop before trying to handle any more matters. True gains are made *only if they have time to become solidified.* Giving someone too many things to do (especially during a first visit) often discourages and confuses him. In such cases, the visit may be considered a precounseling contact. It may be considered to be successful if the problem emerges, the householder shows concern for honoring God in the matter, initial steps are taken to begin to deal with it, and agreement is reached to begin a series of more formal counseling appointments.

When during a visit it becomes apparent that no special problems will be raised, the pastor should consider the call to be at an end[4] and should make an effort to bring it to a close. He may close a visit in several ways. Usually, the formal house call can be closed simply by saying, "Before I say goodbye, let me read a portion of the Scriptures and have prayer." Upon doing so, the pastor should arise immediately, head slowly for the doorway (or request his coat) and *without lingering* leave. Some pastors, to the exasperation of their members, try to conduct a second discussion in the hallway. That is no place to talk. When a pastor announces his departure, he should be as good as his word. The usefulness of what he has done during the visit can be destroyed by such dawdling. Many men waste as much as twenty minutes per call because of this bad habit.

Bible Reading[5]

It is always good form to use the householder's Bible whenever it is readily available. The pastor then may insert a tract or pamphlet at the place from which he read so that the member may reread for himself at his leisure. This is especially crucial whenever there has been a necessity to discuss the application of a passage of Scripture during the previous conversation. This should be a regular practice, not merely occasional, since few people know how to make personal application of the Scriptures themselves. Sometimes it is also necessary—when the Bible is not at hand—to jot down the Bible reference on a card or tract and leave that instead. In one way or another, it is important to direct the householder to ways in which he may further reflect upon the discussion of his life in the light of God's Word.

At any rate, whatever Bible is used, the Scripture reading ought to grow out of and be appropriate to some aspect of the discussion. A brief portion, read at times with a crisp explanation (whenever necessary), is best. Whenever in the discussion itself a particular Scripture passage was read, explained and applied, it is wise to use this same passage again for the closing Bible reading ("Let me remind you of what God says about love by rereading that passage in I Corinthians 13 . . ."). Long readings (and especially without explanation) are rarely productive.[6] The pastor will have a

---

[4]Unless, of course, he suspects that problems exist but that the householder is refusing to mention them. Then, in a proper way, he may broach the subject himself. Cf. *The Christian Counselor's Manual,* pp. 290-293.

[5]The pastor can make the mistake of talking about the Bible while failing to show clearly that (and how) the authority for his advice comes from the Word of God itself. He must never *assume* that references to verses, passages or teachings of the Scriptures will be understood or accepted as such. Therefore, it is essential to establish every major thrust in a pastoral discussion or counseling session by direct reference to and explanation of the principal scriptural passages themselves.

[6]People often learn to tune out the Bible since they do not understand it. Better to read, ex-

growing list of passages appropriate to various situations that he uses frequently with profit.[7]

Prayer[8]

As with the Scripture reading, the prayer should *focus* upon the discussion. Yet, the prayer may (indeed should) range beyond. It should seek to bring the whole of God's concern into relationship with this family. It should go beyond human needs and speak dominantly of the ultimate concern of all believers: to glorify God. Thanksgiving should be mingled with earnest supplication. Doxology should balance confession of sin. While man is sinful, God is holy; while our problems may yet be unsolved, God's purposes are victoriously unfolding. There is, then, always a note of joy and triumph possible in any call, and it is upon that note that it should end. That triumph and joy are found in God; but we who know Him may enter into it too, for the Kingdom of God is righteousness and peace and joy by the Holy Spirit (Romans 14:17).

Some Thoughts on House Calls

It is plain that house calling either can become a blessing or a burden to the pastor. Unless he learns to say "no" to the incessant thoughtless requests of some members to make unnecessary house calls,[9] and unless he develops the biblical view of visitation that puts house calling in its proper but limited place, the pastor will, like many before him, carry about the unnecessary and crushing load of the guilt of the unmade call. Proper scheduling (q.v.), a biblical perspective and a reasonable plan for house calling will remove the load. I mention this burden again because it is so widely felt by so many pastors and has been such a large contributing factor in the decision of many to leave the ministry. Do not allow the Adversary to gain a beachhead here. Together with a proper program of study and sermon

---

plain and apply one proverb (e.g., "Better is open rebuke than hidden love." Proverbs 27:5) than to read the whole 119th Psalm! Long readings, like long prayers, can readily lead to formalistic religion.

[7]See the Exercises at the end of this Chapter for a suggested way in which to list passages. The pastor should be careful to maintain visiting records on which he records the date of each visit and the Scripture read. Duplication of readings is possible otherwise. 3 x 5 cards as part of his general filing system (q.v.) afford one useful method of record-keeping.

[8]Prayer, like Bible study, links the sheep directly to the chief Shepherd. Apart from these two endeavors, it is too easy for the householder to conclude that the comfort, encouragement or advice is merely human. The pastor, therefore, should always, by the use of prayer and the Scriptures, bring the member of the congregation into direct confrontation with Jesus Christ.

[9]He must courageously say "no" when he simply *cannot* make another call or *shouldn't* make the one suggested. At times he may respond, "I am very heavily scheduled just now; if the call is so crucial, will you visit for me, since you are concerned?" If he is conscientious he will gain respect rather than lose it by agreeing only to as many calls as he truly can (and should) make.

preparation, correct practices of visitation and house calls will give a freedom and release to one's ministry that nothing else can provide. The formal call should never deteriorate into an inquisition. As A. H. Baldinger once wrote:

> To be sure, the pastor of today is not the pastor of former days, neither indeed can he be. It is sometimes difficult for older members of the church to recognize the changed conditions amid which pastoral work must be done, or to adjust their minds to the fact. Time was when the pastoral function consisted principally of periodic visitation of the homes for the purpose of exhorting the parents and catechising the children (provided he could get hold of the latter before they ran away and hid). It was a solemn day for the family when the minister called.[10]

While changes in practices of house calling have occurred, many of these have been based upon something less than biblical principle.[11] All changes in pastoral work must arise out of an effort to better understand and better apply the scriptural norms to a changing society. Each change in society that creates problems for pastoral work should send pastors back to their Bibles to reexamine the scriptural injunctions in an attempt to make the new applications that are demanded. Sometimes in return, new insight is gained (especially is this true in the area of pastoral work, about which so little scholarly study has been done). But the pastor always must be careful not to bend the Bible to the circumstances. Neither the Bible nor the pastor may become a mirror to reflect the times; rather, they must become a force to mold them.

Surely, however, the sort of "solemn day for the family" that Baldinger describes as typical of the calling of the pastor in the homes of his members, we may be glad has all but disappeared (in some tight-knit ethnic circles it still persists[12]). Such fear of the minister and the elders, such gloom over the coming of the shepherd who comes in the name of the Good Shepherd to do good to His sheep has no biblical support. It was wrong and always shall be wrong. The solemn visit can be considered a welcome loss, hopefully never to be brought to light again. The coming of Christ's shepherd should be a time of hope and even of joy. The discussion should be conversational and substantive, never dictatorial or inquisitorial. A biblical balance of authority, desire to minister and loving concern provides the proper attitude. However, it should be noted that the original *intention* behind the

---

[10]*The United Presbyterian,* November 30, 1933, p. 5.
[11]Baldinger seems to be reconciled to change that grows out of changing societal conditions.
[12]Just this past week the pastor of such a church explained that members of his church still literally tremble when he stops by. Some of the women clean house for three days beforehand.

formal pastoral call, which may have misfired by being transformed into an inquisitorial session, must *not* be lost. Too often in reaction the baby goes out with the bath. The formal solemn visit had behind it the proper biblical intention of inquiring into the state of the lives of the members *in order to help*. Unfortunately, the means had become the end. Yet, discovering needs, we have maintained all along, is one Scriptural purpose of true pastoral concern. But this biblical objective best can be reached and the end kept clearly in view, by grasping the wider biblical notion of *visitation* and by making the house call one means toward that end.[13]

While it is true that house calls may uncover information that demands exhortation or even censure, and while it is possible that many calls may (should) develop into a solemn discussion of sin and its consequences, that is quite a different matter. It is one thing to enter the house—every house—with a solemn chip-on-the-shoulder, and it is another to enter as Christ's servant coming to offer help from His Word in the name of the Lord.

Most disciplinary matters are handled best by scheduling a special call, clearly demarked ahead of time as a visit in which the topic of discussion is known to all parties beforehand, and which is clearly differentiated and distinguished from a regular pastoral call.[14]

It is vital for the pastor to avoid carrying gossip about the congregation as he visits; otherwise he will become a spiritual Typhoid Mary. Not only should he keep his own mouth closed, but he must be quick to stop the mouths of others who would like to fill his ears with such pollution. A gentle rebuke, often *implied* in the pastor's refusal to receive gossip as soon as he is able to identify it as such, will silence it and help a thoughtless member for years to come. Others must be dealt with more directly. Sometimes the only way to handle the problem is to interrupt and warn, "If I continue to listen to this, you recognize that it will obligate me before God to go and talk to Phyllis about this problem; and, of course, I must reveal my source of information."

---

[13]No such situation ever could have developed if the house call had been placed in its proper biblical perspective as one among many of the ways and means of exercising oversight and care for God's flock. Its unscriptural exaltation to the be-all of pastoral activity ("the pastoral function consisted principally of periodic visitation of the homes") so highlighted the call for both pastor and people that this anti-biblical view of visitation developed.

[14]It is best, of course, to hold such disciplinary discussions in the study whenever possible. This allows for full control of the environment, assuring all concerned of privacy and eliminating harmful distractions or annoying interruptions. Yet, in disciplinary cases, particularly where stubbornness and rebellion complicate the picture, it is not always possible to elicit agreement from all parties to come. That leaves the pastor no other alternative than to go. Cf. *The Christian Counselor's Manual*, pp. 58, 59.

The old saying, "A house-going pastor makes a church-going congregation," is only partly true. Many pastors who have bought the simple statement merely at face value have discovered that its mechanical application did not pay off such handsome dividends. Instead, they found that the hours were long and exhausting and the returns were few. What they (and possibly the wit who first put together the proverb) failed to understand is that it is not house-going *per se* that leads to church-going. Rather, looking at pastors who visited faithfully by making house calls, they assumed that the call, in and of itself, was what made the difference. To a small extent, doubtless, the showing of interest in ("remembering") does pay off. But what they failed to see was that the all-important factor was *what went on* during those visits. Certainly in those cases in which substantive help was offered and given, in which the calls were the prelude to more intensive follow-up during counseling sessions, etc., *that kind of* house-going led to a meaningful kind of church-going. Church attendance growing out of superficial calling ("I covered fifteen houses today!") will tend to be of a kind with it.[15] Persons whose allegiance is gained in this way come just so long as the pastor feverishly makes the rounds to say "hello and good-bye" every two or three weeks. They are won by the attention of the pastor, and not often to faith in his God. But when a minister has called, uncovered a serious problem and dealt with it in depth over six weeks of consecutive follow-up counseling sessions in the study, and a marriage has been saved as the result, or a boy has been rescued from drugs, and the counselees have been drawn close to God, *that* family is more likely to become a church-going family that will continue to come and to listen and to grow whether the pastor ever visits them again or not. They are there because he led them to the Chief Shepherd, not to himself. It is the quality and the content of pastoral visitation, not merely the fact of calling, that count.

The pastor who keeps in mind the three basic purposes of pastoral calling, (1) to uncover sins and needs; (2) to show God's concerned interest in His sheep and (3) to deal with simple problems, will not expect too much from making house calls (leading to disappointment and discouragement). Nor will he depend too heavily upon pastoral calling (leading to the false notion that making house calls = shepherdly visitation[16]) as the one and

---

[15]Cf. J. H. Jowett, *The Preacher: His Life and Work* (Baker Book House, Grand Rapids: 1968), p. 185: "I have no confidence whatever in the ministry which calculates its afternoon's work by the number of doorbells it has rung . . . I attach little value to the breathless knocking at a door, the restless, 'How do you do?' and the perspiring departure to another door . . . even less value to a sharp, short series of afternoon gossipings which only skim the surfaces of things. . . ."

[16]Surely it is of significance that nothing approximating the house call is inherent in the two fundamental passages that most fully describe pastoral care (Psalm 23; John 10).

only means of pastoral care. He will be concerned instead to develop and use every other general and specific means possible for assuming this responsibility.

Commenting upon Acts 20:20, the text most pertinent to pastoral calling, John Calvin (as he so often did) wrote what so far might be considered the definitive word:

> This is the second point, that he did not only teach all men in the congregation, but also everyone privately as every man's necessity did require. For Christ had not appointed pastors upon this condition, that they may only teach the church in general in the open pulpit, but that they may take charge of every particular sheep.[17]

In conclusion, it may be said that the formal house call is a (1) biblical, (2) useful and (3) necessary part of every faithful pastor's ministry. Yet it must neither be equated with visitation, nor should a minister spend too large a proportion of his time engaged in making house calls. Instead, he must concentrate upon pastoral visitation (of which making house calls is but one part) and determine what the priorities must be in the concerned care of each particular flock that he is called upon to shepherd. These will be determined not only by the standard ministerial activities required by every congregation of the Lord Jesus Christ, but also by the specific needs of each congregation as they appear from the pastor's concerned analysis of them.

While he will not depend upon pastoral calling as the one-and-only means to accomplish the work of shepherdly care and discipline, he will by virtue of a narrower focus expect to accomplish more through house calls than he did formally. If he *restricts* his goals to the three aforementioned, he can *concentrate* upon them. Instead of attempting to accomplish everything by means of house calling (and thereby actually accomplishing very little), by *focusing* upon showing God's interested concern ("remembering"), discovering problems and meeting simple needs, he will do much more. Clear goals and purposes lead to more actual achievement for Christ. The man who calls, not knowing what he wants to accomplish in a call, more often than not, is likely to go away not knowing what did happen. By centering upon specific objectives in depth, the pastor can determine (1) whether or not he has achieved the ends that he had in view, and if not, (2) what hindered him in doing so.[18] Focus and concentration

---

[17]John Calvin, *Commentary Upon the Acts of the Apostles,* Vol. II, H. Beveridge, trans. (Edinburgh: Calvin Translation Society, 1884), p. 244.

[18]Self-evaluation and improvement thrives under conditions where the goals are clearly in focus, for then the pastor cannot deceive himself as readily about whether he was successful in his endeavors.

are important: one can do so much more of less. The narrower the goals, the more fully they can be accomplished. Samuel Shoemaker rightly observes that "a clergyman today often fails . . . from scattering his shot too widely."[19] Therefore, above all, know and pursue definite realistic goals in making the formal call. Then, the "widespread scepticism and . . . constant revolt"[20] against making house calls will vanish, for they will become what they ought always to have been: one profitable, fruitful means for pursuing the work of pastoral visitation.

EXERCISES

For the Student

1. Arrange to go along on several house calls with an elder or pastor. Observe, question, discuss and evaluate what took place. Write out your conclusions below.

---

[19]Samuel Shoemaker, *Beginning Your Ministry* (Harper and Row, Publishers, N. Y.: 1963), p. 54.

[20]Charles E. Jefferson, *The Ministering Shepherd* (Y.M.C.A., Paris: 1912), pp. 35, 36.

2. Arrange to make several house calls yourself. Afterwards, evaluate these, noting strengths, weaknesses and what you may do to improve.

Strengths	Weaknesses	Improvements

For the Pastor

In the boxes below build up a growing list of verses for various visiting situations for use as ready reference.

Situation	Verses

CHAPTER XIII
SPECIFIC CONGREGATIONAL MINISTRY

In Acts 20:28, Paul exhorts the elders to care for "all of the flock." Clearly a flock is composed of individual sheep, but it is also an entity itself—a *flock* (he does not say "each of the sheep"). Thus, the object of the pastor's work is the flock (the body, the building) as a whole, as well as each member in particular. But, as the letters to the seven congregations in the Book of Revelation indicate, each congregation has its own peculiar problems and needs at any given time. These require specific care and ministry adapted to each situation that goes beyond the general on-going concerns of regular congregational visitation that are necessary for the well-being of every congregation.

Planned programs, endeavors, etc., aimed at filling in the holes and repairing rips are in view here. Visitation of the congregation in this sense implies the sort of concern that leads to congregational analysis in order to uncover and understand its peculiar problems. This analysis, in turn, leads to creative adaptation of the program of the church in ways that are calculated to solve those programs. Often, this may require program innovations growing out of and consistent with biblical principles. For instance, the example of lack of fellowship and the various suggestions about how to solve the problem that has been the major interest of the last few pages, is an excellent example of a more intensive attempt at pastoral visitation-in-order-to-bless. The pastor works on various levels (one of which may include the house call) to help the flock meet this problem. Other activities of a sort programmed at the congregational level, such as the institution of regular fellowship dinners, home Bible studies, etc., may be devised to meet the need for fellowship.[1] All of this work, it must be noted, however, is to be done to build up the congregation in a way

---

[1] As well as other needs, of course, the home Bible study may serve to meet many needs at once, as can readily be seen. Generally speaking, in a day when time is so rapidly consumed on transportation, etc., it is wise to combine as many functions as possible. It is rarely wise for a minister, or for a congregational program, to plan to do merely one thing at a time. Multiple-telic programming is a vital consideration that cannot be ignored.

that pleases God and brings honor to Him. Unless this emphasis is kept central, and unless the pastor himself constantly reminds the congregation of the purpose of Christian fellowship, etc., the care can disintegrate into mere activity and self-concern.

It is vital for the pastor to read, analyze and react to congregational needs and trends. In scriptural terms, he is to be a "watchman." Cf. Acts 20:28, as well as many references in the Old Testament. Enemies come from without and from within. When heresy is stalking the flock like a hungry wolf, he should be aware of its presence and guard the sheep from its every attack. Hebrews 13:17, among a wealth of other passages, also speaks of watching over souls. "Watch and pray" suggests the twofold direction of the shepherd's task: he must be alert and seek God's grace to meet those challenges that confront the flock. If congregational attendance at morning/evening services, prayer meetings, the Church School, etc., is down (or up), it is his business (1) to discover why, and prayerfully (2) to do whatever is necessary to remedy (or encourage) the trend. If workers cannot be found to staff the Vacation Bible School, for example, he must ask: "Is the problem

(1) not enough interested, dedicated personnel?

(2) not enough trained personnel?

(3) a poor choice of dates for VBS?

(4) poor material or facilities for VBS?

(5) bad past experiences with VBS?

(6) waning response from families and children?

(7) dissatisfaction with former leadership in VBS?

(8) a combination of these and/or other reasons?"

Congregational giving may reflect general attitudes in many ways; he is sensitive to these. He knows also that an index of congregational lack of interest in missions may mirror failure on the part of the pastor to challenge the congregation about missionary concerns, dissatisfaction with the missionary program of the denomination, lack of love coupled with self-centeredness, etc. There can be multiple causes of one result. It does no good to challenge the congregation to greater giving, for instance, when there has been great disappointment over the presentation and general quality of the work of the last three missionary representatives who spoke at the church. An entirely different approach to the problem will be needed. But, apart from concern to analyze and to discover the true factor or factors that caused and that continue to feed a problem, it is nearly always impossible to remedy it. Therefore, the shepherd will build watchtowers. From these a general survey analysis of the state of the congregation should be made periodically to assess the situation and to take measures to meet any problems that seem to be emerging.[2] This information may be gleaned in many ways. Yearly overnight retreats with the elders and with other leaders in the congregation aimed at gathering such information may help. Time regularly spent at each elders' meeting in discussion of aspects of the life of the congregation may (1) make elders' meetings more vital and at the same time (2) help the elders to take a greater interest in and responsibility for the welfare of the flock. But no matter what else is done, the minister should get out among the rank and file members of the congregation to take a sampling of ideas, attitudes, etc.[3] In part, the regular house call, the casual coffee-and-dessert discussion and other measures calculated to hear from the members themselves will provide the basic information needed. Whatever methods are adopted, however, must be developed *fully* and utilized *regularly*. Skill in sighting potential enemies and preparing for their attack is vital. The good shepherd will obey God and take the time to build and use his watchtowers (developing the best ways and means for overseeing the flock) and to develop his skills of observation and analysis. A flock with a watchful pastor may "fear no evil" though he must lead them "through the valley of the shadow of death."

When Ezekiel pictures the unattended flock neglected by its shepherd, he says, "They became food for all the beasts of the field when they were scattered" (Ezekiel 34:5b). In these days of heresy, liberalism, secularization, psychologizers, occultism, radical ideologists, etc., flocks whose shepherds fail to watch become prey for every kind of wild beast. Many sheep have been devoured. Let every shepherd, therefore, heed the warning of Ezekiel 34:7ff.

The Care of Families

Perhaps the most pertinent need of many congregations today is the preservation and care of families and marriages. Every pastor will discover that fully eighty per cent of his serious counseling problems will directly

---

[2]Our Lord set the example for such concern by the writing of His seven letters to the seven churches in Asia Minor.

[3]Pollsters can teach us here. They take *samplings* rather than talk to everyone. The minister should develop a network of key representative persons who reflect a cross section of the congregation from whom he can readily obtain a valid picture.

involve marriage (husband/wife) and family (child/parent/in-law) problems. We shall reserve further comment about marriage and family counseling for a later section. But here, the concern is more basic. Recognizing that the basic attacks of our day are upon marriage itself and the institution of the family, the pastor must guard his flock from them and endeavor by every biblically legitimate means to instruct, cultivate and foster strong Christian marriage and family relationships. His pastoral task in this regard then is

(1) to recognize the basic nature of the contemporary attack upon the foundation of God's Church and society in general: i.e., upon marriage and the family;

(2) to take every measure to insure that these attacks are blunted by the teaching of the pure Word of God, which alone affords the power to defend one from the fiery darts of the Evil One;

(3) to instruct covenant youth about the fundamentals of marriage and family life, since in modern society they will be "educated" (by TV, magazines, college professors, the general gossip of the day, etc.) in views that see marriage and family life as optional, open, subject to any and all modifications, and who knows what next. If they are to receive thorough biblical instruction about marriage at all, it will almost certainly be obtained from the church, for the previous generation rarely received it or knows how to impart it in the family context itself.

This instruction must not be concerned with the esoteric or fine questions about marriage, but rather must concentrate upon the biblical basics themselves. It should be a deliberate part of the program of every pastor today not only to preach frequently about biblical solutions to marriage and family problems, but also to spend a definite period of time instructing covenant youth in the fundamentals of marriage and family living. Time off from Sunday School, youth meetings, catechism, or whatever seems best for a period of no less than twelve weeks, in which the pastor himself (or some *very* capable elder) takes the time to give such instruction, is mandatory in our time.[4] Pastors must become deeply concerned to operate preventively rather than settle for patching things up later on.

(4) Pastors should become concerned about developing ways and means to implement Titus 2:4: that the "more mature women (v. 3) . . . train the younger women. . . ." Much of this may happen at home, as indeed it should. But it is hardly likely to happen spontaneously in our day of biblical ignorance unless the ways and means of promoting it are developed. It is vital

---

[4]An instruction manual, Jay Adams, *Christian Living In the Home* (Presbyterian and Reformed Publishing Company, Nutley: 1972), has been prepared for use in such courses, as well as for use in marriage and family counseling.

to note that Paul does not say "mothers" but "older (more mature) women." That means, probably, the development of week-day morning courses for women to help them to learn how to instruct their daughters. But it cannot mean only that. Something more ought to be done, for Paul did not say "to train their daughters," limiting the responsibilities to the instruction of one's own children; he wrote that it is up to "mature women . . . to train the younger women." The referents in view are *all* of the younger women of a congregation. This is necessary because

(a) not all of the younger women have converted mothers to teach them;

(b) not all converted mothers are capable of teaching for various reasons;

(c) not all converted mothers themselves are living as they ought or know God's Word as they should;

(d) not all converted mothers excel in the same gifts. By pooling the gifts of each of many women to teach all of the younger women, much more help can be shared generally among the members of the congregation;

(e) often younger women will best receive instruction about some skills from a woman other than their own mother.

Therefore, some programs at some time (perhaps for a quarter of each year during the Church School hours) should be devoted to fulfilling this vital task. Up until now, women (as well as *male pastors*) have neglected this all-important task. It is high time for conservative pastors to see both the need and the opportunities that this whole untapped area affords. All too often the women's societies are looking for something worthwhile to do. Who can offer a suggestion for a more important project for them to undertake? What other project is so clearly assigned to them by God in the Scriptures? Yet, we find women bored to tears, wondering what to do![5] Here is an exciting, challenging, vital task almost totally ignored in the history of the church. In our day, no pastor can afford to neglect this untapped potential for good.

(5) Older men must also take on the task of teaching the younger men. God in Titus 2 is explicit about that point too. Indeed, there can be no

---

[5]There will be far fewer problems with the excesses of women's lib activities, or women seeking to take over functions that do not belong to them, if they become occupied in fulfilling the tasks that have been assigned to them by God Himself.

more important work for the pastor to do with families than to train the heads of those families. If priorities must be weighed, the pastor must give heaviest weight to the work that he does with men, especially with husbands and fathers. As a standard practice, he should from time to time communicate with families through their heads.[6] Not *every* announcement should be made to *everyone*. At the beginning of a chapter of the boys' brigade in the church, it might be well for the pastor to gather all of the fathers of boys together to announce its formation and to challenge them to assume the responsibilities of operating it and sending their boys. Special courses for men to discuss the meaning and implementation of headship in the modern home might well be conducted during the Church School hour at least once every year. I have discussed many of the basic issues that might be considered in *Christian Living in the Home,* so I shall not develop these here.

(6) Couples' classes (or courses) are a must. Not only can family conferences and weekend retreats be held once each year, but regular weekly or monthly meetings at which practical problems ("How do we provide for aging parents?" . . . "What is the best means of discipline in the home?" . . . "How can we prepare for grief?" . . . "What are the biblical principles of sexual relations?") may be aired, and at which instruction from the Scriptures can be given, are vital. Fellowship, sometimes of the finest sort, often flourishes in such meetings. It is important, however, to be sure that these gatherings do not deteriorate into Encounter or Sensitivity Training sessions, with all of their attendant dangers.[7] This is God's work; in all of it He must be focal, not merely in name but in fact.

To sum up, then, the pastor has a preventive ministry of sensing the needs of his time, their particular manifestations as problems in his flock, of guarding and inoculating the sheep against them, and of caring for the whole flock, every family and each individual.

---

[6]It is important at every opportunity to single out the heads of families *as such* and to work with them in a special way to make them aware of their responsibilities as heads of homes.

[7]For more specifics about such dangers, see Jay Adams, "Group Therapy or Slander?" *The Big Umbrella* (Presbyterian and Reformed Publishing Company, Nutley: 1972).

EXERCISES

For the Student

1. Interview five pastors and try to discover from them a number of specific problems or needs peculiar to each congregation.

2. Choose one problem or need from each congregation and write a paper suggesting ways and means of meeting (at least in part) those needs by special efforts of pastoral care (visitation).

3. Give a part of the paper (that pertains to his congregation) to the pastor of each congregation and ask him to write his evaluations on it. Return the paper, together with the evaluations, to your professor for final evaluation.

For the Pastor

If you are convinced that a program for women modeled on Titus 2:3-5 is necessary, use the space below to sketch a plan for expediting it. Include steps to take in organizing together with a schedule for organization, and names of specific persons who might be contacted to launch the program.

CHAPTER XIV
PERSONAL MINISTRY: COUNSELING

Personal ministry largely consists of counseling, ministering to the sick and to the bereaved and dying. Since we shall have more to say about counseling and the visitation of the sick and dying at subsequent points, here it will be sufficient to make only three general preliminary observations about counseling.[1]

1. *Counseling is best carried on in the study, not in the home.* While the pastor must be flexible, and must be prepared to counsel anywhere, he will endeavor to restrict all intensive counseling to formal sessions in the study. There are many reasons for this.

(a) It is important for the pastor to be in control of the counseling situation. In homes, pots boil over, doorbells and telephones ring, TV sets distract, and children come running through the room. Often the seating arrangement makes it most difficult to counsel effectively. A counselor needs to concentrate fully upon the counselee's problem and cannot afford for himself or the counselee to be distracted. In the study, because he is in control, the pastor can arrange the counseling environment to avoid most of these interruptions. This allows him more readily to close a session, obtain handouts (counseling materials, booklets, Scripture portions, etc.), make necessary phone calls ("We'll just phone the doctor and see what he says about . . ."), etc.

(b) It is a way to serve more persons more fully. In our busy world in which a congregation is sprawled out all over the map, the pastor who does not use his study fully wastes his time and money (neither of which are his but the Lord's[2]) and the time of the congregation by chasing all over a city to make counseling visits. By asking members to come to the study[3] for

---

[1] In the next volume I discuss various aspects of pastoral counseling that I have not considered elsewhere. In particular, a substantial section will be devoted to premarital and marital counseling.

[2] He should set the example of good stewardship of the Lord's time and money.

[3] Cf. Jay Adams, *The Christian Counselor's Manual* (Presbyterian and Reformed Publishing Company, Nutley: 1973), pp. 221-225, for further suggestions on training a congregation to come to the study.

counseling, the pastor gives them the very best kind of counseling in the best counseling environment, can provide more time for counseling, and best serves the Lord by best serving the whole congregation. Non-members should be urged to come too; this has the secondary benefit of getting them into the pattern of coming to the building where the congregation meets.[4] Familiarity with it may make it easier later on to attend services.

(c) Counselees are better prepared when they come to the study. Because they are already acclimated to the idea that when they go to the physician's or lawyer's office they must prepare themselves to make known their needs, counselees also more readily get down to brass tacks in the minister's study than elsewhere. They talk less about the time of day, Aunt Susie's sore toe and the like, and more often about their real concerns. The more businesslike (not cold or professionally sterile) atmosphere means a more businesslike approach to problems.

2. *In general, it is better not to announce set hours for counseling.* If the pastor plans such hours for his own schedule, he can make these known (when necessary) to those who seek help at the time of making the appointment. But, as a rule, if the pastor can be flexible enough to switch study time (for instance) for counseling time, he will be wise to allow for such change in cases (1) where there is a true emergency; (2) when, if he does not strike while the iron is hot, it may cool too rapidly. However, he should be careful *not* to make such concessions for persons who persistently take advantage of his consideration. To do so is only to contribute to their problems by reinforcing their lack of consideration for others. If the pastor makes his counseling appointments according to his *own* unannounced schedule, therefore, he may so arrange his appointments as to restructure the habits of thoughtless persons (which is an element in the counseling process itself[5]).

3. *The pastor should learn to use God's untapped resources in counseling.* I have written elsewhere about the use of the Scriptures and prayer and the importance of employing Christ's authority and discipline (all in the power of the Holy Spirit) in counseling. All of these resources have been virtually untapped for two generations. Only today are conservative

---

[4]For gathering basic information from non-members, the Personal Data Inventory is invaluable. See *The Christian Counselor's Manual,* pp. 433-435.

[5]Counseling involves the whole relationship from beginning to end. How appointments are made and kept can make a great deal of difference in how the counseling will proceed. If the pastor is sloppy or confused about these matters, he communicates this *at the outset.* His procedures (whatever they may be) should be well thought through and followed faithfully. From the beginning he should be *on top of* such matters. This instills confidence at the outset. A secretary who can learn to be gently firm about such matters is invaluable.

ministers beginning to awaken to the vast potential of counseling help that *they*—rather than the non-Christian counselor, psychiatrist or clinical psychologist—possess. Through these resources they

(1) know man's basic nature: a creature created in God's image;

(2) know man's basic problem: sin;

(3) know God's basic solution: salvation (including not merely justification, but the ongoing process of sanctification as well);

(4) know what man's purposes in life are: to glorify and enjoy God forever;

(5) know how a man's life must be patterned: according to the life of Jesus Christ, who alone perfectly exemplified the meaning of the commandments by loving God and his neighbor as they require;

(6) know the One who provides the power to live according to God's requirements: the Holy Spirit.

All of this, and all that it implies, belongs to the Christian pastor as counselor. He must not, therefore, defer to another who has set himself up as a counselor, with neither the divine commission nor resources to do so. In contrast, the authorized Christian counselor is "thoroughly equipped" by God (II Timothy 3:17) for every good work.

There is, however, one resource about which little has been said and about which I wish to say a word or two. That resource is the Church itself.

When considering counseling, it is easy for the pastor on the one hand to forget (or ignore) the social needs of counselees and on the other the latent power of a congregation of God's people to meet such needs. The counselor must grapple seriously with the mighty force that the congregation itself can become, either for good or for evil; either to further or thwart the sanctification aimed at in the counseling. He must discover, by God's grace, how to harness and direct that force. The congregation is never neutral; the force it exerts will help or hinder, or do some of each. Therefore, the counselor must reckon with this power and learn to bend and mold its potential for good. When he does, he will discover the excitement of doing counseling, not alone in the cold impersonal context of an office, but of working together with flocks and families to help each member who is in need. He must remember Ephesians 4:11, 12.

In dozens of ways congregations exert pressure. In disciplinary cases, for instance, the way in which a repentant offender is received by the congregation can make all of the difference in his reclamation (cf. II Cor. 2:5-8) and future usefulness in the Kingdom of God. The standoffishness of the congregation at Jerusalem would have excluded the potential apostle of the gentiles from its midst if it had not been for Barnabas (cf. Acts 9:26-28). The pastor must learn how to follow the lead of Barnabas, whether he is bringing into the church a converted persecutor like Paul, or whether he is seeking to reinstate a repentant failure like John Mark. Barnabas was truly a "son of *paraclesis*," i.e., one who was outstanding for the ways in which he learned how to stand by those who needed him in their hour of need, regardless of who thought to do otherwise. Fearlessly, he cared for others in the face of intimidation and opposition. In this way too, God calls upon the pastor to function.

Yet, if he spends time beforehand molding the board of elders, the leaders of organizations, and the congregation as a whole, by his preaching as well as in group discussions and personal confrontation for such work, he will have less opposition and more cooperation. And that is just what he wants: a congregation that enthusiastically seeks to cooperate with him in the work of counseling. A congregation like this is one that responds warmly when he asks for an elder to spend an evening in a home helping a family to get started on family devotions. When he needs a home in which a new convert who has just thrown off his drug habit can stay for two weeks, he gets more offers than he needs. When Barbara, who was unfaithful to her husband, repents and is forgiven by God, by her husband and by the board of elders, returns to the women's organization, she discovers that they have forgiven her too.

Congregations like this grow only under the ministry of a man who sees a need for them and, because he recognizes the potential, calls upon them frequently in dozens of ways to exercise their gifts to help him do his counseling more effectively. Rarely do the members of congregations learn to "stimulate one another to love and good works" apart from the guidance of a shepherd who, by asking them to do so in scores of concrete situations, leads them into the joys and blessings of such work. By preaching and practical application that emphasizes the true message of the parable of the Elder Brother, members of a congregation can at length be taught to rejoice with the angels that Christ has sought and found His stray sheep.

Discovering how to use the diaconate fully for ministries of mercy, not only to the sick, but to those with other needs, is perhaps one of the best ways to begin to activate a congregation to the responsibility that Christ has given to each member of His flock to be his brother's keeper.[6]

---

[6]For a full discussion of this subject, see "You Are Your Brother's Counselor," *The Big Umbrella*. A discussion of diaconal work may be found on pp. 351, 352 of this combination volume.

EXERCISES

For the Student

Write an essay on the place of counseling in the care and discipline (visitation) of members. You may wish to compare the benefits of pastoral counseling with traditional views of house calling.

For the Pastor

1. Draw up a personal policy statement for counseling. State goals, objectives, times, ways, means, etc.

2. If you have not already done so, begin to organize a file system for counseling notes and records. For help, cf. *The Christian Counselor's Manual*, pp. 228ff., 237, 258, 263ff.

STATEMENT

_____

_____

_____

_____

_____

_____

_____

_____

_____

_____

_____

CHAPTER XV
VISITING THE SICK

All Should Visit

It is the duty and privilege of all Christians to visit (i.e., to be concerned about and care for the needs of) the sick. Matthew 25:36 makes this plain. God has served notice that He expects elders to be available for such work in their official capacity (James 5). And the pastor in particular, as a teaching elder, is obligated *as shepherd* to look after the sheep in times of such need (Zechariah 10:2, 3; 11:15, 16; Ezekiel 34:4).

In connection with the visitation of the sick I have noted already that the concept of visiting is broader than that of making house calls or, as in many instances of the visitation of the sick, hospital calls. That the obligation does involve this in part, James 5 makes certain, but Matthew 25 (as well as the whole thrust of the biblical notion of visitation as concerned care) expressly prohibits us from identifying calling with the *whole*. In Matthew 25:36, Jesus literally says this: . . ."sick, and you looked after me *(episkeptomai)*." The word used must be contrasted with the word used in the latter part of the verse concerning the prisoner: "in prison, and you visited (or came to—*elthate*) me." The former term also is used in James 1:27, where truly religious man is designated as one who "looks after" or "takes care of" widows and orphans. Clearly this cannot mean merely to pay visits to or make calls upon widows (or orphans!).[1] Visitation of the sick, then, means far more biblically than making hospital calls. Yet, tragically, in the recent history of the church it has degenerated to that. Entire clinical pastoral educational programs built upon this partial view of visitation have been developed. Seminaries have spent inordinate amounts of time and effort

---

[1]Moreover, *episkeptomai* is used in 1 Peter 5:2, 3 to describe the work of the elder in *exercising oversight*. It cannot be translated *"making house calls* not under compulsion but voluntarily, according to God's will; and not for sordid gain, but with eagerness, nor yet as lording it over those allotted to your charge, but proving to be examples to the flock." Clearly, in that passage, the work pictured is larger. One proves to be an example to the flock in "caring for" or "exercising care over" the flock.

training men in bedside manners, etc. Yet, how *little* time has been devoted to the development, growth and maintenance of programs for the total care of the sick (not to speak of orphans and widows).

There can be little question that a total ministry of mercy that is led by the pastor, carried on largely by the elders and deacons, and that enlists all of the members of the congregation is what is needed. At points this may lead to the development of hospitals, adoption agencies, etc. At the very least, it will insist upon seeing that all physical and other needs are met. Galatians 6:10 is an imperative sadly neglected by churches today. There may be instances in which it might be necessary to raise large sums of money to meet the needs of indigent Christians who become ill. At other times, it may mean taking out a health insurance program for impoverished members. Whatever the solutions reached—and these must be thought through much more creatively in the light of the new shape of modern problems than we have done so far—visitation means *looking after* the needs of God's flock.

While there is a desperate need to explore and exploit this biblical concept of visitation to the full, at the same time there can be no lessening of the ministry of the Word. Yet, the third (and largely inadequate) substitute for both that so often has been described as the ideal for the visitation of the sick will not do. The sort of feeble, effete sympathizing with destitute believers, who are staggered by overwhelming medical and hospital costs, which offers no more help than sympathy alone, is a far cry from the biblical concept. On the other hand, writing off one's obligation by writing a fat check quarterly for the deacon's fund will not discharge one's duty either. Somehow the giving of one's time and self must be coupled with the giving of his money. Most of all, the giving of the Bread of Life must be, first and last, the fundamental focus of all. And that is exactly where pastoral leadership comes in. By preaching and teaching, by planning and enlisting, the pastor will develop and maintain a program that creatively provides for both the care that is needed and the opportunity for *every* member to participate in exercising that care. When he prayerfully gives his time, his heart and his prayer to the institution and maintenance of such a program, he will discover that he can accomplish more in the long run than he can by running all over the community for hours on end making sick *calls*.

The Pastor's Task Today

I do not wish to suggest for a moment that the pastor should not make calls upon those who are ill. Particularly is it necessary for him to make hospital visits and especially visits to those who call for him or who *should* do so (cf. James 5:14). Such opportunities for the effective ministry of the Word are rich and must be mined deeply for the blessing of the sheep and the honor of their Chief Shepherd. Yet many aspects of calling visitation as they are now carried on by pastors could be conducted by elders, deacons and others within the congregation—to the great benefit of all involved. It is just simply a fact that if the pastor does not mobilize the *entire* congregation for the work that all can (and ought to) do, it will not be done, what is done will be partial and spotty, and the pastor soon will find himself carrying about the load of guilt of the unmade call. Therefore, perhaps the chief task of the modern pastor in helping the sick consists of planning for and instructing, training and encouraging a congregational ministry to them.

Perhaps one of the main reasons why pastors leave their congregations so frequently these days is to escape from the ever-increasing weight of unfulfilled obligations. The answer for both pastor and people is not flight, but reconsideration of obligations and a reorganization of the congregational visitation program through a mobilization of the gifts of all of the members to meet the needs of all. After all, what does Ephesians 4:11, 12 mean when applied to the text in Matthew 25:36 if it does not require the pastor-teacher to enlist, instruct and train his entire congregation (Matthew 25 applies to *all* Christians, not just the church officers) for this ministry?

To meet specialized problems, such as severe illnesses and those occasioned by sin in which experience and ability for counseling are needed,[2] the eldership in general and the pastor in particular must be available and willing to make every house or hospital call required by the situation. But if the pastor wastes his time doing what other members of the congregation could do as readily or even better than he, he robs everyone of blessing. On the one hand, spotty and partial calling upon shut-ins and convalescents, for example, will cause them to miss the blessings of a *regular* ministry. A couple of members bringing a tape recording of the weekly Sunday messages, sharing in a discussion of the joyful news of the congregation, and regularly speaking of the needs of the sick member can accomplish far more than a busy pastor, no matter how noble his intentions may be. He simply does not have the time to devote to all of these activities, most of

---

[2]Cf. James 5:14ff. I do not intend to discuss the meaning of this passage here since I have developed a full interpretation of that passage in *Competent to Counsel*, XIV, pp. 105-110, 121, 204, 207. I should like to point out, however, that the church officially (that is, through its officers) assumed responsibility for the welfare of the sick member, meeting not only his psychosomatic needs through prayer and confession, but prayerfully administering medicinal help as well. Pastors should be aware of the need for frequently raising the question of whether or not sin may lie behind the illness as part of the problem.

which are not limited to pastoral work, but are activities in which any believer may share. Moreover, whenever the pastor tries to do what a member can do, he robs the member of the blessings of using his gifts in ministry. Remembering that "it is more blessed to give than to receive," the wise pastor seeks to lead every member of his congregation into the fulness of these blessings. And, in turn, he—as a true pastor who recognizes that it is a part of his ministry to encourage the ministry of all according to Ephesians 4:11, 12—receives the blessings of having "given" *this* to the members of his congregation.

That the task of the pastor does not consist only of personal ministry to those in need is borne out by a careful reading of the pastoral epistles (to Timothy and Titus), in which these two pastors are instructed again and again to engage in the work of developing the personal ministries of all members (cf., for example, I Timothy 1:5; 2:1, 7, 10; 3:15; 5:1-16; 6:17, 18; Titus 2:1-10, 14, 15; 3:2, 8, 14). Those verses paint the picture of a pastor busily cultivating his own life before God in order to instruct, organize, develop and fully employ the gifts of the whole congregation.[3]

Pastoral Calling Upon the Sick

While the ministry of "looking after" the sick is larger than that of making calls upon them at home or in the hospital, nevertheless that is one aspect of the work to which a pastor has been called. Much has been written already about this task in many places[4] (most of which wrongly sees it as the all-in-all of the visitation of the sick and which, therefore, must be evaluated in the light of that failing), and I do not wish to duplicate that which is available elsewhere.

Plan for the Visit

To pray intelligently and plan adequately for the visit, the pastor should discover as fully as possible beforehand (1) why the patient is in the hospital; (2) how serious his condition is. These factors will determine the urgency of the visit ("Should I drop everything and go, or can I wait a day?"), the proposed length of the visit and the selection of appropriate scriptural passages to use during the visit. Before visiting, the pastor

---

[3]Cf. *The Christian Counselor's Manual,* "Gifts That Differ," pp. 344-347.

[4]Cf. especially Richard C. Cabot and Russell L. Dicks, *The Art of Ministering to the Sick* (The MacMillan Company, N. Y.: 1938). This is the landmark book in the field. The content is theologically liberal, but nevertheless gives a good picture of the hospital situation and problems faced in ministering to the sick. While the biblical pastor will (should) not concur in many of the views or approaches suggested by Cabot and Dicks, he will profit from thinking through from a scriptural viewpoint the issues that they raise.

should pull the sick member's visitation card(s) from his file to discover what passages have been used previously. A card record should be simplicity itself; all complicated records discourage use (see more *infra* on a simple card filing system). One suggested method that fits the total filing system to be recommended later uses 3" x 5" cards as follows:

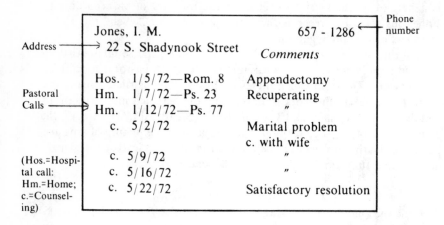

Address → 22 S. Shadynook Street

Phone number

Pastoral Calls →

(Hos.=Hospital call: Hm.=Home; c.=Counseling)

Jones, I. M.		657 - 1286
22 S. Shadynook Street		*Comments*
Hos.	1/5/72—Rom. 8	Appendectomy
Hm.	1/7/72—Ps. 23	Recuperating
Hm.	1/12/72—Ps. 77	"
c.	5/2/72	Marital problem c. with wife
c.	5/9/72	"
c.	5/16/72	"
c.	5/22/72	Satisfactory resolution

Go Upon Request

Calvin's principle, when ministering in Geneva, was not to visit unless he was requested to do so in accordance with James 5:14: "Let him send for the elders of the church." There are some good reasons for adopting a stricter adherence to this principle than has been characteristic of the pastor in recent times. First, the principle is biblical. However, while the pastor is *required* to go only if requested to do so, the biblical principle does not *forbid* his paying calls upon sick members when his presence is not requested. In going *only* upon request, Calvin possibly went too far. Especially would this sort of rigidity be erroneous now. For in these days when Christians are so poorly instructed, the pastor must at times go even when not asked. Yet (and this is crucial), he should teach, through preaching, bulletin announcements, etc., that it is as much the duty of every sick member (or his family) to call for a pastoral visit as it is to request the services of the physician. People do not expect the physician to take the initiative; why should they expect the pastor?

Secondly, pastors should explain that they are neither omniscient nor omnipresent and that in our modern urban communities they simply do not receive information about sickness soon enough in many instances.[5] The congregational grapevine unfortunately functions well about some matters (usually those that should never be communicated) but often poorly in conveying such information. Strictly speaking, each member of one's congregation *must be taught* that there is no one to blame but himself if he fails to receive a call from the pastor because he has not requested it.

The problem of who takes the initiative is a third reason for stricter observance of the biblical injunction "let him call." When he is *ready* to see the pastor (or elders) he can then make that known. If there are problems (or sins) connected with the illness that must be discussed, it is well for the one who is sick to have initiated the counseling situation by requesting the call. A request for visitation should not be construed merely as a request for a quick call to hold hands. Instead, both the patient and the pastor should approach it from a biblical stance involving whatever total ministry may be necessary.

The pastor who properly trains his people in these matters will save both himself and his members many headaches and heartaches. There are numerous ways of reminding the congregation besides the usual mention of the point in pew cards, church calendars and bulletins and in teaching and preaching. For instance, take the situation in which a member asks his pastor to visit a sick non-member. What should the pastor do? One way of handling the situation is to say to the member: "Will you please contact Mary first in order to discover whether she would like to request that I come?" Here, on the one hand, the pastor may avoid making many unnecessary and unproductive calls while, on the other hand, encouraging more serious (and more fruitful) visitation. Whenever a member (or his family, in case of his inability) *fails* to ask for a call, the pastor would be wise to phone before going (unless there is an emergency) and say something like the following: "I hear that Tom has been taken to the hospital; but since I haven't received a request to visit, I was wondering whether there was any special reason why you (family member) or he did not want me to come at this time." The added effort, consistently made in circumstances like these, at length will pay large dividends. Training takes time, as well as consistent conscious effort on the part of the trainer.

---

[5]Again, like many of our present outmoded practices, in past years the idea of relying upon the village grapevine was adopted as a fairly efficient substitute for the biblical pattern. But much was lost, for the biblical injunction to call not only involved insuring the communication of information, but also the fact that the one who sent for the elders took the psychological initiative, which in many cases—as James indicates—is vital.

Goals in the Visitation of the Sick

The general goal of all Christian activity is the glory of God. Visitation in general, and making calls in particular, are no exceptions. But all too frequently the way in which the words "the glory of God" are used is virtually meaningless, for as a pious platitude they cover fuzzy thinking and abstract notions. Were the impertinent question asked, "How may I glorify God?" probably nine out of ten of those who utter the phrase so glibly could not muster anything like an adequate answer.

How does one glorify God? More specifically, how does he glorify God in the visitation of the sick? And, most pointedly, how does he glorify God through making calls upon the sick? In the answers to these questions lie the goals sought.

Glorifying God means two things that grow out of a third more basic fact. First, glorifying God means spreading the knowledge of His glory among those who do not know Him.[6] This is spread by the witness of one's life and words to His matchless Person and to His wonderful works. Secondly, God is glorified by doing those things which please Him. That is to say, He is glorified (whether or not others see and hear[7]) by obedience to His will as it is revealed in the Holy Scriptures. Thus, glorifying God consists both of witness and obedience. Or, to put it another way, to glorify God is to give witness to God and to others of His majesty and honor. Lastly, and basic to both, is the verbal acknowledgement of God as God. Thus, the phrase "glorifying God" means virtually the same as honoring or praising Him.

So then, by what short-term goals may one glorify God in the visitation of the sick and how may he seek to enable sick members of God's flock to do the same? The answer simply is that God may be glorified by the pastor (1) by adequate care that demonstrates the love of Christ to the sick member and to the world in general; (2) by pastoral care that pleases God, even if not acknowledged or appreciated by the sick member or others.[8] The sick member may be helped to glorify God (1) by pastoral assistance in handling his sickness in a manner pleasing to God (i.e., in a biblical way); (2) by learning to share the implications of sickness with others. Thus, the pastor visits to confront a sick member in such a way that he (1) becomes

---

[6]To glorify God does not mean to *add* anything to the weight of His glory. Rather, it means so to live and to speak as to unveil the eyes of men to God's glory (i.e., the effulgence or brilliance of His majesty and honor).

[7]Cf. Colossians 3:22-25, Ephesians 6:6-8 and I Corinthians 10:31, where it seems clear that to glorify God does not mean merely to spread the fame of His name among unbelievers, but also includes that which is done for Him and in His presence alone.

[8]E.g., the sick member may resent rather than appreciate the offer to discuss any sinful basis for the sickness (in accordance with James 5) or any disciplinary measures connected thereto.

aware of his biblical responsibilities to God and man in the sickness and (2) is strengthened and encouraged in the biblical ways and means of doing so.

This concept of visitation differs in several ways from the usual concepts of paying a call to empathize with the patient, to read the Scriptures and to offer prayer. One of those differences lies in this: the biblical notion of visitation has a specific focus—the pastor visits to help and to encourage the member to realize these responsibilities. The pastor knows that every true member of Christ's flock, by the power of the Holy Spirit who indwells him, and by the instruction of the Word, can do so. As a minister of that Word, whom the Holy Spirit uses as he ministers the Word, he appears on the scene *for that purpose.* He is a ministering friend, but he does not come principally as a friend. He comes as a fellow Christian, but not even primarily as such. Rather, in his capacity as an officer in the Church of Jesus Christ (cf. James 5: "let him send for the *elders*," not "let him send for a brother") he comes in Christ's name (i.e., in His full authority) to minister His Word. That is one (perhaps the major) reason why it is important for the sick member to initiate the visit. This request, in effect, amounts to an act of faith and obedience in which the sick believer requests Jesus Christ to help him through the use of the authoritative means that He Himself ordained. It is an acknowledgment of Christ as Shepherd to request the presence and help of His undershepherds.

When the pastor comes in Christ's name with the explicit purpose of helping the sick member to face and handle the sickness and any problems that may be connected with it biblically, he should recognize that he is entering into nothing less than an official counseling relationship. This is not merely a social call. What should take place in that relationship will depend upon the particular problems and needs. If the sick member has done and is doing all of the right things, the minister's task will be minimal: he will offer comfort and encouragement. If, on the other hand, there is unconfessed sin, rebellion toward or bitterness against God, resentment toward others, or a complaining attitude, the task may be maximal. Whatever situation that is found must be met biblically.[9] At times, his visit will focus upon the need for patience (cf. Romans 8:18-28) in a world of sin and misery. At other times, he will appear as healer (when there is need for confession of sin that led to the sickness).[10]

---

[9]I shall not discuss the "how-tos" of meeting bitterness, fear, etc., in this place, as I have done so elsewhere (cf. *Competent to Counsel; The Christian Counselor's Manual*). Rather, I shall concentrate upon those factors which are peculiar to the sick room. The *totality* of need should be the concern of the shepherd who wants his sheep to lack *nothing* (Psalm 23:1).

[10]Sometimes there is an opportunity to witness or otherwise minister to others in a ward or semi-private room. Often roommates will request prayer. Frequently the best result is that

The Use of the Scriptures

The pastor will find himself using certain passages of Scripture frequently.[11] Among those used (not merely read, but explained and applied[12]) again and again may be the following:

I Corinthians 10:13
Psalm 23
Romans 8:18ff
Psalm 119:50, 52, 67, 71, 75, 92
Psalm 38
Psalm 77
Psalm 32, 51
Psalm 107:17-22
James 5:11, 13ff
II Corinthians 1:3-7
James 1:2-4
I Corinthians 11:27-34
I Corinthians 15:51-58
Hebrews 2:14-15; 4:15-16
Job 42:10, 12
Job 1:20-22; 2:7-10

The Scriptures must be used not as if they were a collection of mysterious books that accomplish their work in magical ways—merely by being possessed or read rather than by being understood and applied. Too often not only do laymen use the Bible in this way, but ministers unwittingly encourage them to do so by failing to explain the Scriptures to them. It was when Jesus "opened" (explained) the Scriptures to them that the disciples' hearts "burned" within them (Luke 24:32). Until then, they had failed to see how He was the subject of "all" of the Scriptures (Luke 24:27). Like the

_____

such a visit opens an opportunity for the sick member to witness to his roommate. Tracts, etc., can be left for him to use.

[11]Be sure to note each use of each on the member's visitation note card to avoid unintended repetition upon subsequent pastoral calls.

[12]There is a time only to read. When the sick visitee is so sick that there is no opportunity for explanation or expanded application, the wise pastor chooses a passage that is susceptible to instant understanding and application. Yet, even in the most serious cases, where because of the severity of the condition one can spend only a few moments with the sick, it is usually possible in not more than a sentence or two to interpret and apply. Sometimes this is done best in prefacing: "John, let me read a verse or two that gets to the heart of the matter of Christian patience and endurance in suffering." (He then reads Romans 8:22-27.) Then his brief prayer makes the application: "Oh Lord, help John to patiently endure this pain. Help him to look forward to that new body that Christ promised us at the resurrection. Relieve him from pain and suffering in Your way and time. In the meanwhile, teach him how to pray and help him by

Good Shepherd, it is the task of the undershepherd to "restore" the sheep by the law of the Lord (cf. Psalm 23:3 and 19:7)[13]Like Him, therefore, they must "open" the Word to sheep to build hope and give strength and sustenance.

As in all good preaching, the wise counselor of the sick will seek to be concrete rather than abstract in his explanations. He will discover that the use of good illustrations (examples, analogies and instances) will be most helpful in making biblical truths clear, vivid and memorable. In this he will follow the communicative methods of the chief Shepherd, who spoke of doors and water, of lilies and a man who fell among thieves to drive home vital truths and make them understandable and memorable.

EXERCISES

For the Student

1. Arrange to make a sick call (this may be done together with another student). Be prepared to report to the class on the visit. The report may be given as a brief role play.

2. Make another visit after class evaluation, and write up the second visit as a short report to be turned in to the professor. In this report, include a self-evaluation.

For the Pastor

In the space that follows (1) give an assessment of your present sick member visitation program together with (2) suggestions for making it more biblical.

Your Spirit in those prayers, as well as in his witness to the hospital staff, to honor Christ . . . in whose Name we pray."

[13]The Hebrew verb is the same in both passages.

CHAPTER XVI
THE HOSPITAL CALL

An abundance of material is available concerning hospital visitation. I shall try not to duplicate much of that, but rather shall touch mainly on points of disagreement or issues of importance that have been neglected.

When to Visit

First, when does one visit? The answer is soon; in emergencies even sooner (i.e., as soon as possible). Death takes precedence over all other demands; emergencies (illnesses, severe marital disruptions, etc.) run a close second.[1] When an operation is pending, the pastor who wants to meet needs will recognize the patient's need for faith and comfort and his need for divinely-given strength to combat fear[2] and doubt. Consequently, he will try *always* to see the sick member *before* the operation (preferably *before* entering the hospital and, in emergencies, in the hospital *before* the operation). He will want to be present soon after the operation also (as soon as consciousness and the initial recovery permit). But his work at these times will consist not only of the primary task of ministering pertinent portions of the Word of God to the *patient;* he will discover that there is the possibility of a vital ministry to relatives in the home or hospital as well. Often, important counseling or evangelistic opportunities may develop

---

[1]But counselors soon become aware of the fact some people are always having "emergencies." These usually turn out not to be emergencies at all. The pastor should structure his scheduling of calls to such persons accordingly. If he caters to their emotionalism he teaches them to cry "wolf, wolf"; moreover, he solidifies their bad behavior and allows them at a whim to rearrange important schedules and to steal time from the rest of the members of the congregation as well as from the pastor. Reinforcing inconsiderate behavior is sinful; the pastor must not be a party to it. If more rigorous scheduling does not itself accomplish the desired end, the pastor must speak directly to the member about the problem.

[2]Studies have shown fear to be a paramount problem of the hospitalized. Cf. Vance Packard, *The Hidden Persuaders* (Pocket Books, Inc., N. Y.: 1958), pp. 205, 206. The wise pastor tries to anticipate and meet the problem of fear by his words, prayers and actions, even when it has not been expressed openly. He is aware of the sometimes troublesome feelings of helplessness and dependence that are experienced by hospitalized patients, and seeks to point them to the One who is altogether dependable, the only sure Helper of those in need (appropriate Scripture might be Psalm 70:5; 121:2; 124:8; 46:1; Hebrews 4:16). 1 Corinthians 15:54-58 is most pertinent.

from these contacts. Pastors should be sensitive to such opportunities and allocate time for seizing upon them. It is often wise to *plan* to visit with immediate relatives before or during serious operations. The key factor to keep in mind is that *serious illness usually affects more persons than the one who is sick* (e.g., worry, financial burdens, etc., may become complicating factors during a period of serious illness); therefore, the potential for ministry must be conceived of as being as large as the whole need and opportunity.

Following the operation or onset of the illness, during the early recovery period, much of the most productive work of ministry may be carried on. The dynamic here and in the period of later convalescence is much the same as in the second or third stages of grief. Because I have already outlined some of the matters that should be of concern to the pastor during these periods in another place, I shall not repeat that material here.[3] It should be sufficient to emphasize that those pastors who devote the bulk of their time and activity to the first, emergency or crisis period, in which often, because of severe pain, unconsciousness, drugs, etc., there is little that can be done to discuss the illness with the patient, miss the vital opportunities afforded by the periods of early recovery and later convalescence.[4]

Hospital calls during the period of early recovery and during convalescence may be made at almost any time.[5] Some knowledge of local hospital routines, cleanup and bed-making periods, mealtimes, etc.[6], should be acquired (a simple phone call to the hospital at this moment would do it) in order to enable the pastor to choose visiting hours which

---

[3]Cf. "Grief as a Counseling Opportunity," *The Big Umbrella,* pp. 63-94 (esp. pp. 78ff).

[4]Some pastors busy themselves about administrative details: "Can I drive you to the hospital?" etc. They usually endear themselves to those whom they thus befriend, but they also thereby neglect the essential elements of their ministry of the Word. In accordance with Acts 6, such matters ought not to be neglected but rather should be *delegated* to a well-oiled and smoothly functioning Board of Deacons so that the pastor/teacher may devote himself fully to the ministry of the Word and to prayer.

[5]But mornings usually are not good for several reasons, all having to do with the fact that this is the busiest time for the patient and for the hospital staff. Some pastors have neglected what can be a welcome break in a long night for many patients—a late night call. At this time routine hospital chores are over, visitors are gone and the patient may find himself bored as he faces the prospects of the long night ahead (sleep patterns often vary in hospitals). This can be a convenient time for pastors as well. One fact that the pastor should keep in mind is that the hospitalized person (or shut-in), unlike others whom he visits, is always "at home." The visitation of sick persons, within limits of consideration for all concerned, therefore can be scheduled more readily at the convenience of the pastor. Since this is a rare situation for pastors, they should take every advantage of the situation that is legitimate.

[6]Mealtimes are a good choice when the pastor wishes to do most of the talking. He may say, "No, please go right ahead and eat and I'll talk to you."

will avoid interruptions during conversations with the sick member and out of consideration for the hospital staff. One time that the pastor ought *not* to make calls (unless he has a special reason for doing so) is during the regular hospital visiting hours. At such times relatives, neighbors, friends, visitors who have come to see someone else in the ward or semi-private room are likely to be present or to drop in. Visiting hours, therefore, rarely afford opportunity for fruitful counseling or ministry. The pastor is allowed access by the hospital to the patient at other times, and he should use (not abuse) this privilege assiduously.[7] Perhaps the best time is at a period somewhat before or at a time considerably later than the visiting period. Very sick persons often are tired by visitors. Relatives and friends frequently tire the patient by overextending their visits, and sometimes by the nature of the call that they make. The sick person may have just breathed a sigh of relief to rid himself of such company, only to have the pastor arrive on the scene. Needless to say, not only does this imperil the health or recovery of the patient, but it affords the worst possible context for fruitful pastoral ministry.

Developing Hospital Habits

When the pastor arrives at the hospital, he should present himself as such (carrying a sizeable Bible helps to establish the identification; clerical garb is not at all necessary as some wrongly suppose) to the person at the information desk, if he does not know the patient's room number, to obtain the same.[8] Next he proceeds to the floor on which the patient's room is located and looks for the nurses' station that is nearest to it. Here he stops and asks

---

[7]Rarely (if ever) will he find this privilege denied. Now and then he may encounter a tired or an officious nurse who tries to do so. Politely he should request the reason. Possibly, in extremely rare cases, he will discover that the reason is valid. In others, he may find either that no reason is offered, or that the reason sounds contrived, arbitrary or artificial. In such cases, he should not argue or assert his rights (cf. Titus 1:7). He should quietly inform her that he must take up the matter with her supervisor if she does not change her mind. If she remains adamant, he should note the name of the nurse who has denied him access to his patient, go at once to the head nurse or supervisor of the hospital, and report the facts, including the name of the nurse and the course of events that followed. The author has heard of no case in which satisfaction has not been received when this procedure was followed. It is important for the pastor to remember that, although the sick member is under the care of the physician and the nurses, that member prior to and coincident with that care is also under the *care and discipline* of the Church of Jesus Christ. That means that the authority of the pastor's shepherdly care does not disappear when the sheep enters a hospital. Rather, it not only continues, but takes on new dimensions appropriate to the new situation that has arisen. Medical care neither supersedes nor annuls pastoral care. At any point where the two are pitted against one another, human authority has entered the picture seeking to usurp the authority of God. In such cases the human authority (whether imposed as medical or, for that matter, as pastoral) must be rejected.

[8]If he does, he may proceed directly to the control desk (on the proper floor) that is responsible for the care and oversight of the patient.

for a nurse who can give him whatever information might be useful to help him to determine the nature and length of his visit.[9] To check before entering the room is always essential when visiting a woman. It can be embarrassing for a woman to be partially disrobed, bathing, etc., when the pastor suddenly steps in. Nurses often will tend to be vague about the type of information that they divulge, but if the pastor shows that it is out of consideration for the patient and for the hospital staff that he wishes to obtain the data that he seeks, he will be likely to obtain better and more definitive information (not: "What is Mr. Jones' condition?," but: "I do not want to overly tire Mr. Jones; can you give me some indication of the severity of his condition?").

When the pastor enters the room, Mr. Jones may be napping. This presents a dilemma. It may be unwise to awaken him, since sleep may be precisely what he needs most at the moment (in such cases a personal note scribbled on the other side of a tract or calling card may be left; this at least shows the patient that you cared and came[10]). On the other hand, some hospitals are very boring places and many patients spend a good deal of the time napping for no other reason. If the pastor is unsure about the situation, he should return to the nurses' station, state the dilemma and ask for her advice. More often than not he will find that she will advise awakening the patient. When he does so, he can explain: "The nurse said she thought you would want me to do so."

Length of Visit

The visit should be no longer than (1) the need warrants and (2) the patient's physical condition can endure. In general, the rule will be: the more serious the patient's condition, the shorter and more often the visits. These two factors demand the making of pastoral judgments derived from the available information at hand (from doctors, nurses, family, patient, chaplains, observation, general knowledge of the type and severity of the illness) and that which develops during the course of the hospital call itself. In nearly all instances (deathbed situations clearly must be excepted), it is better to err (if not sure) on the side of brevity. The rule during the early stages of illness or recovery is to visit briefly often. Frequently, the best judgment can be made by the patient himself. It is wise often for the pastor at the outset to invite the sick member to indicate when to close the interview ("Bill, if you begin to get too tired, I'm counting on you to let me

---

[9] In some hospitals there is a chaplain's office. The chaplain may have on hand much information that cannot be obtained from a nurse. It is wise (in many cases) to stop by his office prior to going to the control desk or nurses' station.

[10] In some cases, the nurse may be requested to inform Mr. Jones of the visit, especially if he

know"). Sometimes, he will notice eyelids closing, the patient's conversation wandering, or other signs of weariness. Under such circumstances, it is better to postpone the rest of the conversation until a later visit. There are times, of course, when one is so sick that all that is appropriate is an appearance, a pat on the hand and a brief one-line prayer. Sensitivity to situations, born of prayerful experience and post-visitation evaluation, is the only way of acquiring the wisdom necessary to arrive at many such judgments. The pastor might take to heart the gracious invitation of God:

> But if any of you lacks wisdom, let him ask of God, who gives to all men generously and without reproach, and it will be given him (James 1:5).

One fact to remember is that a patient in a coma, unable to respond and seemingly unable to hear, *may* (after all) be able to hear.[11] Two important facts grow out of this: (1) the pastor must be careful about what he says to others within hearing distance of the patient; (2) the pastor must not despair over ministering the Word to those in such a condition under such circumstances, but despite the lack of visible response should speak and pray as though heard.

EXERCISES

For the Student

Interview a physician, nurse or hospital chaplain about hospital procedures and the place of the minister. Write out any helpful suggestions obtained in the space below.

---

is in a condition where he cannot read. But even then, if the pastor leaves the card and note with her, his request is more likely to be honored.

[11]Cf. John S. Bonnell, *Do You Want to Be Healed?* (Harper and Row, N.Y.: 1968), p. 59. See also Cabot and Dicks, *op. cit.,* p. 309. One patient said, "I knew everything and heard everything, but I couldn't move or talk. You gave me up too soon."

For the Pastor

1. Do you know the varying policies of the hospitals to which your members go? Now, or on the next visit to a hospital, check into these. Knowledge of hospital policies may have some bearing upon your own.

2. What happens in your congregation whenever someone goes to the hospital? *Who* is activated to do *what, when* and *how*? Do you know? Do the members of the congregation know? Lay out a plan, if you have none, obtain agreement from all parties involved and advertise the procedure regularly to the members of the congregation.

What Happens?

_____

_____

_____

_____

_____

_____

_____

_____

_____

_____

_____

_____

_____

CHAPTER XVII
VISITING IN SPECIAL SITUATIONS

Visiting Convalescents and Shut-Ins

Emergency and crisis visitation is one thing. Visiting during the early stages of the illness or recovery from it is still another. In both of these the tension will be greater. The need for immediacy of help and information will be large. All is said and done against a background of urgency or pressure or great pain or fear.

Convalescents and shut-ins provide a different sort of problem. They have time—much of it—and it is all on their hands. They will have a hard time understanding why you don't come more often and stay longer. They may have lost contact with the realities and responsibilities of busy every-day life, and may need reminding of the fact. This is particularly true when, as is so often true, the pastor finds that they are wasting valuable time in meaningless sinful activities or non-activity. One of his most important tasks (in addition to discussing the illness in relationship to God), then, will be to help such members to learn how to use their time productively in the service of Jesus Christ. Books and literature may be brought regularly by other members of the congregation who also come with church bulletins and weekly tape recordings of the Sunday services. Convalescence periods often provide precious time for the study of the Scriptures. Shut-ins and convalescents need to be brought up to date on the news (but not gossip) of the congregation. The pastor must assiduously avoid spreading personal information about others. He must be alert to being "pumped" for such information. The pastor should not merely steer the conversation away from gossip, but when necessary he should directly confront the shut-in or con-valescent about the matter ("I am sorry, but I have no right to reveal such privileged information"). Prayer requests also may be provided (what valuable time for the important work of prayer shut-ins have available.[1])

---

[1]The pastor may say, "God has given to you an abundance of the greatest commodity of all—time. The rest of us have so little because of our daily responsibilities. He has removed many of these from you for a purpose. Let's see how you can best use this time as a good steward of God."

There may be unique opportunities in the hospital for evangelistic outreach among other patients. Members of the congregation may wish to provide the convalescent with tracts, booklets and other gospel literature to help in this endeavor.[2] Addressing envelopes for a church mailing, phoning members to remind them about an important meeting, and a dozen other such useful and productive ways of ministering can be imagined. But, whatever else is done, the Christian convalescent and the shut-in *need above all else* to become as meaningfully productive in God's service as their present strength and condition allow.

The pastor's visits to such persons ought to thin out as he helps them to deal with their illness and as this productivity increases.[3] Other persons in the congregation (deacons and those enlisted and trained by them) may take over the (important but not peculiarly pastoral) social and administrative aspects of visitation in his stead. The pastor who organizes a diaconate that actively functions in such ways will multiply his efforts many times over, bring blessing to many members, and far better provide for the needs of the sick than he could were he to attempt to do the impossible task of meeting these needs alone.

Visiting Sick Children

The opportunity (not to speak of the obligation or need) that is missed by many preachers to pay a visit to the lambs of the flock (and thus reflect the loving care of their Good Shepherd) when sick is deplorable. Such visits by the pastor make a great impression upon the child and strengthen the lines of communication among the members of the covenant community. The lambs are in the sheepfold; they are members of the visible church, and as such are under the care and discipline of the church (cf. Genesis 17:14)[4].

---

[2] A deacon's fund for the purchase of such literature is important.

[3] Pastoral visits to shut-ins and convalescents should be made at random, not according to a fixed schedule. The patient should not be able to discern patterns of time, date or frequency. If he does, and if the pastor fails on occasion to follow such patterns (even without promising to do so), the patient will often reprimand him.

[4] The child was circumcised as a sign of membership in the fold, or covenant community. If the parent failed to circumcise his child, he would be "cut off" from the people. Children of believers ever since have been included as part of the covenant people. That is to say, they share all of the rights and privileges of care and discipline. Membership in the visible community does not save them; saving faith in Christ alone does that. But the church is obligated to minister to them, so that together with the prayers and ministry of their parents, the church also must seek to bring them to faith in the Lord Jesus Christ. Part of the background for that evangelistic opportunity is the care and concern shown by the church (and in particular by its official representatives) for the children of the covenant. Not only were children not excluded from (thrown out of) their membership in the flock in the New Testament period, but at its inception their continued membership was reaffirmed in the very terms of this Abrahamic promise (Acts 2:39). Moreover, the shepherding concern for the lambs of the flock (and it should be noted that in the Scriptures they are viewed as such) is evident in Christ's threefold restoration of Peter to his pastoral call (John 21:15).

The pastor will not pay a visit upon children for every childhood disease or minor injury that they suffer. If he did so, he would find his time fully occupied in doing this alone. What he will always be alert to is the *special* problem: the broken leg, the tonsillectomy, the appendectomy, etc. Here is an unparalleled opportunity to teach, to evangelize and to show Christ's care for the lambs in His flock. From the store of literature provided by the deacons, he may take along a Bible portion—perhaps the Gospel of John and a simple booklet (depending, of course, upon the age of the child), such as one of those Bible story booklets appearing in the Concordia Press series. C. S. Lewis' Narnia tales—with some explanation—might be excellent reading for older children who have already made a profession of faith.

Visiting Those With Contagious Diseases
There is rarely any need to visit those who are contagious; moreover, the number of occasions for such visits grows smaller each year. The pastor's best policy in such cases is to forget all of the unnecessary heroics and pay a visit *by way of the telephone.*

If, in cases of emergency, he is required to visit in person, the hospital will provide special garments, including a face mask, to be worn while in contact with the patient and to be discarded before leaving. The pastor also should observe the following precautionary rules:

1.   Make the visit as brief as possible.

2.   Do not touch the sick member, his bed, or anything else in the room (stand at a distance, do not sit).[5]

3.   Wash hands and face thoroughly as soon as possible upon leaving the room (down the hall in the men's room; don't wait till you get home).

Visiting the Dying
Here is where a pastor finally knows whether he has what it takes or not. When he stands by the bedside of a man who appears to have but a few hours to live, what does he say and do? I did not ask, what does he feel? Even those who are most bold and most faithful find that their feelings betray them from time to time. The question is: how faithfully does he minister to such a person? And behind that one, what constitutes faithfulness?

---

[5]My colleague, Dr. Clair Davis, frequently observes that it is of importance not to sit on the patient's bed—whether there is fear of contagion or not. In a real sense, the bed is the one personal piece of property possessed by him in the hospital (it is his oasis in the desert; his island in the sea) and must not be invaded.

First, he seeks to speak to the sick member alone. Interference, tears, outbursts of weeping from others can be very distracting.

Secondly, he never says that he *knows* that another is dying; he does not know that. There are plenty of cases on record where the former "dying" patient attended the pastor's funeral!

Yet, he deals with the sick member as if death were a distinct possibility; it is. This means that he speaks directly about death and eternal life. If he does so frequently anyway from the pulpit and in ordinary pastoral conversations, it will not be so difficult to do so here. He rehearses the gospel message in simplicity and with clarity. He reminds the patient of the need for a Savior that sin brought about. He rehearses the wonderful message of good news that God—out of pure grace—sent His own Son to die in the place of guilty sinners, taking the punishment that they deserved for their sins. He speaks of the resurrection as God's stamp of approval upon the work of His Son on the cross, and our certain assurance that our frail bodies shall be raised, transformed, and together with our souls shall live forever. He clearly outlines the means by which a man enters into the promises of eternal life: through simple faith in Christ. Then, he asks, "You are trusting in Jesus Christ as your Saviour, aren't you?" or "Are you ready to meet Christ if God should call you to do so?"

When a true believer triumphantly reaffirms his faith, the pastor comforts and reassures him of the great hope that is his by reference to any of the many marvelous promises of the Scriptures. Prominent at such times are such passages as John 3:16; 3:36; 5:24; 14:1-8; Psalm 23; 90.

If problems (doubts about salvation; the need for confession of some sin) arise, or the sick person gives no evidence of salvation, the pastor must straightforwardly deal with the issue (or issues) involved. He should warn of his danger, present the gospel clearly and call upon the unsaved patient to believe in the Lord Jesus Christ.

In ministering to the dying believer, the pastor should keep in mind the possible mixes of pain, fear, sorrow, worry, weakness, helplessness, anger and guilt that may be present. In looking for the dominant strains of each of these (e.g., bitter complaints, "Why did this have to happen just when we moved into our new home?" or anxious concern: "What will happen to Mary and the little one?"), the pastor will discover the concerns and needs that must be met. It is his task to do so as fully as he is able in the remaining time that God allots. He can call to repentance and forgiveness; he can promise to look into and attempt to settle any matters that the dying believer is now unable to handle for himself. He can point to the relevant words of God in the Scriptures pertaining to his problems or attitudes. But most of all—and uppermost in the pastor's thinking—always must be the need for rehearsing the simple, but wonderful story of the gospel of Jesus Christ. The plan of salvation as executed by the Lord Jesus should be the *theme* of any and all conversation with the dying, no matter what other subjects may be of importance as well.

Now, let us consider a current problem that many pastors discover only too late to do anything about it: the problem of the use and misuse of modern medications. Frequently, by the time that the pastor and/or family arrives at the hospital upon learning of the pending death of a loved one, he has been so doped up with medication that a sensible conversation of the sort just described is nearly impossible. The true shepherd, anxious to minister, is stymied. This problem may become a source of great regret to all and should become a matter of real concern to a pastor who cares. What should he think about this and what may he do?

First, it is important for every person who has contracted what is now called a "terminal illness" to know that fact. The pastor can urge the physician and members of the family to be honest and tell Frank *from the beginning* that he has cancer. Lying about this can never be condoned. But never can it be more destructive than under such circumstances. Families that could spend weeks (or months, or years) making the most of their last earthly hours, drawn more closely together, resolving tensions and differences, and planning for the future, instead grow apart, become cold toward and fearful of one another because of the great secret that is covered by a thousand lies. Seeking to know and seeking to tell, the sick and the well reach out to one another only to find that the other has moved apart. Instead of drawing close, they are driven asunder; instead of understanding and discussion, the great lie closes all significant communication. Instead of grieving together, the surviving partner must bear the grief alone—and in a context of drifting apart amidst untold unresolved issues.[6] This *should not be* among the saints of God. Lies are wrong; lies hurt. So, if his last hours are likely to be spent in unintelligibility and insensitivity to those around him, the "terminal" patient must be told of his condition in plenty of time to take care of all such matters beforehand.

Fear of injurious psychological impact must not deter. True ministers believe the Scriptures. They know that I Corinthians 10:13 assures the believing patient of sufficient resources and that there is ample comfort to be found in passages like I Corinthians 15:54 - 58. People who stress the

---

[6]Cf. "Grief as a Counseling Opportunity," Appendix A for further implications of this question. Pastors must consider how impossible it is to function as members of a body (the church or home) apart from truthful communication (cf. Ephesians 4:25).

hard effects of learning the truth usually fail to recognize the bad effects of not divulging it.[7]

Secondly, every man is entitled to know it when he is likely to die soon. Why should everyone else but the dying one know? Christ took time on the Mount of Transfiguration and in the Garden of Gethsemane to prepare for His death. In these two places He discussed it with others and with God. True, His death had implications greater than all of the deaths of all of the men of all time lumped together. But, for weak, fearful sinners, though in no way approximating His, one's own death is the most formidable encounter he will ever face in this life. If He needed to prepare for His death and to discuss it with God and with others, so too do we.

Moreover, superimpose upon this discussion the patriarchal scene of Genesis 49. The dying Jacob gathers his children round about him and speaks to each about his future. Contrast that with the most common modern mode of dying, in which the father and husband disappears from the scene as a deceived, doped, deluded and despairing person—dying alone without a parting word on his lips for anyone. Everyone is separated and alone; no one can reach through to touch or hold. There is little to carry away but doubt, regrets, unresolved problems and a gnawing sense of guilt over the grand deception. Which is more Christian?

Christian pastors must begin to instruct members of their congregations to insist upon changes. Medical personnel often have claimed rights and prerogatives at this point that do not belong to them. Christian families not only must begin to stand up to such matters as (1) the insatiable prolonging of life under vegetative and artificial conditions when its maintenance is merely mechanical, (2) they also must begin to require physicians and hospitals to tell the truth to the patient and (3) should request the use of medication that will permit him to function with mental clarity as long as he desires in order to speak with God, his wife, family, minister and friends.[8] Physicians must be told that pain is not the only evil, and that it must not always become the principal target of attack, taking precedence over all else. Moreover, medication exists today which, in most cases, will relieve a patient of pain without surrendering consciousness.

The pastor must consider what to do when faced with a choice between family, medical and scriptural viewpoints. Picture a (not unusual) situation

---

[7] Cf. Samuel Staudard and Helmuth Nathan, *Should the Patient Know the Truth?* (Springer Pub. Co.: N.J., 1955) pp. 40, 42, 65, 72, 77f.

[8] It is true that there may come a time when the words of Proverbs 31:6, 7 become pertinent. But Christ's rejection of such an anesthetic potion (Mark 15:23) in order to retain full consciousness and sensibility during His unique and incomparable task shows clearly the secondary, rather than primal, concern over pain.

in which a husband has cancer, and has been declared "terminal," the likelihood being that he will not live another six months. The physicians have told the family, but together they have decided to deceive the sick man. "Your problem is curable," they have informed him, "but conditions may become worse before they get any better." Joe, the patient, is a believing member of your congregation. The family tells you his condition and what they have done about it. They assume that you will go along. What will you do?[9] As a faithful minister of the gospel, you must do something like the following:

1. Tell them that this lie is a sin against God, against Joe, against his wife and family, and against the church (which is hampered thereby in exercising its proper ministry to him). An attempt should be made to persuade them to tell the truth (many of the reasons above could be cited—the benefits of the last weeks' planning and growing together, the ability to grieve with one another rather than in the bitterness of isolation, his right to know and his need to prepare himself, his affairs and his family—but none of these should take precedence over the fact that to lie to Joe is a sin, perhaps the greatest deceit that ever could be committed against another human being). The pastor may even offer to be the one to break the news to Joe (Joe may already know or strongly suspect—as in so many cases). To do so takes boldness to be lovingly frank. The pastor who does so must ask God for tender courage. But to do so is also to have the privilege of helping Joe to handle the problem as a Christian. It means to help him to sort out his relationship and responsibilities to God, to his family, to his church, etc.[10] A pastor must not think of pulling the stopper on the truth, only to walk away unconcerned about the results. There may be a period of heartache and sorrow at first. There may be bitterness and resentment to work through, but the faithful shepherd remains at hand guiding, bringing to reconciliation, helping to plan and (in general) assisting him in every way that he can.

---

[9] Of course, it is better to prevent this problem whenever possible by speaking about the matter beforehand from the pulpit, in Sunday school, in couples' club meetings, etc. Members of a conservative church should (themselves) demand of physicians and the family that they be told the truth.

[10] Every minister should be ready and able to give help and direction to dying members (or others) who seek advice on willing a portion of their estate to the church, theological seminaries, or other Christian organizations. Such information often can be obtained readily from officers of the organization itself. Mr. Robert den Dulk, of Westminster Theological Seminary, who is an expert in such matters, has expressed his willingness to give help to pastors who would like to learn how best to handle the many problems connected with this matter. He may be contacted at the seminary: Westminster Theological Seminary, Chestnut Hill, Philadelphia, Pennsylvania, 19118.

2. But, what must be done when the family refuses? Especially, how does one face the argument, "But the physician said that we should not tell him; and (after all) Joe is under his care." First, the pastor should note that the decision, though it may have medical implications, is not fundamentally a medical one. The physician has no special expertise, knowledge or authority in the matter. His viewpoint, therefore, always will be personal, not professional.

When all persuasion fails, the pastor must make clear to the members of the family that the impasse must be broken. The matter cannot be avoided. He may turn to Hebrews 13:17: "Obey your leaders, and submit to them; for they keep watch over your souls, as those who must give an account." In direct application of the passage, the pastor may state, "Long before the physician took Joe under his care, Joe asked us in Christ's name to take him under *our* care, which is a perpetual and more basic one; it is a care in which we have obligated ourselves to 'watch over his life' and for which we must 'give an account' to God."[11]

If the members of the family are Christians, who themselves are under the same care, the first part of the verse also may be stressed ("Obey them that have the rule over you"). If ever there were a good example of the kind of situation in which a clash of views is to be resolved by the authority of the church of Christ mentioned in this verse, this is it. In any case, their refusal to divulge the truth must be countered by (1) a similar refusal to join in the lie; (2) a willingness to wait prayerfully and patiently for a time while the family is urged to discuss and pray about the matter; but (3) in the event that there is an ultimate refusal by the family to do so, a warning that the pastor himself will be under obligation to tell Joe.

It is in such matters as this that the difficulties of the work of the ministry come into clearest focus. When the issue is joined between the authority of God and the authority of man, the pastor must not compromise. It is in standing firm out of faithful obedience to Christ and love for His sheep that men (sometimes for the first time in their lives) discover that it means something to belong to the Church of Jesus Christ. They learn that Christianity is not a religion with a set of ceremonies to be observed, but a life (and death) commitment to the Lord Christ to whom every believer promises submission. They learn that Christ has given authority to His

---

[11] The general question should have been discussed and settled with the other elders in the church long before this particular instance arose. Their commitment to back up the pastor in such situations at times could be vital. Their failure to do so could be devastating. Such issues will be handled best when a pastor has taken the time to instruct, cultivate and work with his board of elders.

church and that its officers have an obligation to take "charge over" the flock "in the Lord, and to nouthetically confront"[12] whenever necessary (I Thessalonians 5:12).

In short, in caring for the dying, the pastor must never merely float with the current, being *told* what to do and what to say. As a minister of the Word of authority, he can never do that. Instead, he must introduce the biblical message of redemption where it is needed, stress the importance of resolving outstanding problems, and straightforwardly pursue a ministry that confronts rather than by-passes the hard issues, to the honor of Christ and for the welfare of His sheep.

Visiting the Bereaved

Because I have already treated the subject of grief and ministry to the bereaved extensively in an article entitled "Grief as a Counseling Opportunity" in *The Big Umbrella*, I shall not seek to duplicate that material here. Rather, I shall include that article in a revised and annotated form as Appendix A.

EXERCISES

For the Student

Read C. S. Lewis' *A Grief Observed* (Seabury, N.Y.: 1961) and using the material presented in the Scriptures and in this volume (especially in Appendix A), write a paper describing the sort of pastoral ministry that Lewis needed, but did not receive.

For the Pastor

Plan *now* (do not wait till it is too late) to:

1. hold some lectures for married couples concerning ministry to the dying, raising the ethical issues considered in the foregoing pages.

2. preach a series of sermons on death and grief if you have failed to minister to the congregation in this area.

---

[12]Cf. *Competent to Counsel*, pp. 41-62, for an explanation of the work comprised under this term.

APPENDIX A

Grief as a Counseling Opportunity

Grief as a Counseling Opportunity[1]

A pastor does no counseling that is considered more exclusively his own than the counseling of people in grief (although recently physicians and psychiatrists have been usurping his right by moving into this area). If grief still is peculiarly within the minister's province, you must be deeply interested in the nature of grief and what God wants you to do to help grief sufferers. As ministers, you and I need to think, speak and write definitively about grief.

More Than A Technician

Yet, just because grief is your specialty, you must studiously avoid becoming technicians in death. If you should become merely that, you would be like the funeral director. His job is to handle death merely as a technician. He performs certain technical services, and that is that. Ministers who perfunctorily make two or three visits before or after death, and who perform expected rites and ceremonies at the funeral and at the grave, likewise have become technicians in death. That is one way of handling the problem of grief. But such ministers are not true to Christ's calling.

Today we shall take a hard look at grief. Even a casual acquaintance with grief indicates that grieving persons need the help of someone who will go beyond the work of a technician. They need the ministry of the Word of God. Nothing less than a word from God Himself can adequately meet the needs of a grief-stricken man or woman. That, then, is my concern today: to discuss some of the ways and means by which we may minister that Word in time of grief.

---

[1]An address delivered to a ministerial conference at the State Mental Health Center, Norristown, Pennsylvania, March 16, 1971 and originally published as a part of *The Big Umbrella*. Here it is reprinted in a revised and annotated form.

What Grief Involves

Grief may be called *a life-shaking sorrow over loss*. Grief tears life to shreds; it shakes one from top to bottom. It pulls him loose; he comes apart at the seams. Grief is truly nothing less than a life-shattering loss.[2] A mere technician can get a body underground, but a pastor who functions as such can never sew a severed soul together again.

Grief is a life-shaking sorrow, but usually grief is not *simple* sorrow. Plugged into the sorrow are other emotions. During grief, emotions of anger, guilt and fear often are involved. When anger, guilt, or fear becomes tangled together with the deep, penetrating soul sorrow of such a loss, a pastor finds himself with a counseling problem of some magnitude. It takes more than a few perfunctory visits or ceremonies to handle this kind of problem. It will take more extensive counseling than usually has been offered.[3]

Grief may be occasioned by a loss of any sort. Significant losses may shake Christians dramatically. First, there is the loss of *persons*. It could be the loss of a person by death, through a move, by a marriage, or because of a divorce. A pastor must not fail to recognize that these other losses of a person sometimes can be just as devastating as loss by death. Often the complications that are involved in a divorce or at the marriage of a child are greater and more difficult to handle than those that occur at death. A child may leave the home and the community in anger (or perhaps while he remains bodily, he leaves psychologically; he may cut off the family as truly as if he had run away). Any significant loss of communion with a person may occasion serious grief responses.[4]

Grief also may be occasioned by the loss of a *position*, as, for instance, when one loses his job. We have begun to encounter this phenomenon more and more frequently today, now that tight economic squeezes have come upon us. It is possible that we shall see much more of this sort of thing in the near future. Loss of status also may lead to grief when one loses his good name. So you see, it is not only through the loss of a person by death that grief occurs; loss of possessions, money, a job, house, or whatever a person holds dear, may be the occasion for grief.[5]

---

[2]Cf. the etymology of the interesting English word *bereaved*. To be reaved literally is to be broken up.

[3]The problem is that few pastors have considered grief as an opportunity for counseling. Rather, the all-too-deeply-embedded pay-a-visit-or-two mentality has prevailed.

[4]That is not to say that every such loss *should* occasion grief. In some instances of this sort, the pastor's task may consist largely of pointing toward a more biblical response.

[5]Again, his sense of values may need challenging.

You and I are called to minister (in a peculiar way) to persons in grief situations of every sort. We must not forget the broad scope of grief and the opportunities for counseling that this affords (and demands of us). But today I am not going to talk about all kinds of grief. Instead, I have been asked to discuss the limited area of grief caused by death.

Your Attitude Is Important

To begin with, if you wish to help persons in grief caused by death, you must have a proper attitude toward death. Now I must assume as a fundamental presupposition that a pastor whose own attitudes about death and grief are shaky will be unable to offer true comfort and help. Because of that uncertainty or ambivalence, he may be of minimal help only, or, as is more likely, he actually may become a harmful complicating factor in the situation. He may confuse the bereaved person more than help him. Each one of us who thinks of ministering to a person in grief first must ask himself about his own beliefs concerning death. We cannot avoid expressing an attitude growing out of those beliefs; we cannot be neutral. This is because each one of us himself is involved in death. When he ministers to another's grief, a pastor thinks also of his own coming death. Since we think about these matters, we all have attitudes toward them. We shall minister out of those attitudes.

Those attitudes may be clearly articulated, or they may be very fuzzy or even unknown to us. Since I teach preaching at Westminster Theological Seminary as well as pastoral work, I must discuss style (language usage) in my courses.[6] Students, I have discovered, sometimes talk about "acquiring" a style as if they were purchasing a brand new typewriter for the first time. The fact is, the minute they first opened their mouths, they had a style. The only legitimate sorts of questions about style are whether one is conscious of it, whether it is good or bad, whether it is canned or refrigerated, whether it is green and growing, etc. What I mean is that those are the only legitimate kinds of questions, since everyone already *has* a style. You would think that students would know this, but frequently they have to be awakened to the fact. It is not a matter of packaging something into an empty space; rather, in helping someone to acquire a good preaching style, the task requires repackaging and retraining. The same is true about attitudes toward death. You *have* an attitude toward death (and also toward grief). Since this is so, you must become familiar with (and may find it necessary to alter) your own attitudes. If you are not, you may be doing things by those attitudes that you don't even realize.

---

[6]Cf. Jay Adams, *Pulpit Speech*, Presbyterian and Reformed Publishing Company: Nutley, 1971, p. 111.

In framing a good attitude toward death and grief, it is most important to settle your own theological stance toward life, death, grief, sin, guilt and, of course, toward God. You cannot avoid these issues. In fact, one's own personal relationship to God and his theological beliefs are central. If one's theological beliefs and his life clearly come together at any point, it is here. Here is the moment of truth for every preacher. Death and grief test a minister's true commitments. Each one of you knows that he is going to die. What you believe about death, the future, salvation and God will make a significant impact as you minister to a grieving person.

Today I can speak only from my conservative, Calvinistic viewpoint as a Christian. I want you to know precisely where I stand so that you will be able to evaluate what I have to say. I happen to believe that what the Bible says about death is literally true. I believe that the God who created this world is going to do something for His people throughout all eternity, not just for the brief period of time that they live upon the earth. All that I have to say is influenced by the fact that I believe in sin and judgment, heaven and hell, the resurrection of the body, eternal life, and that redemption through Jesus Christ is the only answer to man's need. He died on the cross in the place of guilty sinners that through repentance and faith in Him they might have the forgiveness of sin and eternal life.

Now all of that has a large influence upon my attitudes toward life, death and grief, and, therefore, upon what I say and do when I sit beside someone who is going through a period of grief; indeed, it has the controlling influence. If you believe differently, what you believe also will have an overwhelming influence upon what you do at that time. That is why you must become aware of your personal-theological stance toward death and grief. If you do not have a biblical faith, I do not know what you will say to those to whom you seek to minister. The poverty of a skeptical or fuzzy faith is never more apparent than at the graveside.

Grief, Not Despair

There is a biblical distinction between grief and despair. Because I believe this distinction is fundamental to all help, I try to communicate it to grief sufferers. Grief, on the one hand, is proper and good according to the Scriptures; despair, on the other hand, is quite wrong. In I Thessalonians 4:13, God revealed to Christians the basic information about death and the resurrection that they need precisely in order to prevent sorrow from turning into despair: He spoke of "grieving" but "not as others who have no hope." The Greek word *lupeo* that is translated either "grief" or "sorrow" is simply the general word for "pain." Paul says that Christians should experience pain over loss, yet not as others who have no hope. He is interested in steering the true course between an unbiblical stoicism that stifles emotion and the despair that comes from lack of hope. Christian grief lies in between. This grief is a painful sorrow that issues in an honest expression of one's feelings; yet even in the midst of these intense feelings, the Christian may look with confidence beyond the tragedy to its solution in Christ.

Faith in the midst of grief looks to the *not yet* and says, "I believe that it *shall be.*" The Christian, therefore, has anticipation in the midst of sorrow. His tears only magnify God's revealed future for him.

It is just this element of hope or anticipation that is lacking in despair. Indeed, faith and hope may grow tall in the rich soil of grief. Being mixed with grief, hope and faith are needed to give balance to it and to bring about the proper resolution of grief. It is precisely here that one's theological position makes all of the difference. If the ministry of the Word, then, requires a ministry of biblical hope, the minister himself must possess such hope.

To prevent grief from turning into despair, the pastor must share the Christian hope with the grief sufferer. He must remind grief sufferers that the Christian hope is firm, for it rests upon the death and resurrection of Jesus Christ. He must point them to that which is beyond death. He must show them again that there is more to life than physical life. He must remind them not only that there is a life after death, but also that there will be new physical life at the resurrection.

According to the Scriptures of both the Old and New Testaments, sorrow is proper. Every emotion is good. God has created man and gifted him with the capacity for expressing all of these emotions. Each is proper in the appropriate situation to which it corresponds. The loss of a loved one is a sorrowful event, so it is improper to hold back one's emotion of sorrow at the time of death. Yet, despair over the loss is inappropriate for the Christian who has God's sure word of promise to comfort him.

At the grave of Lazarus Jesus wept. His emotional responses were so apparent that others standing by commented about them. They said, "See how much he loved him." Sorrow visibly released in the form of grief is, therefore, a very good and proper emotion that expresses one's love and shows that he cares.

Removing Fear From Death

But let us now consider the scriptural concept of hope.[7] In I Corinthians 15, after discussing the resurrection of the body at great length, Paul closes his discussion with a quotation from the Old Testament in which (in a great apostrophe) he addresses death itself: "O death, where is your sting?" He acknowledges that there is a *sting,* that is, something *painful* about death.

---

[7]See also *The Christian Counselor's Manual, op. cit.,* pp. 45-46.

The Greek word translated sting is *kentron*. This vivid word is used in other places in the New Testament. For instance, it refers to the sting of the scorpions mentioned in the book of Revelation. I don't know whether you have ever been stung by a scorpion or not, but I once had that unhappy experience in Texas. (Incidentally, I understand that the sting of our American variety of scorpion is not quite as painful as that of scorpions in Palestine, but that is hard to imagine!) I crawled into bed that night as a green Easterner not realizing that this eventuality could occur, and a scorpion had already blissfully gone to sleep in the bed before I arrived. He must have resented my disturbing his nap, because he soon let me know it! For three days I walked around with a fiery red spot as large as a frying pan on my right leg. During the remainder of my stay, every time I got near a bed or a shoe or a shirt or tie or anything, I checked it out first before putting it to use. I immediately learned to respect scorpions because of their *sting*. The sting was painful, and I wanted to avoid it at all costs. Because of its painful aspects, I took every necessary precaution to make sure that I would not get involved in another similar experience. That is the picture in I Corinthians 15. Men shy away from death because of its painful aspect; they do not want to get near it or have anything to do with it.

The word *kentron* is used also of the goads employed to herd animals along the road. These goads were long sticks with sharp points on one end. The word occurs in the book of Acts (chapter 9). The risen Lord, addressing Saul said, "It is hard for you to kick against the goads." The picture here is of an animal that wants to go his own way. The herdsman is jabbing him with the goad to drive him back onto the path. But he is annoyed by this goading, so he gives the stick one good hard clout with his foot. The sharp point sinks deeply into his flesh and then he really gets the feel of the *kentron!* That pain is so severe that he will never kick it again. He has learned to respect it; he will avoid it at all costs *because of the pain* that it inflicts.

So in I Corinthians 15 Paul says to death, "Where is your sting? Grave where is your victory?" He continues, "The sting of death is sin and what gives sin its strength is the law." In other words, Paul notes that people are afraid to die. They fear death because of its *painful* aspect. They are afraid to die because they know that they are sinners, that they have not kept the law of God, and that they must face God at death as lawbreakers. Men avoid death because it is painful.

Paul's words, however, indicate that one need not fear death. He himself was able to address death without such fear. For him the painful aspect was missing. Christ has conquered death and removed its stinger. The Lord

Jesus Christ came to die for sinners. Although His people had broken
God's law, He bore the penalty for their sin. Death held no such fear for
early Christians, then, since it was their firm conviction that death's stinger
had pierced Another; it came loose on the cross. So the great specter is
powerless and the fearful scorpion who once held the keys to death and
Hades has had them snatched from him (Rev. 1:17, 18). The risen Christ
now says to His people: "Fear not."

That is the Christian viewpoint toward death. While the sorrow of loss
remains, the hope of eternal life, the resurrection of the body, the anticipation of the reunion of believers, and most of all the hope of living in the personal presence of Christ also share space with it. Indeed, these realities
must triumph over grief.

The biblical view is found also in Hebrews 2:15. There the writer says
that the Lord has released from bondage those who "all their life long were
held in the bondage" of the fear of death. Christ's first sermon was preached
from Isaiah 61:1-2. That passage predicts that He would come to comfort
all who mourn. He came to deal with this question of death. His coming
"brought life and immortality to light through the gospel" (II Tim. 1:10).

The pastor who believes this biblical teaching, therefore, will bring the
balancing note of victory into the milieu of grief. He will not find it possible
to sound that note of victory at all times and in all places in the same way,
but if he believes with Paul that "to die is gain" (Phil. 1:21), and that death
means "to be with Christ, which is far better" (Phil. 1:23), all that he says
and does will convey this viewpoint. It was only the victory of Christ over
death that allowed Paul to speak to death as a defeated foe. It is that same
fact that makes the great difference between hope and despair; it is the only
hope that can make such a difference.

Using the Grief Process

So much, then, for the attitude of the pastor toward death and grief. To
be helpful, a pastor also must understand, evaluate, confront and learn to
use the grief process. Again, it seems necessary to take a closer look at these
matters through Christian eyes. Many points of view about grief have been
adopted wholesale from the studies of psychiatrists. The work of Eric
Lindemann, who made the classic study (1944), has been the basis for most
of the discussion since. This study had severe limits, yet very few
acknowledged those limits. Geoffrey Gorer is an exception. For twenty
years, nearly everyone accepted Lindemann's view as the description of the
normal grief process. But Gorer, in his book, *Death, Grief and Mourning,*
challenged this assumption.[8] He has charged that the use of Lindemann's

[8]Geoffrey Gorer, *Death, Grief and Mourning,* Doubleday and Company, Inc.: New York,
pp. 141-152.

study made by most subsequent writers is invalid. Gorer points out that most of the mourners in Lindemann's study were bereaved through war or the disaster of the Coconut Grove fire. The husbands of the surviving widows had all been fifty years old or younger at the time of their death. Gorer observes that it is possible that grief over a death that is considered more "natural" (e.g., due to age and infirmity) will differ from the patterns occasioned by sudden unexpected deaths. Some of the elements Lindemann noted in the grief experience when the death is premature, may be missing. Gorer challenged Lindemann's findings because they differed markedly from his own. Since the results of his studies differed significantly from some of the conclusions to which Lindemann came, Gorer has cautioned, rightly, that there may be good reasons why Lindemann's description of the grief process should not be considered the norm or standard. Because of the failure to recognize these facts, the model of mourning in most of the existing scanty literature is very heavily biased toward premature and unexpected bereavement. Gorer found, in contrast, that hostility was not always present in more "normal" deaths.

It would seem important to ask the kind of questions that Gorer has asked. It is time to take many second looks and to ask many more questions. There may be some facts about the grief process that can be learned from Lindemann and from others. I am suggesting then that the pastor should take in account the fact that subsequent writing almost monolithically has been based upon Lindemann's work. Much work needs to be done, therefore, in the study of grief. This should be the conclusion of anyone who has studied the literature in the field. Certainly the last word has not been spoken; I shall not speak it today. It may be necessary to revise most of what has been said so far.

Christians ought to ask questions from the distinctively Christian viewpoint. Basic questions like, "What were the researcher's assumptions?" and, "What were his basic presuppositions?" have not been whispered. Yet those kinds of questions really are vital. What one looks for usually is what he finds. And every finding is evaluated from the vantage (or disadvantage) point at which one stands. What can Christians do by working from Christian presuppositions? The study of grief from a biblical viewpoint will elicit entirely different results. For example, Paul himself insists that the Christian faith will make a difference (I Thess. 4:13ff.); he distinguishes between two kinds of grief. He speaks not merely of one, but of (1) a grief in despair, and (2) a grief in hope. Lindemann and most others fail to recognize any such distinction. Yet, Edgar Jackson, in his book, *For the Living,* cites some interesting studies that may have to do with this very question. He notes that there has been a difference in the rate of recovery between those who have hope and those who do not.[9] The distinction between those who have hope and those who do not also should influence the manner in which one approaches a grief sufferer.

As Christians, we should not accept at face value the results of any studies that are based upon non-Christian presuppositions. Instead, let us who believe the Scriptures take our stand there and look at what others have said from that vantage point and also ask the questions that must be asked. Preachers too readily "buy" what psychiatrists and medical doctors say. There is another viewpoint, another stance and a whole new dimension to be brought to the problem. The Scriptures give us that perspective. Although we may learn much that is valuable and useful from others (if we know how to evaluate their work by the standard of biblical principle) we must not be intimidated by them into conforming our ideas to theirs. But what we do and say must not conflict with the Scriptures.

Prepare for Grief

Turning now to how we may help our congregations, first let me note that much can be done by pastors to *prepare* others for the grief that inevitably will overtake them. So often we have failed our congregations by not preaching and speaking frequently enough about death and grief. We hear much today in churches as well as elsewhere about the facts of life. We teach courses, hold conferences, engage in studies, and publish books and pamphlets about the facts of life. We encourage young people's groups to discuss the subject. But where is there a course, a book, a study or anything else on the *facts of death?* Death is more universal than the begetting of life, and yet we say virtually nothing about the facts of death.

Previous instruction concerning death and grief helps. Indeed, it helps immensely. That is why Paul wrote I Thessalonians 4:13ff. Notice how he opens the passage: "I would not have you to be ignorant, brethren, concerning those who are asleep . . . so that you may not grieve as others who have no hope." Then he offers detailed information calculated to bring hope out of despair, to give answers to problems, and to give comfort in the time of sorrow. He closes that section with the words, "Comfort one another with these words." So information, detailed information, is crucial. I do not think that our congregations hear enough of this information. No wonder that there is often so little comfort. We have failed to prepare people for death and grief. Hope that will carry them successfully through the time of grief must have time to mature. It cannot grow fast enough in the

---

[9]Edgar N. Jackson, *For the Living,* Channel Press, Des Moines: 1963, pp. 78, 79.

overly rich soil of grief alone. There must be a mix. Grieving is affected by hope or the lack of it, and hope is affected by information or the lack of it. Hope does not grow out of misunderstanding and ignorance. Hope is based on information.

Grief should be discussed beforehand. Why not discuss the subject of grief with a young couples' group? These couples have parents who soon may die. As a result, they soon may face grief. In such groups the subject may be discussed at some length with great profit.

When I teach beginning Speech to students who have had no Speech courses at college, one of the things that I must explain is the process of stage fright. I talk to them in detail about it to help them understand the dynamics of what is happening and, *through understanding,* to alleviate the fear of it. If a speaker's mouth dries up like cotton, his tongue sticks to his jaw, his heart begins to pound, his hands get clammy, his knees knock, and he feels butterflies in the stomach, he is likely to become frightened by these bodily responses unless he understands them. When I explain that these are normal anticipation responses, similar to those of pilots before they take off for combat duty, that they are the same kind of responses that football players experience before going out on the playing field, and that they approximate the responses of people starting off on a long trip, it helps. The feelings that I have just mentioned are the sensations associated with mobilizing the body for a challenging experience. They indicate that the body is geared up for that experience. What you feel in your stomach, for instance, is not butterflies of course; it is the cessation of the comfortable peristaltic movements of the stomach that move your food along. When these cease, you get that hollow feeling in the pit of your stomach. All of these changes take place in order to *prepare* the body, and that is exactly what a speaker needs. He does not want to be so completely relaxed that he drapes himself all over the pulpit; that would show a lack of concern for his subject and his audience. But if he stands up alert and prepared, anticipating what he has to say, and able to fully concentrate all of his forces (both mental and physical) upon his topic, he is ready to speak. The anticipation response of the body, then, is part of what makes him ready to speak or preach. He should welcome this bodily change, not fear it. When you explain this to a student, it makes a tremendous difference to him. If sometime later he begins to feel a cottony mouth, he is not likely to become as upset about it as if he did not know these facts.

The same is true with grief. In fact, in C. S. Lewis' book, *A Grief Observed,* this very point is made. In this book Lewis records his own grief as he experienced it at the death of his wife. Listen to his very first words:

"No one ever told me that grief felt so like fear." Note, he says, "No one ever told me." Perhaps some of the problems that he experienced in that period of grief against which he rebelled so strongly, that he found so difficult to handle and that caused him so much fear, might not have occurred if someone *had* told him. I think that we must take a cue from C. S. Lewis and start talking to people about grief. That will mean, among other things, talking about:

The Process Itself

It is time to take a look at that process of grief. But we must look at it differently from the way that some others have. We shall not consider it as "grief work" that has to be done. This is the standard approach of Lindemann and the many who have followed him. We shall not discuss grief merely as so many things that have to be done in such and such a way in order to get through this process successfully. Those who adopt the "grief work" view think of the process as fairly uniform so long as one is certain not to short-circuit it or delay it or divert it into some wrong channel. They have conceived of the grief process too mechanically and too uniformly, and too superficially. We must learn to understand the process in all of its complexity if we would use it for the welfare of the one who is suffering grief.

The various stages of the grief process may be divided in different ways; for example, some see four stages, others three, etc. Three stages, at least, must be distinguished. All studies (probably correctly) show at least three stages in the process. For the sake of convenience I shall call these three stages Shock, Disorganization and Reorganization.

SHOCK

The first is *Shock*. The length of this period variously has been computed as lasting from one to two hours. This is the period from when you hang up the phone, having been told, "He's dead," to the time when you come to your senses and say, "Yes, he is dead." During that period one may experience numbness, the feeling of being stunned, hysteria, a near or an actual paralysis and bewilderment. Some persons, however, take such news quite coolly. One biblical example of a very strong reaction to the shock of the news of death may be found in I Samuel 4:19-21. Ichabod's mother was still carrying him as an unborn child when news reached her concerning the capture of the ark of the covenant. She was told that, in connection with that sad event, her husband and her father-in-law had died. In shock, she gave birth to the boy, named him Ichabod and died on the spot. What a dramatic and forceful account of the initial shock period in grief! The combination of factors was overwhelming, too much for her body to stand.[10]

The pastor during this period sometimes may be more present than active. This is something that you hear said all of the time, of course. I hesitate ever to say that about a pastor, and yet this seems to be the one place where we have to say it. The pastor normally ought to be far more active as a counselor than many advise. But here is one of those rare occasions where frequently there simply is not very much that he can say or do. He can handle discussion at this point only to the extent that it is possible to do so. But again, what he does will depend upon the particular individual involved and how he or she is reacting.

If the pastor enters the picture during this early stage, either during shock or during the next few hours as the sufferer moves into the second stage (Disorganization), sometimes he may be subjected to harsh treatment by the sufferer. Not everyone is likely to respond in this way, but now if the bars are down, the restraints have been removed, and the first glimmerings of what has happened begin to sink in (and particularly if there are other problems like hostility or guilt mingled with the sorrow), some sufferers are likely to spill their feelings upon the pastor or others who may be among the first to enter upon the scene. The pastor should be aware of this possibility. He should also be prepared for it.

This kind of a response needs to be handled properly. What does a pastor do? Well, to begin with, he must not think merely of himself. He should neither let his feelings be hurt, nor respond in anger, nor turn on his heels and walk away from the situation. He should not begin an argument or ordinarily attempt a discussion. Instead, he can do at least two things. First, he can give a gentle, corrective rebuke in which briefly he may explain that he does not think that the charges that have been made are correct and that at a later time he would like to take up the matter. This leads naturally to the second point. *Later* (the pastor should refuse to discuss the matter at this point) the pastor may raise the issue. It is wrong to avoid the problem or to let the matter drop as so often has been advised. Something came to the surface that needs to be dealt with. Postponement will provide a good opening for later counseling about the anger or fear or guilt that may have slipped out when the sufferer's defenses were down.

DISORGANIZATION

Let us now turn to the second stage: *Disorganization.* There is much that needs to be discussed about the questions of length and duration and even about the concept of stages itself, but I cannot do so today. The second phase may last from seven to ten days. Let us take a look at the symptoms

---

[10]It clearly demonstrates that there is no uniform grief response. Cf. also Zechariah 12:10, where the mourning over an only son is distinguished as particularly bitter.

that *may* occur during this period. All of these (as in the period of Shock) may not appear in every case. I do not think that in every instance they should. Certainly a devout Christian and an unbeliever should respond differently.

Physical distress may come in waves of bodily discomfort down deep inside. There might be twenty minutes worth of this, then a break and then more in an hour or so. Such feelings may include a tight feeling in the throat and a feeling of being suffocated. A number of people have talked about deep sighing. The sufferer may not even realize how often he sighs. He might go around saying, "Oh, my," or something like that. A sensation of desert dryness may plague him. He could possibly suffer from limpness of the limbs and little mobilization of the muscles in general. Then there is likely to be a drained emotional state, emptiness of feeling and a sense of unreality on the part of the person in grief. Perhaps at times he will wander off into a dream world. A "this can't really be true" attitude may begin to grow; whatever he is doing, his heart is likely not to be in it. There may be loss of spirit, zest, joy, initiative and motivation. In such cases he will do things mechanically. He will become very stiff and formal even toward his closest friends. He will appear standoffish (seeming not to care about others) or even be discourteous. He may not give much thought to manners and courtesy or care much about tact. Now, of course, if he gets a good bit of sedation during this period of time (which may be very unwise), the whole process might be prolonged or altered. It might be wise even to chat with the physician about this matter if you notice such a problem.

Guilt and Grief

If guilt is plugged into the picture, serious complicating problems may arise. For example, if a bad relationship existed between the sufferer and the person who died and attitudes had become bitter and hardened with much resentment between the parties, most likely there will be added difficulties. It will be your task to discover such matters during grief counseling sessions. When necessary, you should probe directly into the question. This matter ultimately must be dealt with by confession and forgiveness and a subsequent change of life pattern.[11] May I say that in counseling every

---

[11]See general remarks in *Competent to Counsel* concerning confession. However, since no confession may be made to the deceased, the pastor may experience a dissatisfied attitude on the part of the repentant confessor. If that is encountered, the problem may be due to the fact that there is no opportunity to experience reconciliation with the deceased. A new relationship cannot be established as when one confesses to a living person.

This means that the counselee is unable to establish a new way of life *in relationship to* the deceased, but he senses the need for a new pattern of life none the less. Two things may be done to meet this problem: the pastor may urge the counselee to (1) do whatever can be done to right continuing wrongs (cf. David's kindness to Mephibosheth, II Samuel 9:1-13); (2) con-

week I find that there is much bitterness and resentment between people? Let's face this fact: many of the problems that we have with others never get resolved. Instead, they usually end up as hardened bitternesses, cast iron resentment. When someone dies with that kind of relationship still existing between the two of them, the survivor may have a hard time handling the problem of grief. God may use the death to bring about genuine repentance. But it will be complex, not simple as it might have been if repentance had occurred prior to the loss. The way of the transgressor is hard. Mixed together are the feelings of sorrow and guilt over the fact that this relationship was never resolved and now cannot be resolved. The resentment, if not dealt with before God, may continue. A genuine pastor will call the grieving one to repentance. This may seem cruel or harsh, but in truth it is the kindest act of all. Simple sorrow over loss is hard enough; it can become unbearable when complicated by unresolved guilt.

Perhaps the problem of telling the patient that he was dying had been solved in an all too typically unchristian manner: by lying. For two or three months, or even a longer period, the family knew that he had what is so coldly called "a terminal illness." Everyone had been informed that he was expected to die, but the physician said, "Don't tell *him* ." Because the family agreed to this cruelest lie of all, they did not tell him, and a false, artificial relationship (everyone was always afraid that he might find out) began to grow. Most dying persons know anyway, but everyone (all around) was

---

sider other relationships in which the same patterns may yet exist. He must do all that can be done (Rom. 12:18) to be reconciled and to establish proper relationships to these persons. Part of the dissatisfaction may come in such instances from requiring an inadequate form of repentance that demands confession but no "fruits" (changes in the repentant one) appropriate to repentance. Such change must be effected wherever possible. Cf. *The Christian Counselor's Manual,* pp. 268 f.

The friend of a young girl who was suddenly killed sought help. He said that he had failed to use many opportunities to witness to her about Christ. Now it was too late. He had become deeply depressed over this matter and had come to believe that he was guilty of sending her to hell. Nothing anyone could say would relieve the depression that had developed. Help came in the form of three things that had to be done: (1) He needed to repent and to confess his sin of failure to witness. Truly he had sinned against God and against the girl. He was guilty of this and had to be called to repentance. (2) He needed to get his theology straightened out. He was not responsible for the eternal destiny of that girl, although he was responsible for witnessing to her. She did not go to hell (if she did) as the result of his sin; she went to hell for her own sin. *She* was responsible to God for her sin; *his* responsibility was to witness to her about it and about her need for a Savior. Each was guilty of separate sins. Truly his sin entered into the question of her eternal state, but she would suffer eternally for her sin, not for his. (3) He could do nothing about the past, but to repent, yet genuine repentance would lead to fruit fitting to repentance: if his repentance over the sin of failure to witness was sincere, he would do differently in the future. As a matter of fact, genuine relief came only when he made a list of persons to whom a witness was long overdue and began to do what he could to make up for lost time.

afraid to broach the subject. No significant communication between husband and wife or children and parent took place. The problem got in the way every time they were together. They could never really talk about the expected death or about what was going to happen after death. Fear grew in the one who was to be left that the deceased might have been able to relieve by his wise help and careful planning during those last few months. On the other hand, a vital ministry of love and help was withheld from the dying loved one who was effectively cut off from everything he needed. The physician and the family meant well, but because they violated God's law, they destroyed all that might have been good. They could not plan together for the eventuality of death. There could be no last words to the children.

This terrible situation so often exists today. One person dies and the family is left with *that* as the last memory. They remember the lies, the hard days, the emptiness and fear. *Grieving together before death* was not possible. Nothing relieves and helps grief more than this. Failure to grieve together is hard for all. But it is particularly difficult for the bereaved, since much of the heartache of grief could be removed by proper Christian communication prior to death. If a husband and wife discuss the expected death beforehand, grief can be lessened by open exchange, reconciliation (if necessary), planning, preparation, warm moments and honest joint prayer and ministry of the Word. There can be pleasant memories of these last weeks or months, in contrast to the empty dread that accompanies the lies. Children can be challenged to duty and devotion as they were by the dying patriarchs. When people need one another so desperately, why should pastors agree to sin by maintaining the lies that drive them apart?

The dishonesty and guilt of non-discussion doubtless is one serious cause of complication in grief. We must question seriously the whole matter of lies or even silence about possible death. Certainly lying about it is taboo for you as God's shepherd.[12]

Resentment also may arise over the death itself. "He's left me now just at this time when I needed him so much," one bitter woman may say. "What will happen, now?" another asks in fear. To further complicate matters, pastors must recognize that fear of the future may be mixed with anger. The survivor may become angry at the one who died, and yet be sorry that he

---

[12]Pastors should warn congregations well in advance that they intend to tell the truth. The warrant to do so, in spite of family or physician, comes from God. The pastoral relationship demands a truthful ministry of the Word. The possibly dying parishioner is not only a member of a family; he is also a member of Christ's Church for whom you and the session have a pastoral responsibility. It is important, however, to speak of preparation for the *possibility* of death, for no one knows when another will die. Many surprising recoveries have occurred in God's providence when a patient was all but pronounced dead.

has died. He may be angry that he has been left alone to face the fearful future. Trust in the providence of God alone can solve problems of fear. The ministry of hope stemming from the conviction that God is sovereign is needed at such a time. In the third stage, that hope will be solidified as the pastor helps a fearful, lonely sheep plan for the future according to biblical principles.

What Grief May Do

Because grief tends to knock down defenses, the grief sufferer may seem to become a quite different person than you have ever known before. When inhibitions are removed, the real person may emerge. The real person may be very different from the manifest person that others previously have seen day by day. The sufferer has been able to hold under his real character until the life-shattering experience shook down the walls. His neighbors and friends and even his family may have thought him to be a very fine person. But now that the lid is off and he becomes outwardly everything that he was inwardly, he may not be very pleasant to have around. Fear may drive him to desperate means; he may speak harsh or foolish words or take irrational actions. The pastor's ministry of the Word may be extended markedly if this occurs. Possibly kindly admonition and rebuke may be called for.

Preoccupation with the image of the deceased (so often mentioned by Lindemann and sometimes by others), which may be very vivid, may possibly occur. In the daydreaming inner world into which he may retreat, this image may at times be so vivid that the bereaved person may even think that he has seen or heard the dead person in a visitation. Where this occurs as a problem, the pastor must steady the sufferer with sound biblical doctrine. He may wish to push beyond the problem itself to see if it is connected to a complicating difficulty like unresolved anger or guilt toward the deceased. He should inquire also about possible sleep loss. Two or more days of significant sleep loss (of R. E. M., or rapid eye movement sleep) can cause any or all of the perceptual difficulties associated with L.S.D. In every instance, it would be wise to urge adequate sleep. Sin against the body by pushing it beyond its limits can add unnecessary heartache, confusion and fear to the grief period. Grief readily can lead to sleep loss, so keep this important question in mind.

During this period of disorganization, you will be watching a very unpleasant thing. You are involved in helping a member of your flock through a very difficult period. It will not usually be pleasant. It is hard to watch a life come apart at the seams; it is heartbreaking to see the stuffings come out; it can be disillusioning to go through the wall behind which this person lives day by day and discover him for what he really is. It would not be pleasant for you or them if others were to look behind your walls. Yet that is often what you will see happening during this period.

When one is bereaved, the old ways are being destroyed. This is truly a period of disorganization. Old fields are being plowed up; old roads are being rerouted and old buildings are coming down. Factors that once seemed so secure now come crashing down around the grief sufferer and all is becoming rubble. He realizes that there must be radical changes, that he can no longer go on as he once did. Now that her husband is gone, now that his wife is dead, the survivor recognizes that much of life necessarily will be entirely different. A new life has to be built; he knows that. The old patterns will no longer suffice. But what will the new be like? The uncertainty may cause acute fear where faith is small or lacking. It will also take time for the transition to take place. The period of Disorganization is itself the first part of that transition period. It is the negative side that must come first.

A period of disorganization is a *negative* period, because it is the time when things come apart. It is a time of falling down, tearing up, and uprooting. But it is a necessary and important period: the remnants and the rubble of each collapsed building must be cleared before something new can be built on that same plot of ground. The pastor may help enormously in this process. A break has to be made with the past, and Christians must see to it that in every way this is a *clean* break. The unsettled sin of the past must be dealt with. The ground must be readied for the future sowing of seed and the building of new edifices. If they are to be good crops and sturdy buildings, all must be readied first.

Disorganization is just that; a life-shaking experience has disorganized the grief sufferer. It has shaken his life to pieces. He has lost his moorings; he is adrift on the sea of life. During this period, one's whole life comes under review. He takes a new look at himself; he can't help it. Here is where the pastor can be of real help. It is not so important (as many of the studies have insisted) to get grief sufferers to talk about the deceased.[13] Instead, what you need to do is to encourage the grief sufferer to talk about his *own* relationship to the deceased. It is really his life that is cracking at the seam;

---

[13]Particularly if the last weeks together have been open, honest and warm. Where unreconciled conditions remain at death, indeed, this must be discussed and handled biblically (even then the emphasis is not upon the deceased but upon one's own relationship to him). But assuming that has been done, or that the grief was simple (not complex) to begin with, then what I am about to say follows. The concept of *grief work*, from which the idea of talk about the deceased emerges, is erroneous. It has false cathartic notions underlying. Talk alone does not solve problems; indeed talk may serve only to intensify grief if that talk does not issue in biblical courses of action calculated to solve the problems discussed.

the other person is gone. If he wants to discuss the deceased, good, but also very soon you should move that discussion to the matter of his *relationship* to the deceased. And you can hardly do that without also talking about his relationship to God, and without talking about his own coming death. These are all pertinent subjects because a grief sufferer inevitably thinks about them. He will be thinking frequently about his own death during this period.[14] He will also talk about the kind of life style that he has led up until this period. This is important and usually it will grow naturally out of the discussion of these other topics.

Such a look at himself, in which he re-evaluates himself from top to bottom, may reveal that he has been an *angry* person. The pastor may need to point out how he has expressed anger toward God, against his relatives, or concerning someone at work. He may still be angry at the one he has lost.

The pastor also may need to show him that he is a *guilty* person. He may have great guilt over this anger and the bad relationships that he has sustained to the deceased and others. There may be guilt over other things that he has done in the past that come to him with renewed impact during this period of re-evaluation.

He may dicover that he is a very *fearful* person, with little or no trust. As a wise pastor, you will take note of fear, particularly fears arising from uncertainty. A widow may say, "I depended so much on him, how can I go on into the future? What will happen to the business? What will happen to the children?" Here is a person filled with fear. You ought to be looking for this. When you spot it, you will want to deal with this problem, especially looking forward to the next period in which you will help to allay many of those fears by stressing the faithfulness of God to His own, and offering concrete help from the Word of God. Since this is a period of breaking with the past, the goal for the pastoral counselor (as I said) ought to be to help the grief sufferer to make a clean break with the past. He must help him to deal with sinful patterns of living that he has fallen into over the years, not only by righting all wrongs between himself and God and others, but by sorting through the rest of the rubble so that he may help him to build something entirely fresh and new for the future.

Counseling in Disorganization

What I am calling for means a good bit more counseling than most pastors give to their people during the time of grief. But it is needed to do this job properly. The time and effort expended are well worth it. Rarely at any other time do you see a person in this condition. Rarely do you see a life

---

[14]This fact should awaken pastors and other Christians to the possibility for evangelism that exists in the ministry to those in grief.

come apart so completely. Rarely can you help one pick up so many pieces and put so much back together to form such an entirely new picture. Grief providentially affords one of the greatest opportunities to help persons to finer living for Jesus Christ than they have experienced before. Remember that this is the opportunity for ministry that God affords you every time a death occurs in your congregation. You ought to seize the opportunity; move in on it with all of the resources of God and allot all of the time needed to do the job well.

Here is one way to go about counseling in such circumstances. See if you can get the grief sufferer to agree to meet with you for a series of eight or ten weekly counseling sessions, if at all possible. Listen; ask questions about the recent past and then move backward. Always take a grieving person very seriously about his sin and guilt. Do not minimize his negative evaluations of himself. He is likely to be more open and honest than at any other time. Agree that he is sinful, but thwart depression by pointing to the biblical solution to each sin rather than by minimizing. Then help him to move in that direction. If necessary, you may have to help him to confess his sin to God and seek forgiveness from God. You may need to stress reconciliation with God and others. It may be necessary to sit down with two or three members of the family and work out some matters between them. Instead of this becoming a time of squabbling and fighting over who is going to get what after dad has passed on, at this point a wise pastoral counselor may be able to *reconcile* estranged relatives. This should be the very period of time in which those members of the family who have been far apart may be brought together again. The opportunity exists as it hardly does at any other time. So let me also suggest the thought of bringing *families* (or portions of them) in for counseling. Deal with the members of the family who are intimately involved and who will live in intimate relationship in the days ahead and counsel them *as families*. This point could be vital.

Certainly during this period you will counsel the grief sufferer(s) not to make hasty decisions. The widow should wait, if at all possible, to decide about such matters as selling the business or moving. If she says, "I could never live in this community being reminded of John by everything," caution her to get some perspective on this matter. Say,

"Wait until you've built the structure for a new life; then make those decisions. Don't make them now. So often people have sold everything and moved to Florida and four months later they remembered that all of their friends are back in Norristown. Because of a decision made before they were *ready* to make it, they have lost their church fellowship and good friends. The people and things that really mattered are irretrievably lost. They are ever after sorry that they made that move." One talented soloist, at the untimely death of her son, resolved that she would never sing again. She might have kept this hasty resolution if it had not been for the wise caution and encouragement given during this period in counseling by her pastor and the elders of her church. Today, her greatest joy is to sing of the victory of Christ over death. It is very important to advise people not to make weighty decisions until the period of disorganization and disorientation has passed.

REORGANIZATION

At the end of that seven to ten-day period, or whatever time it might cover, comes a third period or stage in the process of grief. I have called it *Reorganization*. This is the most neglected period of all, and yet it is the pastor's most opportune one. It is really the flip side of Disorganization. It is the positive part of grief. Yet this is the time when everybody begins to forget. By this time friends, neighbors, relatives and usually the pastor as well, disappear from the scene. They have all been very solicitous during the seven to ten-day period following death, but now that has ended. And rightly so; most friends can't continue to spend the same kind of time with the grief sufferer that they did before.

But what is deceptive is that since the grief sufferer now seems to be getting over it, since he can go back to work or begin to function fairly well again, everyone thinks that the grief process has ended. That is false. This third period is in one sense more crucial than the second. It is during this period, when he is forgotten by everyone else, that the grief sufferer usually, on his own, has to undertake the hardest task of all. This is a huge order, usually too large for somebody who has just come through an exhausting and disorienting life-shaking experience. It is too difficult to handle alone. He now must plan, lay the foundation and begin to build the structure for a brand new life; that is his work during the next few weeks. He must make many decisions; he must start up forces that may continue to work throughout the rest of his life. Everyone has forgotten him. Yet, he is very tired, sometimes very confused, and often very fearful. He is still looking at everything quite closely, and yet during this period he has to begin to make long-range decisions; he has to put his life together again. It is hard to get perspective alone. How important, then, for pastors to conduct regular counseling sessions from the earliest point following the death through the next two stages. If the time periods for stages two and three vary greatly among individuals, that will not matter, for if regular weekly sessions were set up initially after the death, they would carry you well into this period no matter when it begins.

This is a very opportune period because this is the period of planning and building. This is the positive period. This is not the look back, but if the break has been a clean one, the pastor can help to make this a marvelous and often exciting period of fresh, new growth. He can help the sufferer to look into God's future with faith and to plan a revised life style according to the Scriptures. During this period, radical change will take place; it must. So you may reckon on the fact that the bereaved is prepared for radical change; he knows that it must come. That big gaping hole in the home is there, so there must be radical change. Where he depended on her, he can no longer do so; change must take place.

If radical change must come, here is the pastor's opportunity to point to the radical changes that *God* requires. The person is *ready* for radical changes, he *knows* that they must be made, and he *will make them.* How important, then, that he make the right changes. You must move in to help him to do so; you can be of lifelong help to him by doing so if you help him to love and serve his Lord more dearly than before.

Change

It is important when we think about change to realize how change takes place. Change does not take place through talk alone. So much advice about counseling has centered (wrongly) upon talk. No one can be opposed to talk; talk is important. But talk alone can be very harmful; it can be destructive. Talk alone simply confirms the fact that there is a serious problem that is yet unsolved. Much talk that goes for counseling does far more harm than good. If that talk in the end does not issue in biblical courses of action, it is counterproductive. Change is a situation that grows out of talk that is oriented toward seeking and implementing biblical solutions to problems. Talk that does not only amplifies the problems. Don't just talk, then; rather, talk through the problem to a biblical solution. Otherwise, talk can be like tearing off a scab and poking your finger around in the bloody mess. That makes a wound all the sorer. That is what talk alone may do. A counselee may feel relieved for twenty minutes because he has got the pressure off his chest, but at the end he takes another hard look at it and he says, "I just see more clearly how difficult the problem is. We've reached no solution; we've not talked about anything to do."

So when you talk, always talk to a person about *change* and talk in concrete terms of *what* God says must be done and *how* to do it. Then, you will truly bless men's lives.

How can you best help the bereaved through this period? Here is one basic suggestion: you can help him to lay biblical plans prayerfully. To do so, you may begin (1) by helping him to set biblical objectives for the future.[15] Then (2) you may help him to list his problems, specifically those difficulties that he must overcome in order to reach those objectives. It is usually good policy to *list* problems so that both of you know specifically what you are talking about. Also, in the process of writing, a person has to formulate and define problems more clearly. Sometimes the answers come as a result of the writing. In days ahead, progress may be judged by the list as he is able to scratch off one here and another there. When he sees the list diminish, he gains hope. When he sees it not doing so, he knows that he has not done his job. Then (3) you might discuss and decide upon the biblical solutions to those problems. But, as I said, you may never leave it there. Quickly (4) help him lay out a course of action to take, including the scheduling (by date) of the initial steps to take and the means for checking up on him to make sure he is taking them.

If this or similar help is given, you are not likely to run into the kinds of difficulties of which so many of the studies speak. If people never get over their grief, or are sidetracked, or a variety of other such tragedies occur, perhaps one reason is that pastors have failed to minister in a thoroughly biblical and, therefore, adequate manner to those who suffer grief. Why not resolve that by the grace of God you will enter into the opportunities and meet the needs?

---

[15]Always with the holy caution of James 4:13-16 that delights in God's blue-penciling.

2
PASTORAL COUNSELING

INTRODUCTION

THE SPADE, THE MIRROR AND THE DOG BISCUIT

"I insist that it is best done with mirrors!"

"Well, you may cling to your view if you wish, but, personally, I prefer the archeologist's spade."

"You are both wrong; what really counts is a dog biscuit."

This, in a nutshell, is today's argument between the Rogerians, the Freudians and the Skinnerians.[1] The not altogether facetious argument above deals with the best *method* for helping men solve their problems in living.

But, why begin with method rather than with theory? Why start with solutions rather than with problems? There are several reasons for this. Consider Perry London's observation:

> . . . the analysis of techniques serves understanding more than any other possible approach to this discipline, mainly because techniques are relatively concrete things, and . . . also more relevant indices of what actually goes on in therapy.[2]

Methodology and practices plainly reveal what is truly central to a theory. The consideration of a counselor's or therapist's actual practice enables one most incisively to slice through the extraneous to the core material. What is considered truly operative (regardless of rhetoric or theoretical trappings) will find its way into the basic everyday methodology of a practitioner. Other materials, though interesting, usually form a large residue of non-operative material. To say it the other way around, it is not in affirmations

---

[1] Followers of Carl Rogers, Sigmund Freud and Burrows F. Skinner.

[2] Perry London, *The Modes and Morals of Psychotherapy*, Holt, Rinehart and Winston, Inc., N. Y.: 1964, p. 32.

that one always may discover the fundamental presuppositions and foundational beliefs upon which a system is built; these may be dimly perceived, faultily stated, or even intentionally clouded. Again, what one *does* for his client in counseling or therapy most pointedly shows what he believes the client's real problem to be.

Methodology then is where it's at. All sorts of people can agree upon noble goals, but when the question arises about how these goals may be attained, they soon begin to part company. Conflicts over methodology plainly expose the true differences between therapists and between counselors. When men agree upon goals, they may only have agreed semantically. They may agree that the client must be helped to become happy, well-integrated, etc. When they begin *working* toward these goals, however, they soon discover that they may be travelling in different and even opposite directions. The reason for this is because each poured different content into the common words that they used to describe the goals. When one man says "car," he thinks of a VW, while another pictures a Cadillac. When one says "mental illness," he thinks of a strange indefinable non-organic problem, while another thinks of brain damage or some similar physical disorder. Thus we shall begin with a brief consideration of the methodology of the three systems mentioned, turn to implications of these concerning presuppositions about man and his problems, and conclude with a capsule critique of each.

"It Is Best Done With Mirrors"

Carl Rogers, phase II, is best known today for his intimate involvement with the Encounter and Human Potential Movements. But in complete harmony with these feeling-centered endeavors that seek the good life through the realization of one's full potential is Carl Rogers, phase I, whose previous work probably still undergirds the practice of more marriage counselors, social workers, ministers, nurses, psychiatrists and clinical psychologists than that of any other.

The wide acceptance of Rogerian practice by so many persons in various helping professions is based primarily upon two factors: (1) its relative simplicity: it is very easy to learn; (2) the lack of risk involved: no advice is given.

In Rogers' Reflective Therapy, through mirroring the client's expressed feelings (rather than responding conversationally to the content of his speech), the counselor seeks to create a psychological atmosphere in which the client feels accepted, directs the interview himself, weighs the issues, gains insight (largely an increased understanding of himself), and makes decisions out of the personal storehouse of resources that he himself possesses. Taboo is any advice, direction, interpretation or persuasion on the part of the counselor. The client's personal autonomy must be preserved at all costs. The counselor, instead, is viewed merely as the one who holds the mirror; he is a catalytic agent who, by reflection of feeling, enables the client to solve his problems for himself.

The following dialogue illustrates the mirroring methodology:

Counselor: "Then, you feel that getting a job might be of importance to you?"

Client: "Well, that's what I've been wondering. I need the money to support the family....But...uh, I can't seem to get along with people at work. What do you think my problem might be?"

Counselor: "You'd like me to interpret the situation for you."

Client: "Yes, what do you think that I should do?"

Counselor: "Hmmmm."

Client: "After all, when you can put together the ideas of several people, it helps you make a decision."

Counselor: "You feel that you need to make a decision."

And so it goes. The counselor doggedly refuses to offer an opinion; instead, he reflects the feeling of the client, even when asked directly for advice.

What is going on here? Why is Rogers concerned about mirroring? Why does he refuse really to give counsel? What does the reflective methodology point to? The answer to all of these questions is found in the basic presupposition of Rogerian thought to which the Rogerian methodology plainly points: *Man has all of the resources that he needs to solve his problems within himself.* Hence, the title of the newer movement, "Human Potential." Rogers once described the ideal counselor this way:

He makes every move in accordance with one fundamental conviction—that the client is capable, once he is freed from tensions and has achieved a clearer insight, of formulating and carrying through a sound solution of his life's difficulties.[3]

---

[3]Carl Rogers, writing in an introduction to Charles A. Curran, *Personality Factors In Counseling*, Grune and Stratton, N. Y.: 1945, p. xix.

Thus Rogers himself acknowledges what his methodology reveals: he believes that man's problem is his failure to realize his own potential. Counseling or psychotherapy, then, becomes the practice of midwifery. The counselor merely assists at the birth of ideas and solutions of which the client is delivered.

The naive and arrogant assumption that each man possesses the answers to all of his problems stands diametrically opposed to a fundamental premise of the Christian faith. Christianity teaches that man is not self-sufficient and consequently needs both a revelation from God and redemptive help to enable him to live according to it. The central act of history was the death and resurrection of Jesus Christ, in whom God also became man to do for man *what he could not do for himself.* Rogers scorns the biblical teaching concerning man's inability and utter need for a Savior. Christians believe that Jesus Christ died for the sins of His people *in their stead.* But Rogers denies the substitutionary atonement. Christians hold that the biblical call to faith in Christ is an acknowledgment that man cannot solve the problem of evil for himself, but rather must depend wholly upon God for the solution. The need for the Scriptures, which Christians accept as the divinely revealed Word of God, also gives evidence of the clear-cut antithesis between the Rogerian and the Christian positions. Unfortunately, some Christian ministers have adopted Rogerian methodology in counseling, failing to recognize that their eclectic approach is inconsistent with their own most basic convictions.

"I Prefer the Archeologist's Spade"

Sigmund Freud wrote thousands of pages in which he theorized about scores of human problems. His positions changed from time to time, some of his views contradicted others, and his cumulative works have kept scholars busy ever since attempting to understand and codify the Freudian system. In his lifetime, and particularly since his death, schools of Freudian thought and practice have developed in which lesser leaders have emphasized, amplified or supplemented some aspect or aspects of Freudian thought. How, out of this mass of material, then, can one isolate a central core of Freudian thinking? Again, by turning to methodology.

The one process that makes a Freudian practitioner identifiable as such is what Freud called *analysis.* As the one essential tool for doing analysis, all true Freudians carry the archeologist's spade. They all are interested in the archeological expedition. Though it may be conducted in many ways, this expedition always has the same objective. The methodology consists of a trip back into the patient's past in which at each dig the attempt is made to unearth the persons, forces and influences that led to the present "neurotic" or "psychotic" behavior of the "patient."[4] Always persons out of the past are discovered (parents, teachers, grandparents, etc.) who, through their baneful influence, wrongly socialized the patient. For some reason(s) or other, under their tutelage, he has developed an overly strict *superego* (conscience; the oughts) which has come into collision with his *id* (primitive desires; the wants). The internal conflict that has arisen explains his disturbing attitudes and/or behavior.

Once the archeological expedition is over, psycho*analysis* progresses to psycho*therapy*. Psychotherapy consists of watering down the strictures of the superego. As the superego is weakened, the conflict with the id is resolved, guilt is removed, and the patient becomes well. The therapy is achieved by resocializing the patient through siding with his wants against his oughts, thus bringing the latter into line with the former.

This methodology clearly points to the basic presupposition of Freudian thought: *man is not responsible for what he does.* His behavior, his attitudes and his difficulties all stem from bad treatment by others. He cannot be blamed if he lives poorly, since he is the product of poor socialization. He is a victim, not a violator of law.

Since Freudianism excuses man from his responsibilities toward God and his neighbor, puts a premium upon the expression of his sinful nature and endeavors to destroy law and conscience, its basic orientation also is antithetical to Christianity. Christians, of course, acknowledge the importance of the early influence of parents and society upon a child. Yet, they hasten to point out that a man is responsible for allowing that influence to continue to guide and direct him throughout his life, and moreover, that a radical change called *regeneration*, which enables one to put off (or exchange) his former manner of life in favor of a new one, is entirely possible. Christian responsibility to God and Freudian blame-shifting manifestly are incompatible.

"What Really Counts Is a Dog Biscuit"

Of greatest significance to our brief survey is B. F. Skinner's behaviorism, the modern revival of the views of Bacon and Watson, which represents the most formidable contemporary challenge. Everywhere, in education, politics, etc., as well as in counseling and psychiatry, behaviorism (or as it is often styled, Behavior Modification) is rapidly gain-

---

[4]The medical model is adopted; Freudian "patients" are considered to be "mentally ill." For a fuller discussion of this question, cf. Jay Adams, *Competent to Counsel*, Presbyterian and Reformed Publishing Company, Nutley, N. J.: 1970.

ing ground. Purporting to be the scientific panacea for the world's ills, Skinnerianism is making headway in a day in which disillusioned men are willing to grasp at almost any straw (even if it is ultimately dehumanizing) in a hope against hope that Walden II somehow can be realized. Man's problem, says Skinner, is that he has been willing to trust science in all other areas (with amazing success), but until now has refused to allow science to control human behavior. That is why progress in meeting human needs and combating human problems has been impeded. Now, perhaps at last, man is ready to listen to science before it is too late. Indeed, there is no other place to turn. Skinner messianically calls for a hearing: *he has the answer*—the *only* answer.

Yes, Skinner says there is an answer. But, fairly enough, he warns, before rushing to buy you must count the cost. Man can have Utopia only if he is willing to surrender the age-long myths of human freedom and dignity. Along with all notions of values, of mind, of morals, and dozens of other non-existent concepts that correspond to nothing capable of being observed, quantified or predicted empirically, these religious or semi-religious myths must be scrapped. A whole new view of man and reality, complete with a new vocabulary that rejects "mentalist" views, must be adopted. Utopia is possible only on scientific terms. When man is willing to drop all pretenses and allow science to define and control him according to experimental data, many of which already have been acquired, then, and then only, will peace and good will come.

And what is it that has been and may be observed about man? Not freedom, not dignity, not mind . . . only *behavior* (defined as *all* that goes on inside of as well as outside of one's skin). Science has been gathering such data about man and has developed from these a series of hypotheses that indicate that man is controllable. What is needed is to discover the pertinent contingencies in a given environment; manipulate these properly, and any man can be made to perform in any way that his physical organism is capable of responding to these stimuli. When the proper rewards and aversive controls (Skinner refuses to call painful experiences that are feared, punishments) are scheduled according to known laws of behavior, predicted results will occur. Man is the product of his environment; therefore, control the environment *scientifically* and you can control man. Indeed, the Skinnerian thesis must involve the conclusion that if he can discover the proper type of dog biscuit and feed her appropriately according to schedule, any husband can train his wife to bark three times, roll over twice and go out and retrieve the evening newspaper in her teeth!

The methodology makes all plain: Utopia is scientifically possible because science has shown that *man is only another animal.* That is the fundamental Skinnerian presupposition. More complex than other animals, more difficult to control, man may be, but more than an animal?—no! Since he is not, he can be trained and controlled as every other animal may be: by the manipulation of its environment. Skinnerians are avowedly anti-religious and totally unwilling to admit the existence of values of any sort, as we have seen.[5] Values are not empirically observable. All that there is to man is behavior, and the sooner that we all learn this the better. By a rigid evolutionary determinism, Skinner describes human development which he thinks has reached the point where at last the control of man's behavior is in his own hands. By operant conditioning, determined man may determine his own predictable future!

Christians must protest strongly. Skinner not only sweeps aside all responsibility, but denies that which gives dignity to man: the image of God in which he was created. Skinnerians see no place, therefore, for the Christian essentials; sin and salvation are myths. Man is to be manipulated, not converted; reinforced, not persuaded. There is no place for the work of God, Christ or the Holy Spirit in the changing of human lives. Indeed, Jesus Christ Himself, according to a Skinnerian reading, becomes nothing more than a highly advanced animal, conditioned wholly by his environment. One cannot help wondering what contingencies led to sinless living and what brand of dog biscuit enticed Him to the cross.

Christians will not be taken in by the impressive results that may be advertised by the behaviorists. They will expect to see more results, however, than the followers of Rogers and Freud were able to realize. Experimentalism is certain to yield some. Man is partly animal, it is true. To the extent that man may be manipulated by behavioral controls, Skinnerians will see results. But Skinner, and those who now follow him so optimistically, will be disappointed. Man cannot be classified merely as another animal. Because of the uniqueness of his divine creation, the moral relationship that he sustains to God and to his neighbor, and as the result of his ultimate destiny, man neither can be satisfied with nor defined by the demeaning content of the Skinnerian presupposition. The dog biscuit will never replace pie-in-the-sky-bye-and-bye (which, incidentally, Christians begin to slice and enjoy right now).

---

[5]Skinner does seem to acknowledge the survival of the human herd to be the one retainable value, although he fails to identify this value as such.

Biblical Counseling

Christians must reject the reductionism that is evident in these three systems of counseling. In their place must be proposed the biblical presuppositions and methods, which, because they have been revealed by the God who made man, work. The Scriptures speak of counseling under the Greek term *nouthesia* ("nouthetic confrontation."). The New Testament. word is untranslatable since there is no English equivalent large enough to carry all of the freight that it bears. *Nouthesia* incorporates three ideas:

1. There is something wrong in the counselee (sin) that God says must be changed.
2. The counselor seeks to effect that change by biblically appropriate verbal confrontation.
3. The change is attempted for the benefit of the counselee.

Each of these elements, *change* through verbal *confrontation* with Scripture out of *concern*, is directly opposed to a fundamental presupposition of each of the three prominent schools that have been considered:

Non-Christian Presupposition	Christian Presupposition
1. Freud: Man is not responsible for what he does.	1. Christ: Man is a responsible sinner who needs to be changed.
2. Rogers: Man has all of the resources within himself.	2. Christ: To change, man must be confronted by My Word in the power of My Spirit.
3. Skinner: Man is but an animal whose only value is his contribution to the survival of the human herd.	3. Christ: Each man was created in God's image and must be confronted, persuaded and changed for his individual benefit.

It has not been possible to *argue* the issues between Christianity and the three major schools of counseling and psychiatry. My purpose, rather, has been to expose sharply the antitheses that exist. For too long biblical presuppositions and methodology either have been ignored or blurred by eclecticism.

Too many so-called Christian professionals thought that by an eclectic approach they could make Christianity acceptable to the world; by now they should have discovered that to beat the drum for the world's latest fad as a Johnny-come-lately has impressed no one, has obscured the biblical antithesis, and has made it impossible to mount a viable alternative. Hal Brooks, pastor of the North Richland Hills Baptist Church, Fort Worth, Texas, put it well when he said, "If you don't know where you are going, any road will do." Skinner won't use Rogerian Methodology; Rogers won't use Freudian. Why? All three know their objectives plainly and they are unwilling to travel by roads that lead elsewhere. Christians who espouse eclecticism, simply show that they do not know where they are going. Methodology is the road to somewhere. If Christians are concerned about where they are going in counseling, if they want to reach God's destinations, they will travel none but God's ways.

That there can be no moral neutrality about methodology by now should be apparent. The issues of the day in which we live are too great, too crucial, too basic to be obscured. Every man must make his choice. Those choices depend upon presuppositions that, in the end, are accepted by faith. When he chooses, however, he should do so with understanding and not in ignorance. The stakes are too high. The choice that we have discussed is between a mirror, a spade, a dog biscuit and . . . a cross.

All of this leads to a second question: How did the antithesis become obscured?

When they are consistent, Christians view life from a perspective outside of themselves. They seek to interpret the world and to live according to God's revealed Word. This Word, they believe, God has recorded as the Scriptures of the Old and New Testaments, which He has declared to be the inerrant and authoritative Standard for faith and life (belief and practice). During the past generation, incursions of psychiatry and clinical psychology into areas that require one to determine ethical norms as the basis for the alteration of attitudes and behavior, therefore, should have been met by a significant response from the church. The fact that there has been until recently little or no such response needs explanation.

Only a constellation of factors, at once converging and combining, could have so dulled the church that she could have allowed the ethical structure upon which she stands to be undermined by views and practices so antithetical as those to which I have alluded. Such was the case. Among those forces which impinged upon the church were the following:

1. The struggle with Darwinism and with higher criticism commanded major attention. This is understandable since the dangers in the views of these opponents were more apparent and their attacks upon the church were more direct. The battles on these fronts did not go well and occupied much time and energy, thus diverting attention from the more subtle inroads of the mental health movement.

2. The weakening of the church due to liberal advances, natural apathy and a general willingness to "let George do it," combined to pave the way for a psychiatric takeover. Personal counseling is exacting, time-consuming work. Much effort is not immediately productive, and the problems that one encounters on the exterior, at least, are frequently baffling. It was easy for an exhausted church to step aside and make room for others who so willingly offered a helping hand.

3. This was particularly true since the product which was sold was falsely labelled. Thomas Szasz, in the first two chapters of his book, *The Myth of Mental Illness*,[6] has traced the history of what in recent years has come to be called the *Medical Model*. A host of persons, who previously would have been considered to be in trouble because they had failed to handle life's problems properly, under Freud and Charcot instead were declared to be "mentally ill." This medical orientation provided an acceptable, if not attractive, packaging for many who were only too willing to defer and refer. Under the false belief (or rationalization) that such persons with non-organic illnesses (a contradiction in terms) were truly sick, Christian pastors could salve their consciences with the thin balm that "I may do more harm than good if I try to help them."

4. With notable exceptions, there has been a general failure of the church since apostolic times to enter into the study and pursuit of personal counseling with the enthusiasm and vigor that must characterize any serious endeavor. No large body of theoretical thought or case study data had been accumulated. The meager amount of discussion concerning the work of counseling that has been preserved seems to view counseling as little more than a subhead of Church Discipline. As a result, personal counseling was carried on largely in unsystematic ways.

It is no surprise, then, that personal counseling by ministers so readily was supplanted by psychiatrists. Yet in recent years the failures of psychiatry have occasioned persons both within and without the discipline to take a second look at the problem. O. Hobart Mowrer, William Glasser, E. Fuller Torrey and others have been exposing the fundamentally non-

---

[6]Thomas Szasz, *The Myth of Mental Illness*, Dell, N. Y.: 1960.

medical nature of the psychiatric enterprise for more than a decade and have awakened even many sleeping members of the church to the reasons for the growing disenchantment and disillusionment with psychiatry. Increasingly, the basically ethical nature of psychiatric activities has become apparent and has resulted in a growing concern over the attendant dangers involved in an uncritical acceptance of these activities. Belatedly, a new generation of conservative Protestant ministers, unimpressed by psychiatric pretensions, whose ministries have been reaping significant results in a day of waning liberalism, have begun to move back into the territory usurped by psychiatrists and clinical psychologists. While they work closely with physicians out of a concern to distinguish behavior that is organically determined from that which is not, they are firmly convinced that the establishment and alteration of values are a part of the task assigned to them by God and refuse to refer counselees for "more professional help" to psychiatrists, marriage counselors and clinical psychologists. They maintain, instead, that the proper background for counseling must include biblical and theological training. Indeed, they have determined that it is *they* who are (or must become) the "professionals."[7]

[7]Recently I had occasion to describe this counselor to Christian physicians as follows:

Let me partially describe this new pastoral counselor. First and foremost he will have an unshakeable confidence in the power of the Spirit working through His Word to solve the nonorganic problems of living caused by the eventual failure of sinful living patterns into which men drift. Secondly, he will use the Scriptures in counseling in a practical fashion that at the same time exalts Christ and meets human needs. He will not give out passages like prescriptions or dispense platitudes like pills. Rather, he will use (and teach his counselees to use) the Bible in a plain and practical manner that enables them to see *how* God has provided solutions to their problems. Thirdly, he will have a humble confidence, acknowledging that any benefit accruing from his counseling is ultimately attributable to the work of God and not to himself. Yet, at the same time he will strive continually to improve his knowledge and technique, recognizing that God ordinarily works through human agency. When he does not understand a problem, he will honestly admit it, but he also will search the Scriptures to discover the answers that previously eluded him. He will tackle nearly any problem that previously might have been referred to a psychiatrist, probably with a significantly higher rate of success and certainly in much shorter periods of time. He will work enthusiastically with Christian physicians and will frequently send counselees for medical checkups.

Brethren, something has been happening, and you should be aware of the fact since you may be able to enlarge the effectiveness of your own ministry as a physician by achieving a significant alliance with a minister (or ministers) to whom you confidently can refer patients for counseling.

Do not expect this new pastoral counselor to have all of the answers, any more than you would claim answers to every organic problem, but look for a man who can do far more to help complement you in your medical ministry than many pastors whom you previously have known. I encourage you to explore this possibility to the full.

The *Christian Medical Society Journal*, Fall, 1971, pp. 10, 11.

Nothing could have set the problem into perspective more vividly than the publication of *Beyond Freedom and Dignity* by B. F. Skinner. This manifesto, in which Skinner squared off against the very concept of values, has caused great concern among Christians, as they have come to recognize that Skinner's objective is nothing less than total scientific control of human behavior. His more recent volume, *About Behaviorism*, has only confirmed the reasons for such concern. And this quest on which the behaviorists have embarked is being carried on by men like Skinner who want to scrap as myths the very notions of the freedom and dignity of man. According to Skinner, these myths, along with all other such value-myths, must be abandoned since they stand in the way of the advance of the human herd toward utopia (Walden II). A truly scientific view of man focuses upon the one tangible factor: behavior. There is no other. From the empirical observation of behavior, Skinner thinks that the future of the human animal can be predicted and thus controlled by the manipulation of the environment of which his behavior ultimately is the product.

As the result of Skinner's challenge, the uneasy rapprochement of Christianity and psychiatry has now been strained to the breaking point. Skinner has helped to bring the true issues and the inevitable antitheses into clearer focus. This development must be welcomed, since the alliance between Christians and psychiatrists, as we have seen, had been formed for unsound reasons. Thus, the growing number of Christians who have gone back to their Bibles to study afresh what God has said about counseling have discovered a wealth of neglected and untapped resources that they now are beginning to treat systematically and practically. Perhaps today more Protestant ministers are doing counseling, or preparing to do serious counseling, than at any time since the Reformation. Though not yet subject to statistical studies, there seems to be mounting evidence that these ministers are having a significantly higher rate of success than the psychiatrists. The results of work done in our own pastoral counseling center support this observation.

The future of the relationship between the mental health movement and conservative biblical Christianity (the only form of Christianity that it seems will survive modern pressures) can hardly be predicted. But it would seem that in the period immediately ahead the antithesis between clinical psychologies and psychiatries that are based upon non-Christian presuppositions and biblical Protestant Christianity will come into sharper focus, thus separating the two into distinct camps in which the issues that divide them and the discussions that shall ensue will center about the ethical question.

Rather than a peripheral matter, then, this ethical question, as Skinner correctly observes, is fundamental. Those psychiatrists and psychologists who have sought to avoid the issue are likely to find it increasingly more difficult to do so as they discover that the very existence of their occupation is being challenged precisely at this point.

CHAPTER I
PASTORAL COUNSELING

Pastoral counseling is a special, but not separate, area of pastoral activity; indeed, biblically it is close to the heart of shepherding. It involves the extension of help to wandering, torn, defeated, dispirited sheep who need the "restoring"[1] mentioned in Psalm 23:3 ("He restores my soul": "my soul" is a poetic phrase frequently used in the Psalms that means simply "me": "He restores me"). The good shepherd "strengthens" and "heals" (Ezekiel 34:4, 16);[2] conversely, the poor shepherd fails notably in the performance of these very tasks (cf. Zechariah 11:16: "who will not care for the perishing, seek the scattered, heal the broken, or sustain the one standing,"[3] NASV). In similar terms, probably reminiscent of Zechariah, Paul wrote of the elders (shepherdly overseers) as "leaders in the Lord and your advisers" (I Thessalonians 5:12, Berkeley). (The word advisers as readily might be translated "counselors.") Their "work" is described in words echoing Zechariah in verse 14.

Too frequently in the recent past God's shepherds have abandoned this ministry of preventive and remedial counseling. As a result, the sheep have

---

[1]This restoration is shepherdly work and, therefore, uses shepherdly means—"the law of the Lord is perfect, restoring the soul" (Psalm 19:7). "Restoration," in these passages, means "refreshment." It constitutes the work of putting new life into one by convicting and changing, encouraging and strengthening after trial, defeat, failure and/or discouragement. One is restored by the shepherd's use of the Word of God. Pastoral counseling, therefore, must be scriptural.

[2]This passage affords no grounds for use of the medical model in counseling; the "healing" here is figurative; surely it can be pressed to mean no more than healing (solving) those problems of God's flock, the people of His pasture, that are occasioned by failure to meet life's problems biblically. The restoration and healing in view is that which can be brought about by the Word (see the previous footnote).

[3]Sustaining the "standing" one probably refers to preventive measures taken to avoid difficulty. Such activities as premarital pastoral counseling (q.v.) would fall under the rubric of sustaining the standing ones.

suffered greatly and presently are in dire need.[4] In His providence, however, He is raising up other shepherds—men whose hearts have been touched by the plight of God's scattered, torn flocks—who truly desire to meet these needs. Yet, many of them lack knowledge and skill. Determined to rely no longer upon the "equipment of a foolish useless shepherd,"[5] they are demanding biblical training in counseling in seminaries, buying those books that explain the use of the Word of God in counseling, and rejecting the views of those who have sought to restore souls according to unscriptural principles, by means of the world's gear. We may thank God for this significant change and, as a result, look forward to new and better days for the Church of Jesus Christ.

One segment of the new movement has been centered in the pastoral counseling done at the Christian Counseling and Educational Center of Hatboro, Pennsylvania, by John Bettler, George Scipione, Howard Eyrich, Tom Tyson and myself, and that is taught at Westminster Theological Seminary, Chestnut Hill, Pennsylvania. Because I have been writing extensively elsewhere about counseling in general and about certain aspects of counseling in particular (see *Competent to Counsel, The Big Umbrella, The Christian Counselor's Manual*), and because these books are all available, I do not intend to duplicate here what I have written there. Instead, I shall consider some aspects of counseling that pertain especially to the work of the *pastor*, focusing particularly upon the work of premarital counseling. Picking this book up by itself, with no previous knowledge of the aforementioned volumes, will make this decision seem arbitrary and the materials presented both spotty and out of balance. Those who are acquainted already with the other books, however, I think will welcome this approach.[6]

---

[4]This is one reason for the phenomenal growth of psychiatric encounter group and cultic healing activities, all of which have had a generally detrimental effect upon the church. The faulty understanding of "visitation" (examined in Vol. I, q.v.) largely has contributed to this lack. Particularly is this true where house-calling has been *equated* with pastoral care. Commenting on this error, Phillips Brooks once wrote" . . . by an understanding with my people I expect to . . . get rid of what I hold to be very unnecessary work, the spending the best part of the day in running about making calls." In Alexander V. G. Allen, *Phillips Brooks 1835-1893* (E. P. Dutton & Co., N. Y.: 1907), p. 163.

[5]Zechariah 11:15. What these instruments were we are not told. But doubtless their use would destroy and injure rather than heal. The point is that foolish shepherds use means other than those ordained by God. This is, at the very least, a salient warning against eclecticism.

[6]Also, other books are in various stages of preparation, including such topics as Crisis Counseling and The Use of the Scriptures in Counseling. An all too brief section of this book concerning the place of the church in counseling' may be developed later on into a fuller volume.

Counseling and the Pastor

The nouthetic[7] counseling approach employed by the biblical writers requires men who have the qualities that are requisite for all ministers of the gospel. They need no more, but also no less.[8] Counseling is a work that every minister may, indeed *must*, perform as a faithful shepherd of Jesus Christ. He must plan to do counseling, must learn how to do counseling and must make himself available for counseling. Referral, except to another faithful shepherd, is out of the question. Better than referral is personal growth on the part of the pastor through discovering and ministering God's answers to the problems encountered in pastoral counseling. The Scriptures contain all of the principles that are necessary for meeting the needs of sheep. The Bible is the textbook for teaching them how to love God and their neighbors (which is what counseling is all about).[9]

But how does a pastor handle the situation in which he does not know what to do next? It is true that many ministers have not been taught to counsel biblically. Moreover, the art of counseling improves not only as information is acquired but as skills are developed; these are not attained all at once and, in particular, not gained apart from doing. So then, what does he do when he does not know what to do? The answer to that is simple (but not necessarily *easy*). First, he says so[10] ("Frankly, I am stymied about some aspects of the problem and I want to spend this next week praying and thinking about the question in the light of the Scriptures; I hope you will pray too"). Secondly, during the week between counseling sessions he does just that. He pours over the Scriptures to discover God's answers. He dare not fail to do so when he has promised. By the next session, hopefully, in most instances he will have mended his net (and he himself will have grown). Of course, the pastor will use whatever additional help he can get from books, discussion with other pastors, etc. Only as a last resort, when all else has failed, will he refer the counselee to another pastor.

---

[7]From the Greek noun *nouthesia* and the verb *noutheteo* used in the New Testament to denote a verbal counseling confrontation in which change in beliefs, attitudes and behavior is brought about by practical use of the Scriptures in order to honor God and bless the one who is confronted. Put succinctly, it is biblical *change* brought about by *confrontation* out of *concern*. See *Competent to Counsel*, pp. 41-64, for further discussion of *nouthesia*.

[8]Cf. *The Christian Counselor's Manual*, pp. 21-30. For a summary from a somewhat different perspective, cf. Rodney R. Kamrath, *A Critical Evaluation of Jay Adams' Theory of Nouthetic Counseling* (Unpublished Master's Thesis at Trinity Evangelical Divinity School: Deerfield, 1974), pp. 80-85.

[9]II Timothy 3:16,17; II Peter 1:3. Cf. *The Christian Counselor's Manual*, pp. 92-97.

[10]People do not lose confidence in a counselor who, when he knows something, speaks with assurance and who, when he does not, says so. They know that they can trust him. Moreover, when he does speak with assurance, they are more likely to respond. Bluffing not only

However, if he was unable to solve the problem biblically himself, could he not have gotten the help he needed from that same pastor during the week so that he himself might carry on personally? Probably. So, in most instances referral is unnecessary. But, assuming that on rare occasions it must be done, the pastor should arrange as part of the referral to be present himself during the counseling sessions that follow. This is (1) for the protection of the counselee from any wrong or harmful doctrine and advice, (2) to maintain continued care over him during this period, (3) to be fully informed so as to be able to make a smooth transition back to his own counseling sessions (referrals should be temporary, only in order to get the counseling process over the hump), and (4) hopefully to learn how to solve some problems that heretofore he did not know how to handle.[11] All in all, whenever any other counselor enters the picture, he should agree to do so only in a consultative or specialist capacity. A pastor never should relinquish his own personal shepherdly care and concern for his member. Always he must remain the counselor-in-charge of the case at hand (cf. John 10:4,5).

Thus, it is the task of every pastor to become competent to counsel, even if he has not received adequate training and even if he is not now adequate for the task. Training in biblical counseling not only is becoming increasingly available, but it is true also that men who have been trained in it now are located in various parts of the U.S.A. and some in other lands. Many of these men, who themselves are busily engaged in doing nouthetic counseling, would be capable of helping those who have not received similar training.[12] Moreover, in addition to direct instruction, books, pamphlets for use in counseling, tapes,[13] a newsletter (Confrontation), and counseling materials (The Christian Counselor's Starter Packet) are all available for those who would like to improve their counseling abilities. Pastoral seminars are held in various parts of the country upon arrangement. There are now enough ways and means available to the average

is a form of lying, but also breaks down confidence; counselees are very good at detecting such bluffing.

[11]It has been our policy at C.C.E.F. to allow their pastors to accompany counselees into counseling sessions. Sometimes pastors are requested to come in order to make a transition back to their own studies again.

[12]A list of men trained at C.C.E.F. is available to pastors upon request (write to John Bettler, director, C.C.E.F. 151 W. County Line Road, Hatboro, Pennsylvania 19040.) Some of these men, upon satisfactory arrangements, might allow other pastors in their areas to sit in on counseling sessions for training.

[13]For information on a tape-book coordinated instructional program designed by the Christian men of the Pentagon to train Chaplains and Christian servicemen, write: Mr. Robert DenDulk, Westminster Theological Seminary, Chestnut Hill, Pennsylvania, 19118. The 14 tapes include lectures I have given at Fort Belvoir during the summer of 1974, two question-and-answer periods, three role-playing sessions and homework assignments.

pastor to enable him to develop and use his counseling skills to meet most (if not all) of the weekly counseling challenges in his congregation.[14]

While at one time there might have been some excuse for referral or simple frustration, the last vestiges of that excuse are now quickly swirling down the drain. Any pastor to whom God has given the gifts and has called to do pastoral work can develop those gifts and prepare himself by using the ways and means that have become available over the last few years, so that if he takes advantage of these resources and applies himself to the work, within a year or so of continued active counseling he should be doing a *very* effective job (more effective than local psychiatrists and psychologists).

Counseling in a Series of Sessions

The average pastor to whom I speak tells me that he does not counsel in a systematic and organized way. This is a mistake; sloppiness in counseling brings sloppy results. A pastor must help the counselee to recognize by his efficient, business-like, take-charge (though not officious) approach and by his demand for a commitment to counseling (as well as his own willingness to make it), that the counseling relationship into which they are entering is not a casual take-it-or-leave-it matter.[15] Instead, by the love and concern that he shows by responding to a request or by initiating counseling, and by the care with which he arranges and begins the counseling, the pastor makes clear to the counselee *from the start* that he expects things to happen. He communicates the fact that he expects commitment and effort on the part of all concerned. By this manner, and by his own full (and often sacrificial) commitment as well as by his words, he says, "This is God's work; it must be done well."

If your counseling leaves something to be desired, at the outset perhaps few factors need to be stressed as strongly as the need for mutual commitment to a well-structured series of counseling sessions, whatever the length of the series may be. I have discussed elsewhere the advantages of a closed- rather than an open-ended series.[16] I have also suggested that the series or-

---

[14]A book, *The Christian Counselor's Casebook*, has been prepared as a workbook to help seminary students, pastors and other counselors to learn the principles and procedures of biblical counseling. The *Casebook* may be used individually, but perhaps is used most fruitfully by groups of ministers.

[15]One reason the materials in the *Starter Packet* (available in any quantity from the publisher of this volume) were made accessible to pastors was to strengthen their ability to do so. Printed materials, including handouts and a structured method by which to proceed, provide additional help. Everything possible must be done to establish among Christians the truth of the fact that by God's ordination the *pastor* is the professional counselor.

[16]*The Christian Counselor's Manual*, pp. 232-241.

dinarily should be limited to a maximum of twelve weekly sessions (the average will be somewhere around eight to ten sessions for very serious problems, although, at first while he is still in the early stages of learning, the counselor may find that more often than not difficult cases will take from ten to twelve weeks). Within four to six months of regular counseling, however, he will discover the average number of sessions growing fewer. Thus, the picture of counseling begins to take on *form*: The commitment that counselor and counselee make is to something concrete.[17]

The counselor may look at counseling as a step in the process of the sanctification of a believer. The change contemplated, therefore, is twofold: dehabituation (putting off) and rehabituation (putting on[18]). It may be viewed (ideally) as follows:

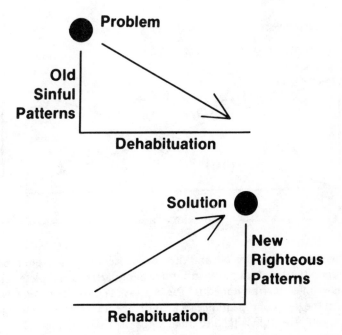

---

[17]Frequently in the first session it is wise to spell out just what sort of things you will be doing in counseling and to indicate the probable length of time that you have in mind. This will help you and the counselee to set bench marks by which to make commitments and to gauge progress.

[18]Cf. *The Christian Counselor's Manual*, pp. 171-216.

But notice, these do not come together to form a strictly linear sequential pattern that could be represented this way:

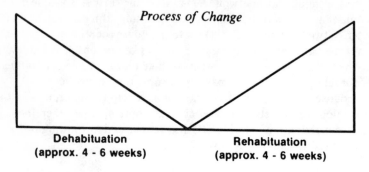

Process of Change

Dehabituation   **Rehabituation**
(approx. 4 - 6 weeks) **(approx. 4 - 6 weeks)**

Rather, the processes usually are (roughly) coeval:

Process of Change

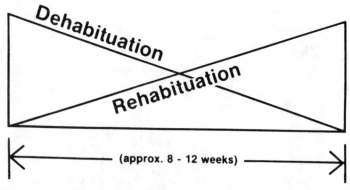

(approx. 8 - 12 weeks)

Whenever repentance occurs, the new process begins. Note especially that rehabituation does not wait *until* dehabituation is complete. The two processes must be simultaneous. The process of counseling may be said to begin at the point of repentance (★). Until repentance occurs, change does not begin. The fuller picture then appears to look more like this[19]:

---

[19]The first process will be unnecessary whenever the counselee(s) begins counseling repentant or under conviction. However, it is never satisfactory to *assume* repentance. The counselor at the outset should seek to determine whether, in fact, the counselee is repentant. Sometimes preliminary homework assignments will provide the additional data necessary to give some indication. Since man looks on the outward appearance and only God can look on the heart, the counselor's determination always will be subject to revision. In love (1 Corinthians 13:7), he always gives the counselee the benefit of the doubt (cf. also Luke 17:4; note: "saying." The one who *says* he is repentant must be believed on the basis of his *word*).

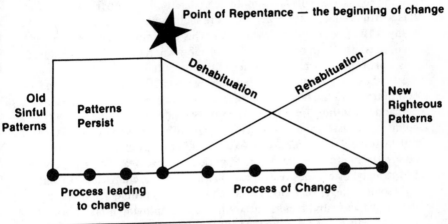

In other words, the process of change through putting on and putting off may not begin until the second or third session, or whenever the counselee, before God and man, acknowledges his sin and seeks God's help to right past wrongs and replace sinful patterns by righteous ones.

The whole process rightly may be called counseling, since the confronting work that is done in the first week (or weeks) to bring knowledge and conviction of sin by the ministry of the Word (cf. II Timothy 3:16—"Scripture is useful for teaching, for *conviction*..."[20]) clearly may fall under this general head.

---

[20]Cf. *The Christian Counselor's Manual*, pp. 93ff. The word "Conviction" is a legal term meaning to prosecute successfully so as to bring about recognition of guilt. In connection with this matter it may be interesting to note that there is a hyper-dispensational teaching abroad in counseling circles today that under the guise of teaching pure grace, instead teaches what can only be seen to be an antinomianism. According to this view, Christians who sin should not feel guilty over that sin nor should they seek forgiveness from God for it. Not only is Matthew 6:12, 14-15 misunderstood (the passage does not teach *judicial* forgiveness but *parental* forgiveness; note the emphasis on God's children seeking forgiveness from their "Father"), but it is also rejected as a standard for Christians. Confession, we are instructed by those who propound this unsound theology, is not for the purpose of receiving forgiveness. The idea runs counter to I John 1:9. There too, it is the *Father* who forgives; cf. vv. 2, 3. James 5:15 also shows how Christian brethren ought to be encouraged to confess sins in order to receive forgiveness. Counselors should be on the alert for the possible ill-effects of such teachings. They are confusing both to sinning counselees and to parents who are to pattern their relationship to their children after God's relationship to His children.

A process like this does involve the commitment of both the counselor and the counselee. This fact should be understood by both from the outset. It is worth taking the time *then* to secure such commitment, as this will save many wasted hours of agony later on. This commitment, to be complete, then, must grow out of repentance and submission to God's Word. Just as it is worth spending as much as a full session initially giving hope,[21] so it is worthwhile to devote an adequate period of time to securing full commitment to the biblical change that is necessary. Indeed, hope and the demand for nothing less than change are two sides of the same coin. When a counselor insists upon setting as the goal nothing less than change, spells out in some detail a biblically based plan[22] for realizing it, and calls for commitment to the hard process that it involves, he wittingly (or unwittingly) offers the greatest reason for hope. The counselee sees that the counselor believes that God has a solution to his problem and that he has developed ways and means based upon and employing biblical principles and procedures for reaching the solution.[23] In contrast to his own failures, the non-specific approaches of other counselors whom he may have consulted previously (particularly those of the talk-only types[24]), and the present despair in which he may find himself, the structured counseling session itself should offer great hope. A counselee cannot be called to commitment to anything less. The counselor, then, must be a man with a plan who, in humble confidence, sets goals and knows how to reach them, relying upon well-thought-through biblical ways and means.

EXERCISE

For the Student

1. Find someone whom you can counsel. (You might "advertise" your availability at a youth group, etc.)

2. Find a pastor who will provide backup help if you should need to turn to him and who would accept the counselee upon referral (with you present) should that eventuality become necessary.

3. Set up counseling, and make and get a commitment and begin.

4. Report the results to the class (flatten out all reports so that the counselee and his situation are utterly unidentifiable).

5. As an alternative to (2) and (4), use the class and the professor as backup and bring weekly reports for discussion and suggestion.

---

[21]*Ibid.*, pp. 39ff.
[22]Cf. "The Use of the Scriptures in Counseling," Part III, *Bibliotheca Sacra*, July, 1974.
[23]Cf. *The Big Umbrella*, pp. 157-174, for a description of the counseling process.
[24]Cf. *The Christian Counselor's Manual*, pp. 243ff.

For the Pastor

1. Consider the last five series of counseling sessions that you have conducted. Ask:

    a. Were they successful?

       (1) If so, what made them successful (success to be governed by biblical standards)?

(2) If not, what made them unsuccessful?

b. What could I have done to have structured the basic format of those sessions differently that might have helped?

2. What do I need to do to prepare for the next series of sessions to be sure that I do the maximal job God requires of me?

CHAPTER II
MUTUAL MINISTRY IN COUNSELING

Elsewhere I have argued for pastoral counseling over against counseling done in a counseling center.[1] I shall not repeat that argument. However, let me remind you of its basic thrust. The argument runs this way: God ordained the minister to be the counselor of His flock and provided him with full resources for carrying out this function (II Timothy 3:16,17—"man from God" is a phrase used to designate the pastor-teacher). Rather than consider himself inadequate for this task, necessitating dependency upon extra-pastoral resources, the Scriptures indicate that the Holy Spirit has provided all that he needs to equip him for "every good work." The Bible is the Textbook for counseling since it contains all of the principles necessary for learning to love God and one's neighbor. Extra-biblical data, therefore, are either unnecessary, irrelevant or contrary to those data provided by the Scriptures.[2]

I have consistently asserted that all of the principles and all of the information necessary for adequate pastoral counseling are found in the Scriptures (and I wish to reaffirm that viewpoint with vigor[3]). However, it is necessary in this volume to make an important distinction that I have reserved for this place and that I have not made elsewhere. Although the Scriptures provide all of the data necessary, these very scriptural data point to resources that God has provided in order to bring about His purposes for His children that are delineated in the Bible. Those resources (the Bible

---

[1] *The Christian Counselor's Manual,* pp. 11ff.
[2] Of course, illustrative, applicatory and extensional information that follows biblical principles may be used. E.g., the Bible enjoins the believer not to harm his body, the temple of the Holy Spirit (I Corinthians 6:19,20). Not all possible ways of harming the body are delineated in the Scriptures. Therefore, studies concerning the effects of drug abuse, significant sleep loss, etc., upon the body may be useful so long as their results are not accorded biblical authority.
[3] According to II Peter 1:3,4 God has "granted us *everything* pertaining to life and godliness." These things were "granted" (he continues) in "precious and magnificent promises" of the Scriptures.

teaches) largely are deposited in gifted men, strengthened by the Spirit, who believe and minister the Scriptures. Primarily these are ministering shepherd-teachers ordained for the purpose of devoting their lives to the public and private ministry of the Word. I say primarily because, as I have shown elsewhere, the Bible teaches that all believers, although they are not called to counseling as a life calling, by virtue of their general office as believers, possess gifts, knowledge and authority adequate to counsel.[4]

Here I wish to observe that this occasional counseling function not only may be exercised individually in crises or in situations encountered by the individual believer alone (such as those described in Galatians 6:1ff.), but also in consort with the pastor as part of the total "one another" (or mutual ministry[5]) that all are called to exercise as members of the same body. It is this joint, or team, effort headed and coordinated by the pastor as an adjunct to his own counseling ministry that I now shall pursue.

Why must a pastor conceive of his counseling as purely a one-man task? In his work, Paul used a number of traveling companions as assistants, as well as the resources that the Spirit provided in the members of local congregations, to help him to carry out his work.[6] Because we speak so frequently of what God accomplished through *Paul* doing this or that, we tend to forget that it was not Paul alone, but Paul at the head of a traveling team, and Paul as the activator of local help, who accomplished the remarkable feats attributed to him. From the evidence in his letters (constantly he gratefully mentions those who labored with him; "fellow workers" is a favorite term), one can guess that Paul would have been the first to acknowledge that it would have been impossible to carry out these tasks alone. To give credit to the many others who worked with him is to take nothing from the honor due to Paul. Indeed, it is to his credit that he recognized his own limitations and turned to the resources that God provided in others.

Modern pastors, most of whom readily would acknowledge that they are considerably less endowed with personal resources than the Apostle Paul, ought not to hesitate, therefore, like him to draw upon all of the resources that God has provided among the members of the flocks over which He has made them bishops (shepherdly overseers).

---

[4]Cf. *Competent to Counsel*, pp. 41ff.; *The Big Umbrella*, Chapter VI.

[5]The words "one another" occur frequently in reference to the mutual ministry of the saints. A thorough analysis of each occurrence, together with a consideration of the various duties enjoined, makes a profitable study.

[6]Cf. Romans 16:1-16, 21-23; I Corinthians 16:10,12,15-18,19; Philippians 2:19-30,4:3; Colossians 4:7-17; II Timothy 4:9-13,19-21.

Mutual Ministry in Practice

Having recognized something of the necessity for bodily coordination in ministry, let us consider (suggestively only) a few ways that this broader ministry can be developed. Theory is essential to practice, but useless without it.

Elders

Begin with your Elders. It should go without saying that Elders can be trained to help carry the load of counseling.[7] Most directly, they can enter into the work with the minister since, jointly with him, they share in the oversight of a congregation, an oversight that includes counseling. Paul's words in I Thessalonians 5:12,13 are of special importance in this regard. Here Paul speaks of the leadership of a congregation in pluralistic terms. The oversight is a joint one. Elders, of both the ruling and the teaching/ruling varieties, were appointed in every congregation it seems. And here it is apparent that they all ("*those . . . who admonished you*") counseled. The word variously translated "admonish" or "instruct" is *noutheteo* ("to confront nouthetically").[8] This word is one of the principal terms used by Paul to denote pastoral counseling.[9]

It is part of the "work" (v. 13) of every elder to counsel. A pastor who becomes properly involved in *biblical* counseling will find that his efforts will result in time saving. Such counseling simply does not take the months (or years) that must be devoted to, say, Rogerian or Freudian counseling. Thus he will be able to counsel more persons in less time. But he will find that the more persons receive help, the more others request it. Sooner or later, the demands will exceed his ability to meet them. At that point he should be ready to turn to his prime source of relief: trained elders.

Since *nouthesia* is part of the overseeing function of an elder, the pastor should not wait until the demand reaches a point where he must call for help to train his elders. From the beginning, elders should be trained to do counseling. This training best can be given by bringing them into counseling sessions as team counselors (at first as participant observers, then as counselors-in-charge, and finally as counselors on their own, able to train others who team counsel with them[10]). Elders who are participating in the life and welfare of the members of the congregation in this manner will be happier, more vital persons, in touch with the realities of the work of

---

[7]In their origin as a functioning body, elders were committed to the task of lightening the burden for Moses by *sharing in his ministry*. Cf. Numbers 11:14-17; Exodus 18:13-27.

[8]Cf. *Competent to Counsel*, pp. 44ff. for a full explanation of the term.

[9]Others (e.g., John) use *parakaleo* in a similar way.

[10]For more information about team counseling, cf. *Competent to Counsel*, pp. 203ff.

Christ's church and less likely to cause some of the difficulties that pastors often complain about. Many of the dissatisfactions that elders express toward pastors stem from their diminished position as mere spectators and monitors of the pastor's work. Moreover, less criticism arises from those who share like problems. They begin to understand the difficulties with which he grapples. A role that allows for decision-making and oversight merely from a distance, but that does not allow for direct participation in the lives of members of the congregation is at the root of most of the dissatisfaction. Not only would better men be screened for the position were it known that they must learn to function in this manner (lesser men would tend to withdraw their names from consideration), but the dormant ministries of many of the better men who are now in the position would flower. Elders must come to see that their work too is *pastoral*. I know of no better way to promote this biblical viewpoint than to get them to counsel with needy sheep.

"But how can I get my elders to do this work?" you may ask. There is no *one* answer to this question. Some will respond gladly and eagerly to the simple suggestion. Others will come forward to meet your need for help. Still others will demur altogether. All will need training. You must *offer* and *provide* the training necessary. You must take the time to persuade, educate and train. You may need to begin with *one* elder who is willing and show that it can be done in order to persuade others. You cannot expect all of your elders to jump at the suggestion. The biblical concept is new to the modern church, and the wrong traditions are deeply grooved. In most instances, patience in effecting change will be required.

"Where can I begin?" Two excellent situations come to mind. These are not the only places to begin or necessarily the best in every case, but because they grow out of material discussed in other sections of this volume, I offer them as part of a package that (hopefully) will take shape as we explore the entire work of shepherding. They are: (1) in cases of counseling single women; (2) in premarital counseling.

I shall not now rehearse the reasons why it is desirable to have an elder present when counseling single women.[11] Here I simply wish to add that most elders can understand the argument for protection and will be willing to "sit in" on such cases in order to help the pastor in this way. They may (or may incidentally not) know that they are receiving training. Perhaps, in this way, at first they can begin to share in counseling as the process is modeled by the pastor and as he calls upon the elder from time to time for

---

[11]Cf. *infra*, Chapter VIII.

comment upon points on which he is sure that he can contribute something. This participation will be minimal at first, but as he sees that he is able to do so, the pastor may involve the elder more and more, until one day—perhaps when it is impossible for the pastor to schedule a session (he may be off to Presbytery)—the pastor may ask the elder to take the session himself (possibly by now with another elder "sitting in"). Thus, either as an *announced or unannounced* program for training elders, the pastor may set out to and may, in fact, achieve his purposes.

The second area, premarital counseling, affords an opportunity too. If the elders buy the plan of sending one of their number to conduct family devotions[12] in the home of the newlyweds, later on the pastor may observe that participation in the prior counseling by that elder could make the entire program more meaningful. Indeed, in time, some of the postmarital visits mentioned *infra* could be allotted to the elders. Perhaps some stages of the premarital counseling program also could be placed in the hands of various elders, who especially concentrate on matters involving finances, church attendance, or whatever they consider areas of particular expertise. Indeed, among a body of elders inclined to participate eagerly, various topics could be apportioned to each man for special study and work so that each soon may become especially competent in counseling about these. Such a joint effort at premarital counseling will impress every young couple with the importance of this work and with the concern of the church for them. Moreover, the pastor is less likely to get static from his elders over negative decisions regarding proposed marriages when they have been participants in the process and the decision-making that led to those decisions.

The objection that "my elders would do more harm than good" only serves to point out the need for elder participation in counseling. Either the wrong men have been chosen ("after all, what does an elder do? he's only a figure head"), or the right men have been allowed to stagnate while their gifts atrophy and their interests and concerns deteriorate.

I do not think that all of the changes will come overnight; that is why I have urged patience. Yet change will never come unless you begin. Begin. Begin today. Begin planning. Begin with the first step of a program (if necessary) that starts with the persons and the situations that are most likely to produce early success and gradually build upon these. In this way you will move more rapidly into more difficult achievements, with considerably less friction. Yet, while advising caution I wish also to

---

[12]Cf. *infra*, Chapter VII.

summon courage. Too little shepherdly courage has been exhibited too often. After all, a shepherd is required to lay down his life for the sheep if necessary. You must teach, challenge and even rebuke when necessary; but *never* do so unless (along with it) you are willing to provide a discipleship-type training program in which those who agree with what you say can find the help that they need to develop and to exercise their gifts of oversight.[13]

One of the most exciting groups that a minister can teach is his elders. Both he and they, and those to whom they minister, will come alive under such a program. The basic need of most congregations is a revival of its leadership. In few ways can this revival be achieved more effectively than by bringing elders into vital ministry to their sheep. In the long run, pastors will do far more for their people when they learn the importance of devoting a large share of their time (at least initially) to the discipleship training of their elders (who in turn will disciple others). Jesus spoke to the multitudes and to the individual, *and* to his disciples. His teaching was not confined to public ministry. Some of the most important information in the Gospels was given to the disciples alone. For three-and-one-half years He discipled them so that they in turn would know how to "*make disciples from all nations*" (Matthew 28:19).

Others

While the pastor should concentrate his efforts upon training his elders in the work of counseling, neither he nor they can be satisfied to stop there. The passage in I Thessalonians 5:12,13, referring to elders, significantly is followed by an exhortation to all Christians ("brethren"). The same word used in verse 12, *noutheteo*, describing the "work" of the elder (i.e., his function *as an overseer*), also is used in verse 14 of the everyday members of the congregation: "brethren, nouthetically confront the unruly." I shall not take the time to discuss the point in detail, as I have already cited references to passages in which this has been done *supra*, but I shall simply mention that Colossians 3:16 and Romans 15:14 are two other significant verses that either enjoin *nouthesia* upon all Christians or commend them for engaging in it. The pastor, then, must encourage general occasional counseling activity among all of the members of the flock. The number of exhortations to such mutual ministry (often alluded to by the use of the words "one another"[14]) is striking. But it is not to the casual, occasional ongoing

---

[13]On discipleship training, cf. *Competent to Counsel*, pp. 258ff.; *The Big Umbrella*, pp. 249ff.

[14]A study of these words (recommended in a previous footnote) provides an illuminating commentary on how fully the brethren in a congregation ought to be "stimulating one another to love and good works" (Hebrews 10:24).

practice of counseling by members of the congregation that I wish to allude in this section. Rather, in addition I am concerned to see various members *work together with the pastor* in ways similar to those who helped Paul and his helpers as adjunct counselors. These need not be only elders or deacons (who, incidentally, can have a great counseling ministry to the sick, the poor and the needy), but also non-ordained members of the congregation.

I am not proposing that others than elders (and possibly deacons) be trained to do counseling *with* the pastor, nor that they sit in on his counseling sessions. What I am proposing, however, is that there should be laymen who are ready and able to be called in to a given session by the suggestion of the pastor (and agreement of the counselee) to assist in some specialized way, using gifts in which they excel. Or the pastor, as part of his counseling, may know that he can send a counselee to confer with such a member about a question; or that he may be able to make arrangements through such persons to provide for the specialized counsel or help needed. This all sounds rather vague, I am sure, so let me begin to concretize it.[15]

Suppose, in the course of counseling a woman who has been suffering from depression, the pastor discovers that she (1) neglects unpleasant chores like ironing and that (2) even when she attempts to do her ironing *against* her feelings, her mind wanders to thoughts of self-pity, jealousy and envy. He may suggest to her that she find a friend who (1) will iron with her every Tuesday morning, thus routinizing the process (a necessity for those who tend to be "undisciplined" [Cf. I Thessalonians 5:14], and as a result become depressed) according to schedule, and (2) who will talk to her about uplifting topics consonant with the standard given in Philippians 4 (thus training her how to use her mind fruitfully). The counselee may not know of such a person. But if a woman in the congregation, possessing the gifts to minister in these ways, is "on call," the pastor may be able to engage her help in this or in other creative ways. Of course, the help will be temporary, will attempt to train, and will be withdrawn as the counselee learns to solve her problem on her own.

Similarly, a woman with a disorganized home (everything is piled everywhere) might receive just the boost necessary to change her entire future from a team of women who stand ready to be engaged by the pastor to help. (1) They may move in and help her clean and straighten up; (2) one or more members of the team then may follow up with consultations to show her how to organize her home and her work for the future; (3) one may check her out for a number of weeks thereafter in order to assure the

---

[15]Cf. also Vol. I of this series, pp. 107, 108.

progress and continued maintenance of the new procedures and to answer questions until the new ways become habitual. What the woman needed from the pastor was biblical directions about her obligations as a wife; what the pastor needed from members of the congregation was expertise and follow-up in helping the counselee to effect and carry out the change. Thus, together, pastor and members of the congregation were able to exercise a more effective ministry than either could separately. Together, they had most concretely carried out some of Paul's admonitions that are found in Titus 2:1, 3-5—in this case those that pertain to a phrase in verse 5:"workers at home" (the King James version, "keepers at home," is incorrect). If you think that I am picking on women by these examples you are missing the point; I am trying to show how women in the congregation may become "fellow workers" with the pastor as he does counseling.

Let us consider another all too common situation these days. A young person, addicted to drugs, becomes a Christian and wants to get off the stuff for good. How can he be helped? For a while (a couple of weeks or more) he will need day-by-day help and monitoring. The pastor cannot give him this help in one-hour counseling sessions alone. The Scriptures continually stress hospitality. But most hospitality is extended to persons who are desirable. Yet, it is some of the "undesirables" who need it most. If the pastor knows that there are persons who, while they have no gifts, let us say, for public speaking, nevertheless are willing to share their house and the structure of their Christian family with those in need, he can counsel more effectively because he knows that he has a place in which to lodge such persons while helping them.

Deacons may be used to develop and to organize such congregational services for the pastor as well as to enter into labors of the sort in a peculiar way themselves. All that the pastor should need to do is to express the desire to have such a program, and the deacons should organize and manage it. One of the great ministries of the diaconate is administrative. In this way, the pastor and elders can concentrate upon giving the counsel itself, while others arrange the circumstances for carrying it out. It is in such cooperative enterprises with his people that the pastor and the flock grow together in the joys of loving ministry.

I shall not multiply examples; necessities and needs point to the programs to be initiated.[16] But one can see readily that persons with

---

[16]That is precisely what Titus 3:14 means: "And let our people also learn to engage in good deeds, *to meet pressing needs*, that they may not be unfruitful." Programs are best inaugurated, many times, out of necessity. Alert pastors will *recognize needs as opportunities* upon which to build programs and in which to challenge members of the flock to ministry.

financial acumen can help others who in counseling reveal that they are having trouble with budgeting. Businessmen who have learned to schedule their hours with care may help those who suffer from nickel-and-diming their minutes away in idleness. Young mothers, having trouble with child raising, can be assisted by others with more experience. All sorts of persons may move in to render various services in crises. (I hope to devote some space elsewhere to a fuller discussion of counseling in crises in a book on the subject.) All of this—and much more—can involve the entire congregation in a conjoint counseling ministry with the pastor. Indeed, since there is no Christian who does not have something to offer by way of help to others, there is no lack of resources for the pastor. His task is to mobilize and to use them. The more he searches out the persons possessing potential sources of skills and abilities, and according to Ephesians 4:11,12[17] challenges and channels them to use these in a conjoint ministry with him, the more blessing and power that there can be in his counseling ministry.

When one contrasts the possibilities of such a *total* counseling ministry with that which can be carried on in only one hour per week in a counseling center, he can begin to see additional reasons why I have strongly set forth the former over against the latter. Only the pastoral context is fully adapted to meet the needs of counseling (which in many cases demand specialized follow up, courses of instruction, prayerful concern, the devoting of time, etc., which the counselor by himself cannot offer). The pastor who (1) has the conviction to do so, who (2) recognizes the potential in various members, who (3) preaches about the ministry of each member and challenges him to discover and develop his gifts, who (4) sees arising needs and problems as opportunities to help not only counselees but also members who can be challenged concretely to exercise their gifts to join him in ministering to these counselees, eventually will mold a congregation that will exert great power in its community for good. Such a church bears a powerful witness as the body of the powerful Christ. Such congregations, however, do not arise automatically. They are brought into being by God through His servants. They must be developed, molded, and guided by shepherds who have their eyes fixed on the goal and through discouragement and temporary failure never waver from that goal, but with patience press on toward it. In time (often after much of it

---

[17]In this passage, it is clear that the officers are given in the church not merely to minister, but rather to help each member to discover, develop and to deploy his gifts for ministry, so that the whole body builds itself up in love (Ephesians 4:16).

may elapse), if they persevere, God may honor those efforts far beyond expectations.[18]

If the goal seems terribly remote as you think about *your* congregation, do not lose heart. As I said before, begin somewhere. Start small. Begin, with some easily attainable short-term goal, to take a step in the right direction. Find persons who are ready to cooperate or who could be successfully challenged to do so and start with them. Any effort in the right direction is movement toward the goal. Remember, it was Jesus who revealed the principle that he who is faithful in small things will be given the privilege of handling larger ones. One reason why some pastors never succeed for Christ is that they want to begin with too much. Never forget that large changes (in perspective, attitude, belief, etc.) can occur through small changes in the situation; *principles*, applicable to much larger matters, usually are taught and learned best by application first to smaller matters. Begin somewhere, with *one* tree, today. Soon, by God's grace, you will have felled the entire forest.

EXERCISE

For the Student

1. Ask yourself: In what ways could I engage in assisting my pastor in his counseling ministry right now? Do not *push* yourself upon him, but offer to be of help in whatever ways you now may be able to do so. List several possibilities to suggest to him below:

---

[18]Brief pastorates often prevent significant change of this sort from occurring. Conversely, one reason why pastorates tend to be so brief is that pastors (unaware of the true reasons why they are failing to see significant changes in their congregation) conclude that they are in the wrong place. Instead of continually moving about with no real plan for engaging the entire congregation in active, happy participation in Christian service, they need (rather) to become deeply involved in developing a biblical program for mutual ministry.

2. Make a study of passages using the words "one another" or suggesting the one-another concept. Record your findings below.

For the Pastor

In the space that follows list in the left-hand column counseling projects for which you now think that you could have used assistance from members of the congregation. Add to the list as new needs arise. In the right-hand column list the names of persons who might be asked to help. When their agreement to do so has been secured, place an exclamation mark after their names.

Projects	Persons
1. (Sample) Help in following up a husband who has committed himself to pay his bills on time by reminding him toward the end of the month and by "checking him out" on the first of each month.	1. (Sample) Fred Jones!

Projects	Persons

Projects	Persons

CHAPTER III
CONDUCTING A CONGREGATIONAL
COUNSELING PROGRAM

Much more may be said about congregational and lay counseling. But in this place I shall attempt to unpack but one final theme from a pastoral base: the concern for developing a formal counseling program throughout the congregation, as well as the encouragement of universal informal counseling.

Informal occasional (i.e., brought forth by occasions) counseling, practiced by increasing numbers of parishioners, ought to be encouraged by the pastor in sermons, by conducting classes in the basics of counseling, etc. The justification for counseling by all lies in such directives as those found in Galatians 6:1, Colossians 3:16 and Romans 15:14. Since I have mentioned this obligation frequently and discussed the problem elsewhere in depth,[1] I shall not rework what I have handled before. Instead, I shall simply repeat the need for the pastor:

(1) to educate the congregation to the necessity for total congregational counseling. The idea is foreign to most members of evangelical churches and, therefore, needs to be taught patiently and preached persuasively;

(2) to instruct all members in at least the elements of counseling so that they may know what to do, how to do it, what to avoid and when to call in an elder or the pastor for aid;

(3) to motivate members to do counseling. Knowledge is easier to impart than conviction, but conviction is easier to attain than action. Teaching alone will not motivate. The need to encourage, warn and demonstrate is equally as great as the need for good instruction.

It is not the informal aspects of congregational counseling that I wish to emphasize, however, but rather the necessity for providing special training for leaders[2] so that in conjunction with their teaching (in the church school,

---

[1]Cf., "You Are Your Brother's Keeper," *The Big Umbrella*, Chapter Six.

[2]I am not here thinking of elders and deacons, whose very offices demand ability in dispensing wise counsel, but of others whose influence for good or evil can be great. Elders and deacons should be trained by the pastor at an early stage of his ministry (see comments on the training of elders, *supra*). When they have been trained, their help can be enlisted in the training of these other leaders.

the youth group, etc.), and other leadership functions that bring them into contact with people and their problems, particularly where they exercise an advisory role, they may offer effective counsel that will preventively and remedially enable them to make significant contributions to the work of Christ.

How can this type of program be carried out? Probably, unlike the training given to elders and deacons, these leaders cannot be invited to sit in on pastoral counseling sessions conducted by the pastor. Therefore, their training largely will consist of:

(1) *theory* taught in leadership and teaching courses conducted by the pastor or by an elder. Parts of *Competent to Counsel* and *The Christian Counselor's Manual* might be useful for such course work. Information on marriage and family problems may be conveyed by outside reading in *Christian Living in the Home*;

(2) *case study and simulated counseling sessions.* Use of selected cases from *The Christian Counselor's Casebook*[3] that can be studied individually or in groups in conjunction with the *Manual* and that can be presented as reports or role played and discussed by the class, will provide the nearest thing to actual participation;

(3) *participant observation.* Some situations (perhaps *all*) provide opportunities for participant observation. For instance, ideally the new youth leader, church school teacher, etc., should be selected far enough in advance to allow him to spend a period of time observing and working with the previous leader. During that tutorship (or discipleship) period, he will have the opportunity to observe, participate and perhaps even to do counseling (under supervision).[4] All persons leaving leadership positions should be instructed in the need for grooming the leaders who will succeed them. Once the discipling process is accepted as a teacher training aid and gets under way, it will become automatic.

---

[3]Jay Adams, *The Christian Counselor's Casebook* (Presbyterian and Reformed Publishing Company, Nutley: 1974).
[4]Other benefits accrue from the tutorial period.

EXERCISE

For the Student

1. Ask the pastor of your church how you could best participate in a congregational counseling program.

2. Tell him about the material that you have been studying and ask about the possibilities (appropriateness, feasibility, etc.) for introducing such a program into your (his) congregation.

3. Write out his comments, including questions, objections, suggestions, etc.

For the Pastor

1. Develop a program for the promotion of congregational counseling. Use the space below as a worksheet for outlining it. State (a) goals, (b) steps to be taken to achieve them and (c) personnel to enlist in the process.

WORKSHEET

Goals (long and short range)	Steps (in random order)	Persons

WORKSHEET

Goals (long and short range)	Steps (in random order)	Persons

2. Using the material in the worksheet above, lay out the program, assigning a target date to each step and each goal as it is placed in proper sequence and attaching names to each step as the persons are actually enlisted.

PROGRAM

PROGRAM

CHAPTER IV
COUNSELING MEMBERS OF
OTHER CONGREGATIONS

What should be the biblical ethics governing the counseling of a member of another congregation? How may one determine whether to do so in the first place? The answer to this crucial question boils down to the issue of what constitutes the violation of another church's discipline. How does one handle the issue of sheep stealing? That latter phrase has been used loosely but ought to be defined clearly in every pastor's mind. It is totally wrong to steal sheep from another flock and another shepherd of Christ. To do so creates division within the body of Christ, breaks down church discipline, allows Christians to run from problems, permits other pastors and their congregations to escape from shepherdly responsibilities toward straying sheep, and greatly endangers the receiving church. Few practices that have become more or less standard among Bible-believing churches have had more destructive effects than sheep stealing, and yet it continues apparently without much recognition or concern.

But while I have said that no true shepherd of Christ may steal sheep from another shepherd, every true shepherd will be careful to consider whether the potential counselee's "pastor" was truly a shepherd. "Sheep stealing" has been the persistent cry of liberals, cultists and others who were preaching "another gospel." But the cry is hollow if the sheep is "stolen" from such a fold. As a matter of fact, "stealing" is an altogether inappropriate word to describe what is happening. The fact, in such cases, is that the sheep has been *rescued* from a "wolf" in shepherd's clothing. He has been enabled to see that the devil's servants often come as "angels of light."

Because counseling involves an intimate relationship between the counselor and the counselee, a counselor who counsels the member of another congregation successfully, whether he knows it or not, often exerts a strong pull upon the counselee. This may be quite unintentional. This effect particularly may occur when the counselee's pastor previously was unsuccessful (or where the counselee thought that he might be). That this influence, tempting the counselee to consider moving his membership, may be strong should lead every pastor to consider carefully when and under what conditions he will undertake the counseling of the member of another congregation.

(1) He will *always* counsel with those whose membership is held in a church that does not believe the Scriptures to be the inerrant Word of God and in which the gospel of Christ is denied. Indeed, it should be a counseling objective to raise these very issues at the appropriate time (this time will vary according to circumstances). That is to say, part of the counsel will be to show the counselee his need for a Savior and for the ministry of His church (or, if the counselee is a Christian, his need for fellowship with the people of God as they enjoy the ministry of God's Word and together seek to worship and serve Him according to that Word). The pastoral counselor who is true to the Scriptures will wish to use the influence exerted to point out the contrast between a true ministry of Christ and a pseudo ministry. He will have no qualms about "Sheep stealing"; he will be glad to rescue them from a wolf.

(2) There are many times, however, when a pastor will be approached for counseling by the member of another Bible-believing congregation. Here is where he must be very cautious of the violation of the discipline of that congregation and of unintentional "stealing." How may he handle the situation?

(a) He should explain that he makes it a policy to counsel the members of other true congregations of Christ only after informing their pastor that he has been requested to do so and obtaining his agreement.

(b) If there are objections to this policy and the potential counselees seek to raise problems that have occurred that made counseling with their own pastor inexpedient, or if it becomes apparent that the pastor of the other church could not handle these problems, the pastor may agree to begin to discuss that issue with the understanding that it may require him to recommend the counselee's returning to his pastor, holding a conference with the counselee and his pastor, disciplinary action, or whatever else is appropriate. No privileged information should be received.[1] Above all, he will see to it that no slanderous accusations are made against anyone not present. Ordinarily he will discover, quickly, that the counselee's only proper course is to return to

---

[1]Cf. p. 292.

deal with the problems from which he may have fled. Occasionally he may learn that part of the problem truly is that the first pastor did not know how to give counsel. In such cases, he should invite the other pastor to sit in on the sessions, and at the first appropriate point return the counseling to him. In other words, he will always be willing to counsel the member of another congregation about his reasons for seeking counsel from him.

Frequently, needed pressure can be exerted upon another church to handle disciplinary matters that they have been seeking to avoid, by sending the counselee back to pursue the course of action outlined in Matthew 18. This advice, when followed, may lead to great blessing and strengthening of the counselee and the counselee's congregation.

Carelessly receiving persons from another Bible-believing congregation without inquiry and investigation about the reasons for their change may lead, as has been the sad experience of many, to the reception of trouble-makers who could not get along where they were and will not get along in the next church either. People moving from churches for the proper reasons[2] and with Christian attitudes always will wish to do things in a decent and orderly fashion and will not object to, but will welcome, attempts to bring about reconciliation, exercise biblical discipline, etc. Beware of those who refuse to heed such counsel. Ordinarily, therefore, the contemplated change from one Christian congregation to another should be greeted (at the very least) by a thorough discussion of the reasons, and more often than not will eventuate in a series of several counseling sessions. If ever conservative churches could work together on anything, it should be in the recognition and exercise of church care and discipline. Herein lies the possibility of a new era for true ecumenicity among believers, based upon the common denominator of the authority of Jesus Christ in His Church.

---

[2]E.g., such as a major change in doctrinal beliefs.

EXERCISE

For the Student

Interview ten pastors about their policies and practices in counseling/accepting members from other evangelical churches in the community. Report in class on these (evaluatively). Jot down notes in the space below.

For the Pastor

1. Visit personally (one by one) all of the evangelical pastors in your community to discuss the practical ways and means of showing mutual respect for church discipline, particularly as it involves the movement of members from one church to another and the need for counseling.

2. Call a meeting of as many of these pastors as express an interest to try to develop guidelines for implementing the considerations outlined in the earlier discussions.

CHAPTER V
EVALUATION AND UPGRADING OF
PASTORAL COUNSELING

A wise fisherman always mends his net. A wise counselor learns from every counseling session and is better prepared for the next as the result. Whether there was failure or success, much can be learned if the pastor takes time afterward to *evaluate*.

What does evaluation involve? There is no one answer to that question, because different cases may require particular types of evaluation, but (in general) at least the following elements will be present in any satisfactory evaluative process:

1. Review of the case. Begin with a consideration of the notes taken during the counseling sessions.

2. Time for reflection upon these notes. Evaluation cannot be done hurriedly. It takes time, usually at more than one or two sittings.

3. Identification of areas of particular successes and failures. These should be listed (in writing) and briefly explained.

4. A general written evaluative summary[1] (put it in the manila folder together with your notes) stating,

   a. *goals,* ultimate and proximate, and whether they were reached;

   b. *progress,* including obstacles encountered and methods used (successfully or unsuccessfully) to overcome them;

   c. *outcome* and present situation (Did it stick? Is there need for further follow-up?, etc.).

From such an evaluation the pastor may abstract principles and methods. These he ought to record in a counseling notebook, on 3 x 5 cards, in the margins of his favorite counseling textbook next to the subject, or in whatever place he finds that it is most useful for him to preserve them.[2]

---

[1]It may be headed the GPO (goals, progress, outcome evaluation).
[2]At the conclusion of this discussion, for those who wish to use it, I have provided space for such a record. .

Evaluation can be deceptive. One can be too critical of himself, justify failures, blind himself to problems, misunderstand the operative factors in a case, misinterpret causes, oversimplify the dynamics of a problem, etc. It is wise, therefore, for the pastor to suspend judgment until he is sure about an evaluation. It is better to write tentative *suggestive* explanations in the summary than to guess. It is better simply to record, "I do not understand what happened," than to give an interpretation of the case that is faulty. Then, the principles and methods that he abstracts are likely to be accurate and useful rather than self-deceptive. What one says often enough, and especially what he writes, he tends to believe. We all have an uncanny ability to persuade ourselves, even when our ideas do not seem very persuasive to others. Therefore, the pastor should be assured that the principles and methods growing out of the evaluation that he records are solid before he records them.

Making a distinction of this sort between firm conclusions and tentative ones (or matters about which not even tentative suggestions yet can be made) allows for growth in two ways:

1. The recorded principles and methods become reminders for future counseling situations.

2. The tentative (or totally inconclusive) statements in the evaluative summary provide agenda material for further study. Rather than lose these in filed manila folders, it would be well for the pastor also to abstract written statements of problems for further study. These could be written out on a separate sheet of paper, in a notebook, etc. He may then study these to find the biblical solutions to them. As he discovers God's answers, the problem may be scratched from the sheet and the solution recorded in the place where he keeps notes on solidly settled principles and procedures.[3]

In evaluating a case, the counselor may find two or three lists helpful. They are found in the reference section of *The Christian Counselor's Manual*:

1. Reference 4, "Fifty Failure Factors," pp. 459-461.

2. Reference 5, "Some Don'ts in Counseling," p. 462.

3. Appendix B, "Counselor's Check List," p. 436.

Also of some value may be the list of reasons for seeking counseling (pp. 277-279), including a list of problems peculiar to various groups of persons.

---

[3]For further information on evaluation, particularly stressing the helpfulness of the joint evaluation of a trainee or team counselor, cf. *Competent to Counsel*, pp. 204-208; 56-59.

These lists may be found suggestive in several ways. For instance, the counselor may ask himself, "Can I pinpoint the reason(s) why Mary came?" His ability or inability to give a clear response to this question more plainly than anything else may help most in giving initial direction to the evaluation of the case. Looking over the list of difficulties frequently encountered in counseling singles, he may inquire: "How many of these did I detect in Bill? Could I have missed any?"

The ability to be self-critical, to see and to admit one's own mistakes, weaknesses, and to mend the net, more than anything else may lead to improvement and growth. Counseling *develops*; it is much more, but it is (nevertheless) a skill that takes time and practice (of the biblically correct procedures) to acquire. Self-evaluation leading to personal improvement programs is an essential factor in that development. No successful counselor finds that this comes easily (or quickly), but if he perseveres he will learn how exciting such development can be as one discovery leads on to another.

To take just one example, remember that it is possible to learn even from failure. Indeed, when one has felt the heartaches of failure, the experience *vividly* impresses upon him the principles and procedures involved in it and, if the failure was due to his ineptness, he doubly recognizes the need for improvement.[4]

To learn from failure the counselor must ask and answer the following questions:

1. Was there truly a failure?

2. Who failed? Was it I, the counselee, or both of us?

3. What brought about the failure? Was it one major factor? Was it a combination of factors?

4. How could it have been prevented? Make a mental rerun of the experience, trying out other ways of conducting the crucial session or sessions that led to failure.

5. What must I do now to prevent such failure in the future?

As a profitable exercise, it might be worthwhile to consider case II-3 in *The Christian Counselor's Casebook*[5]:

---

[4]The difference between the pastor who grows and the one who will not largely lies in the difference of response to failure. The first, though disheartened, determines that by God's grace he will not fail Him or his parishioners in that way *again* and prayerfully digs in.
[5]Pp. 128, 129.

"Now let me get this right," says the counselor. "You only had three conference tables, and two of them blew up in arguments?"

"Yes, that's right," Paul and Jan reply simultaneously. "And what's more, the third one wasn't very profitable," Paul adds.

"What caused the first blowup?"

"Well, we were talking about finances, and I got mad at something Jan said."

"What was that, Jan?"

"I just said that we are in financial trouble now because Paul has never helped me or given me *any* leadership in organizing the budget."

"And when I saw her attitude I didn't want to talk any more," Paul blurts out. "Besides, it wouldn't have been any use. She didn't want to talk. She wanted to criticize."

"Now was the second blowup over the same issue?" asks the counselor.

"No, it was different," says Jan. "I wanted to discuss Paul's defensiveness with him. The thing that happened at the first conference is typical for him. Whenever Paul's failures are mentioned, he becomes defensive and stops talking."

"And what happened when she mentioned this, Paul?"

"I got mad and walked out. I don't have to stand for that kind of stuff!"

Now without answering the discussion questions on page 129 of the *Casebook* in depth or fully discussing the case, let me make at least one or two observations relevant to learning and growth evaluation. First, in this case the counselor was at fault (as well as the counselees). He had failed to explain the conference procedures adequately, especially those that would have helped them to avoid problems or handle problems if they arose.[6] He *now* can take occasion to give those instructions, *pointing out the demonstrated need* to follow them. Just as failure vividly impresses such needs upon the pastor, it also can be used to vividly impress the need for

---

[6]For a thorough discussion of these procedures cf. *The Christian Counselor's Manual*, pp. 321-332. Anticipating and meeting possible problems in giving homework assignments is vital.

change upon his counselees. After pointing out to the counselees where they failed and where he failed them, he may continue:

"O.K., while we can never be happy about sin, in one sense we can be glad that this happened; it provides an opportunity for us to do several things:
1. Discover how God wants us to straighten out wrongs;
2. Learn His ways of preventing future failure even before it begins;
3. Find out how He expects us to deal with an argument once it has begun."[7]

After evaluation, the counselor may wish to write in his procedures column: "Never assign the conference table without giving a full explanation of it." As an additional impetus he may add: "Remember Louise."

The counselor has failed in other cases described in *The Christian Counselor's Casebook*. Case II-14 also is a good one to ponder to discover where the counselor has gone wrong, to see how he can recoup, and to discover what he can learn from his failure.[8]

All in all, there is too little evaluation of counseling principles and procedures. It is essential for Bible-believing ministers to become the most highly self-critical professionals that there are. I do not refer to morbid introspection or to some preoccupation with self-recrimination; far too much profitless and, indeed, counterproductive self-flagellation is already carried on in Christian circles. No, the kind of self-criticism to which I refer constitutes a relentless self-evaluation of one's practices and operating principles, stemming from constant review in the light of ongoing research, development and application of biblical understanding.

Of all persons, whether it has to do with his preaching, his counseling, his pastoral care, or whatever, the conservative minister of the Word should recognize this need. He knows (1) that he is a sinner who will never be perfect in thought or deed in this life (although *counted* perfect before God in Christ) and (2) that he has a Book revealed by God that contains more truth than he can fully comprehend in a lifetime. Therefore, he knows that both his understanding of and his ability to apply that Word must continue to enlarge every day. He must *never* think that he has arrived. But unlike others, simply *because* he has an inerrant Standard of faith and practice, as a minister of *that* Word, he always has an infallible rule against which to

[7]*Ibid.*, pp. 316ff., for methods of recouping and pp. 197-201; 355-367, on resistance and restraint and redirection of anger.
[8]*The Christian Counselor's Casebook*, pp. 150, 151.

measure his ministry. He does not need to waste time debating whether what he reads is true or not, as every psychologist or psychiatrist must whenever he reads Freud or Rogers or Skinner or Harris or Perls. He *knows* that the Book is true. All that he must do is to understand it and learn how to apply what he understands. This is an enormous advantage. And, because he is able to grow through scriptural self-evaluation, he is encouraged rather than discouraged by the evaluative process. Counselors with no Standard by which to judge their beliefs and practices tend to become discouraged after a while by the confusingly large number of counseling options that appear on the market. And each of these options on any given point is antithetical to the beliefs, principles and evidence supposedly supporting others. Apart from a final, absolute, God-given revelation, there is simply no way to know how to love God or how to love man. And that means, there is no way to know how to counsel men to do so.

The minister of the Word, as a consequence, must not minimize the great privilege and the immense advantage that an infallible Standard provides. He must not neglect the opportunity ever to learn and to grow from truth to greater truth.[9]

In order to emphasize and explain what I have been saying pointedly, I shall close this chapter with an address delivered earlier this year at a Christian college.

Don't Be Short-Changed[10]

I thought at first of entitling this address, "Anyone who goes to a psychiatrist ought to have his head examined," but then thought better of it and settled for "Don't Be Short-Changed."

Counselees, or those who initiate counseling for them, are interested in change. In one way or another, the uppermost concern is to change their lives.

—Perhaps they have *had it* with wives/husbands/parents/children... They want a change.

—Possibly they seek relief from depression or worry or fear or mysterious voices speaking out of nowhere.

—Or... they are anxious to learn how to get along with others/how to

---

[9]The formation of an accrediting association for nouthetic counselors is under consideration. The association would require continued growth and competence of its members and would develop ways and means for attaining it.

[10]An address delivered to the student body at Westmont College, Santa Barbara, California, March 29, 1974, and later at the Philadelphia College of the Bible, November 8, 1974.

control tempers/how to communicate with persons they love/how to keep a job/how to rope and tie a runaway sex drive. Any one of these. . . or dozens of other problems. . . impel people everywhere to seek counsel of others, hoping they will provide the change that will bring peace and joy.

Counselors are people who try to help them effect that change. Many of these people who counsel are well-meaning and enter the field from altruistic motives; others are themselves confused, seeking answers; some are in the work for the prestige, the power or the money, and some for the gratification of baser desires.

But in this attempt to effect change, profound and urgent questions arise, such as: Who sets the standard for change? The counselee? The counselor? Someone else? Does the counselee know enough? May the counselor's values be accepted? And—who answers the question about who sets the standard? Who effects the change? Counselee? Counselor? Both? Another? What means will be used for bringing about the change? All those that work? Then is brainwashing acceptable? Surely, there must be *some* limitations in *some* directions— but that's just the problem: where shall the lines be drawn?—and who shall draw them? These and many other similar questions inevitably arise in the minds of all thoughtful counselors.

The trouble is—there isn't one in a thousand who can begin to answer them. Yet, without answers, where are we; what shall counselors do; and what of the counselee?

Counselors read, experiment, debate, write, yet they are no nearer to agreement on these questions than when they first began. Seated in his plush, expensive study, lined with learned tomes, the average counselor, seemingly serene and secure, is nothing of the sort if he is a man of integrity and a diligent student of his profession. Daily he is harassed by the silent but strong protests over every action he takes and every word that he speaks coming from the authors who observe him from their perches on his shelves. "Too directive," cry some. "Why don't you reflect his feelings?" shout others. "Get rid of all of that nonsense about value; focus on the behavior," demands a third. From all sides competing 'isms and 'erapies woo and warn. In his better moments he tells himself: "Toss the whole business overboard. After all, who can know what is right—I don't even have time to learn all of the systems, with their presuppositions, principles and practices, let alone try them out! Why, there are classical Freudians and Neo-Freudians, Adlerians and Jungians, Logotherapists, Integrity Therapists, Reality Therapists, Radical Therapists, Rational-emotive Therapists, Contract Therapists, Primal Screamers, Laingians, Transactional Analysts, Skinnerians, Behaviorists by the buckets, Rogerians,

Group Therapists, Family Therapists, etc., etc., etc. Why in the world should I think that what I am doing is right?"

And... think of the poor counselee—in confusion meandering from one counselor to another—looking for someone who can help him. In the process he is diagnosed, misdiagnosed and rediagnosed. He may be told that he is sick, or that he has been poorly socialized by parents and peers, or that he has been wrongly conditioned, or that he has failed to live up to his full potential. He may be assured that the problem is illness, or bad training, or learned behavior, or emotional immaturity, or chemical, or interpersonal or existential or whatever in origin. Appropriately he will be treated or trained or encouraged or taught or medicated in widely varying ways. "Let it all hang out," says one. "Tell me about your childhood, your sex life and your dreams," says another. "Take these pills four times a day and see me in six weeks," or "Renegotiate all of your personal contracts," or "Get rid of those inhibitions—find a man with whom you can have successful sexual relations," or "You must have a series of E.S.T. treatments (i.e., electroshock therapy—or, to put it more realistically, grand mal seizures, artificially induced)," or "We shall recondition your behavior," or "Hypnotism will help," or "Get a frontal lobotomy," or "Talk it out," or "Scream,"... or... that's just about what one feels like doing when he hears even so small a portion of the whole as this.

In the process, persons have been advised to urinate upon their father's grave, punch pillows until the feathers fly, file for a divorce if they don't get along with a life partner, and just about anything else one could imagine. Before he is through, a counselee may run the gamut, being assured that all will be well if only he medicates, or copulates, or urinates, or meditates or ventilates!

What is he to *do*? In whom shall he *believe*? Where is he to *turn*?

And... in the face of all of this uncertainty, don't fail to notice what it is all about. Remember, all of these views, all of these persons, all of these methods are concerned about changing people's lives! If physicians were so divided and uncertain, would we entrust our bodies to them? If airlines and airline pilots differed so widely about flying principles and practices, who would fly? Yet, think, people by the millions turn to such counselors to *change their LIVES*! That means—to change their values; to change their attitudes, to change their beliefs, to change their behavior and to change their relationships to significant persons! DARE we allow anyone to meddle in such matters when all is in flux?

Think about the trick a psychiatrist played upon his fellow practitioners—he sent twelve persons—sane as you or I—into twelve of the nation's leading mental institutions for the expressed purpose of discovering how accurate psychotherapeutic diagnosis is. What do you think happened? You guessed it; some of them were wrongly diagnosed as having serious mental illness. How many do you think? Would you believe half? Wrong. Would you believe three-fourths? Still wrong. Would you believe all twelve? Right! All twelve! A one hundred per cent failure!! And, listen to this, of the twelve diagnoses, eleven were a diagnosis of schizophrenia! Moreover, these "patients" made no attempt to deceive, but acted normally during the entire period of diagnostic evaluation! No wonder Karl Menninger, commenting on the fiasco, said: "Schizophrenia is just a nice Greek word."

Surely, by now we should be asking not only where can counselees find help, but also—how can they be protected in their gullibility and vulnerability from misguided (even though well-intentioned) persons, from incompetent individuals, and from foolish and from unscrupulous practitioners? Who or what will preserve them from making changes of thought and action that can only disappoint and that may lead to ill consequences equally as bad or worse than those previously experienced?

And, surely, all of this confusion, contradiction and chaos must not only give us pause before approaching or sending someone to the self-styled experts or professionals, it should make us ask an even more basic question: What is behind the disorder or (as Zillborg called it) the "disarray"? Other fields, while having healthy disagreements, seem to make progress and seem to be able to tack down many areas of common agreement. But there is nothing like a consensus on anything in counseling. Is there not something radically wrong in the discipline of counseling? *What could it be?*

As I gather it, you have asked me to come in order to answer that question. As you might suppose from what I have said, that is no small task. Indeed, after hearing something of the various opinions and ideologies to which I have alluded, you may wonder why I came—how I could accept the invitation and what brings me here anyway. Certainly I could not be arrogant enough to imagine that I had the final word, could I? Do I come to make another vain thrust and thus stir up more sediment to further foul the pool? Dare I even think that I could introduce the idea that would clarify the situation and point toward a pathway that emerges from the fog? No, if I came with another such word I should be not only a fool but a charlatan. I do not so come.

"Then, what brings you here?" you ask. Answer:

To point to the path leading to the clear light and sunshine; to explain what is behind the confusion and how it may be swept aside; to herald a new day of counseling that has already begun to dawn—and about which you may possibly hear much more in the not-too-distant future; to challenge some of you to join the ranks, and to hope that this meagre effort may bear some fruit toward these ends!

"Wait a minute," you reply:

First, you said that you were not bringing in another opinion or ideology; yet now you seem to say just the opposite. You'd better explain—and make it plain; I've heard just about all I want to take of confusion and contradiction for one day!

OK; OK—I'll give it to you straight. I have not come to offer one more opinion, system or ideology. I would not dare, and I wonder continually at the audacity of those who do. Instead, I have come with good news. There is hope in the midst of the chaos, but it is not found in *my way*.

Remember the question I asked but did not answer earlier? It went something like this: since other disciplines (engineering, business, medicine and even non-clinical and non-counseling psychology) seem to be able to arrive at some measure of order and cohesion—enough at least to produce some concrete results—must not something be radically wrong with counseling? The answer to that question is "yes." Something *is* radically wrong with counseling, and *this is it*: almost to a man counselors have rejected the only true standard of human values, beliefs, attitudes and behavior. Yet those matters comprise the stuff of which counseling is made. They have *looked* everywhere else, *tried* everything else, but have totally ignored the one Book that can bring order out of chaos. Only a word from God Himself can properly tell us how to change. In the Bible alone can be found the true description of man, his plight and God's solution in Christ. Only the Scriptures can tell us what kind of persons we must become. Only God can command, direct, and give power to effect the proper changes that will enable men He redeems to renew the image corrupted by the fall. Two Skinnerians in a room with their latest sausage grinder, by which they claim to be able to make any sort of sausage one wishes, cannot agree about what kind of sausage they want, what sort of man to produce. Each wants sausage like himself. God not only has *told* us what man must become, but has *shown* us in Christ! In short, counselors are in their present state of confusion, swayed by every new fad, precisely because they have rejected the one and only perfect and lasting textbook on counseling.

"*Textbook* did you say? The Bible a *textbook* for counseling?" Yes, the Bible is God's basic text for living. It contains "all things pertaining to life and godliness." In it is all that a counselor or counselee needs to know in order to honor God by loving Him with all that he has, and by loving his neighbor as himself. As a matter of fact, on those two commandments— and on the scriptural explanation of how to fulfill them—hangs all of the work of counseling.

In counseling—per se—we do not find many persons presenting problems about the trouble they are having with things ("You see, Doc, there's this chair that I have been having difficulty with . . ."). When the organic difficulties have been eliminated by sending such persons to physicians, what is left is that large number of people who are in trouble in one way or another with other *persons*—with God and their neighbors.

"But," I can almost *hear* the objection, "you don't use the Bible as a textbook for engineering or architecture or medicine, do you?" Of course -not. "Well, then, why do you use it as a textbook for counseling?" Because, while the Bible was never *intended* to be a textbook about business or engineering, God Himself, in the passages cited, as elsewhere, tells us that it *is* a textbook concerned precisely with the problems encountered in counseling. And from the confusion seen uniquely in that field, it should be evident that just such a text is desperately needed.

How extraordinary, indeed, it is for Christians, those who claim to believe in the inerrancy and authority of the Scriptures, and who have been saved through faith in the Savior, whose death for their sins is recorded therein, to doubt the fact that the Bible is the textbook for living—and, of course, every *change* in living! How could it be otherwise? God alone can tell man what values to espouse; after all, no one else originated the Ten Commandments! God alone can disclose the chief goal of man, explain the core of his problems and offer the fundamental solutions to them. If counselors, apart from the Scriptures, could do so, the Bible—and, to be sure, Christ Himself—would have been given in vain! But counselors *cannot.* That is precisely why we are presently in this thick soup.

Well, then, what is the alternative? "There is hope, you say? Then tell me about it—I shall listen cautiously."

To begin with, everywhere in the Scriptures God commands change: "Be perfect as your heavenly Father is perfect" (Matthew 5:48); "You must walk no longer as the heathen walk" (Ephesians 4:17); "Grow by grace, even by the knowledge of our Lord and Savior Jesus Christ" (II Peter 3:18). I could go on and on, but you know already that this is true. What you may not have realized, however, is that every biblical exhortation, every demand for change, implies hope. God never demands of His children that which He has not provided power for them to do. We are not only *saved* by grace, but our sanctification (i.e., our continued growth and change from sin toward righteousness) as Christians also is the result of God's grace. As Paul told the Galatians, we did not begin the Christian life by grace . . . only to complete it by our own efforts. No, all is of grace. That means, therefore, that God Himself has provided the instructions and the power to live and grow according to them. The instructions—the goals, values, presuppositions, principles and practices—are found in the Scriptures; the power for Christians to live by them is provided by His Spirit. That is the good news about counseling that I bring today. And everywhere—throughout the country—and even elsewhere in this world, Christian ministers are awakening to the fact. And the same Book that says that God has provided what is needed for counseling says also that it has been provided for the equipping of ministers for the work of changing lives: "that the *man of God* (or," man from God," a term picked up from the Old Testament and used in the pastorals to refer to the pastor/teacher) may be adequate, thoroughly equipped." While every Christian should do counseling, it is to the minister that He has assigned the task as a life work.

No wonder there has been confusion! The wrong persons, using the wrong standards, have tried to do all sorts of wrong things without power.

But to be more specific, just what *does* the Bible provide? Let us look a bit more closely at II Timothy 3 to see.

In this fundamental passage concerning the Scriptures, it is important first to note that their twofold "*use*" or "purpose" is described *in terms of change*:

(1) Salvation: they are able to make one "wise unto salvation"; and
(2) for those who *are* saved, they provide four things:

(a) Teaching—they become the standard for faith and life; they show us all that God requires of us.

(b) Conviction—they show us how we have failed to measure up to those requirements in our lives. The original word is a legal term meaning more than to "accuse" but speaking of pursuing the case to its end *successfully*. The Scriptures show us our sin; they flatten us in repentance.

(c) Correction—the word means (literally) "to stand up straight again." While it is true that the Bible knocks us down, cuts and bruises, and rips up and tears down, it is equally true that this is done only to prepare us for its work of picking us up again and heading us in God's proper direction. The Scriptures also bind up and heal; they plant and build. By God's Spirit, who works in and through them, they not only help us put off sin, but also enable us to put on righteousness.

(d) Finally, they "train us in righteousness." It is not enough to quit the past ways, break old habits and stop sinning. If that is all that occurs, one will find himself soon reverting to past ways. He must not only quit past ways, but learn *as a way of life* to do the new ways (Ephesians 4:22ff.).

And what does all of this amount to? Change. We have been describing the process of *change*. Change in depth. Change as profound as one could imagine. Eternal change. And it is all found in God's Book, the Bible.

I urge you—consider the facts—and make the decision. Perhaps God is calling some of you to such a ministry of vital change. If so, answer in faith. With such powerful resources available why should counselees be short-changed?

Notations Abstracted From
Case Evaluation

Principles	Procedures

Principles	Procedures

EXERCISE

For the Student

1. Using the principles and procedures columns that precede these exercises, consider what you have learned from self-evaluation during counseling sessions this year. Make several entries in each column.

2. From these entries develop a personal progress paper of four to five pages in length in which you discuss thoughtfully your own immediate needs for development as a counselor.

For the Pastor

Using the principles and procedures columns that precede these exercises, enter any information that grows out of an evaluation of your counseling cases from the past six months. Go through the files you kept and evaluate your work; study problems unsolved (or partly solved) and what to do about them—all in the light of the Scriptures.

CHAPTER VI
HOW TO TAKE PASTORAL INITIATIVE

The pastor, unlike other counselors, does not need to wait until matters have grown so serious, so miserable and so complicated that persons *seek* his counsel. In God's providence, as shepherd, he may be used to detect early signs of difficulty in time to nip these in the bud. Often he is able to head off problems that otherwise, if they persisted, might lead to dire consequences. Yet it is this very great advantage that God has given him that many pastors neglect. They must learn that they may not do so and yet be counted good shepherds. The shepherd "watches" (i.e., is alert) for problems and anticipates needs.

Straightforwardness

How does a pastor suggest counseling to those whom he thinks need it but do not seek it on their own? The answer is by straightforwardly suggesting it to them. "But won't they be offended if he does?" you ask. The answer to that is not uniform. Some will, some won't; more will if he does it poorly, fewer will if he does it properly. Still fewer will (1) if they know (from other encounters) that he has a true pastoral concern for them, (2) if they recognize that he is not making unfounded accusations but is coming in a lovingly tentative fashion, and (3) if he approaches them in the spirit of gentleness mentioned in Galatians 6:1.[1]

What does straightforwardness mean? It means a bold, clear statement of one's purpose without hedging and without apology. Such an approach is appreciated by most persons, since they recognize that their pastor is thereby seeking to please his Lord and to help them. Those who do not appreciate it but become angry or are offended—assuming that the approach is made in the gentleness of loving pastoral concern—*thereby demonstrate their need* for counseling. The fact may be pointed out to them.

"But I really don't know how I would ever be able to approach a member of my congregation with a suggestion for counseling." Really, it is not all that difficult. The greatest difficulties that you have are:

---

[1]Cf. *The Big Umbrella*, pp. 19, 146ff.

1. Straightforwardness is uncomfortable to you because it is new; you have not walked in these shoes before. They may pinch at first, but when they are broken in, you will be much more comfortable wearing them. Remember, though, they will never be broken in if you keep them in the closet.

2. Straightforwardness is uncomfortable because you fear the possible consequences. Yet this is an unworthy motive for refraining. Fear will never be conquered by submission to it; it is one enemy that can be defeated only by a head-on attack. Since we know that love is greater than fear (indeed, love throws fear out![2]), the pastor's combined love for the God who called him to shepherd and for the sheep who is in need of help will prevail. After all, it is the love of God Himself that has been shed abroad in the believer's heart to enable him (like Christ) to risk his own life for others. Pastors, like their Lord, must be willing to lay down their lives for the sheep.

The Approach

But, precisely, how does one go about approaching a member *straightforwardly*? That question certainly deserves a straightforward reply.

Straightforwardness (or as the Bible calls it, "openness, boldness"[3]) consists at least of:

1. a plain statement of the facts,

2. a tentative statement about their apparent meaning,

3. an evident concern for the person confronted.

I could unpack each of these three concepts individually, but, instead, the simplest way for me to demonstrate and for you to understand what I have in mind is to sample a situation in which all of these elements appear:

Suppose that a pastor becomes concerned about Bill and Leslie, a middle-aged couple in his congregation. He has no hard facts that conclusively show that the marriage is crumbling, and yet from circumstantial evidence he cannot help but conclude that either there is something radically wrong or, if what seems to be a present combination of factors persists, the likelihood is that it will not be too long before serious trouble will arise. Here are the data that he has:

---

[2]1 John 4:18.
[3]Cf. Acts 4:29, 31 (the word is *parresia*); see also Joshua 1:6, 7, 9; Jeremiah 1:7-10, 17.

1. Between the two of them, one or the other seems to be out of the house (for meetings, etc.) every night in the week. He wonders: "Are they purposely avoiding one another or have they unwittingly allowed themselves to become caught up in the rat race?" Either way the problem of biblical priorities in scheduling seems acute.

2. He overheard their son tell his son, while the two were playing, about a "terrible fight" that "mommie and daddy had." But, he also knows that children tend to exaggerate such events, and yet . . . .

3. He has noticed that whenever Bill and Leslie joke in public, they use personal barbs. This may be only in fun, but it *could* stem from bitterness and resentment.

All of this information may add up to serious marital difficulties; on the other hand it may spell only potential trouble. Either way, he sees the need to do something—if not remedially then preventively. How would he take the initiative? Here is one possible way of proceeding:

1. Phone Bill (not Leslie; Bill is the head of the home. Phoning him stresses this fact and the responsibility that it entails) and make an appointment for him to drop by the study on his way home from work.

2. When he arrives, explain the concern, stating clearly all of the facts mentioned above.

3. But be sure to *explain tentatively*: "Bill, let me outline for you why I have asked you as the head of your home to come today (and by the way, I want you to know that I have not spoken to Leslie about this). There are three, and only three, factors that have come to my attention that may—or may not—add up to something significant. I don't know. I haven't tried to make a judgment, but because these matters could spell trouble I wanted to mention them to you to see what you had to say. Perhaps they can all be explained in an entirely different way from the possibilities that I fear. So let me tell you what this information is and then you can respond. First. . . .

"So, Bill, in conclusion, you can understand why I called you. If there is something that I can help you and Leslie to work out, just say so. If there is no problem I'd be happy to hear that. Whatever the situation, I want you to know that Jesus Christ and His Church are concerned about you."

In this example you can see that all three elements are operative. The nouthetic concern is evident (1) in the pastor's initiative itself (he could have said nothing), (2) in the manner in which he set up the appointment with the husband, and (3) in the language he used. The tentativeness of judgment both in approach and statement is so apparent throughout that it would be superfluous to say more about it. And yet, there is nothing uncertain about what the pastor has called his parishioner to discuss. He does not fudge: he is concerned, things look bad to him and he wants to help. The making of an appointment itself formalized his concern and prepared both for a substantive encounter (the member easily might have passed it off for a casual comment if the pastor had attempted to confront him in a less formal context). The plain and open statement of the facts from which the concern grew allowed the member to make an immediate evaluation concerning the sources and types of evidence that the pastor had in mind. He could see the reasoning behind the pastor's concern and, therefore, had no need to grow suspicious or to speculate about any unmentioned sources of information (gossip, slander, etc.).

There are few situations in which a similar approach (translated into the "language" of each particular situation, of course) will not be found to be satisfactory.

Your immediate response to this approach may be that it seems hard and that it demands courage that you are not sure that you have. Two things may be said in reply: (1) If you do not develop such pastoral courage after a reasonable length of time, perhaps you should question your calling.[4] It is instructive to notice that in his letters to Timothy Paul continually plucks this string of the need for pastoral courage. (2) If you do not prayerfully begin to do what you know God wants you to do (whether you think that you possess the courage or not), you will *never* develop the requisite courage for such pastoral counseling. Ordinarily, courage is given in the doing; as a pastor steps out in faith to obey the directives of God's Word, he too will find Paul's words true: "I can do all things through Him who strengthens me" (Philippians 4:13). Certainly such work is not easy, but God did not promise that the pastorate would be easy. He (as your Shepherd) promised only to supply your every need. A pastor will find, nevertheless, that in the long run it is much *easier* (as Spurgeon once said) to crush the egg than to kill the serpent. To deal pastorally with problems that are only getting under way, to anticipate and prevent others, rather than to be spending hours repairing seriously broken lives, is of the essence of the best pastoral care. This is what good pastoral visitation (or concerned inspection and care that leads to meeting needs) is all about. The pastor who learns to do the "hard" thing *now* will save both himself, and those sheep to whom he ministers, hours upon hours of agony and much more difficult problems later on.

---

[4]Cf. the discussion of "The Personality of the Counselor" in the *Christian Counselor's Manual*, pp. 18ff.

EXERCISE

For the Student

Interview five pastors and discuss their approaches in taking initiative with members of their congregations who need counseling. Jot down notes on what they say and report from these notes to the class.

For the Pastor

Make a list of all of the persons in your congregation who ought to be contacted about problems (or possible problems).

1. Lay out a schedule for contacting and dealing with each one (include time for prayer).

2. Determine *how* to broach the question in each instance.
3. Tell your elders what you plan to do and enlist their prayer and/or help.
4. Fearlessly (but cautiously) take the initiative—make the first phone call.

CHAPTER VII
PREMARITAL COUNSELING

It is unnecessary to rehearse the deplorable statistics on divorce, illegitimacy, etc. They change so rapidly, anyway, that by the time this book goes to print statistics probably would be outdated. Nor is it necessary to mention or describe the many homes loosely held together in deep unhappiness. True shepherds all too soon become well aware of such facts.[1] What is of importance here is to discuss some ways and means of preventing such difficulties among the members of God's flock. Every counselor who encounters the same marital problems again and again, most of which could have been avoided by providing proper instruction at an earlier point, before long wishes that he could do something to avert their occurrence. The pastor (as counselor as well as in his role of preacher and teacher) in God's providence is uniquely able to do precisely that. His position as one who also is a teacher and preacher of God's Word enables him to work preventively as well as remedially. He may warn and instruct from the pulpit, in classes and in private. People expect this and come for this sort of help. Once again, the fact, pointed out in previous books, that it is to the pastor that God has assigned the task of counseling as a life calling, comes to the fore.[2] It is only a pastoral ministry that is designed and equipped to provide full-orbed help.[3] It is essential, therefore, for pastors to recognize this fact and neither fail to engage in every sort of remedial work that is biblically warranted, nor to avail themselves fully of all of the many resources that God has provided to do so.

---

[1] A pastor who is not acutely aware of the extent of problems within his congregation should read Chapter Twenty of *The Christian Counselor's Manual.*

[2] *Ibid.*, pp. 11ff.

[3] Other counseling, which is wholly remedial and limited to one hour per week, cannot compare favorably with God's ordained counseling context. It is partial, truncated and single-sided. It places emphasis upon repair rather than upon avoidance, precaution and proper use in the first place.

Pre-pre-marital Counseling

Marriage counseling must be early, educational and preventive. It consists largely of the work of establishing and encouraging the growth of proper attitudes toward marriage based on scriptural principles. It also provides for guidance in decision-making and problem-solving in conjunction with contemplated and recently consummated marriages. The former is accomplished principally by effectively providing good models and conveying information concerning biblical principles to young people from the earliest time possible—certainly beginning long before they become involved in dating or have selected their life's partners. There are three principal areas in which this may be accomplished:

1. *The Home.* The key here is for pastors to *teach parents to teach.* Parents first teach, of course, by their own marriage. If they do not give priority to cultivating their marriage, all that they say will be undercut by what they do. First, then, the pastor does pre-pre-marital counseling by helping young couples to establish biblical marriage models. Models will enable children to see not only what to do to avoid sin, but also how to handle sin God's way.[4]

Parents too will teach directly and indirectly (out of the milieu) by word of mouth. Many do not know how to do so. In this also pastors may help parents to prepare their children for marriage. They may do so directly by instruction given in young couples' groups, by providing literature, etc., and indirectly by teaching teachers of parents how to help them.[5]

In all of it, parents must be shown that children do not exist for parents, but parents for children. A parent must recognize that God has given him children, not to cement his marriage together, nor even principally to nurture. Rather, God loaned children to him to prepare for a life of loving service for Himself. The parent's task is to nurture, train, discipline, prepare, etc., with *that* goal in mind. One major task is to lead children to faith in Christ. Another is to prepare them for Christian marriage.

2. *Church School.* Teachers should be alerted to the need to deal with matters concerning marriage. They should be instructed not only about *what* to emphasize, but *how* to do so effectively at each age level. Usually

---

[4]E.g., it is vital for children to hear parents *resolve* the problems that they have heard them express as differences in their presence. Often the altercation is public but the solution private. That means that parents provide children only a model of problem-raising but not of biblical problem-solving.

[5]Cf. *The Big Umbrella,* "Parental Sex Education," pp. 195ff., for one phase of this question. The facts of sex should be taught by the home; the many biblical principles of sex should be taught by the church. But the pastor often must help parents to assume their responsibilities in this matter.

teachers below the High School level do not consider it their task to teach about marriage. They must be shown otherwise. Instead, *all* teachers—from the cradle roll ("here is a picture of a mommy and daddy who love each other the way God wants them to") up—must be taught to consider premarital counseling one major emphasis of their instruction.[6]

3. *Youth Groups.* This ministry is vital. Courses on the home, dating etc., should be part of the youth program from the time that a youngster enters Junior High School. The selection of youth group leaders must be of prime concern to the pastor and elders. They should be good models themselves, carefully trained for the work and in close communication with the pastor about such questions *at all times.* The youngest couple in the church is not necessarily the best couple to select for this task. Surely one overriding qualification for such leaders is harmony and Christian vitality in their own marriage. The pastor frequently should discuss new ways and means for conveying Christian truth about marriage with these leaders.

Some of the basic questions that need to be dealt with in greater or lesser depth over the Junior High/High School/Post High years are:

1. Marriage "only in the Lord" (I Corinthians 7:39; II Corinthians 6:14ff.). Christians are explicitly forbidden to marry unbelievers; if they do so they will reap only a sad harvest of trouble. This must be spelled out in detail. A further implication of this fact is that youth groups and churches must provide a wide range of contacts among *Christian* young people.

2. The fundamentals of marriage mentioned in Chapter 4 of *Christian Living in the Home,* "Bible Basics About the Family." One reason why this textbook was written was to provide a basis for such study. If the book is used with a youth group, however, the section on single persons, Chapter 6, should be expanded. Today the very foundations of marriage and the family are under attack in schools and in society in general. If young people are to learn a Christian value system and Christian principles concerning marriage and the family, these must be taught by the church and the home. And they must be taught with new vigor since society today increasingly is becoming actively antithetical to Christian truth about the home.

3. The myth of "compatibility" and the dangers of "falling in love." All sinners are incompatible; only the grace of the Lord Jesus Christ can make them compatible. (Cf. *Christian Living in the Home,* pp. 63-66.)

---

[6]Incidentally, it is rare that teachers are made aware of the sorts of goals and objectives to seek to attain in teaching. Precisely articulated instructional aims, determined by the elders and (in written form) communicated to each new teacher, could help immensely. It is difficult to attain your goal when you aim at nothing!

4. The Hollywood/*Playboy* illusions about love must be shattered:
   (1) Love is not feeling first (as they allege).
   (2) Love is not a happening (as they allege). Love is a thinking attitude and activity to be kept under control (love is commanded in the Scriptures, showing clearly its volitional base).
   (3) Love is not getting, but giving.
   (4) Love demands effort and must grow.

5. Two Christians are ready for marriage *only* when they have demonstrated adequately in concrete situations that they (1) desire to and (2) are able to solve problems *together* God's way from His Word. In order to enable them to do this, young people must be taught how to use the Bible practically to meet life's problems.[7]

If these basic themes are held in front of young couples from the outset, (i.e., long before they become couples) together with the usual (vitally important, but here assumed) teaching concerning the need for prayer and Bible study in the home, many later tragedies will be averted.

Pre-marital Counseling

Unfortunately, it is necessary to urge pastors to *insist* upon premarital counseling. Not only do many couples assume that a pastor automatically will perform a wedding upon request, but some pastors also act as if this were so. Premarital counseling takes time; so it is easy for a pastor to rationalize his failure to provide it by the ready acceptance of all sorts of excuses.

Let it be said from the outset that while marriage is divinely ordained, the form for weddings and the need for a minister to perform them are not. The commission to conduct a wedding ceremony does not come from God as a part of the duty of a minister. When he participates, he does so as his own personal decision for which he alone is responsible before God. The decision as to whether or not he will conduct a worship service at which two persons solemnize marriage vows before God in all cases is his. No minister can be forced against his conscience to do so. No congregation, no board of elders,[8] no presbytery, no denomination can demand this of him. He is the one who ultimately is responsible to God for the decision. Therefore, it

---

[7] Hopefully, a volume for instruction of this sort will be made available in the next year or two.

[8] However, although they cannot require him to perform a wedding, the elders and presbytery may exercise a negative control over this decision-making power, for they (together with him) are responsible for the conduct of worship. They may, of course, exhort him about such matters.

behooves him to act cautiously in participating in so vital a service. In properly assuming this responsibility, almost without exception, he will wish to counsel with every couple in whose wedding he participates. Here is his opportunity to make at least one small contribution toward arresting the moral decay of the home and toward guiding one future family toward those God-given channels that run between the reefs and shoals upon which so many marriages have been shattered. And, it is just because he is *not* commanded to perform weddings that the pastor may insist upon premarital counseling.[9]

Insist upon premarital counseling, I say. Why? Because so often today couples come to the pastor's office totally ignorant of the principles of Christian family life and entirely inexperienced in its pursuit. And on top of that, they come to discuss the wedding rather than the marriage. They are caught up in problems concerning the ceremony that initiates the marriage, not in the life that must be considered its object..

If objections are raised, the pastor may tactfully, but firmly, ask two questions in return:

1. How much time have you spent planning the wedding and preparing for it? The answer (if seriously considered) usually will yield a surprisingly substantial number of hours. Whereupon, the pastor may further inquire: Do you not think that at least an equal number of hours ought to be spent in discussion and planning for the marriage itself?

2. Which, after all, is more important: the wedding (that will last for less than an hour) or the marriage (that God says must last for life)?

Only on the rarest occasions, when, for instance, the pastor knows that someone else already has given adequate counsel, should he agree to officiate in a wedding that was not preceded by premarital counseling. In this day of unprecedented pressures, false teaching, and superficial idealism it should be his vital concern to make every attempt to launch this marriage successfully to the honor of Christ. After all, two young persons who refuse the offer of premarital counseling in a day like this without adequate reason may thereby give indication of the very sort of attitudes that so frequently lead to disaster in marriage. The attitude that "we know it all; no one else need bother to give us any instruction, so thanks anyway," can hardly help but remind one of Proverbs 16:18: "Pride goes before destruction and a haughty spirit before a fall." The wise pastor will give warning in accord with I Corinthians 10:12, "Let him who thinks that he stands take heed lest he fall," and will seek to persuade them to enter into

---

[9]Since God does not require him to perform marriages, he may set the terms on which he does.

counseling. He would be unwise to participate in their wedding otherwise. [10]
If he holds before them the high ideal of Ephesians 5, that a Christian
marriage should reflect the marriage of Christ to His bride, the church, he
should be able to point out the seriousness and solemnity of the estate into
which they are planning to enter. No one can be instructed too often, nor
can he properly afford to reject any and all assistance that may be offered to
help him to fulfil that high calling.

Having established this the pastor may outline what he has in mind. He
may say something like the following (depending upon the particulars of
the marital counseling program that he devised):

"We shall meet on at least three occasions prior to the marriage, and at
least three times following the marriage. Of course we shall attempt to deal
with problems that are uncovered, during those sessions, but if necessary
additional sessions may need to be scheduled."

The three basic premarital counseling sessions have in view three major
considerations: (1) *Qualifying the Counselees for Marriage;* (2) *Uncovering
and Handling Problems*; (3) *Discussion of Sexual Matters and the
Wedding Ceremony.*

The Qualifying Session

The pastor must make it clear from the outset that his agreement to
participate in the marriage will be conditioned upon what is discovered
during the initial session or sessions of premarital counseling. To enter into
such sessions must not be considered tantamount to such agreement. The
very first concern of premarital counseling will be to qualify the parties for
marriage. This should be made known from the start. One way to do so is to
speak plainly of the first session as a "Qualifying Session."

There are three basic qualifying questions which should be asked
explicitly and discussed as thoroughly as is necessary to arrive at a
satisfactory explanation. They are:

1. Are there any reasons why there may be a question regarding the
propriety of this marriage?

Here the concern is to ferret out any matters that possibly could lead to a
fraudulent situation: unknown sterility on the part of one or the other
party, the fathering or mothering of illegitimate children, an abortion, a
crime, etc. There is also the opportunity to express a concern for dealing

---

[10]A pastor should have discussed his policies with his board of elders *before* he is faced with
such a refusal. He will be wise to seek their backing in all such matters since it could be crucial
to his ministry and to the welfare of the congregation.

with guilt over premarital sex and possible pregnancy.[11]("Are there any sinful sexual relationships that need to be cleared up before we go on?") Sexual matters, not so handled, will cause difficulties such as suspicion, continuing guilt, or a bad sexual relationship later on. The occurrence of these sorts of problems in the Christian community, unfortunately, is growing more (not less) frequent. The session affords opportunity to divulge such information in a context that allows for forgiveness and healing. Fear to tell the truth combined with underlying guilt often plagues one or both partners. The opportunity to reveal such information before someone who could help pick up the pieces is often most welcome. Pastors, who care, will give opportunity ("Fred, is there anything that has ever happened in your life that you have been afraid to tell Penelope, but that you feel guilty about and that you know you *should* tell her?").

Depending upon the information revealed, and the immediate response to it, the pastor may suggest postponement of the wedding (or at least of the next regular premarital counseling sessions) until a point at which the matter can be set to rest before God and all others who are concerned. Special counseling sessions directed at helping the couple to come to grips with the issue and to make a resolution of it that pleases God and one another may intervene.

2. Have there been any previous marriages?

More and more today the pastor will encounter divorced persons seeking remarriage. Many, if not most of these divorces, he will discover, were not obtained on biblical grounds (adultery; desertion of a believer by an unbeliever[12]). Even when grounds may have been biblical, the manner in which the issues involved were handled (exercise of church discipline, attitudes, attempts at reconciliation, etc.) may not have been proper.[13] *Before proceeding to perform any second marriage* (except where the former one was broken by death) *be sure that all matters in the past have been settled biblically.* In most cases, the pastor will find that there are still loose ends that must be tied up biblically. He must not move ahead until these have been settled. He must warn, urge and encourage. I Corinthians 7:27,28 clearly speaks of remarriage. Paul here writes of a man properly

---

[11]If the girl is pregnant, that sin must be dealt with. But, having done so, it is still possible to qualify them for marriage. Pregnancy does not always demand marriage. When, let us say, the boy is an unbeliever it is not proper to advise the girl to commit further sin by entering into marriage with an unbeliever.

[12]For a thorough discussion of the question of divorce, see John Murray, *Divorce* (Philadelphia: Presbyterian & Reformed Publishing Co., 1961); Guy Duty, *Divorce and Remarriage* (Minneapolis: Bethany Fellowship, 1967). Duty's book contains valuable information.

[13]Cf. *The Christian Counselor's Manual*, pp. 60-62.

"loosed from a wife" (one of the expressions used for divorce) remarrying without sin. While his point is to say that even though in a time of distress and persecution (v. 26), when it is better to remain single if one has the gift of continence, he does not sin if he marries, it is important to note that this is true not only for those who have never been married before, but (he says) even of those who have been divorced. It is wrong, therefore, for a pastor to counsel that there is no case in which remarriage is possible. To hold to such a position is to try to be more pious than Paul. Indeed, in I Corinthians 6:9-11 he assures us that one can be washed and entirely cleansed, *even of adultery.* When this has happened, what God has cleansed, no man has the right to call unclean.

On the one hand, therefore, it is essential not to qualify those whom God disqualifies because of previous marital obligations. Fundamentally they are those who have not done *all* that the Scriptures require in order to put the past entirely into the past by reconciliation, church discipline, or whatever obligations yet remain. But when, according to God's Word, there is an official statement on the minute book of the board of a disciplining Bible-believing congregation to the effect that the party (or parties) concerned has done all required to satisfy God and man and that the matter is closed, qualifying him (or her) for remarriage, no evangelical pastor should refuse to remarry the person. On the other hand, no minister *on his own* should undertake to determine the matter; it must be resolved by the church, acting officially in Christ's name. But when a true Church of Jesus Christ acts, that decision must be respected. It is not only presumptuous not to do so but tragic. Few enough congregations do their duty. Let us not discourage them by disregarding their decisions when they *have* made them. The pastor is not (himself) guilty if, *unknown to him,* wrong has been perpetrated by the court of Christ's Church; the guilt for any wrong falls rather upon the board of elders who adjudicated the matter.[14] If there is reasonable evidence that this board attempted to handle the matter scripturally, the pastor dare not take it upon himself to disregard the authority of Christ duly exercised by His Church. However, apart from an official study and pronouncement of the Church to this effect no pastor should proceed to perform a wedding involving a divorced person. The

---

[14]Of course, the pastor may not ignore a *known* wrong; he must call any such wrong to the attention of the body of elders who knowingly or unknowingly proceeded in a wrong manner. Yet when he has no knowledge of the facts or any wrongdoing concerning a matter that has been settled by a congregation that exercises scriptural church discipline, the pastor of another congregation has no right to reopen a subject that has been declared closed. He does not need to know all of the details; he has no right to retry the case personally. Upon receipt of such word from the clerk of the board of elders he should cease making further inquiries.

pronouncement is for the protection of all. This, again, may require postponement of marriage and the pursuit of the matter by the Church (a previously attended one or his own) until fully settled. A holy future marriage cannot be built upon a yet unclean past. Indeed, it is for the welfare and protection of all that these matters should be fully settled before proceeding further. Haste cannot be countenanced.[15] Careless handling of the obligations of one's past, and unwillingness to take the time to put all in order, should (in itself) be a warning to the other party that he (or she) is entering into a marriage that without change cannot turn out satisfactorily. It also may reveal attitudes that need to be dealt with before it is possible to qualify one for marriage.

3. Are you both saved?

This third question, of course, is the most basic of all. Yet, surprisingly, there are many views among conservatives about whom they may rightly advise to marry. There are three possible relationships to consider.

1. Two believers

2. Two unbelievers

3. A believer and an unbeliever

Nearly all conservative pastors are agreed that they cannot in good conscience before God aid and abet a believer to sin by helping him to violate God's commandment to marry "only in the Lord."[16] Therefore, they refuse to marry a believer and an unbeliever. In this refusal they are correct. However, there is wide divergence about how to qualify two believers or two unbelievers.

Consider first, relationship number 1: The proposed marriage of two believers. While there is every reason to believe that two believers can make a satisfactory marriage and overcome all problems that stand in their ways because they possess the Scriptures and benefit from the power of God's Spirit working within,[17] nevertheless they are neither qualified nor fit for marriage at all times and under every and any circumstance simply by virtue of their salvation as we have seen already in the discussion of the two previous questions. For any number of valid reasons a pastor might (1) refuse to marry two Christians who are not qualified for marriage because

---

[15]Indeed, willingness to do whatever is necessary to satisfy God in such matters is one clear mark of genuineness. Unwillingness may lead to early detection of the opposite spirit.

[16]I Corinthians 7:39; cf. also II Corinthians 6:14 ff.; Ezra 10. But see *infra* about the evangelism of unbelievers who seek marriage.

[17]Cf. *Christian Living in the Home*, Chapter 5.

of attitude toward God and others and/or because of unresolved problems in their lives; (2) strongly advise a couple against marriage *now*, and/or might refuse to participate since he personally cannot do so in faith (cf. Romans 14:23). While no pastor should refuse to marry two Christians except for the gravest reasons, he must recognize that a Christian profession *alone* does not qualify them for marriage.

Let us now turn to relationship number 2: The contemplated marriage of two unbelievers. Here conservative pastors are widely divided over the practical question. There is little or no disagreement over the fact that the marriage of unbelievers to one another is proper, desirable and recognized by God. Is that a satisfactory basis, however, for the participation of a Christian minister in the wedding ceremony? Some say "yes." They maintain that since the practice is proper, the minister's participation is also. Others distinguish between the minister as an agent of the state in performing marriages and an agent of Jesus Christ in ministering the Word, and insist that it is purely as the former that he officiates in such cases.

Against these views, several things may be said. First, the Christian minister is requested to perform the wedding *as a minister* and *not merely as an agent of the state*. (When have you *ever* known anyone to request that you act only in the latter capacity?) That is why his services—rather than those of a justice of the peace—were sought. Because of superstition, sentimentality, or whatever, the church wedding frequently is chosen over the purely civil one. Moreover, the pastor may be able to make precise theoretical distinctions in his own mind, but the persons present at the ceremony will not. To think that a minister conducting a wedding ceremony can adequately convey to participants or to the assembled gathering that he is acting solely as an agent of the state in a merely civil capacity is (to say the very best) self-deceptive.

But of greater importance is the fact that a Christian wedding—with vows taken before God, with the reading of scriptural portions that refer to Christians only, exhortations that pertain to believers alone, the pronouncing of the blessing of the triune God upon the man and his wife together with His benediction—all of this constitutes far more than a civil ceremony! Indeed, it constitutes so much more that it may be said to be nothing less than a Christian worship service. It is the performance of a sham, or of a mock Christian wedding, by persons who are not Christians. When a Christian minister assists non-Christians in taking vows before a God whom they do not know, he participates in hypocrisy and encourages and aids them in the perpetration of a lie. And, as a final thought, it is necessary to ask: why should a Christian minister care to function merely as an agent of the state anyway—particularly when he runs such a great risk of being misunderstood?

What does one do when he finds that the persons who have come to the first session do not qualify? First, he tells them so in loving, clear terms and explains why. Whenever there is reason to do so, he holds forth realistic hope. ("Let's meet several times and discuss the gospel.") That is to say, the unsaved persons (or person) may be evangelized. Upon a genuine profession of faith followed by acceptance into the membership of a disciplining church, the qualifications for marriage change. Moreover, a Christian—unqualified because of past matters yet unsettled—may by God's grace deal with these and thus remove his disqualifications.

Ministers who turn unsaved persons away with no attempt to evangelize them miss an important opportunity. At this crucial turning point in life, it is sometimes true that God in His providence chooses to work powerfully to bring about the conversion of His elect people and to restore wayfaring Christians through repentance.[18] The opportunities for such ministry must not be lost. Disqualified persons ought not to be simply turned away. Postponements, opportunity to counsel fully about what stands in the way, aid in assisting the prospective man and wife in clearing up past problems, ought to be suggested and pursued.

Beware of Rice Christians

But—and this must be marked well—the pastor ever must be on guard for "rice Christians." The so-called rice Christian was named this because on the foreign field he made a pseudo profession of faith merely in order to receive the bag of rice that the missionary of former days handed out. Fortunately contemporary missionaries have largely abandoned the dangerous practice. But the shower of rice that follows a church wedding is so dearly prized by some that they too will make a false profession of faith in order to receive it. Such premarital counselees might just as appropriately bear the name. Christians too may follow various scriptural directions mechanically (without genuine repentance) as a gimmick or as a technique in order to acquire the same end.[19]

---

[18]People contemplating marriage and its responsibilities often think more basically than at other times. They are forced to do so by the necessity to grapple with the large changes that are impending. It is not that this somehow makes one more susceptible to the gospel; spiritually a dead man cannot believe unless given life by the Spirit of God. However, God often chooses to use such situations to bring about His sovereign purposes of redemption and He calls upon us to be wise not only in the manner in which we present the gospel, but also in seizing opportunities for doing so (Colossians 4:5, 6).

[19]Cf. *The Christian Counselor's Manual*, pp. 98, 99, 204, 205.

How can the problem of the rice counselee be avoided? Well, one can never wholly avoid the problem since sinners the world over will act true to form. Moreover the counselor cannot judge motives: Man looks on the outward appearance; only God can look on the heart. However, strong warnings about the problem, coupled with careful probing, and the examination of the fruit that is appropriate to repentance over some time, combine to give the pastor some assurance about the legitimacy of one's profession. It is always a good policy to discuss this problem of rice-Christianity thoroughly as well as to probe deeply. But in the end, unless there is strong external evidence to the contrary, an intelligent profession of faith followed by evidence of some change of life must be accepted.

Where the evidence causes reasonable doubt, the pastor should honestly assert his reasons for doubt and should discuss these in depth with both parties. Should this doubt not be cleared up in that discussion, he would be wise to urge the believing party to postpone any plans for marriage until such time as these doubtful matters have been dealt with. In cases where the pastor is uncertain then he may advise delay.

However, since it is necessary for the new convert to make a credible profession of faith as he unites with the visible church, the issue again is not left solely to the judgment of the pastor; he will be assisted in this matter by the combined judgment of his board of elders.[20]

It is apparent, then, that there are a number of circumstances in which the pastor will be called upon to exercise discretion, faithfulness and courage in the pursuit of even so seemingly simple a matter as agreeing upon the performance of a wedding ceremony. Increasingly in our day it is becoming more evident that there are ministers without the God-given capacity to withstand the many pressures that will be exerted upon them. They should carefully reexamine their call to the ministry. Struggles and tensions are not going to lessen. Too many men have been encouraged to enter the pastorate who have never seriously considered exhortations like the following:

1. "Be strong in the grace that is in Christ Jesus" (II Timothy 2:1).
2. "Suffer hardship with me, as a good soldier of Christ Jesus" (II Timothy 2:3).
3. "...kindle afresh the gift of God that is in you...for God has not given us a spirit of timidity, but of power and love and discipline" (II Timothy 1:6,7).

---

[20]The pastor who will not marry unbelievers will, of course, not perform a marriage ceremony for new converts until they make a profession of faith and are received into the membership of the church.

4. "These things speak and exhort and reprove with full authority. Let no one disregard you" (Titus 2:15).

The church cannot survive another generation of weak, fearful, compromising ministers who will continue to foster the weaknesses that could end in her retrogression into another period comparable to the dark ages. She needs men who not only will preach the truth of the Scriptures and all of the doctrines contained in them (thankfully, there seems to be a resurgence of concern for this), but men who (as fearlessly as they preach) also will *apply* that truth in the hard concrete situations of life to which it is directed. It is one thing to win the Lord's battles *verbally* from the pulpit; it is another to win them *experientially* in the everyday affairs of pastoral work. Sadly, there are all too few who exhibit the courage to exercise church discipline, to say "no" in practical matters of judgment and to evangelize in counseling when they know (all too well) that this is exactly what is needed by the persons to whom they speak. Instead, there are all too many who rationalize, and in the name of love, sympathy, compassion, etc., compromise God's truth in actual practice. There is too much of the fear of men. The Church needs men who fear God more and, therefore, fear men less. Only such pastors can remain faithful to Him and effectively minister the Word in love both to saved and unsaved sinners.

Counseling that courageously comes to grips with the problems of individuals, and that dares to stand firmly on God's truth in dealing with them must increase, or the claims that are made in the pulpit will fall on deaf ears. Preaching always must be backed up by loving, fearless application to become effective. It is precisely at such points as in qualifying persons for marriage that the difference between true and false Christianity is seen. It is here that others recognize that Christianity is not mere words, but that it *makes a difference* in life. Care must be exercised neither to refuse what God permits nor to permit what God refuses. The decision is not always easy, but that is why God has called pastors to be leaders of His flock in helping the sheep to walk in the right pathways as they are described in His Word.

Outlining the Basics

Whenever a couple has been qualified for marriage—at the conclusion of the first session or following subsequent *ad hoc* sessions—they are ready for the next step in premarital counseling: a discussion of the basics of marriage and family living. Such a discussion, thoroughly outlining the fundamental scriptural principles that are pertinent, followed by later "in depth" discussions of any of these that raises particular problems that must be handled before marriage, is vital.

Because I advise that the next step that should be taken is to hand out a book to be studied (preferably one that contains exercises to be done, so that you may be reasonably sure that they have given adequate study to these principles) and because I have published such a text, I shall not go into the sort of content that is necessary for such a study.[21] This book may be assigned for use following the session at which the couple is qualified and prior to the next session. The pastor may suggest that the chapters be read by both (possibly together) and then discussed by them in terms of the applications to their lives that they consider to be most pertinent. He may request that they write down, and bring to the next session, all questions, problem areas, and any other matters that this study has brought to light. Usually these two homework assignments are sufficient.[22]

The Problem Session

All matters raised by the reading assignment should be considered first. It is important to give adequate time to the discussion of any questions that the couple consider important—even if it means that it will be necessary as a result to schedule an additional session or two.

During this session, or at a special one that follows, above all other matters, the counselor should cover the following: (1) future family relationships; (2) problem-solving from the Word of God; (3) communication. *Christian Living in the Home* provides sufficient data for triggering the discussion of each of these. A discussion of future family relationships can grow naturally out of inquiries about the material on pp. 51-56. Biblical problem-solving may emerge as an upshot of data on pp. 64-66. Communication is treated in an entire chapter (pp. 25-41). In stressing these three areas, there are particular emphases which need to be made concerning each.

(1) *Future Family Relationships*

Not only should the pastor emphasize the need to make a break with the counselees' parental homes, but he must be careful to note that one of the principal reasons for the break is that marriage brings into being a new decision-making unit that is directly responsible to God, and that in this

---

[21]*Christian Living in the Home* is brief, but contains basic materials and exercises. If it is not used, I suggest that the pastor find a book that covers roughly the same ground. Whatever text he uses, the pastor should see to it that the church budget provides for the purchase of a substantial number of books for giving away in counseling and evangelism. Since my text does not contain information concerning finances or church fellowship the pastor may wish to prepare to discuss these verbally when using the book.

[22]The counselor, however, should stress the importance of doing these assignments well.

unit the husband and wife are responsible also to put each other first before any other human beings.[23]

Again, it will be important to show the need for this break with former parental authority to be a *clean* break, Christian in every way. Frequently marriages begin with clouds hanging heavily over the young couple because the break with one or both of the families was not effected properly. *This must not be so.* Any marriage today has enough other pressures exerted upon it that it can ill afford to have to bear up under these strong emotional strains as well. Therefore, the pastor should probe carefully and fully to be sure that all difficulties or conflicts with parents may be uncovered and resolved *before* the wedding.

Losing a child—even in marriage—can be a cause of grief for one or more parents, especially if either has attempted (sinfully) to find the satisfactions in a relationship to the child that properly can be found only in a spouse. Add to this the normal emotion that marriage occasions and you can have a highly explosive situation. The pastor may find that he must send one or both of the young people back to seek forgiveness from parents for words spoken in anger or haste. He may need to hold additional sessions bringing together parents and children to help heal wounds and to facilitate reconciliation. But, whatever he does, he must do everything that is scripturally legitimate to bring about a resolution of any outstanding problems between the generations.

Above all, the children must enter into the marriage with a clear conscience, knowing that they have done all that they should before God and their parents to reach a biblical resolution to every problem. Otherwise, they will jeopardize their marriage from the outset. The twin burdens of God's disfavor and parental disfavor are too heavy to expect any fresh marriage to bear. The pastor, then, must help them to enter into a marriage that is truly fresh, free from such impediments, and bright with the favor of all. There are few things that a pastor can do to counter the tide of divorce that are as vital as this. The goal must be to carry nothing detrimental from the past into the future marriage.

In conjunction with this purpose, the pastor might mention his intention to set up postmarital counseling sessions (see *infra*) during which, among other things, he will want to see that a good Christian relationship with parents is being maintained and growing.

---

[23]Cf. Genesis 2:24.

(2) Biblical Problem-solving

Little can be said about this matter, although much *needs* to be said.[24]
Here, I should like to make but one point that the pastor also must
communicate with clarity and force: *A Christian marriage will succeed and
prosper only if the partners in that marriage are willing and able to solve
every problem together from the Bible*. This point should be stressed and
the pastor may wish to develop a brief lecture of his own on how to go
about doing this. He may wish to make an appointment for an elder to visit
in the home soon after the honeymoon to give such instruction, and/or he
may wish to develop and hand out literature to assist.[25]

(3) Christian Communication

Since I have devoted a full chapter to the subject in *Christian Living in
the Home* I shall say little here about Christian communication. Probably
the stress in this discussion should fall on free and open communication
and the need for avoiding a communication breakdown. Lines are kept
open when (a) neither party blows up or clams up, (b) both regularly discuss
their problems together in a systematic way, and (c) seek to solve them
together from the Scriptures. The conference table concept is probably
most useful for a young couple to develop from the beginning of their
marriage. Material on this is available in several places.[26] If either party
senses the beginning of a communication failure that is not being overcome
by joint effort, he should seek help quickly. The pastor should emphasize
his availability for such purposes. ("Call right away. It is easier for *everyone*
when the quicksand is only up to the ankle. It is tough when all that the
counselor can get hold of is an ear!")

At the conclusion of the problem session, the pastor may wish to set up
additional sessions (1) to handle matters for which he did not find time
previously, (2) to delve further into difficulties encountered, etc. If the
session goes swimmingly, and he is ready to proceed to the final session (or
if the counseling has proceeded through additional sessions to this point)
the pastor may wish to assign homework such as the following to be completed in preparation for the final session. Homework: (1) Optional: take

---

[24]Hopefully, at a later date a book on *The Practical Use of the Scriptures* designed to meet
such a need as this may be forthcoming.

[25]See the previous footnote. There are books that have sections which may be useful for this
purpose, but if the pastor uses a book that is not simple, informative and practical he may
discourage rather than help.

[26]*The Christian Counselor's Manual*, pp. 16, 321ff.; *The Big Umbrella*, 159-173 (this
chapter may be found useful to give to certain counselees, or even to young married couples as
post marital reading to help them to recognize something about the purpose and process of
counseling).

the *Sex Knowledge Inventory* in the next room before you leave today;[27]
(2) Make a list of ideas and questions about the wedding.

The Final Session

The final session should begin with a cleanup of any unfinished business
and then should proceed rapidly to two subject areas: (1) The Christian
View of Sexuality in Marriage; (2) The Wedding Ceremony.

(1) *Sexuality*

Since I have outlined fully the biblical data that need to be discussed in
The Christian Counselor's Manual (pp. 391-399), I shall not repeat these
here. I urge any who are interested, to reread that section prior to the final
session (particularly the seven principles on p. 392).[28]

If the couple have taken the Sex Knowledge Inventory, they will want to
know the results. Usually, the pastor will reassure them that they came out
in about the same way that most couples do (most do, of course!). Then, he
may wish to mention any item or items that seemed to need further
attention. However, if serious lack of knowledge or strange attitudes were
noted, the pastor will wish to say so and focus upon these. He may find,
however, that embarrassment or other extraneous difficulties led to the
failure and may want to suggest this possibility. Serious lack of knowledge
may lead the pastor to recommend a book (or books) on sexual functioning
and/or techniques.[29] In some cases he will wish to recommend a discussion
with a physician. He will *always* do so, for instance, when questions arise
about the kind of birth control measures to use. Beyond expressing
disapproval of any method that utilizes the abortive day-after-the-night-
before principle, he will probably wish to relegate the matter of
methodology to a physician.

---

[27]The S.K.I. is a test designed to determine knowledge and attitudes toward sex. When used
judicially by the pastor (1) according to his own preferences and (2) *without placing too much
weight* upon its validity or findings, it can give certain insights into possible problems and can
afford a good jumping-off point for the discussion of sex at the final session. The S.K.I. may be
obtained from Family Life Publications, P. O. Box 427, Saluda, N. C., 28773.

[28]The pastor may wish to read over these in the session, make additional comments and
clear up any misunderstandings. These major principles are reprinted in the appendix to a
useful booklet by Harry McGee, M.D., *Scripture, Sex and Satisfaction* (Presbyterian &
Reformed Publishing Co: Nutley, 1975). This pamphlet is designed for use as a counseling
handout in marital and premarital counseling.

[29]Few of these exist from a Christian perspective. He will probably want to qualify his
recommendation and for some spell out clearly *what* he does and does not endorse in the
book. Counselors still run into some counselees who are virtually totally ignorant of proper
sexual information. The pastor should have copies of such books on hand to lend to couples
contemplating marriage.

(2) *The Wedding Ceremony*

I wish to reserve a discussion of the elements, the conduct, and the form of wedding ceremonies until a later point in a subsequent volume in this series. Therefore, I shall say nothing more about this matter at this point except to note that the discussion in this final session should focus on the meaning and the form of the wedding (and a discussion of the reception must not be omitted. The couple should be charged to be sure that this *also* is Christian; so frequently a wonderful service has been grossly marred by what follows). The date for the rehearsal should be set at this time (more must be said about this also in the proper place).

For homework, the pastor may wish to assign the following.

1. Set the dates for postmarital counseling (see infra):
   a. One week after the honeymoon an elder comes for supper. He explains family devotions, and demonstrates how to conduct family worship. This (1) shows the concern of Christ's church for their home, (2) gives the couple an elder as a special friend and helper to whom they can turn when they need to, (3) leads the elder to take a special interest in them during days to come, (4) gives the wife an opportunity to try out her culinary arts while teaching the new couple to show hospitality.
   b. Two weeks to one month after the marriage the pastor calls. The couple is to have kept a list of all problems that they wish to discuss during the interim. Handing out a homework book (or some other prepared form) in which to keep the list always helps to remind the couple to do their work. The elder, at his visit, also may issue a reminder. Together, the pastor discusses with them the items on the list in the light of the Scriptures. Additional counseling sessions may be scheduled if needed. A six-month checkup may be scheduled if necessary.
   c. One year after the marriage (as close to the anniversary as possible) the pastor returns. At this time he may reread the vows and discuss the marriage.

2. Set the dates for the rehearsal and for the wedding.

Note on Postmarital Counseling

The setting of dates for postmarital counseling sessions (whenever possible) may turn out to be the most important part of the counseling program. During premarital counseling, a young couple with stars in their eyes, and who have not yet experienced the problems that inevitably will come, may tend to hear selectively only what they want to hear. One year, six months, or even one month later the stars may have moved up over their heads.

If this program for marriage counseling sounds too ambitious, remember its preventive nature.[30] It is much better in every way to spend time beforehand than to devote weeks later on to repairing what need never have broken down.[31]

EXERCISE

For the Student

Interview ten persons who had premarital counseling to discover what, if any, help they were given. Jot down ideas below. Be prepared to report useful ideas or warnings to the class.

---

[30]Of course, in practice, not every item in the program needs to be covered as thoroughly for every marriage couple. Knowledge, commitments and ability to solve problems differ. The counselor will want to be sure about his own reasons when he omits any items. He must avoid making rationalizations in order to save time and effort, etc.

[31]Incidentally, pastors should clear Saturdays during the latter part of May and early June since this a favorite time for weddings.

For the Pastor

1. Interview a number of married persons in your congregation to determine (1) what they would like to have been told in premarital counseling but were not, (2) what they were told that they have found most useful, (3) what they were advised that was harmful.

2. Discuss premarital counseling with your couples' group (its values, its goals, its problems, etc.). Ask for suggestions.

CHAPTER VIII
CARE IN COUNSELING WOMEN

During the last few years, a disturbing number of instances in which Bible-believing ministers have become sinfully involved with female counselees have come to attention. Fortunately, to date, none of these ministers was using nouthetic counseling. While nouthetic principles and procedures themselves help the counselor to avoid many of the hazards into which other approaches lead a counselor,[1] no approach in and of itself can safeguard the man who will allow himself to become involved.

Present within the counselor is the potential for committing all sorts of sin. David ever stands as a sturdy reminder of this. Perhaps, however, the warning found in Galatians 6:1 is most pertinent.[2] In this verse, Paul, speaking to well-meaning persons, urges them to seek the proper ends and to use correct means in order to avoid temptation in counseling. He warns, "Look at yourself, so that you may not be tempted as well." In view of this warning, it should not be thought incredible by any counselor that true concerns could develop into sinful ones. Counselors, periodically, should read I Corinthians 10:12.

That women, dissatisfied with their own husbands, through fantasizing about how wonderful it would be to have the interest of a marvelous Christian like pastor so-and-so, do "fall in love" with him should not be doubted by any fledgling minister. Too many pastors (and female counselees) testify to the fact for it to be ignored. And that they can become a serious attraction to him is also the testimony of many pastors, as well as part of the message of Galatians 6:1.

If these facts are true, what can be done to avoid all such problems? The following advice may help:

---

[1] For instance, some approaches invite disaster by their insistence on one-to-one sessions, the stress upon feeling, their views that sexual drives underlie most problems, and especially their use of transference ("tell me how you feel about me").

[2] The passage refers to temptation in counseling in general, not only to sexual temptation. A drowning person can be dangerous and can pull his would-be rescuer under the water. The lifeguard must handle the situation correctly or both may drown. (I am indebted to David Cummings for this very apt analogy.)

1. *Always* try to have husbands present whenever they will come.

2. *Never* counsel a woman alone whom you in any way even suspect to have any improper interest in you. Instead, in such cases *always* invite an elder to be present as a team counselor. (No explanations for this are necessary. If questions are asked, simply state that this is a matter of counseling policy.)

3. If for some reason (e.g., the elder couldn't show up) such a single woman or a wife must be counseled alone, be sure that your secretary (even if you have to engage a temporary one for such occasions) is in the reception room next door. If the rooms of your church are not properly laid out for such an arrangement, you may have to think out a new arrangement for such situations, such as doing counseling in another room of the church that has a connecting room in which the secretary may work during the hour. Always counsel at the church study, never in the counselee's own home.

4. Handle the subject matter of counseling carefully. When sexual issues *must* be discussed, it will be necessary to have the husband, another minister, or an elder present in most instances. *How* the discussion is carried on is altogether important. This is the one time to wear a white-coated, clinical manner in counseling. Say what must be said factually, without an emotionally laden vocabulary and/or examples. Discourage any discussion of unnecessary details. Immediately end any session in which the discussion is beginning to wander afield.

5. Avoid all personal references (to clothes, hair styles, etc.). Such references easily can be misinterpreted as romantic or sexual advances. Follow I Timothy 5:2 scrupulously.

6. Remember Joseph and Potiphar's wife. Ask God regularly to preserve you from such a trial.

Meeting A Proposition

Should a woman make an outright proposition or sexual proposal to you, there is only one thing to do. You must know what to do beforehand and be prepared to do it. Do not hesitate—call in the secretary and tell her what has happened, then phone an elder in the church immediately, tell him what has happened, and as soon as possible together with him speak to the woman and attempt to straighten the matter out once and for all.[3] Do not spread the fact to others; do not keep it to yourself. She needs help; you need protection. Both goals must be sought conjointly. You should be concerned about securing adequate witnesses whenever it is possible that

[3]In the event that an elder cannot be reached, phone your wife, another pastor or some other responsible party.

accusations may be made (cf. I Timothy 5:19-20).[4] Your wife should be notified by you *and* by the elder (or secretary).

The following incident occurred. A pastor received a late evening phone call from a woman in his congregation requesting a pastoral visit. She put it this way: "I have some records on, come on over." What should the pastor have done? What would you have done? (Why not stop right here and think about it.)

"Well," you might reply "One thing I would *not* do is clear; I wouldn't go. I would say 'no.' " Frankly, I disagree. I think that the pastor should reply: "I'll be right over." "You do?" you may ask. Definitely; otherwise he may miss a great opportunity. "That kind of opportunity I can do without," you may think. I agree, but we are thinking of two different things. This is an opportunity to minister to her, to meet a real need in a way in which it probably could not be met under any other circumstances. The pastor, having hung up, should then phone an elder (or any other responsible Christian man in the remote case where no elder is available), briefly tell him what has happened and should say, "I'll pick you up on my way." The two should arrive at the member's door together as soon as possible.

Dealing with a Special Problem of Women

Recently, a counselee said, "You should know that most of my problem at last week's session was that I was having my period." Male counselors do not have personal experience of menstruation in their own lives, and therefore must learn how to recognize and to reckon with this most persistent problem. In an extended series of counseling sessions, it is possible for the problem to occur on at least two of these. Indeed, what otherwise might seem to be extremely unpredictable behavior is readily understandable when this fact is made known. Yet, many pastors forget the phenomenon and thereby entirely miss it, consequently misinterpreting menstrual behavior as a setback. Instead, they must continually be alert to the possibility that the difficulty encountered is likely to be temporary and occasioned by the occurrence of the menstrual period.

But how can one become aware of it? First, it is possible to raise the matter as a Personal Data Inventory[5] item which might be worded as follows: "Your next menstrual period will occur_____." But, since some women fail to keep track of their periods and could not answer, since others might consider the matter too personal (prior to having met with

---

[4]Witnesses can attest to innocence as well as to sin. If accusations are made, insist that the requirements of I Timothy 5:19-20 are followed scrupulously.

[5]Cf. *The Christian Counselor's Manual* for information on the Personal Data Inventory, pp. 433-435.

you as a counselor, when the P.D.I. is filled out) and since it would in a number of instances be irrelevant, we have left it off of the standard P.D.I. form. Instead, it has been common practice not to raise the matter unless strange, otherwise inexplicable behavior occurs, in which instances the simple offhand question, "Are you having your period at present?" seems always to be accepted as appropriate. Generally speaking, women are not embarrassed (as men often wrongly suppose) but appreciate a man who is considerate enough to ask the question.[6] At present, however, we are handing women counselees a booklet entitled "A Personal Word to Women" following the first counseling session.[7] This booklet deals with menstrual problems.

Now, the real danger (of course) in asking this question is to allow the woman to use her period as an excuse for poor behavior. Many women, who become tigers around the house for three to four days each month, must be confronted about this fact as well as about any other. Only in rare cases does the period itself have a *direct* effect upon behavior. (Menopause and postpartum depression largely fall into the same categories.) In such cases a physician can render aid. Some women will argue the point, wishing to hold on to an excuse for bad behavior. Others will have convinced themselves so fully that the anticipation of difficulty brings it about as a self-fulfilling prophecy. But unless the physician confirms the fact that this is one of those exceptional instances, the pastor may deal with menstruation[8] as follows:

1. Do not allow a woman to shift the blame for her behavior to the fact of menstruation.
2. Assure her that she is responsible not only for her behavior in general during menstruation, but for handling menstruation itself in a proper way.
3. Help her to deal with the unpleasantness of the period by suggesting ways to handle it as a Christian.

In order to do so, it is useful to keep certain facts in mind, the summary of which is that *menstruation itself does not cause grouchiness, temper or depression.*

---

[6]Many men think of menstruation as sexually connotative; women, by- and- large, do not share this view. For them it is more like a discussion of elimination.

[7]Cf. Appendix A.

[8]Substantially the same approach must be taken with a woman undergoing menopause. The major difference here is the protracted nature of the latter and the thought patterns with reference to age that accompany it.

It is true that many women experience a change of personality during the monthly period. They may become depressed, they may become irritable and disagreeable. They may grow uncommunicative and unreasonable. But unless (as we said before) this is one of these extremely *rare* instances, menstruation (or menopause) is not the *cause* but merely the *occasion* for such behavior. In effect the bodily changes which occur do no more than place the stone in her pathway; it is her fault if she allows herself to stumble over it. The menstrual period may be accompanied by fatigue, weakness or pain. Some of this is physical in origin, but even some of these elements may be caused or (as often is the case) exaggerated and aggravated by other factors.

A woman who is having such difficulties must learn that just as it is easier to "let down the bars" when she suffers from a cold, from a severe headache, or from a painful injury, so too it is easier during her period to loosen the restraints on her temper, to neglect her daily duties and chores (leading to depression[9]), and (in general) to become difficult to live with.[10] She must be assured that *while it is harder to control her behavior during menstruation* (or menopause), nevertheless God holds her responsible to do so, just as He holds her responsible for her attitudes and actions in pain or grief or sickness. Patterns of losing control must be broken and new patterns pleasing to God and to her family must be developed. Habits of brawling, getting out of sorts, etc., must be replaced. The Christ, who said, "My grace is sufficient for you," and about whom Paul was able to echo, "I can do all things (i.e., all the things that He requires of me) through Christ who strengthens me," does supply adequate help so that one may overcome the temptation to let down the bars and allow his sinful impulses full reign. The fruit of the Spirit is "self-control"; it is that for which the counselor should urge every Christian woman to pray and structure her life.

How can she be helped to do so? First, she must be convinced of the need to do so. She must be shown the necessity of "putting away" all "bitterness and wrath and anger and clamor" (Ephesians 4:31), together with "abusive speech" (Colossians 3:8). She need not give in to her sinful habits any longer since in Christ she has "laid aside the old man with his evil practices"

---

[9]On depression, cf. *Competent to Counsel*, pp. 116ff.; *The Christian Counselor's Manual*, pp. 375-383.

[10]Menstrual problems in this respect · compare favorably with such behavioral and additudinal difficulties as those that arise as the result of arteriosclerosis, for instance. When hardening of the arteries occurs, the cause of behavioral difficulties is both *direct* and *organic*: restraints are removed and what is inside emerges. The temptation to allow the same thing to happen during menstruation is strong; yet the difference is great—in spite of strong temptation to unlock the gates, a woman need not do so: she holds the key. In hardening of the arteries, the key has been lost. In both instances the common factors are two: (1) the removal of restraints triggers the behavior; (2) what the inner person over the years has become is seen.

(Colossians 3:9). No exceptions to the behavior cited above, either in sickness or suffering or during menstrual discomfort, are made in the Scriptures. Indeed, in a passage particularly of interest to Christian women Peter writes, "In the same way, you wives, be submissive to your own husbands... [having] a gentle and quiet spirit" (I Peter 3:1,4). When he says "*in the same way*," he refers back to the previous chapter in which he had described the control and restraint of Christ during His sufferings (cf. especially I Peter 2:20-23). In this passage Christ's "patient endurance" (vv.20,21) of genuine suffering is set forth as the way in which to handle trials. Now, while Peter is not speaking of the menstrual period in this passage, nevertheless reasoning from the greater to the lesser, if a Christian wife is called upon to endure *persecution* from an unsaved husband as Christ endured suffering, i.e., without complaint and without losing control, so may all believing women be called upon to endure such lesser (though real) discomfort as menstruation may afford. One way in which the wives of unsaved husbands (to whom this passage refers most particularly) may "win" them to Christ by their "behavior" is by beginning to exercise self-control during their premenstrual tension periods.

Secondly, a woman can endure better when she is prepared to do so. Since the monthly period is of regular occurrence, she can

1. Keep a record ahead on her calendar and become aware of the days each month when she is likely to face discomfort;
2. Prepare for these by prayer as they approach;
3. Follow a low-salt diet for about a week before menstruation to eliminate the bloating caused by excess water;[11]
4. Plan to take on no unnecessary stress situations during the three days preceding menstruation. For instance, this is not the time to have dinner guests or a special party for little Johnny. While all stress cannot be eliminated during this period, it is possible to schedule those stressful events which are movable for other times;
5. Let her husband know when the onset of menstruation has arrived so that he can take this into account;
6. Refrain from making any crucial commitments or decisions during this time since they are likely to be highly colored by it (postponement is almost always possible in such cases);
7. Follow responsibilities (before God and man), not feelings (i.e., no matter how she feels, in everything she must do what she knows God wants her to do—*even* if she does not feel like doing it);

---

[11]If this does not help, a physician can prescribe a mild diuretic (water tablet) that will.

8. Not allow herself to get behind in daily chores;
9. Avoid brooding on problems in self-pity sessions and refuse to attend any pity parties held over coffee or over the phone by neighborhood friends;
10. Make a list of special small acts of love and kindness toward her husband and family that she can do during this time (the list may be consulted as menstruation approaches).

Sometimes when it is known that a period of premenstrual tension is likely to coincide with a counseling session, the counselor may wish to skip that session (especially if the session is likely to be a tense one) or reschedule it (with profit to all concerned). Many bad decisions, regretted later, have been made under menstrual pressures. Pastors will do well to counsel women to postpone such decisions.

More could be said about this problem, but it is probably sufficient simply to say that all counselors should be aware of it and know how to handle it both as a problem in itself and as a complicating problem that often can get in the way when dealing with other difficulties.

EXERCISE

For the student

Prepare a paper including:

1. A thorough exegetical study of I Timothy 5:2b.
2. A discussion of the implications of this study for the counseling of women.
3. Ask two or three women to read it and to make notes on the paper.
4. Hand in the annotated paper to your teacher.

Read at least three good medical textbooks on menstruation, menopause and postpartum depression. Most hospitals have a medical library with which every seminary student and pastor should become familiar.

For the Pastor

Ask yourself:
1. Have I been sufficiently aware of menstrual problems in counseling?
2. Do I have an adequate procedure for

a. gaining information concerning this problem?

b. instructing women to handle their discomfort in ways pleasing to God?

3. Have I carefully thought through policies and procedures for counseling women in my particular counseling context? In doing so be sure to take I Timothy 5:2 into consideration.

CHAPTER IX
COUNSELING OLDER PERSONS

There are many problems that arise in old age. One of the greatest of these is coping with change. Another is the fear of approaching death. A third is the loss of community. A fourth is the many possible physical effects of aging. A fifth may have to do with decreased mobility. To mention only one more, often there are problems connected with diminishing finances.

Because each of these problems tends to blend with one or more of the others, I shall not consider them separately. Rather, I shall discuss some ways in which, jointly, these difficulties may be handled by the counselor.[1]

Before proceeding further, however, I should mention two additional factors that may become significant barriers to aiding older persons: (1) embarrassment that "at this age I should have to seek help, especially from a younger person," and (2) the notion that it is not possible to change "at my age." Since I have discussed the second barrier at length elsewhere,[2] I shall concentrate upon the first. Often, indeed, the second objection is merely a cover for the first. But, apart from that and other such aspects of the problem that might be explored, the question to which we must address ourselves is "how does a counselor penetrate this barrier?" Of course, ultimately, in some instances where there is a contumacious unwillingness to forsake sin, he may find it necessary to rely upon the recon-ciliation/discipline dynamic.[3] But, apart from that last-resort recourse, and apart from the basic principles of counseling that apply to all counseling situations, how may a counselor meet the *peculiar* difficulties associated with older counselees, and in particular, the problem of embarrassment because of age differential?

---

[1]Incidentally, counselors will find that this holds true of much counseling; work on one problem and others change with it. Sometimes a basic change of life (e.g., scheduling sleep, work and other activities) will bring about a number of other changes not specifically attempted.

[2]For further information concerning this problem, see *The Christian Counselor's Manual*, pp. 29, 30, 65ff.

[3]*Ibid.*, Chapter 8. E.g., in cases that may involve disciplinary action when unreconciled relationships, divisive activities, malicious gossip and similar matters persist.

Questions like these cannot be avoided. Because of modern longevity, due to dietary and medical advancements, the number of older persons is increasing steadily. Pastoral ministry to older members is likely to become an ever greater part of pastoral work. Pastors, therefore, must come to grips with issues of age. It is important to remember that they too will be grappling with problems of aging themselves sooner than they may realize. Every pastor does well to read Ecclesiastes 12 regularly.[4]

Well, then, what does a pastor do? First, he does not let older persons "despise his youth" (I Timothy 4:12). How does he keep them from doing so? The answer is found in the latter part of the verse: by demonstrating through the maturity of his own Christian life that he knows how to meet the changing adversities of life in Christ's strength. Moreover, he must be able to bring helpful instruction from the pulpit about how to do so, not only to his peers but also to his elders. That is what being an "example" (or "pattern") in speech and behavior means. Thus, when his own exemplary life and counsel exhibit biblically applied maturity, elderly persons will find it easier to come for help with less embarrassment. They also will find it much harder to stay away on the pretext that he is too young to understand.

But this is not all that he must do. In writing to Titus, Paul declared, "Let no one disregard you" (Titus 2:15). The King James version in Titus 2:15 and in I Timothy 4:12 wrongly translates two similar, but distinct words, by the one English term "despise." This translation obscures the point in Titus, even though it is accurate enough in I Timothy. Paul said to Timothy, "Let no one *think down* [or *despise*] you" (*kataphroneo*); but when writing to Titus, Paul said, "Let no one *think around* [or *disregard*] you *(periphrones)*.

The pastor's maturity of behavior and speech overcomes the first problem; his willingness to "speak with authority" overcomes the latter.[5] In his public and private relationships to his flock, he must impress upon them the fact that he is a representative sent by the living God to minister to them.[6] The delicate balance between being a servant (minister) and an authoritative leader of the flock is difficult to maintain, but must be cultivated carefully. The perfect balance was demonstrated by the Chief Shepherd. The pastor may not be looked upon merely as a youth, or merely

---

[4] Which, by the way, is addressed to youth, urging them to make the most of their youthful vigor for God before it has slipped away.

[5] "These things speak and exhort and reprove *with all authority*. Let no one disregard you" (Titus 2:15).

[6] As Paul puts it in I Timothy 6:11 (see also II Timothy 3:17) when he called Timothy a "man of [from] God."

as a servant by elderly members; he must be viewed also as one who has been called and ordained to his work (part of which is to counsel them from God's Word) by the King through His church. That calling, with its authority, must be respected in its own right.[7] Thus, when he exercises the inward authority *(dunamis)* of exemplary life and speech (I Timothy) and asserts (not flaunts) the external authority conferred by Christ *(exousia)* by teaching, exhorting and rebuking with authority (Titus), others (particularly elderly persons) will find it easier to approach him with less embarrassment. He will command respect by his life and by his office. They are less likely to think of themselves as elderly persons approaching a stripling. That notion easily may become a source of serious embarrassment, not to mention a lack of trust and confidence. Instead, they will think of approaching a man of God who seems to have wisdom and maturity beyond his years.

If embarrassment continues, it is better (whenever possible) to make as little of it as possible. This usually may be done by pushing on to the discussion of the problems in an orderly and competent manner rather than by trying to relieve counselees of the embarrassment. Ordinarily, the more attention that is given to the matter of their feelings (assuming these feelings are genuine) the more likely it is that these feelings will persist and even grow. If by (1) digging into the problem or (2) by outlining some of the procedures he plans to follow or (3) by engendering hope[8] in some other way, the counselor can draw attention away from feelings toward the work involved in solving problems, the unpleasant feelings soon will subside. Remember, *bad feelings are always swallowed up by true hope.* If he can give genuine (i.e., biblically-based) hope, therefore, he will succeed in overcoming problems of embarrassment.

"But if such problems—in spite of all of this—persist, what then do you do?" Good question. You will find that very rarely will you have to use its answer, for adequate hope coupled with the right combination of inward and conferred authority most frequently will be quite sufficient to overcome most barriers. Yet, for that rare instance where the counselees *persist* in intruding their embarrassment into the situation let me suggest

---

[7] The word "authority" in Titus 2:15 is *epitage*, which refers not to the passive possession of power to be respected, but to the active assertion of authority to be obeyed. It is literally a "commanding" or "ordering" authority, that is exerted by "teaching" *(laleo)*, by "exhorting" *(parakaleo)*, and by "rebuking" *(elegcho)*. All three of these activities (v. 15) are to be carried on with Christ's *full* authority. This authority is conditioned, of course, by the Scriptures. Its exercise, limits, etc., are all bounded by the Bible. The authority is not merely exercised when preaching to the whole flock, but also when ministering privately to individuals: "Let *no one* disregard you."

[8] Cf. *The Christian Counselor's Manual* for help in doing so, pp. 39-48; 229, 230.

one way for a counselor to handle the problem[9]: let him set his rudder for a direct course toward the source of the embarrassment and sail full speed ahead. He may say, "Well, we seem to be bogged down before we have even begun by your embarrassment (call it by name). Since we can't seem to get past it, let's go through. What do you think may be at the bottom of it?" If the counselee's answers are vague, or he can't seem to come up with answers, or simply shows greater feelings of embarrassment, the counselor may continue: "Then let me make a few suggestions, and hazard a few thoughts and let's see if they ring any bells. First, let's understand that embarrassment grows out of judgments that you have made about yourself (focus not upon the feeling, but upon its cause). These judgments are either true or untrue. If after examining them you should conclude that they are untrue, you should begin to feel different already. If they are true, we can discover what God says to do about them in the Bible and begin to do it, again (I am sure) with considerable relief. Now, let me make those suggestions. Some persons are embarrassed because they think that if they can't solve all of their problems themselves, they are inferior to other Christians. . . . Is there anything like this behind your embarrassment?[10]" Or he may inquire: "Is coming for counseling hard to take because of pride?" Or, perhaps, "Does it seem embarrassing that after all these years you find it necessary to seek help? Well if it does. . . ."

The counselor who takes this straightforward approach usually will do so as a last resort, because it means heading across stormy seas from the outset. But the gales can be weathered when it is necessary to do so! Far better (to change to a more modern figure of speech) to get above the choppy air whenever it is possible to do so. Yet when you can't, fasten your seat belt and plunge into the dark clouds. One side effect that you may discover is that the counselee is glad to get down to a discussion of the main business after flying at that altitude for a while.

One or two other suggestions may be in order. Filling in the pink sheets of the Personal Data Inventory often helps persons say what they find it hard to speak. Sometimes speaking is much more difficult for some persons than writing. Using the pink sheet from the outset in cases where you might expect such embarrassment to occur may help you to avoid the barrier altogether. But in situations where unexpected embarrassment occurs, it is always possible to reach into the desk drawer, pull out a couple of sheets of

---

[9]Assuming this is the genuine problem. If it is a cover-up or a cop-out, however, this method usually will uncover that fact as well.

[10]If the answer is in the affirmative, he can point out that all Christians need counsel sometime (Acts 20:31—note "each one of you"; Colossians 1:28—note "every man," etc.). Cf. *The Big Umbrella*, pp. 126, 138-141, for more help on this point.

paper and some pens and say, "O.K., if it is so hard to say, jot down some of the principal thoughts here, while I'm gone. I'll be back in ten minutes." Then, promptly leave, and return as indicated. More often than not what is written will (1) give you the data that you need to move ahead (thereby getting past the embarrassment) or (2) provide enough material from which to begin significant movement toward obtaining such data. Only *very* rarely will the sheets be blank. Such action might represent one way to move ahead in case No. 8, in *The Christian Counselor's Casebook*.[11]

What To Do About Other Problems

Having begun counseling successfully, by getting past initial embarrassment or other barriers, the counselor often discovers that he is inundated with a plethora of unsolved life problems. They are often tangled, twisted and warped together. He soon gains full sight of barnacle-encrusted bitterness, dry-rotted boredom, stagnant self-centeredness, desert loneliness, plaguing what may be a pain-racked, fear-pitted body. It sometimes seems that everything goes to pieces all at once. It looks that way because often that is exactly the case. In further discussion of the basic dynamic of the collapse of a life pattern, resulting in the opportunity for biblical reorganization, and how to counsel toward this goal, see the information in Appendix A, Vol. 1 of this series, entitled "Grief as a Counseling Opportunity."

Separate problems, like fear and anger, may be faced in much the same manner as one handles these questions when they arise in the counseling of younger persons. There is, therefore, no need for repetition of such material, since I have considered many of these issues elsewhere, and plan to continue to do so in other volumes yet to be published. Problems that grow directly out of old age, like senility, loneliness, meaninglessness, failing health, must be met on their own terms,[12] within the context of old age.

But what does the counselor do when confronted with all of these in profusion screwed, bolted and rusted tightly to one another? Does he get

---

[11]Jay E. Adams, *The Christian Counselor's Casebook*, Presbyterian and Reformed Publishing Co., Nutley, N. J., 1974, p. 15.

[12]Some of these terms have been mentioned already specifically or in principle. For instance in dealing with loneliness and meaninglessness, see information concerning shut-ins. The principles described in ministering to handicapped persons also apply to ministering to those who suffer from ailments, physical weakness, etc. Senility is another matter. Here, there is often a physiological breakdown of the brain resulting in attitudes, speech and behavior that previously were restrained. The bars are down. Outwardly moral men may make lewd remarks, etc. Behavior harmful to one's self, loss of recent memory, etc., may occasion care similar to that given to a child. However, one should be *sure* that he is dealing with physiological deterioration, not merely self-centered, manipulative, attention-attracting behavior.

out wrenches and penetrating oil and try to take them apart, one by one? Or is there another approach?

Sometimes there is nothing else to do but use the wrench; *always* this is true when there are sinful relationships to straighten out (people from whom the counselee needs to seek forgiveness and to whom he needs to be reconciled) before counseling can progress. That is to say, such nuts must be loosened *individually*. Yet there is another way that one often may approach these problems that is not incompatible with but rather complementary to the first. I mentioned this approach at the beginning of the chapter. It is like taking the whole rusted, twisted, tangled mass of nuts and bolts and soaking them in baths of oil until all of the nuts spin freely on their threads and the whole thing comes apart by hand.

Of the several oil baths that might be mentioned, I shall discuss three.

1. Consider Physical Condition

Help the aged counselee to take stock of his physical condition and to make adjustments in all activities and life styles appropriate to the facts. When the facts indicate a change in life style due to physical weakening, he should readily admit it. The counselor may have to help him to do so. Here future comments with reference to handicapped persons growing out of a consideration of Romans 12:3 are apropos.[13] Suggestively helpful is the aged Apostle John's evaluation of the different functions of age and youth mentioned in I John 2:13-14.[14] The strength of Christian youth complemented by the knowledge, wisdom and experience of Christian maturity makes a victorious combination that effectively overcomes Satan.

In this passage John's *shift* in emphasis from the use of the body to the use of the mind in Christ's service (while certainly not *more* than an *emphasis*) should be suggestive. Many older persons must be helped to discover how best to make the shift. Moreover, the apparent *connection* (rather than separation) of youth and age also should suggest the biblical pathway to finding solutions to some of the problems of extremes from which our churches often suffer (e.g., reckless youthful activism, or footdragging geriatric apathy). Together, instead, youth and age can

---

[13]Infra, Chapter XII. But be very careful not to counsel inactivity or the cessation of perfectly valid activities. Physical abilities at *any* given age vary greatly.

[14]The pastor may wish to point out that John wrote out of the experience of a long life lived with Christ. Study the verses cited and be prepared to explain these upon occasion.

provide the *balance* of wise activity. Similarly, clashes over new forms and old traditions may be hammered out into programs that retain the good while reaching for something better. The churches' *need* for the wisdom and moderation that usually accompanies age, therefore, should be stressed when counseling older persons. The opportunity for engaging in various mind-using activities should be explored creatively. The question of how best to work in a church and in a world in which one no longer has the physical prowess or stamina to do what he used to do, but where his mind still soars, itself can be presented as the first challenge to creative new uses of that mind.[15] Suggestions may be given to prime the counselee's pump, but it is better for the counselor to assign the task as homework.[16] One such typical assignment might read: "List at least a dozen ways in which you can spend your time profitably in the service of Christ. Don't hesitate to discuss the matter with other Christians." This homework, given as a challenge, out of genuine hope generated from biblical exhortations based upon the scripturally important place of older persons, can itself become the doorway to a new outlook on life.[17] It may be the first step into a second phase of living.

2. Do Not Retire; Retread

Some persons who retire in good health find it possible to enter into a second phase prior to the one mentioned above. They retire from their first job as soon as it is possible and put their expertise to use in serving a Christian college, seminary or other institution which otherwise could not afford to hire someone so highly qualified. Such organizations often badly need financial, managerial, and other similar services. How much better to become involved in such a ministry than to take the path that leads to TV dry rot!

---

[15]One woman uses part of the time spent in her wheelchair to write comforting letters to people in trouble. In ministering to others, she avoids self-pity and exaggeration of her own plight. Thus, she finds it truly "more blessed to give" comfort than to "receive" it!

[16]On homework, cf. *The Christian Counselor's Manual*, Chapters 27, 28, 29. The pastor might also get some mileage from his suggestions. For example he may line up volunteer readers for monthly sermon-illustration hunting. Five or six old-timers may gather one morning each month at the church to clip, categorize and file illustrations from piles of old magazines. A pleasant time of dedicated activity and good fellowship in a room with a sign entitled "The Clip Joint" can yield rich ore for a busy pastor and an additional thrill for the clipper when he hears "his" illustration in a sermon.

[17]Cf. such verses as I John 2:13, 14; Titus 2:2; Prov. 16:31; 20:29.

I should like to make an observation or two on the question of retirement in general. Retirement, as it is currently conceived, is not a biblical option. Indeed, because God made man with the capacity to receive a satisfaction that comes through work, and through work alone (cf. Ecclesiastes 5:12), every person needs to work so long as he lives. His work may be remunerative or nonremunerative, but he must work. Work is not the result of the fall (labor against thorns is what the fall occasioned); God gave Adam work to do in the garden (to dress it, to name the animals). The redeemed children of God will work in heaven ("his servants shall serve him," Revelation 22:3). So, retirement from a job *must not* be thought of as retirement from *work*. Rather, the Christian must consider retirement from one job as an opportunity to engage in other work which may not have been feasible for him to do before. Retirement solely to recreation, to hobbies and to leisure is not a proper objective. While all of these may increase with retirement, basically the Christian counselor should advise his people to look forward to retirement as *retirement to new work*. In this way many, if not most, of the problems of retirement could be obviated.

3. *Adjust Lifestyle; Keep Making Friends*

Conjoint with a change in activity is the need for adjustment of lifestyle and the acquisition of new friends. Older friends die; new ones must be made. They do not come out of nowhere. Often one of the largest complaints of older persons. . . loneliness . . .is the direct result of their own failure to *make* friends. An older person who does not develop a new life style or friendships of his own, but who depends upon his children to adapt *their* life styles, conversations, interests and activities to his is asking for the impossible. He is shortsighted and selfishly sinful. This problem frequently arises when older parents (or a surviving parent) come to live with children.[18] They must be helped to realize that while their lives can contribute richly to one another, the *activities, interests* and *friendships* of older and younger persons will differ greatly. Neither can (nor should) attempt to mesh life styles too tightly. All will be happier when they do not try. That means that one of the greatest services to be rendered by the

---

[18]Another factor to remember is that older parents must recognize that in doing so they come *under* the authority of the husband in the home, even though previously he may have been under their authority in their home. He is now the head of this decision-making body who is responsible to God for every member in it, even the "stranger within the gates" of his household. Children have an obligation to aged parents. But their obligation is *first* to their spouses, next to their children, then to their parents. Cf. *Christian Living in the Home*, pp. 51-56; I Timothy 5:8,16.

pastor is to encourage the widow (widower) to become a part of a new circle of Christian friends of a contemporary age, who participate in activities and discuss interests common to her (him).[19] Individual congregations (or congregations working together[20]) should provide organizations, meetings, opportunities, etc., for elderly persons to gather in Christian fellowship.[21]

So much more could be written about this ever-enlarging area of pastoral concern, but hopefully this discussion will stir enough beans to the top of the pot for wise pastoral counselors to scoop off.

EXERCISE

For the Student

1. Interview (perhaps in conjunction with previous interviews) pastors and discover what kinds of activities and organizations for the elderly exist in their congregation. Report on these (verbally) in class.

2. Together with a group of 5 or 6 other students spend an hour brainstorming other possibilities for helping the elderly. Turn in an accurate list of ideas at the next class period (annotations should include [1] Scriptural evaluation of each idea, [2] Explanation of ideas, where necessary, and [3] Other comments you think may be valuable; for example: concerning ways and means).

---

[19]"Independence" is the cry of older persons who in many ways must become dependent upon others. So long as the cry is not for a sinful independence growing out of pride, or an independence from God, it is healthy and should be encouraged. What it really means, in such instances, is willingness to be responsible. But older persons must be shown that personal independence depends upon acting independently (not merely talking about it). That is to say, the older person must assume whatever obligations he or she is able to assume, make new friends, plan activities with them, build a life style that is properly independent of others. The counselor's task is to show that such independence grows out of assuming responsibility, not shirking it.

[20]One of the problems is that each congregation seems to think that it must provide everything on its own. In programs for meeting *specialized* needs (for youth, older persons, Christian singles, retarded children, etc.) the rule, rather than the exception, will be cooperation with other congregations.

[21]Even many of the shut-ins now and then can meet at the church for a special service. Properly arranged, it could be an inspiring sight to see a group of persons in wheelchairs, on crutches, etc., gather. The youth group or the Christian singles' society could help to provide transportation and assistance to and from cars.

For the Pastor

Interview key elderly people in your congregation and ask:
1. In what ways is the church best serving you?
2. In what ways is it failing?
3. What do you suggest to improve the situation?
4. What part would you be willing to play in bringing about any desired changes?

CHAPTER X
EDUCATIONAL COUNSELING

There are numerous instances when persons who seek counsel of a pastor basically have need of educational counsel. That is to say, the fundamental problem from which their difficulties stem is a lack of information or distorted information. This is the sort of problem to which Paul addressed himself when writing to the Thessalonians. There Christians had received insufficient and, then afterwards, incorrect data concerning (1) the death of believers, (2) their future resurrection and (3) the return of Christ. Somehow, through a mixture of the false teaching and the limited truth that they possessed, the Thessalonians came to the erroneous conclusion that none of their number would die before Christ returned. But when some did in fact die they were troubled and wrote to Paul out of their confusion. He responded by saying, "I do not want you to be ignorant, brothers, concerning. . . wherefore comfort one another with these words" (I Thessalonians 4:13,18).

Clearly, a proper understanding of the facts was the counsel required to bring the comforting hope needed. Similarly, the pastor will encounter many persons with informational difficulties during the course of a year. The variety of their questions will be almost without number. They will come in distress over lack of assurance, concerning doubts, about perfectionistic teachings, erroneous ideas about divorce and remarriage, thinking they have lost their salvation, supposing they are oppressed by demons, wondering whether they have committed the unpardonable sin, etc. Proper teaching in any one of these instances may be all that is necessary to solve the problem.

There are times, however, when more is needed, when the informational problem presented is but an opener, when it is raised as a faulty understanding of the real problem or when it is only symptomatic of other difficulties.[1] But then again, it is important not to turn a simple, educational matter into something more complex. To create problems for

---

[1] Cf., e.g., *The Christian Counselor's Manual*, pp. 426-428.

the counselee by suspecting or by implying that there is something "deeper" or something "more," for some counselees can be devastating. As examples of cases in which educational counseling will probably provide the solution, cf. *The Christian Counselor's Casebook*, cases 6 and 19.[2]

The question with which the counselor is faced in many instances of educational counseling then is whether the need lies solely in more (or more accurate[3]) information or whether there is something else involved. How can he decide?

It is not always easy to decide. Nor is it always possible to determine right away whether the problem is basically educational. But there are some things that the pastor can do to steer as straight a course as possible between the failure to discern other difficulties on the one hand, and the danger of creating imaginary problems for the counselee on the other. Here are a few:

1. *He can ask.* The simple, straightforward approach is frequently forgotten in the maze of substitutes that often are suggested. Ask: "Is your problem solved by learning these facts, or is there some other (perhaps) more personal side to it?"[4] or "Now that I have shown you what the Scriptures teach on this subject, may I ask: is there any aspect of it with which you are having difficulty in relationship to God or others?" Always, the straightforward question saves time, is generally appreciated, and gets the best results. It is far better than the (not too) "sly" innuendos that radiate from some more oblique approaches.

2. *He can give homework designed to pick up such information.* "Now that we've talked about the issue, perhaps you should go home and think about its implications in your life.[5] Write out any personal problems that this raises for you as well as any further questions that you may have, and bring them in next week. I'd like you to take time for the coffee to perk."

3. *He can state his own problem openly.* Not only in this instance, but in any other when one does not know how to raise a matter for discussion, but knows that he should, he always may begin *by saying so* ("I've got a problem, Joe. On the one hand, I don't want to raise issues where there are none, but on the other hand, I don't want to miss any either. So. . . .").

---

[2]Pp. 12, 38.

[3]Acts 18:24-28 affords an excellent example of such counseling.

[4]The counselor may wish to suggest the sort of thing he has in mind by listing 5 or 6 possible implications ("sometimes others have had difficulty with. . ."). He usually will be wise to do so when he strongly suspects certain difficulties. Then, he may list the problem he suspects together with the 4 or 5 other items.

[5]Even when there is no further matter than lack of information, the emphasis upon the practical implications of truth itself can be helpful to the counselee.

Again, the honest, straight-from-the-shoulder (but with the sharp edge blunted: the counselor says "it is my problem,"[6] not necessarily the counselee's) approach pays off.

4. All or any combination of these approaches may be used. Homework, as a double check, and (in particular) homework that gives the counselee the option of changing his mind if at first he responded too quickly or dishonestly, is especially helpful. And it is easy to see how homework clearly combines with the other approaches as their complement.

Awareness that what may at first seem to be a doctrinal problem might really extend beyond is the important fact to keep in mind. But turning every such discussion into a series of counseling sessions, or even attempting to set up a series of counseling sessions to consider problems that mature Christians themselves can handle once some basic direction has been given them, is a serious error.[7]

Prebaptismal Counseling

One specialized form of educational counseling is prebaptismal instruction. Two issues arise in the consideration of this matter:

1. How does one counsel an adult presenting himself for baptism?
2. How does one counsel the parents of a covenant child who is brought for baptism?

Before considering these matters let us be clear about the necessity for prebaptismal counseling. Because there is so much confusion regarding baptism (its purpose, its meaning, its subjects, its mode and its effects all have been debated hotly among Christians), and because a major purpose of a sacrament is to represent a significant truth symbolically, unless the person applying for baptism clearly understands its significance, the sacrament will fail to serve this purpose.

How much counsel is necessary? That depends upon the knowledge of the applicant. In the case of an adult who has been converted recently the amount of educational counseling required may be maximal; when an elder brings his fifth child for baptism, it may be minimal.

In neither instance should counseling sessions be extended and numerous. The pastor should set forth the biblical truths concerning baptism simply and plainly and, *if there are no questions or problems*

---

[6]"I have a problem. . . ." This approach also is particularly useful when one must confront another about his sin, as in obedience to Luke 17:3, and he does not know how to broach the subject. The approach is honest and straightforward.

[7]For more information on this latter point see "Counsel or Counseling?" *The Christian Counselor's Manual*, p. 251.

raised, should proceed to perform the ceremony as soon as possible.[8] Only unsolved problems that stand in the way can justify delay.[9]

In any educational counseling such as this a clear-cut explanation of the purport of the sacrament ought to be given. All ideas of baptismal regeneration, sentimental notions, superstitious views and the like should be combatted. ("So you see, water baptism has no part in bringing about the regeneration of the soul.")

Since meaning is inextricably bound up in mode it cannot be divorced from prebaptismal discussion. Because so many Bible-believing Christians refuse to baptize children, the pastor must show the biblical reasons for infant baptism.[10]

The child of any converted person (one believing parent is adequate) who belongs to your congregation is a fit subject for baptism. It is unwise to baptize the child of someone not a member of your congregation unless there is agreement with the board of elders who rule the congregation to which the parents belong.[11] Otherwise, it is dubious as to how the child can become a part of the local visible church and be brought under its care and discipline thereby.[12]

---

[8] Both the O.T. and the N.T. give evidence of the early administration of circumcision (the 8th day; i.e., as early as physically practicable) and baptism (for adults, on the same day as conversion).

[9] There is no biblical justification for long delays. For instance, when an applicant questions the meaning or mode of baptism these questions must be resolved. Sufficient teaching, given in plenty of time to discuss all such questions while seeking to avoid such delay, is the ideal. It is not always wise to wait until the *birth* of the first child for instruction. It could begin immediately after the announcement of the pregnancy.

[10] See my "The Meaning and Mode of Baptism" (Presbyterian and Reformed Publishing Co., 1975). This discussion, in part or in full, may be used as a guide for discussion. An additional book, covering the question of Infant Baptism, is planned for future publication.

[11] In such cases, the congregation should not be called upon to affirm responsibilities toward the child that they cannot assume.

[12] Water baptism is the sign of admission into the visible church, not into the invisible church (one becomes a member of the invisible church through the regenerating baptism of the Holy Spirit at conversion).

EXERCISE

For the Student

1. Set up several educational counseling sessions (perhaps with young people in a youth group at your church).

2. From these experiences begin to make a list of biblical principles to remember in educational counseling. Report on these to the class.

List of Principles

For the Pastor

Keep a record of educational counseling sessions (give a thumbnail sketch of each case as a reminder) together with problems encountered and biblical principles learned.

Educational Counseling Sessions

Case	Problems	Principles

Case	Problems	Principles

CHAPTER XI
INSTRUCTION IN COUNSELING

When Paul distinguished the preacher's two prime activities as "nouthetically confronting every man and teaching every man,"[1] he had no intention of dividing these tasks. Indeed, his purpose was to bring them into the sort of close proximity that would show their interdependence and interpenetration. Together, these complementary tasks comprised Paul's ministry. A pastor must not think, therefore, that when he counsels he does not need to teach or that when he teaches he does not need to confront. He does not change hats when moving from counseling to preaching or vice versa. The fact is that each of these activities necessarily presupposes and involves the other. It is not only that in applying the Word individually one thereby learns how to preach (teach) more concretely, and that when one so preaches, people respond by seeking counsel; no, there is more to it than that. Christian teaching—because it concerns God's holiness and man's sin—always confronts listeners nouthetically; and nouthetic confrontation—because it is based upon the Scriptures—always requires both explanatory and applicatory teaching. Just as the change that God requires is the goal of all biblical counseling, so too is that change the goal of all truly scriptural preaching. Each task, in turn, has as its common end the glory of God through the sanctification of God's sheep.

Because scriptural counseling is directive, and counsel consists in large measure of giving information, direction and advice,[2] by the very nature of the case, teaching must be involved in it.

But before going further, let me warn the reader about one vital fact: the solution to the problems that counselees have is not *merely* educational. That means that, for instance, Fuller Torrey's view that counseling should be *equated* with education is false.[3] His substitution of the educational

---

[1]Colossians 1:28.
[2]Cf. *The Christian Counselor's Manual*, pp. 15-17; George Scipione, "Counselors and Counseling," *The Westminster Theological Journal*, Volume XXXVI, Winter 1974, No. 2, pp. 186ff.
[3]E. Fuller Torry, *The Death of Psychiatry* (Chilton Book Co., Radnor: 1974).

model for the medical model will not do. Because counseling involves teaching, the counselor must not conclude that all that the counselee needs is the missing pieces to his puzzle, or that reeducation and/or retraining will solve his problems. Nor must he see education (even in scriptural truth) alone as the sum of counseling. Counseling involves *more*—much more—than instruction, just as preaching involves more. Counselees are sinners who do not always automatically do whatever God wants them to do upon learning the truth. Often they don't (for various reasons) or won't. In addition, there must be reproof, conviction, persuasion, encouragement or whatever any given situation requires; but the point of the present discussion is that always there will be teaching too. And, of greatest importance, is the fact that the teaching, the persuasion, etc., must be within the context of sanctification. That is to say, it must be done by the power of the Holy Spirit working through the various scriptural modes that the counselor employs. So while teaching is an essential element in counseling, it is not the only essential. And, those who are attempting to make it such err.[4]

Having issued a warning, I now must turn to the topic at hand. *How* does one instruct, *whom, when,* about *what* sorts of data in counseling? Of course, those questions cannot be answered, except in generalities, without considering the particulars of each individual counseling situation. Yet there is a place for such generalizing (at least suggestively) in order to stimulate thinking about these important issues (there has been far too little so far[5]).

First, it is essential to point out that the pastor has the opportunity to satisfy instructional needs exhibited by counselees through the use of educational opportunities provided by his church outside of counseling. Often, for instance, the need for instruction in the practical use of the Scriptures arises within counseling. If periodically, two or three times each year, such a course is provided by the church for new converts and others, it is possible (as a counseling assignment) to enroll counselees needing such instruction in the course. When a congregation regularly provides a course

---

[4]The cycle of human wisdom has been turning and there are indications that in the near future we shall experience a new upsurge of old errors which find the solutions to problems in reeducation or retraining. Christians who leave out the other biblical elements err, and especially when they attempt in a naturalistic way to apply means in a non-sanctification context. C. S. Lewis says, " . . .that mere development or adjustment or refinement will somehow turn evil into good. . . . This belief, I take to be a disastrous error. . . . Evil can be undone, but it cannot 'develop' into good." *The Great Divorce*, MacMillan Publishing Co., New York, 1946, pp. 5, 6.

[5]One reason for this lack is the widespread Rogerian error that counseling does not involve giving instruction but rather mainly consists of evoking data from the counselee.

on Christian living in the home, similarly, the pastor may suggest to a counselee that as an adjunct to the counseling sessions, he should enroll in it. This course may supplement and provide a basis for more particular instruction given in the sessions themselves.

However, instruction in Christian living, for example, must be conceived of as consisting of more than theoretical learning, acquired by attending courses. Much learning comes only through discipleship, which involves observation, participation, discussion and critique.[6] Such learning assignments also can be given to counselees within the framework of the congregational life.[7] For instance, the pastor can arrange for counselees who need to learn how to pray to become part of a vital prayer group for a time. A young man who has never learned structured, disciplined living in home or college can spend a month living in the well-ordered home of one of the elders or deacons. A woman who does not know how to organize and schedule her housework can be assisted by a veteran housewife who, as a part of her ministry (in obedience to Titus 2:3-5), may devote one morning each week to such projects. *Instruction*, then, must be conceived widely enough to embrace the effort to help counselees acquire *both* the information and the skills that are necessary to solve the problems encountered in counseling. Some of the instruction can be given in the session, by the counselor; but other instruction may be given by others (upon arrangement by the pastor) during the week between the counseling sessions.

How-to Instruction

Just as instruction roughly can be divided into the teaching of information and the acquisition of skills, from a different perspective, it may be said to be divided into instruction in two basic kinds of content: What-type content and how-type content. Most Bible believing pastors and churches are strong on the *what*, but weak on the *how*. Possibly as much discouragement exists among the members of Christian Churches because of this failure as it does for any other. How many times—after a stirring sermon on the family—have members returned home to make things right with one another and with God, only to end up three days later in deeper discouragement than before, in large measure because they did not know *how to* do so? Indeed, their well-meaning (but poorly-executed) attempts may have led to new and more serious difficulties. How often have members left church fired up to "study their Bibles, not merely read them"

---

[6]Cf. "The Christian Teacher and His Disciples," *The Big Umbrella*.
[7]Cf., for instance, Titus 2:3-5.

(as the preacher said), only to return to the former reading practices by Thursday because they did not know *how to* effect the change? How often have Christians concluded that the Bible is a fine book for Sunday use, from which to retrieve information to aid them in the next Bible quiz, but is irrelevant to most of what they do on Mondays through Saturdays, mainly because they have never been taught *how to* use the Bible practically? One of the crying needs of Christians *across the board*, and certainly in counseling, is for instruction in ways and means, i.e., in the *how-to*.

Counselors in particular must *not* neglect this great need, since, as every counselor (who looks for it) quickly finds out, the inability to develop ways and means growing out of and appropriate to biblical principles is a major problem for counselees. Early he discovers that many counselees often have correct goals and (at times) even exact knowledge about God's will, but in spite of this they are failing from ignorance concerning *how to* do what God requires. More often than one would suspect it is ignorance from which their difficulties arise rather than sheer rebellion. There are times, of course, when modern Naamans think it better to dip in the waters of Damascus rather than in the dirty Jordan. Yet often the problem arises from ignorance. Such ignorance, of course, is culpable; for example, God excuses no one for failure to recognize that modern psychological methods of ventilation of anger are diametrically opposed to biblical teaching.[8] But a major occasion for failure to recognize the unbiblical nature of many ways and means is the failure of Christian pastors to point out what means are (and what means are not) in accord with the Bible. Too many pastors, like too many of the books that they read, speak, preach and counsel about noble goals only. Why? It is easy to discover and agree upon goals; it is a good bit harder to help counselees to devise a scriptural plan for attaining them. Probably most of the improvement upon which pastors need to concentrate in developing better instructional practices in counseling (and elsewhere) will focus upon ability to give godly instruction in *how to*.

"Wait a moment," you say, "you have spent a good bit of time telling me that I must improve in my ability to give how-to instruction; are you going to be guilty of the same fault? What I mean is—aren't you going to spell out the *how-to* too?" That is certainly a fair question. In answer, however, I wish to say several things, some of which (hopefully) will be satisfying and others which I suggest beforehand will not. First, you *should* have been taught how to instruct others in how-to in seminary. Until seminaries

---

[8]Cf. *The Christian Counselor's Manual*, pp. 348-367.

consider the teaching of methods and skills important, unfortunately the deficiency is likely to continue at all levels. Because you did not receive such training—training that involves the elements of discipleship previously mentioned (observation, participation, discussion and critique)—do not think that you can acquire these through studying this book. Neither swimming nor counseling can be taught merely through books. Somehow, somewhere you will need to see and hear someone counsel in a way that adequately takes all such matters into consideration. And, even then, although such training will be of immense help, a certain amount of skill and knowledge will have to be learned in the doing. You will have to work at it prayerfully and patiently until you develop the requisite skills and find many of the answers from the Scriptures on your own.

However, all is not lost. There is more hope than that. For nine years we have been giving just such discipleship training in counseling to hundreds of men at the Christian Counseling & Educational Center in Hatboro, Pennsylvania. That training has continued and is open to seminary students and ministers.[9] Moreover, the ministers who have taken training at the center are now scattered around the United States, Canada and elsewhere in the world. Many of these men are capable of sharing their present skills and insights with others who wish to be trained by them. And, in addition (or if either of the two previous suggestions is not feasible), a pastor may use sections of *The Christian Counselor's Manual* that pertain to "how to" matters like giving homework assignments, etc., in conjunction with a workbook designed specifically to provide a measure of experience that hopefully will improve his abilities.[10]

Times For Giving Instruction

Now let us turn our attention to a brief consideration of some of the *times* when instruction within the counseling session itself seems appropriate. Contrary to what at first may seem apparent, it is often better not to begin with instruction, except when such instruction itself may be the principal means for bringing hope,[11] when it is essential to an initial

---

[9]For further information, write to The Director, C.C.E.C., 151 W. County Line Rd., Hatboro, Pa. 19040.

[10]Certain cases in the workbook are related specifically to the problems of how-to instruction. Cf. *The Christian Counselor's Casebook*, pp. 128, 129, 132, 133, 140, 141, 152, 153, 176, 177, 198, 199, 200, 201, 204, 205, 208, 209.

[11]Cf. *The Christian Counselor's Manual*, pp. 39-48. In dealing with a homosexual or lesbian, it is often quite essential to make a survey of the biblical data in order to give hope, showing (for example) that hope comes from acknowledging that homosexuality is sin. ("... So, you see, even though God has said nothing about altering genes, He has promised to deal with sin in Christ. How thankful we should be, then, to learn that because homosexuality is not a genetic disorder, it can be forgiven.") Cf. pp. 403ff.

homework assignment,[12] or when there must be a negotiation of the counselee's agenda.[13] Also, whenever it is possible that persons might follow directions out of wrong motives it is vital to explain the biblical warrant for the desired action.[14] I am speaking of full instruction, of course. It is always necessary at least to give minimal instruction whenever assigning any homework. When interpreting the data concerning the counselee's problems it is important to give full instruction. However, here is one of those points where the counselor can move too quickly if he is not careful. It is possible to jump to conclusions about the nature and causes of specific problems. ("Your problem is easily explained: just last week there was someone who had a similar situation"—what at first *seems* similar, at length may be seen to be quite different.) It is always wise to hold (if not to state) such views tentatively at first. ("It is possible that what we're facing here is what Paul talked about in I Thessalonians when he said. . . " or "From what you have said so far it seems that significant sleep loss is at least one aspect of your difficulty. However, this is frequently a complicating problem growing out of and aggravating others. So let's look further into the situation to determine what else. . . .") Indeed, one of the better ways in which to learn the dynamics of a situation is to do just that: state a view tentatively ("John, let me explain to you what depression is like; then you can tell me whether or not that rings any bells. You see, first something, legitimately or otherwise, gets you down; then. . .").[15] Hopefully, after a brief description of the depression dynamic John may say, "Yes! That's it! That's the sort of thing I have been involved in." Upon such a response, a fuller description may be given, this time with complete explanation concerning the place of sinful self-pity, responsibility failure and the tragic consequences that accrue to those who follow their feelings.[16]

---

[12]Cf. *ibid.*, pp. 321ff. The somewhat lengthy sample of instruction in this place is perhaps typical of what I have called applicatory instruction. See also pp. 305-306.

[13]Cf. *ibid.*, pp. 276, 277. Also, of course, in cases where the nature of the problem is fundamentally educational.

[14]See warnings about "rice counselees."

[15]Tentative suggestions can be made at any time *so long as they are clearly identified as such.* Failure to do so can give occasion for serious difficulties.

Some counselees are far *too* anxious to understand what is at the bottom of their difficulty, and may fasten on to any explanation, true or false. They then will begin to focus upon and interpret (misinterpret) all subsequent data in the light of the false explanation. Whenever there is a possibility that this may happen, the counselor would be wise to underscore the tentative nature of his feeler-explanation by suggesting no less than two tentative interpretations. ("In a situation like this there are several possible explanations. We could possibly be facing. . . or. . . or. . . John, do you vibrate to any one or two of these?")

[16]For more information on depression and what to do about it, cf. *The Christian Counselor's Manual*, pp. 275-383.

If, on the other hand, John's response is, "Well, perhaps that is my problem, but I don't think that it is really like that," fuller explanations can await further ascertainment of the true cause of the difficulty. In other words, full 15 to 20-minute instruction periods in a 60-minute counseling session ordinarily should tend to appear further along in the series of sessions, and only rarely (some of the exceptions have been noted above) in the first or second sessions. Early instruction will tend to be brief, minimal or tentative and largely related to seeking explanations of problems and giving how-to explanations of homework assignments. Full biblical interpretations of problems often must wait until the counselor is more sure of the fundamental dynamics with which he is dealing.

Since the counselor should be more interested in focusing upon the present in the initial situations,[17] and the past and future later on, emphasis at first will fall upon *what* can be done about the situation and instruction will center around *how* to do what God says to combat the problem. ("Bill, we are more interested at the moment in *what* you must do to straighten matters out with Marie than in *why* you screamed at her. Basically, we know the why anyway. . . because you are a sinner. So let's look at what God says in the Scriptures about the importance of immediate reconciliation; then, having effected that, under less pressure, and perhaps even with her aid and encouragement, we shall be in a position to help you to learn how God directs you to avoid future failure.") Put first things first.

Often, in an early session, repentance, forgiveness, reconciliation and such concepts will need to be explained along with the how-to steps appropriate to each counselee's circumstances. Such explanations should be made clearly, concretely and persuasively (not merely informatively), with a minimum of jargon and technical vocabulary.[18] One of the best ways to explain is by the use of examples. This was Christ's method ("The Kingdom of heaven is like. . . "). The counselor must remember that until the biblical instruction has been given in an applicatory manner the task is incomplete. Until he and the counselee have understood not only what the Bible means, but also what it means in terms of the counselee's situation ("Jeanne, the meaning of this passage for you and Joe is plain: you must break up this illicit relationship"), the counselor's instruction is inadequate.[19]

17Cf. *Competent to Counsel*, pp. 151ff.

18Cf. Jay E. Adams, *Pulpit Speech* (Presbyterian & Reformed Publishing Company, Nutley, N. J., 1972), pp. 46-48, 125.

19Cf. Jay E. Adams, "The Use of the Scriptures in Counseling," *Bibliotheca Sacra*, April, 1974, pp. 104-108. The *telic* emphasis in counseling is vital.

Evaluative Instruction

A favorite method often used by Christ was what might be called *evaluative instruction*. This method is most useful to counselors. In evaluative instruction, at a seminar—after *the fact*—he would evaluate the event (i.e., discuss and analyze what occurred). Sometimes evaluative instruction was even initiated by the disciples (e.g., Matthew 13:36; 17:10, 13).[20] In such instances, they had become so involved in the event that they wanted to know more.

The key point to notice, however, is that involvement in following Christ's directions does not take place only *after* full instruction about the event; rather frequently the instruction is stimulated by and grows out of the experience itself. A classical example of this method in counseling is found in John 9:1-41. When the blind man who was healed insisted, "This one thing I know," he was being honest; Jesus had taught him nothing. He had given merely how-to instruction. Later, after the healing, Jesus explained more about himself (vv. 35-41). Skill in the use of this methodology is vital to much good counseling. To put this methodology into perspective more concretely, it may be well to focus upon some concrete examples. Take the case of a depressed teacher who has been assigned as counseling homework the task of grading all of the papers and tests that have piled up on top of one another over the last month. When she returns after doing so she will feel much better. Then is the appropriate time to give full instruction about the dynamics of doing and feeling. It can be understood, appropriated and remembered much better, and may become something of a paradigm case upon which to hang such (otherwise abstract) principles as "Do not follow feeling, follow God's Word," "Do what God requires you to do no matter how you feel," "Do right and you will feel right," or "Depression comes when we allow small unpleasant chores to pile up because we follow our feelings about doing them." By full instruction, the paradigm case may become the key to unlock more serious difficulties to be encountered in later sessions.

Consider another example: the case of a husband and wife who have lost vital communication. Upon reestablishing communication through the use of a conference table,[21] they are ready to listen to fuller explanations of the value and ways of developing and maintaining communication. Prior to a *taste* of it, the lectures, the explanations and the exhortations concerning communication that a counselor might give, valid, true and persuasive as they might be in themselves, all are likely to fall upon bad soil. Now that the

---

[20]First came the event, then the discussion, finally (v. 13) the understanding.
[21]Cf. *The Christian Counselor's Manual*, pp. 321ff.

flavor of communication has been savored by them, with its possibilities and joys, the counselor will find that the ground has been plowed and is ready for seed.

Instruction at the End

Another time for full instruction comes toward (or at) the end of the counseling series. During the last session or at the six-week checkup that follows it, the counselor would be wise to take the time to do several things:

1. Survey the whole period of counseling, bringing the whole into perspective, giving an evaluation (and reevaluation) of the entire situation from the vantage point of hindsight. Misinterpretations previously made may be corrected, partial or fuzzy understandings now may be sharpened and fleshed out, disconnected observations may be woven together into the whole. No counselor should miss this opportunity (although many do). It is often to the counselee's great advantage to have *him* sum up. Indeed, where it is possible, the counselee may be asked during the six weeks prior to the final checkup[22] to write out such a survey for himself. This can be used by the counselor to evaluate the counselee's understanding of what has occurred and to furnish him with information regarding any misunderstandings or gaps in the counselee's thinking.

2. Give full instruction about what to do to avoid future failure. Clear-cut how-to steps that grow out of successful pursuance of the counseling assignments should be presented in explicit form (usually written) so that in any future temptation the counselee will know precisely what to do to avoid sinning: "Remember, self-pity sessions can be avoided by (1) praying briskly,[23] (2) turning to your Philippians 4 think list and concentrating on a profitable activity instead."

3. Give full instruction about what to do to recoup in case of future failure. Since so long as we live in this world we can never live sinlessly, counselors should remember this fact and anticipate failure (as indeed the Scriptures in a realistic manner continually do) and instruct the counselee about what to do if and when he finds it necessary to follow the instruction.

---

[22]Cf. Jay Adams, "How You Can Get the Most out of Counseling," *The Big Umbrella*, p. 162.
[23]So that the prayer is not turned into a self-pity session.

In presenting the gospel to an unsaved counselee, it is also useful to remember that Christ frequently evangelized with one hand while helping the person out of a dilemma with the other. He healed bodies and souls, cast out demons and forgave sin. The same fundamental method must be used by counselors. Initial help may be offered to solve some pressing problem with which the counselee's mind is preoccupied ("Her bags are packed, she is planning to leave me!")[24] so that the way may be cleared for subsequent instruction concerning salvation. The good news (gospel) is not a non-cognitive message, but contains factual historical elements (cf. I Corinthians 15:1-4). To present the gospel is to give instruction from the Scriptures which "are able to make you *wise* about salvation" (II Timothy 3:15). But in states of high negative emotion counselees usually are impervious to instruction concerning anything other than the problem occasioning the emotion.

Instruction of various sorts also may take a variety of forms: desk turnover charts, chalk boards, written assignments, attendance at courses, booklets, research assignments, interviews and involvement in discipleship contexts are but a few of the numerous possibilities that may be added to the basic stand-by: verbal instruction. Even verbal instruction, however, should be concretized and visualized by the use of applicatory examples and picture language. It is not easy for most counselees, particularly when they are confused, to understand totally abstract material.

EXERCISE

For the Student

1. Watch, particularly, the tendency to give too much full instruction too soon. This is a strong temptation for seminary students.

2. Analyze *what* you are doing in counseling. At the end of each session make analytical notations. For instance,

"Session #2 - 4 instructional units (lengths: 5 minutes, 3 minutes, 10-12 minutes, 5 minutes. Total 23-25 minutes of instruction). Probably too much and too long for this early session."

---

[24]Obviously, a counselee in such emotional turmoil usually will be unwilling to listen to the gospel until the immediate problem has been mitigated at least somewhat.

For the Pastor

Keep a record of successful topics for instruction that you have given during counseling sessions with a brief sketch of each. Refer to these from time to time as reminders for future sessions.

Sketches

Sketches

CHAPTER XII
COUNSELING DISABLED PERSONS

There is no question that physical disability can lead to decided disadvantages, particularly in our highly complex, fast-moving and competitive world. The present connotations of the word handicapped give ample expression to this fact.[1] The handicapped person does not have an easy row to hoe. He knows this, and often, when the disability is of high visibility, so do others. How he and they handle this knowledge can make all of the difference between a productive life of joyous service for Christ and a bitter life of misery and regrets with little to show the Master when He returns to ask what was done with what the counselee may refer to disparagingly as his one talent. Proper pastoral counseling often can be the catalytic agent that brings about this difference.

There are fundamentally two times when counseling of disabled persons is indicated: (1) When the disability has just occurred (the loss of a limb in an accident, etc.) and (2) when a member shows that he or she is failing to cope with a longer-standing disability. ("I've tried and tried and tried, but I can't go on any longer.")

In the first instance, normal pastoral concern during the time of crisis or need will lead to natural counseling opportunities that should not be missed. The section on grief (Vol. I, Appendix A) suggests ways in which to turn such times of difficulty into opportunities for Christian growth. Much of what applies to grief over the loss of a loved one applies as well to the loss of one's former abilities, which also may lead to the loss of a job and/or adequate financial support. All of the fears and resentments mentioned there just as readily may be occasioned by a serious disability. Moreover, the basic principles of biblical counseling concerning self-pity, fear, resentment, etc., all apply.[2] And of great significance is the fact that

---

[1]E.g., observe the current use of the word in sports.

[2]Cf. *The Christian Counselor's Manual*, pp. 368ff., 413ff., 348ff. There is at present a volume on *Counseling in Crisis* in preparation that highlights information on the special factors that pertain to the suddenness and emergency aspects of loss.

disability (as in grief) may occasion the need/opportunity for large changes in life patterns. The counselor's challenge is to help the counselee to enter into the opportunity provided by the change to serve Christ in new and better ways.

When the pastoral concern for counseling members whose disability is not recent arises out of some change in the status quo, gradual deterioration of a situation, or simply a general growing awareness (or suspicion) by the pastor of the failure of the disabled member to handle his disability biblically, other approaches in addition to those suggested in the material concerning grief must be considered.

There are at least two ways in which the pastor becomes aware of such problems: (a) He is informed by the disabled member himself, by a friend, or by a member of his family; (b) the pastor himself notices a possible problem.

Under circumstances in which direct information is given normal counseling procedures may be followed. It is perhaps important to repeat that when it is *others* who draw his attention to a supposed need, the pastor must not receive what might be called "privileged information."[3] As a condition for receiving any information about others the counselor always must insist that informants allow him to cite the source of his information when approaching the disabled member if necessary. ("I want you to know first that I probably shall find it necessary to tell Bob where I heard what you are about to relate.")

Under circumstances where the pastor himself becomes aware of or suspects the existence of a problem, and where *he* therefore must make the approach rather than the counselee, certain words of precaution may be given. First, because persons with disabilities may be overly sensitive about their problems, he should be careful not to offend unnecessarily. It is possible, of course, for the disabled person from pride or self-pity to be so self-conscious that *any* approach, no matter how careful and loving, would be poorly received. If proper care has been taken, the pastor must not reproach himself when he receives such a response, but must continue to minister *in spite of the response*, recognizing the need that this very response itself indicates.

Another factor must be kept in mind: too frequently, others may fall into the same trap that awaits the unsuspecting disabled member—focusing upon the disability as the cause of all difficulties. The counselor must realize that the member is *first* a human being, not first a disabled person

[3]For further discussion of privileged information cf. *The Christian Counselor's Manual*, pp. 269, 270.

(perhaps it is wrong even to use such labels outside of analytical studies such as this). The counselee, quite apart from his impairment, acts as any other sinner does and thus may become involved in various problems for the very same reasons that others do, none of which stem even indirectly from the disability. Therefore, unless he is entirely certain that the difficulty arises from a failure to cope responsibly with the disability (or with its consequences), the pastor should approach disabled persons *in exactly the same way as he approaches others* in his congregation.[4] He will do this by stressing the *observable problem* ("Joe, I've noticed that you haven't been to many services lately"), not the *suspected cause* ("Joe, I'm concerned that you haven't been coming often since your accident"). It may turn out that the cause is quite distinct. ("Well, pastor, my accident has nothing to do with the matter. The fact is, I have begun to question the validity of your Calvinistic teachings.") There is no reason to wave red flags and to run the risk of raising additional problems when it is unnecessary. It is altogether possible that the accident and the non-attendance are merely coincidental. It is also altogether possible that the response about Calvinistic teachings is a smoke screen covering deep embarrassment or resentments over the accident. Further discussion alone may enable the pastor to discover this (e.g., if discussion of Calvinism is totally non-productive; particularly if there is seemingly no real concern for the discussion). All that I wish to point out here is that the pastor always should ask himself: "Is the problem really related to the disability?" rather than to *assume* a positive answer to this question whenever a disabled member needs counseling. In every contact, in every approach, unless the matter plainly relates to the disability, pastors should speak to disabled persons *exactly as they speak to any other member.*

Having raised these precautionary matters, it is now possible to consider some of the problems (or peculiar combinations of problems) that are likely to be encountered when ministering to disabled members. While disabled persons are subject to all other difficulties as well, pastors will find that the following problems occur with sufficient frequency that he should be aware of the possibility of their presence and in counseling should probe to discover whether they *are* present:

1. *Self-pity* — "Look what happened to me: *why* did this happen? I'm no longer good for anything," etc.
2. *Self-centeredness* — "I don't know why they did that; after all I'm a

---

[4]For further help on making such approaches cf. *ibid.*, pp. 220, 221. See also supra, Chapter VI.

paraplegic. I don't go there any more; they refused to build a ramp for my wheelchair," etc.

3. *Manipulation of others* — "How can you go out and leave me alone in this condition?"

4. *Resentment* — (seen in several statements above) toward God or toward others.

5. *Blame-shifting* — (using disability for an excuse) "After all, you couldn't expect me to come in *my* condition; I'm sorry that it didn't get done; obviously I couldn't do it and I don't know why Mary didn't."

6. *Laziness* (cf. 5).

7. *Depression* (stemming from 1, 4, 5).

All of these problems must be faced in counseling. What I have said elsewhere about anger and resentment, self-pity, depression and blame-shifting I shall not repeat here. But since that means quickly skipping over much that is crucial to the counseling of disabled persons, I do wish to urge the reader to review that material in conjunction with this current study.[5] Here, instead, I shall try to point out additional suggestions for adapting the basic approaches outlined elsewhere to the disabled.

Challenge

First, the counselor should challenge the disabled Christian to live up to his full capacity (even if this capacity is now somewhat less than it used to be). The key passage about the body of Christ (I Corinthians 12) can be used with peculiar effect in stressing the need to find a place of ministry to others (ministry to *others* is an essential ingredient in helping self-centered, self-pitying persons to change[6]). Of all persons, the physically disabled person can be brought to recognize with vividness the handicaps that develop when any part of the body is disabled. The application of his own problem to the body of Christ and the need for his ministry in it (whatever that may be) is direct. If he protests that (1) he is now useless or (2) that he can no longer do what he once was able to do, he can be faced with the facts that (1) "Jesus Christ must think differently since He left you here for some reason," and (2) "It may be true that there must now be a change of ministry. But you must not regret the fact, for it means that you have been restationed by Christ for new duties in His service." The counselor may point out that perhaps the most exciting, the most exacting and most

---

[5]Cf. Chapters 31, 32, 33 in *The Christian Counselor's Manual.* Also see *Competent to Counsel*, pp. 147ff, 220-228; 116ff, 141-148; 45-48, 212ff.

[6]They must be shown that they will lose their lives when they selfishly seek to save them and that they find them only in losing them for the sake of Christ and His Kingdom.

productive stage of his life lies right ahead; if he was faithful in little things God may now be ushering him into larger responsibilities. One thing is certain: his future service is needed, may be fruitful and (indeed) ought to be viewed with excitement and anticipation in Christ. Moreover, the pastor may assure him that he can be certain that whatever the challenge and whatever the accompanying difficulties, he will be adequate for them in Christ (I Corinthians 10:13). Christ may in larger ways than ever be teaching him, and others through him, how He makes His strength perfect in our weaknesses. The vessel is earthen—with *all* of its attendant defects—as He said, but the treasure it contains is costly. He may have determined that its beauty may shine most clearly in such a context. Challenge, then, challenge to new and/or renewed service for Christ is a most essential element in counseling newly disabled persons. Their biggest problem may be their unwillingness to change or fear of change. Change is the factor most feared by many, but for the Christian this should not be so.[7]

Discovering Gifts

Secondly, disabled persons need to discover, develop and emphasize the gifts that they are able to exercise. To excel in these, while forthrightly acknowledging limitations, is of the essence. Romans 12:3 speaks of making a "sober" i.e., realistic and emotionally cool assessment of one's capabilities in order to determine his place of ministry and vocation. One who is filled with regrets, resentments, and self-pity is incapable of making a sober self-analysis. Often such sinful attitudes, and the actions that accompany them, arise from pride, or (as Paul calls it) the tendency to "think more highly of himself than he ought to think." That, not so surprisingly when you think about it, can happen even to disabled persons who declare that they "don't deserve to suffer like this."

Blessings of Limitations

Limitations can become a source of great blessing to those who previously dissipated their energies by spreading themselves too thin. Sober evaluation discloses facts like this. A disability can automatically chop out of one's life unnecessary areas detrimental to his well-being. Limitation, positively viewed, means the opportunity and challenge to focus and concentrate, thus giving opportunity to excel. Failure to focus interest and effort is a principal cause of mediocrity. Limiting disabilities thus can remove the temptation into which so many fall.

---

[7]See extensive remarks concerning Change in *The Christian Counselor's Manual*, pp. 161-190.

Closely connected with the idea that limitations allow one to do more with less is the fact that disabilities often lead to the necessity for new discipline. In my pamphlet, *Godliness Through Discipline*, I have explored the importance that discipline plays in sanctification. The discipline *forced* upon the diabetic or the recovered heart patient can be a blessing without disguise. His whole pattern of life of necessity may be changed for good. He must now be careful to observe stricter dietary and/or sleeping habits that can have beneficial side effects in every area of his life.

Disabled persons in finding their place in life are *forced* to consider their *whole* manner of life, as *every* Christian should (cf. Ephesians 4:22), but only too few actually do. Numberless offshoots of blessing may come from intensive self-reevaluation in the light of the Scriptures—changes in habits, priorities, schedules, use of time, etc.[8]

Turn Liabilities into Assets

Finally, it is important to help the disabled to learn to turn their liabilities into assets. Some wit has said, "When God hands you a lemon, make lemonade." Paul discovered how to do this.[9] There are many forms that such activity may take. One counselor learned how to do so in counseling. He would listen long enough to the complaints of counselees about their minor irritations and difficulties to provide them with enough rope to hang themselves; then he would propel his desk chair out from behind his desk, pull up his pants revealing two wooden legs, and say, "O.K., let's talk about your problems!" A counselee, unable to walk, may read textbooks on to tapes to help a blind student through law school. He thereby has found a way to minister to another who is disabled by a different problem. On the other hand, a blind counselee with a keen sense of hearing may find vital work in producing quality tapes for a local Christian tape ministry.

In conclusion, I should like to emphasize two things. The first may be apparent already: it is the need for a disabled person to work at productive, meaningful activity. The second is implied, but not perhaps so apparent: his need for community. Disabled Christians may (1) out of embarrassment (i.e., pride), (2) from difficulty of mobility, or (3) because disability also makes them shut-ins,[10] tend to avoid or lose contact with others. Not only do the Scriptures clearly indicate the need that they have for the fellowship of the saints, but they also point out the need of the whole body for the communion of the disabled saint. He must be counseled never to

---

[8] I am not referring to unstructured morbid introspection, but rather to purposeful focused evaluation in the spirit of Romans 12.

[9] Cf. II Cor. 1:3-6; Philippians 1:12-18.

[10] See comments on ministering to shut-ins, Vol. I, pp. 126ff.

break and always to deepen his relationships with God and his neighbor. The summary of God's law is to love God and neighbor to the full ("with heart, mind, and soul" and "as yourself"). The recluse, the ascetic, the loner and the disabled person who breaks community with others fails to obey (at least) the second commandment (in fact I John indicates that he breaks both since he cannot love God if he does not love God's children[11]). The commandment to love a neighbor *requires* neighborliness as the basis for its fulfillment. Any Christian, disabled or otherwise, who denies his social needs and obligations rebels against the whole of the Scriptures. Therefore, counselors will seek to urge disabled persons to find useful work and to develop mutually beneficial social relationships. When either of these goals (both so important that they are mentioned as essential to man even *before* the fall)[12] is unattained, the disabled person will find himself in serious difficulty.

---

[11]I John 4:21.
[12]Adam was to tend the garden and God said, "It is not good for man to be alone."

EXERCISE

For the Student

Below list ten disabilities together with corresponding opportunities for meaningful occupation and social contact.

Disability	Occupation	Social Contact
1.		
2.		
3.		
4.		
5.		
6.		
7.		
8.		
9.		
10.		

For the Student or Pastor

Below:

1. List all of the disabled persons you know.
2. Divide them into two categories: (a) those who are successfully handling their disabilities God's way; (b) those who are not. Discard names of any about whom you are uncertain.
3. Under each name list the factors that you think are central to their success or failure.
4. Interview as many of the first group as you can to check out your conclusions and to enlarge your understanding of how they are coping with their handicaps. Record your findings.
5. Enlist them as resource persons to assist in helping others.
6. Write out suggestions for helping those who are failing.
7. Set up appointments with each of those in need and try to help them.

DISABLED PERSONS

Name	Failing to honor God because:	Suggestions for helping:

Name	Successful in honoring God because:	Willing to help others in the following ways:

CHAPTER XIII
A FINAL NOTE ON PASTORAL COUNSELING

I should like to close this discussion of pastoral counseling with the statement of a fundamental procedure that encompasses most of what has been said thus far in this volume and elsewhere, but in a different and more complete way. It can be stated as a set of steps (not all of which always should be taken separately) designed to help counselees face and solve problems God's way. Counselors should stress some such procedures with members of their congregations.

What to Do When a Problem Arises.

1. *Think First of Christ.* Ask yourself, "How is this an opportunity to honor and serve Him?" This consideration will lead to a proper orientation toward the problem. It will enable you to see His providential hand in the trial and to focus upon His honor rather than your possible difficulty or discomfort. It also will orient you toward the proper sort of solution—one that honors Him (whether it is to your immediate benefit or not).

2. *Seek Christ's Wisdom and Strength.* Through prayerful study of the Scriptures ascertain His will in the matter. Christ has the solution to your problem in His Word and gives the strength to meet it by His Spirit. Ask Him to meet both needs. When you are sure of the biblical course of action that you should take, step out in obedient faith, whether you *feel* the strength to move ahead or not. The ability often is given in the doing.

3. *Turn to Christ's Undershepherd.* If steps one and two do not succeed,[1] the member should seek counsel of his pastor. Counsel may be given, or a process of counseling thereafter may ensue.

4. *Engage the Ministry of Christ's Church.* Here, the mutual ministry of other believers may be engaged at the suggestion of the pastor for

---

[1] Through the failure of the counselee, of course; God does not fail. Counselees often are impatient, misinterpret the Scriptures, sometimes pray wrongly (cf. James 4:3), etc. The pastor may be able to identify the source of the difficulty to help the counselee to return to steps 1 and 2.

additional help of some specialized sort as previously mentioned, or the elders may be called upon to exercise the privilege of church discipline.

This four-step program, with clear-cut procedures in this, or some similar form, might be posted on the bulletin board, periodically run as a notice in the church paper, mentioned from the pulpit, etc., until every member of the flock becomes familiar enough with it that he knows what to do when problems arise that he does not know how to handle.

CHAPTER XIV
THE SHEPHERD'S EQUIPMENT

Elsewhere I have mentioned Zechariah's reference to the "equipment of a foolish shepherd."[1] The commentators throw up their hands when it comes to giving an explanation of that cryptic phrase. Frankly, I have no new light to offer either. However, a couple of things are clear.

1. Shepherds used equipment. We know of the rod and the staff from Psalm 23. What other equipment might have been in use from time to time is not so clear. Perhaps David's sling represents an additional piece of equipment.
2. Wise shepherds—in contrast to Zechariah's foolish ones—obtain and use proper equipment, wisely.

It is hard to know where to include a unit on shepherding equipment. Does it belong under the heading of leadership and guidance (administration)[2] or somewhere else? After all, we have been talking already about record-keeping and scheduling. Perhaps it belongs to counseling and visitation (shepherdly care). Arbitrarily, I have included the subject in this volume as a sort of practical transition from pastoral care over individuals to the equipment that enables one to exercise such care freely. Yet, so much more could be said about other types of equipment, like slide projectors, chalk boards, overhead projectors, etc.[3] The selection of the limited number of items mentioned in this section reflects, therefore, not a comprehensive treatment of the subject, but suggestively deals with one prominent area that must be considered in the pursuit of the duties mentioned so far. The discussion of other items will be reserved until the appropriate place to consider each.

---

[1] Volume I, pp. 75ff.
[2] Volume III of this series.
[3] Frankly, many such issues as the use of tape recorders, etc., have been by-passed in these volumes.

THE STUDY

The study is primarily that—a study. It is not a Sunday School classroom nor a church office, but first a study and secondarily anything else. Ever since Paul's expressed interest in books (II Timothy 4:13), preachers—as men of *the* Book—have been scholars who (necessarily) have shown great interest in books and in study. The study is the pastor's place to house and to use these books; it is the place where all of the preparatory tasks for his ministry of the Word occur. It is therefore an important part of his daily environment and should be given serious thought and consideration.

Some ministers always have preferred to locate the study in the manse (parsonage); others want their studies in the church building. There are advantages and disadvantages to both locations, with the church (perhaps) having the edge (or better, a combination of a major study in the manse and a counseling room/mini-study in the church building). Some of the advantages have to do with the family situation of the pastor (are there small children still at home or not?), his study habits (one says "I must have absolute quiet when studying"; another, "That kind of silence deafens me" or "puts me to sleep"). At the church (in the mornings at least) as a rule there are fewer interruptions, particularly by small children and the pastor's wife (the last problem can be a serious one for some men). If such interruptions are likely to become a problem, the pastor by all means should locate his study in the church building. The church study, if it doubles as a counseling room, also has another advantage. It is a more neutral and impersonal setting for counseling. Unless the study in the manse has convenient access from the outside by means of a separate entrance, coming for counseling may become too formidable an obstacle for some persons under some circumstances to hurdle. The study in the church building, unless adequately heated by a separate unit, can be forbiddingly cold in some northern climates during the week when the church is not heated to its Sunday temperature. This, by all means, must be remedied at the outset. The pastor always runs the risk of someone breaking into personal counseling records. So if they are kept in a church study, they must be (1) locked and (2) listed according to code number rather than by name. The names of the coded 8½" x 11" file folders may be decoded by reference to entries in the universal 3" x 5" file index (q.v.). The manse study does, of course, offer opportunities to snatch spare moments for study (and they can be important). A study in the manse also makes it more convenient for the pastor to run down at night during moments of inspiration to do a bit of work. This privilege, of course, can become a liability rather than an asset when abused. Probably the ideal situation, for most pastors, is to have two studies, either the main study in the church building, where most of the counseling also is done, with a small study area in a corner of the manse (perhaps in a multi-purpose or guest room), or the other way around. I personally prefer the latter.

The appearance and atmosphere of the study can be important. The pastor should make it look like a place where he would like to be, because it is a place where he will spend a great deal of time. Probably he will spend well in excess of thirty hours per week in this room doing two of the most important functions of his ministry: studying (and preparing sermons) and counseling. It should be an inviting room, conducive to work, prayer, and discussion. It should be warm, cheerful and light. It should, like the pastor's mind, be organized and uncluttered, but not unused. Its appearance may have more influence upon him than he realizes. For instance, the color of the walls *may* have something to do with the colors and hues of his sermons![4]

In the study, besides ample space for books, and books yet to be purchased (congregations have no idea how many shelves are needed—the rule is that whatever they suggest in building shelves always should be tripled at least),[5] there should be plenty of room for files and storage closets for supplies and equipment. Ideally the room should provide space for a large desk (I now have a 14 foot table instead!), at least one table, a sofa and a couple of comfortable chairs. There should be a warm rug on the floor and good lighting. The decor of the study should be masculine. If there is a choice, opt for movable louvered wood shutters at the windows. Some of the curtains provided (often as the result of a compromise following disagreement among various female members of the congregation) may leave much to be desired. Louvered shutters at once provide a remarkable combination of masculinity, durability, light, privacy and air.

Ideally, adjacent to the church study there should be an outer office occupied by the church secretary, in which all of the congregational supplies are stored (these should never be stored in the study itself). If others can obtain access to the study only by reaching it *through* the secretary's outer office (the pastor may want to use a back door), many

---

[4]Avoid solid reds, ice blues or blue-greens. Orange, rich browns and tans and yellows perhaps are stimulating (though not overly so) while also warm and friendly.

[5]After building many shelves, I have concluded that the book space between the shelves should measure no less than 13 inches.

unnecessary interruptions can be avoided and many persons may be intercepted and screened before they ever reach the pastor himself. The phone should be answered by the secretary on the extension in the outer office. Her presence adjacent to the pastor's study provides a large amount of security for the pastor when counseling single women.[6]

RECORDS AND FILING

The pastor must keep various sorts of records. I have noted already the importance of keeping visitation records to prevent duplication in the use of Scripture readings.[7] These same records may provide many other sorts of data as well (e.g., statistics for yearly pastoral reports; information for the pastor on how many hours he spends in house calling, making sick calls, counseling, etc.). He will want to keep 8½" x 11" folders[8] of notes and other information taken during counseling interviews. These, remember, should be coded and kept locked, with access provided for the pastor alone. These are *his* records; they do not belong to the church. They should be taken with him or burned when he leaves the congregation.[9]

But the great question always has been, how can he keep track of the many sources of information that get tucked into manila folders, that are written on scraps of paper, that may appear on counseling records, that are on pages 50 and 98 of hundreds of different volumes, etc.? Many answers have been given to this question. Ingenious file systems have been developed and much time and money have been spent purchasing and trying to keep these (usually very complex) systems up to date. Most pastors have tried several, only to find themselves either becoming enslaved to the system or throwing over all hope of ever maintaining a system at all. What is the answer?

Young pastors (or for that matter frustrated older pastors), let me strongly recommend to you the one unfailing, universal filing system that solves all of the problems! First, it is inexpensive. Secondly, it is quick. Thirdly, it has a built-in factor that forces you to do daily filing and thus keep up. Fourthly, it has extreme flexibility and portability. Lastly, it provides for filing *anything* (you can even file a record of the blue socks that

---

[6]But see further comments on this point in Chapter 8.

[7]Volume I, pp. 89ff.

[8]Cf. information on materials in the Christian Counselor's Starter Packet (see *The Christian Counselor's Manual*, p. 477).

[9]I suggest the former. Wise pastors will find many legitimate future uses for the information in these folders. They may be called upon to supply important data that can be located only here. Of course, in a long ministry, a man eventually must begin to dispose of files that are 10-12 years old. Even then, he may wish to read through and make notations of potentially significant material before he does so. Reading through old counseling files, moreover, can provide challenge and motivation for improvement.

are in your second bureau drawer). That is what a pastor needs in a filing system: simplicity, portability, low cost, universality and, built into it all, a daily reminder. This magical system I call: THE SHIRT POCKET FILING SYSTEM.

Here is how it works. *Everything* (there are no exceptions) is filed alphabetically on normal, inexpensive 3" x 5" cards. In Volume I, I have already noted how 3" x 5" cards may be used for recording pastoral calls.[10] Anything else can be filed similarly. Let us say that eight magazines arrive in the mail on the same day. There is no time to read most of the articles, even though many of them seem to be of interest. Well then, why read them? Scribble off a card for each topic or text (textual materials also are included alphabetically; Jeremiah and Jones are both filed in the "J" section. The various textual passages are simply filed under "Jeremiah, Bk. of" in their order of occurrence: Chapter 1, Verse 1, etc.). Then put your magazines aside. Later on when you preach on that topic or from the text or when studying that subject, the cards will lead back to the magazine articles which at that point may be read for the first time.

Take the problem of reading. Often, a book on one topic contains a brief section of importance on a subject that is not directly germane to its main thrust (it may be only a footnote). It will be hard to *remember* in days to come where that section may be. Or, as many books do, the one you are reading may have sections on several diverse subjects. These too all can be filed topically (or textually) in alphabetical order on 3" x 5" cards. It is good to read with a pile of such cards at hand. Take cards to lectures; then file your notes. Jot down thoughts on cards beside the bed at night. Carry cards at all times for ideas, illustrations, etc. Remember, the one key is to give to each card an appropriate topic heading ("Justification," "Planning, method of," etc.), and then *slip it in your shirt pocket.*

What assures daily filing is the fact that the shirt must be removed each night. If you sleep in your shirt, I have no help to offer! The cards then being removed from the shirt pocket may be placed upon the wallet or other item as it is removed at night. The next morning, the cards are there to be filed right away. Filing a maximum of ten to fifteen cards (already filled out) each day is no chore. If the services of a secretary are available, the pastor simply hands them to her each day to file. There it is—the most simple, cheap, flexible and foolproof system of filing available for a minister (or anyone else, for that matter). If you have no other or are

---

[10]Cf. Vol. I, p.114. I. M. Jones' card is simply filed alphabetically in the "J" section along with everything else. Of course, a separate section of a file drawer may be set aside for the names of members. But the cards provide for flexibility; each man may do as he pleases.

dissatisfied with the one you now use, try it. You will be glad you did.

Here is what a few typical file cards look like (note the personalized abbreviations used throughout):

About the only complication comes when the reference or item to be filed properly belongs under two or more headings (or perhaps it belongs both in a textual and in a topical position). In such cases, a cross reference card may be made out as below (X= "see cross reference card"):

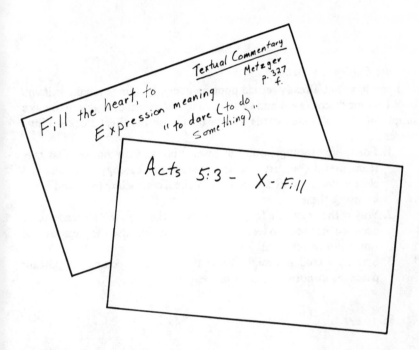

Clippings, tracts and small pamphlets may be placed in folders or (better) in boxes with lids that cover the entire box to its bottom edge. Boxes may be labeled and then shelved in their proper places on the shelf right along with books on the same topic. Cards referring to file folder and box numbers (or titles) are then used to identify their contents.

EXERCISE

For the Student or Pastor

If you have not already settled upon an adequate filing system, or if you have become discouraged and have given up, let me encourage you to buy a supply of 3" x 5" index cards and begin to use the Shirt Pocket Filing System.

1. For topic headings, pull out several books with indexes that may seem useful (be sure one is a systematic theology text, one is a church history text and one is a biblical counseling text) and begin by using these.

2. Stay with the system for six months, so that you will have adequate occasion not only to test the ease of filing, but also the pleasure and simplicity of retrieval.

3. Seminary students might begin to file notes, lectures, important passages in books, etc., from the earliest point.

APPENDIX A
A PERSONAL WORD TO WOMEN[1]

During a series of counseling sessions, the occurrence of the menstrual period sometimes may become the occasion for difficulty that may complicate counseling or lead to temporary setbacks. In order to help you and to help your counselor we would appreciate it if (1) following the first session you will inform either the secretary or the counselor if your menstrual periods are times when you notice that you experience significantly greater difficulties with others who may be involved in your problem; and (2) then please inform us whenever a period of menstrual or premenstrual tension coincides with a counseling session. You may cancel your session if you let us know sufficiently in advance. This is not advisable unless the situation is extraordinary. If you keep your appointment, your counselor will want to know the fact since your attitudes or behavior is likely to be influenced by menstrual discomfort. Prior to any counseling session simply mention to the secretary that you are having your period. She will inform the counselor.

If you are having problems controlling moods and behavior during your menstrual periods, the following information may be of help.

You do not have to become a tiger around the house once a month. Only in rare cases does menstruation *directly* cause such radical behavior change that one may be relieved of her responsibility. (If you think that your case is one of these exceptions after you have read this paper, consult your physician; he can be of help.) In most instances the monthly discomfort can do no more than present you with an *occasion* for sin. It may become a stumbling block in your pathway, but you are responsible if you stumble. There are ways to walk around it, and God holds you accountable for doing so. You must not allow menstruation to become an excuse for becoming hostile, bitter, nasty, depressed, etc. The Bible is clear that the fatigue, the weakness, or the pain that may be experienced is no excuse for failing to

---

[1]Pamphlet available in any quantity from the publisher of this book.

exercise self-control, for allowing yourself to get behind in your chores (which leads to depression), for sulking (in self-pity) or for engaging in spiteful behavior or temper tantrums. While *it is harder* to control your attitudes and your behavior during menstruation (as it is for instance during the physical discomfort of a headache, severe cold or even a painful injury), God holds you responsible to do so. You need not, indeed *must* not, let down the bars.

If over the years you have developed patterns of losing control, these patterns will have to be changed. God's grace is sufficient to enable you to overcome them if you are a Christian (if you are not, your counselor will be happy to discuss the way of salvation with you). Christ said, "My grace is sufficient for you" (II Corinthians 12:9). Paul echoed the truth of these words when he said that he found that in any situation in life he "could do all things [i.e., all that Christ required of him] through Christ who strengthens me" (Philippians 4:13). It is not necessary to allow sinful impulses regularly to have free reign a dozen times each year. The fruit of the Spirit is "self control" (Galatians 5:23), for which (as a Christian woman) you must pray and properly structure your life. You truly can avoid "bitterness and wrath and anger and clamor" (Ephesians 4:31) and "abusive speech" (Colossians 3:8) during this time. No exceptions, either for sickness, suffering, or for menstrual discomfort, are made in the verse. "In the same way" that Christ "endured" suffering, Peter says that a wife must remain "submissive" and maintain a "gentle and quiet spirit" (cf. I Peter 3:1, 4 and 2:20-23; the words "in the same way" refer back to Christ's behavior). If wives are expected to do so during persecution, they can see plainly how this applies also to the lesser discomforts of menstruation. There is responsibility and there is hope in this expectation.

Here are ten guidelines that may help you to endure your monthly trial. You may:

1. Keep a record *ahead* on your calendar and become aware of the days each month when you are likely to face discomfort;

2. Prepare for these by prayer as they approach;

3. Follow a low-salt diet for about a week before menstruation to eliminate the bloating caused by excess water[2];

---

[2]If this does not help, a physician can prescribe a mild diuretic (water tablet) that will help.

4. Plan to take on no unnecessary stress situations during the three days preceding menstruation. For instance, this is not the time to have dinner guests or a special party for little Johnny. While all stress cannot be eliminated during this period, it is possible to schedule those stressful events which are movable around the time;

5. Let your husband know when the onset of menstruation has arrived so that he can take this into account;

6. Refrain from making any crucial commitments or decisions during this time, since they are likely to be highly colored by it (postponement is almost always possible in such cases);

7. Follow responsibilities (before God and man), not feelings (i.e., no matter how you feel, do what you *know* God wants you to do—*even* if you do not feel like doing it);

8. Do not allow yourself to get behind in daily chores;

9. Avoid brooding over problems in self-pity sessions and refuse to attend any pity parties held over coffee or over the phone by neighborhood friends;

10. Make a list of special small acts of love and kindness toward your husband and family which you can do during this time (the list may be consulted as menstruation approaches).

3
PASTORAL LEADERSHIP

INTRODUCTION

Many Christian ministers who believe the Scriptures to be the inspired Word of God and who are concerned about serving Jesus Christ as fruitfully as possible nevertheless seem to have a strange blind spot when it comes to serving Him through Church administration. Some go so far as to decry planning, organization and management as "dependence upon the arm of flesh," while others see it as a wearisome necessity and go plodding along under the sagging weight of a burden that they must carry as "the cross that a minister must bear," or "the price he must pay to be able to preach the gospel."

Certainly for every minister who thoroughly enjoys the work of administration (and there are *some* who get themselves so involved in it that everything else suffers including preaching and pastoral care) there are dozens who can be heard any month at the local ministerium crying the blues over the intolerable load that such work demands. Some call church management a waste of time; others see it as a necessary evil. Many resent the time that it requires which keeps them from the "real work" of the ministry. Yet, in I Timothy 3:1-5 proven managerial ability[1] is set forth prominently as a crucial qualification for the selection of an overseer.[2] Without this ability, Paul says, a minister cannot properly carry out the "work of an overseer" (which includes "taking managerial care of the church of God"). From this verse we can see (1) that management gifts and skills are necessary for discharging the ministerial duties enjoined by God (he must be able to "manage well"), (2) that management is a necessary part of such duties (it is part of overseeing "work," v.1), and (3) that the church suffers when such management fails to be forthcoming (the church needs managerial "care," v.5).

To think, therefore, of planning and church administration as dependence upon worldly or fleshly means is to think in categories not only

---

[1] *Proistemi*—literally "presiding over."

[2] See especially vv. 4, 5. Indeed the word *episkopos* ("overseer") itself indicates that the work of administration is inherent in the ministerial office. The word *overseer* might as readily be translated "manager" or "superintendent."

foreign, but entirely antithetical to the Bible. While church administration *may* degenerate into fleshly dependence upon worldly ways and means, this is in no way a necessary consequence. Indeed, one of the most worldly and unchristian ways of dishonoring God is by the careless, sloppy, confused and confusing manner in which some try to carry on His work. Anything pursued in an unbiblical manner, anything not Spirit-controlled, will become fleshly — whether tightly organized and managed well, or whether loosely thrown together. The Spirit is neither bound by organization, as some think ("If we fail to plan, we may hinder the Spirit"), nor is He unable to work in freer contexts ("Until we work out all of the arrangements we cannot expect God to move"). He sovereignly works when and where and how *He* pleases. We do not have to "free things up" as some maintain (possibly as an excuse for failure to organize). While He may choose to break out beyond our plans and programs, the Spirit thereby does not call us to abandon or to become careless about planning and leadership. When we not only plan, but also submit our plans to the Spirit for His blue-penciling, we do well.[3] We must remember that all that the Scriptures say about the necessity for good leadership (and they say *much* about it) was inspired by the Holy Spirit Himself. It is of utmost necessity, therefore, to recognize at the outset that good leadership, planning and management in the Church of Christ are not merely tolerated or permitted (as one might suppose from listening to many ministers) but required and encouraged by the Holy Spirit. To put it tersely: biblical administration is spiritual.

If the last sentence in the preceding paragraph is true, then ministers dare not speak of administration as a waste of time, or carnal, or of less importance than the other work to which they are called. It is no less spiritual to plan a series of meetings well so that the gospel may be preached than to do the preaching. The one is a vital means for facilitating the other. Indeed, leadership among the people of God, as one may see by reading either the book of Judges or the book of Acts, is Spirit-motivated. It cannot be denied that the Holy Spirit freely uses human leadership, guided by His Word, as the principal means of achieving His purposes. Spiritual leadership is leadership that He empowers to carry on His work.

Nor must leadership, planning and administration be set off from the "real work." This false disjunction has done much harm. Planning, for instance, *is* the real work of the overseer. Indeed, it is so bound up with

---

[3]Cf. James 4:13-17. N. B., James does not *forbid* planning; rather his main concern is to *show how to plan*—by conditioning every plan through a willingness to have God revise or overturn it ("say, 'If the Lord wills. . .' ").

preaching, with evangelism and with pastoral care that it can never be separated from them. The two sides go together. Leadership *is* a part of the work; planning *is* a part of the work; management *is* a part of the work of the minister. If that work is biblical, and Spirit-motivated, it is spiritual work. And, far from hampering the proclamation of the gospel, such work becomes the vehicle that facilitates it. The two go together so closely that, ordinarily, under normal conditions, there will be little or no successful preaching, evangelism or counseling without proper planning, structure and leadership.[4]

In this matter, much depends upon one's viewpoint. Since wrong attitudes quickly grow from wrong orientations let us take a hard look at this question from another angle for a moment.

A general does not consider his army to be a liability, but rather the principal asset that he has for winning the war. Because he clearly recognizes that without a well-organized army he can do nothing to achieve the goals and purposes for which his generalship exists, he prizes his army. He sees to it that every unit is well-disciplined. He sets up networks of rapid communication. He wants not only every division but every soldier in it to be fully skilled and equipped for every task to which he is called. He is deeply involved not only in strategy and command but in organizing a body that will know what to do and how to do it when he determines the proper actions and issues a command.

Why must he be concerned with all of these matters? Because they all hang together; each is dependent upon the other. The general knows that he cannot fight his battles alone. He knows the importance of clear communication, the necessity for training and how essential good discipline is. It is precisely because he is intensely aware that the work to which he has been called must be done *by means of his army* that he busies himself with such matters. It may be said, therefore, that the professional viewpoint of a good general is army-oriented rather than self-oriented. He has come to recognize that just as his soldiers in many ways must depend upon his leadership, he too must depend upon his army; and that means that he will see to it that it becomes a body that is well-trained, well-organized, etc. In short, since he must depend upon his army, he must endeavor to make his army *dependable*.

The bad attitude of many pastors toward administration stems from a faulty viewpoint and a defective vocational orientation. They complain about their congregations, but they have done little to make them

---

[4]Cf. Jay Adams, *Your Place in the Counseling Revolution* (Presbyterian and Reformed Publishing Co., Nutley: 1975), pp. 40ff.

dependable. This attitude surfaces in words and phrases that (although not always expressed quite so boldly) amount to saying: "I can do the Lord's work *without* my congregation" or "If they won't work with me, then so much the worse for them; I'll do it alone."

This viewpoint needs correction in several particulars. Principally, it fails to distinguish between the pastor's obligations before God as an individual Christian and his work *as a shepherd*. As an individual, in some extreme situations it may be possible to continue to serve Christ even when others refuse.[5] But, *as a shepherd*, what can he do without sheep?

An attitude of independence toward the flock is virtual rebellion against the Chief Shepherd; it amounts to a resignation from the task to which Christ called him. Instead, a minister must come to see that his designated task is in its entirety *sheep-oriented*. The great Shepherd of the sheep did not call him to some abstract work called "shepherding," but to the actual earthy task of working with wandering, sick, wounded, smelly sheep. Shepherding is always concrete. That is to say, it involves all of the problems of caring for *sheep*.

And, as is the case with the general, the sort of shepherding to which he is called goes beyond merely tending and feeding the flock for its own benefit. The Chief Shepherd of his sheep wants His undershepherds to nourish, train, mobilize and deploy the flock in ways that *serve* Him and bring honor to His Name. That is to say, the shepherd becomes sheep-oriented in his work because he is already Shepherd-oriented in his allegiance. It is out of love for Him that he serves among His flocks.

As every general knows, it is his task not merely to care for his troops, as an end in itself. His work includes seeing to their welfare and effectiveness *so that they will be ready and able to serve his country*. So too, a good undershepherd recognizes that shepherding is *for a purpose*. He readies and organizes the flock so that the sheep may be able to follow his leadership in fighting the battles of the Lord. The flock, like the army, is the principal vehicle by which the Lord has chosen to carry out His purposes and by which He spreads His glory in the world. Therefore, every pastor must become deeply *committed* to the task of organizing, equipping and leading a well-disciplined flock of God's people in Christ's service. He must become committed to it as a *spiritual* task. When he is so committed, he will not look upon church management as a dull, burdensome and necessary evil, but rather as a vital, exciting and challenging part of the total task for which he has been chosen by Christ.

---

[5] However, no one may dare declare himself independent of Christ's Church (cf. Hebrews 10:25). Also, he must remember, there always are others who have not bowed the knee to Baal.

In the first chapter, therefore, we shall turn our attention to some of the biblical data that show the place and importance of administrative tasks.

CHAPTER I
SHEPHERDS LEAD

To begin with, let me point out that the Scriptures consistently refer to shepherds as "leaders." In one sense, leading may be thought of as the whole task that comprises such matters as training, administration, organization, guidance, motivation, etc. In another sense, it may be narrowed to mean *guidance by example.* I am not going to try to distinguish between the various senses in which leadership may be viewed since the Scriptures themselves seem not to make any such hard-and-fast distinctions. As a matter of fact, the Scriptures seem not to distinguish sharply between any of the functions of shepherdly work. Rather, they view the work holistically even when speaking about its various aspects. Sometimes they use one term and sometimes another to describe the various functions that a shepherd performs in the tending of a flock. It would be unwise, therefore, to try to sharpen the focus too greatly. Instead, I shall simply note what sorts of tasks biblical leadership involves. Perhaps in that way we may be able to develop a view of shepherdly leadership that distinguishes but does not separate functions which of necessity seem to overlap. The essential fact to grasp is that any attempts to lead sheep that ignore, minimize or purposely eliminate any of the several facets of leadership that are scripturally discernible, thereby weaken and dilute both the biblical concept and the actual ministering power of those who make these attempts. In the passages to which I shall make reference in the paragraphs that follow, one can see at least these elements: responsibility, planning, organization, guidance, and example.

The Shepherd as Participant
Notice that when the Scriptures call shepherds "leaders" they continually picture them as *participants* in the activities into which they lead their sheep. They are never looked upon as armchair theorists, but rather as themselves down there on the plain, up there in the mountains, travelling the paths trod by the sheep themselves. Shepherdly leadership is concrete, participative, involved leadership. Shepherds are *with* the sheep—keeping

watch over their flocks by night, passing through the valleys where in every shadow lurks the possibility of death from a wild animal, gently leading those with young and gathering the lambs (cf. especially Isaiah 40:11; Ezekiel 34:15; Psalm 23). It is the shepherd who "leads them out" of the fold and who "goes before them" (John 10:3,4). He defends them from the wolf with his rod. No wonder shepherds are called simply, but pregnantly, "leaders" in Hebrews 13:7,17,24. That is why the writers may urge the sheep to consider their way of life and to imitate their faith (v. 7). The shepherd is an involved example.

The Shepherd as Organizer

It is essential for a proper understanding of this leadership to notice what happens when there is no leadership or faulty leadership. Again and again we are told that as the result of such conditions the sheep are "scattered"[1] (e.g., Ezekiel 34:5). Without leadership, the sheep become confused, each turns to "his own way," and "wanders off." That is why Zechariah was able to portray the disorder among the disciples that accompanied the death of Christ so vividly by use of this shepherdly figure when he prophesied: "Smite the shepherd and the sheep will scatter" (Zechariah 13:7). Indeed, the biblical phrase "as sheep without a shepherd" has become proverbial. Yet like most familiar sayings, we take it for granted and we seldom think of what it means. Consider, for a moment, something of its import. Sheep are helpless and prone to scatter; i.e., to break up into separate single units, to become disorganized and to disintegrate *as a flock*. Unlike "birds of a feather" that "flock together," sheep do not of themselves tend to do so. It is shepherding that produces flocking among sheep. Flocking, or the organization of individual sheep into a definable entity called a flock, is a principal activity of a shepherd. By faithful, personal leadership that involves responsible participation on his part such congregational organization is accomplished. Shepherdly leadership, then, has as one of its chief ends to bring about cohesion and *order*.

The Shepherd as Planner

But notice too, sheep, even where there is a good shepherd, tend to "go astray," i.e., as Isaiah put it, they are prone to turn, "each one to his own way" (Isaiah 53:6). There is, then, a second feature closely related to disorganization. The idea of *wandering* also is prominent (cf. Ezekiel 34:6 and Zechariah 10:2). Sheep not only scatter individually, but as a result

---

[1] *Putz* = scattering, dispersion and confusion. All three ideas are inherent in the word.

wander aimlessly in their own way.[2] It is the Shepherd's work to turn aimless wandering into purposeful travel leading at length to the still waters and to the green pastures. The sheep on his own heads aimlessly in any direction without thought for where he is going or for what the consequence of such a course may be. He thereby exposes himself to grave dangers (Ezekiel 34:8). But the Chief Shepherd is concerned to guide His sheep in the "paths of righteousness." Indeed, in that great covenantal passage where the sacrificial Lamb of God Himself becomes the Shepherd, He guides His martyrs "to springs of the water of life" (Revelation 7:17). So, just as flocking is a shepherdly activity that overcomes the sheep's tendency to scatter by bringing order and cohesion, so too *leading toward a destination* (green grass, still waters) is a shepherdly activity aimed at overcoming proneness to wander by setting forth goals and objectives for the flock. These two activities — organization and biblical goal setting — are so fundamental to shepherdly leadership that they run through every phase of it.

The Shepherd as Ruler

Let us also notice how frequently God calls the minister a "ruler" or "manager," revealing a slightly different facet of shepherdly work. The word *proistemi* ("to preside over, to manage") occurs not only in I Timothy 3:4,5 where proven ability at managerial rule is designated as a requirement for a minister, but also in such passages as I Timothy 5:17; Romans 12:8 and I Thessalonians 5:12. Shepherdly leaders, according to Hebrews 13:17, must be "obeyed." Shepherds were "rulers"; indeed, the thought moves in both directions—kings and other rulers in the Old Testament were often called "shepherds." (Cf. Jeremiah 23, and especially, the remarkable Cyrus prophecy in Isaiah 44:28.) The two concepts are *fused* as God in the second Psalm speaking of Christ declares: "You shall rule (literally, "shepherd") them with a rod of iron."[3] This great prophecy is picked up in Revelation

---

[2]The story of the Book of Judges is the story of wandering sheep without a shepherd. Whenever there was no leadership, every man did what was right in his own eyes (Judges 17:6). When God sent judges to lead, the people followed in the ways of God. Cf. also Deuteronomy 12:8.

[3]The Hebrew of Psalm 2:9 reads,"You shall smash them with an iron bar." A slight change in the pointing of the original text leads to the LXX rendering which agrees with the usage in Revelation. From the ironical play on words used in Micah 7:14,"Shepherd. . . with a rod," there is a reason to see here a growingly close association. So that G. B. Caird, *et al.*, have far less warrant for saying that the LXX and John "made a mistake" in thus rendering the word by *poimaneis* (shepherd) than one at first might think. It is likely that two words— close in sound—had come to be used interchangeably whenever speaking of a forced rule. In smashing the rule of the kings (v. 3) by the missionary preaching of the church (Revelation 19:15),Christ began his rule over the nations (cf. Jay Adams, *The Time Is At Hand*, pp. 80ff.).

2:26,27; 12:5 and 19:15 where in its application the (probably intended) ambiguity also remains.

Of greatest importance is that in all of this, the *leading* work of the Chief and Great Shepherd of the sheep is reflected. It is *God* who *"leads* Joseph as a flock" (Psalm 80:1; also Psalm 23; John 10), who organizes both Jew and Gentile into one flock, who seeks the lost sheep, and who "rules" with the rod of iron.

Shepherdly leadership, then, is responsible participant exemplary leadership that involves:

(1) *Planning* (i.e., the setting of goals and of objectives for the progress of the flock as it seeks to honor God in all of its activities and endeavors; determining where the green grass grows and the still waters lie, and how to discover and guide the sheep into the paths of righteousness that lead there).

(2) *Organization* (i.e., flocking; bringing sheep *together* as a flock, or congregation, teaching and helping them to live, learn, love, and labor together for Jesus Christ).

(3) *Rule* (i.e., the authoritative instruction in and application of the Word of God to the individual and corporate activities of the sheep; management). Other elements either may be distinguished from or subsumed under these, but shepherdly leadership at least always involves these three.

EXERCISE

For the Student

Interview your own pastor (or some other pastor) briefly:

1. To discover his views on pastoral leadership (jot these down, take them on cassette, etc.) and be prepared to share and discuss these with the class.

2. To let him know that you are taking this course, and to ask him if he would be willing to work with you in a variety of ways in the weeks ahead (you might show him some of the assignments in this book that may require pastoral help).

For the Pastor

1. Consider your own attitude toward leadership. Is it

good ☐

poor ☐

inadequate ☐

2. Rate your abilities and performance with reference to:

	good	poor	inadequate
leadership responsibility	☐	☐	☐
planning	☐	☐	☐
organization	☐	☐	☐
guidance	☐	☐	☐
example	☐	☐	☐

3. In the space below, write out suggestions for improvement.

CHAPTER II
LEADERSHIP IN THE CHURCH

All of the leadership activities of the Christian shepherd occur within a given organizational framework: the visible church of the Lord Jesus Christ. While there is plenty of room for individualization by congregations, and for the use of personal gifts among the members of those congregations, nevertheless all such variety occurs within a basic, given structure ordained, built and maintained by Christ Himself. That Church is an organic entity that manifests itself in this world through a visible structure that, for its maintenance, requires planning, organization and rule.

The shepherd must see this Church organization not as an impediment to the smooth functioning of the Church itself, but — as it was intended to be — the very vehicle through which shepherdly work for individuals and families as well as for the whole flock may be carried on. The organized Church is not an evil to be put up with, as some seem to think, but rather the visible manifestation of the body of Christ.

Because it has a visible, organized structure, the Church must be *managed* (I Timothy 3:4,5). And Christ has given officers in the Church to carry out these managerial functions (cf. Ephesians 4:11,12).

Mismanagement, not organization, actually is the evil that so often constitutes the underlying difficulty. It is not easy to bring sinners together into one flock and to maintain the unity and peace of that flock while carrying out the orders of the Chief Shepherd to walk through the barren shadowy valleys toward the grassy pastures that He has mapped out. Not only mismanagement but discouragement, weariness and fear can get in the way. Such work calls for organized guidance through little known paths (that sometimes the sheep do not want to take) toward clear objectives; that is to say, the work calls for good management. Management is responsible, authoritative, organizational leadership.

Let us therefore take a closer look at the authority structure of this flock over which Christ, the Chief Shepherd (I Peter 5:4) through His undershepherds, is the "Shepherd and Overseer" (I Peter 2:25). I shall not limit my discussion to shepherdly images alone, rich as these may be, but shall range over several of the figures of speech used to delineate and delimit the organizational structure of Christ's Church.

Unlike the sort of hierarchical situation that exists in business and in many other organizations, the Church of Jesus Christ is *His* Flock over which He rules both directly and through undershepherds. The rulers of His flock, as well as those whom they rule, all take orders directly from Him. But these leaders are not legislators. He as the Chief Shepherd has appointed leaders and has given to them *His* authority to lead and to manage the flock. This authority is great, yet limited; and it is entirely delegated. No authority exists within the Church except His own.

To each member of the flock, Christ has given gifts through His Spirit and has assigned them tasks to do that are appropriate to those gifts.[1] He has provided leadership for the purpose of helping every sheep to discover, develop and deploy his gifts in ways that contribute to the welfare of the entire flock and that further His purposes in this world.[2] And in accordance with the abilities granted and the leadership requisite for their proper exercise, He has given each member authority to minister in His name.[3] All tasks must be carried out for the honor of the Chief Shepherd. It is clear, therefore, that all leadership in the Church is *functional*. None exists for one's own ends, nor for his personal aggrandizement.

Each sheep in the flock must respect and submit to the authority of Christ, and must recognize that all authority that is exercised legitimately within the flock is His authority. There is no lesser authority. Therefore, he must submit to the undershepherds who manage and exercise oversight as he would submit to Christ Himself so long as they speak in accordance with the Scriptures (cf. Hebrews 13:17). Ultimately each sheep, therefore, submits to Christ alone for it is *He* who is the Shepherd, and they are *His* sheep.

In submitting to the care and discipline of the Church he does so "in the Lord." That is to say, he belongs to a kingdom (to change the figure) that is a constitutional monarchy. It differs, however, from other such monarchies in that the constitution was imposed by the Monarch Himself, not for His own instruction, limitation, etc., but so that every member of the body politic might know the laws and ordinances that He has ordained. By this constitution they may judge the actions and the commands even of

---

[1]Cf. *The Christian Counselor's Manual*, pp. 344-347. See also *infra*, ch. 10.
[2]Ephesians 4:11-16.
[3]Revelation 1:6.

the leaders. While allegiance is to Christ alone, the terms of that allegiance are set forth in the Scriptures. He alone laid down these terms; they have not been acquired through legislation devised by the leadership.

The constitution of the kingdom therefore is not a civil or social contract, negotiated and finally agreed upon by its members after compromises and trade-offs. The Church is neither a democracy nor a republic; it is a theocracy. The Bible is a covenant document divinely revealed and deposited with the Church by the Sovereign Himself. In it are the principles of management that the Sovereign has imposed upon His subjects. The authority of the leadership, individually and corporately, everywhere is conditioned by this constitution, by which also their exercise of Christ's authority is enjoined and delimited. The task of the leadership within the Church, therefore, is to declare, to minister and to administrate. There is no power to legislate.

Every member within the flock must grant to the leadership all proper deference and great respect,[4] but at the same time Christ has made each member responsible to exercise individual judgment concerning the leadership that he follows. That means that the leaders must teach each member adequately enough that he may judge whether those things that they command are truly in accord with the constitution (cf. especially the powerful word of the Apostle Paul on this question in Acts 17:11).

Yet, if a member disagrees with the decisions of the leadership, and because of conscience before God finds that he must refuse to submit to the orders that they give, he must do even that submissively (i.e., in a proper spirit that acknowledges the position and authority that Christ has granted to the leaders of His Church). Moreover, he must recognize the grave danger in which he may be placing himself by such a refusal. It is possible otherwise that:

1. He may be found to be opposing Christ Himself.
2. He may be showing disrespect for Christ, by disregarding the authority that He invested in His officers (cf. I Thessalonians 5:12,13, NASV).

Because of these dangers, only after great care and willingness to be taught and corrected by the leadership as they explain the Word of God to him, may he refuse to submit to them. And then may he do so only if he is thoroughly convinced of their failure to base their case upon the Scriptures. He may not refuse to submit to authority because of personal differences or

---

[4]Cf. Hebrews 13:7,17; I Thessalonians 5:12,13. The respect enjoined in these passages is of the highest level.

because of conflicts of any other sort. He must remember always that the authority to which he submits is not theirs but rather is the authority of Christ. And pastors, difficult as it may seem to them, must teach this submission to their members. Too many congregations have been split because members had not the foggiest notion that such submission is required by God.

Even in those rare instances in which he may find himself basically at odds with the leadership of the Church, a member must be careful about the *manner* in which he differs. He may not do so in a rebellious or independent spirit. Such differences must be stated in a spirit of sorrow and with a willingness to work toward biblical agreement (Philippians 4:2: "be of one mind in the Lord").

All of this is not merely academic; every aspect of it is bursting with practical significance. There are numerous applications of the biblical principles of Church authority that are vital for the well–being of the Church as she endeavors to serve her Lord in the everyday ongoing affairs of life. For instance, consider the following:

1. If Christ expects the members of His Church to respect the authority that He has given to His undershepherds, as I have indicated, they must be *taught* to do so. The widespread lack of respect for such authority in the Church today clearly indicates that there is a mammoth educational task in this regard that must be undertaken by every minister. The fact, then, is that the possession of authority from Christ implies the responsibility to *teach* about authority (cf. Titus 2:15).

2. If Christ expects the members of His flock to obey His undershepherds, then they must *exercise* that authority. They may not preach and act "as the Pharisees," but they must speak as Christ: "with authority." That is to say, the possession of authority requires the need for careful, but courageous, full and firm use of that authority.

3. If Christ has given undershepherds to lead His flock and He expects them to follow this leadership, then ministers of the gospel must *exert true shepherdly leadership*. That is to say, leadership must be personal and involved; such need for leadership implies the necessity for personal holiness of example and walk in the Christian life. The authoritative uniform must be filled by one whose life is submitted to that authority.

4. If shepherds wish to exercise biblical leadership with authority, they themselves *must know and teach the Scriptures faithfully in depth*. That is to say, both leadership and authority imply the need for shepherds with biblical knowledge and wisdom.

5. If they care about exercising powerful leadership, shepherds must be willing to *support every plan, every program and every administrative act by scriptural principles*. That is to say, they will ever study, question, examine and reexamine everything that they say or do as leaders in the light of the Word of God — they will never be satisfied with custom and tradition alone.

6. Whenever they cannot support their actions with certain assurance of biblical backing or whenever they are unsure about the teachings of the Scriptures concerning a given point of faith or life, shepherds may not require compliance from members of the flock to what can be only a tentative (and possibly erroneous) position. That is to say, authority must be used within the limits and according to the teaching of the Word of God, and its use, therefore, implies *the need for great discernment and careful judgment by undershepherds.*

7. Because shepherdly authority and leadership are ministerial, and these elements are sheep-oriented, they exist for the benefit of the flock, and for the good of each member of the flock. They are means for enabling all to grow by grace. That is to say, authority and leadership *must be exercised in love, with care, and with concern* both for the welfare of the flock and of each sheep in it.

8. Since all authority is Christ's authority, it *must be used in His Name and for His glory*. That is to say, authority implies concern for the honor of Christ in every instance of its use.

These eight implications, and their practical effects, are not exhaustive but merely suggestive of some of the more important implications of the concept of shepherdly leadership.

Obedience in Secondary Situations

Questions arise about the secondary aspects of leadership however. Since shepherdly leaders are to be "obeyed" (Hebrews 13:17) and "followed" or "imitated" (Hebrews 13:7), it seems clear that in those matters not specifically ordered by the Scriptures, about which the leaders are obligated to make decisions, the members must submit to their leadership *unless what is enjoined plainly violates biblical requirements.* Otherwise the leadership exercised would be merely declarative and not managerial. For instance, the Scriptures teach that the Church is to meet on the first day of the week for worship; the leaders, therefore, have no authority to decide to hold the regular weekly services on Tuesdays instead. But the Scriptures do not set a specific hour for worship, nor do they require any stated number of such convocations on the first day. Because it is incumbent upon the leadership to see to it that the saints assemble themselves *together* and that in doing so order is maintained and confusion is eliminated (cf. I Corinthians 14:33,40), they must determine how many meetings there will be and when these meetings will be held. The members of the flock should submit to these decisions and order their own affairs to conform to those decisions. Yet, in making such decisions, biblical mandates concerning prudence, concern for the members of the flock, etc., should lead the leaders to consider matters of practicality (e.g., if most of the members are dairy farmers, it would be disruptive to hold services at the milking hour). Members may disagree with the wisdom of the leaders' judgments in such matters and may respectfully request (or even urge) changes, but they have no right to refuse to comply unless they can show clearly that compliance would require them to disobey God. In matters of disagreement about such issues, the elders in the church (like the husband in the home) must have the last word.

But leaders within the Church of Christ do not merely "manage" or "rule." In addition, part of their *leadership* function is to teach, to train, to plan, to organize and to encourage others. And a large share of their work consists of developing the flock itself into a smoothly functioning organism in which each member contributes fully to the operation of the whole (Ephesians 4:15,16). We must turn therefore to the study of a fundamental principle of leadership found in that significant passage. But first, let me issue an important warning.

Management by Divine Direction

While I cannot spend a large amount of space here discussing the problem, I do wish to warn pastors not to adopt business models for the government of the Church of Jesus Christ. There has been too much easy adaptation of pagan principles and practices by evangelical churches in recent times; and the area of leadership and administration has not escaped this baneful trend. One typical sort of problem is the wholesale takeover of Bible-believing congregations by the Management By Objective movement. Some, in the most naively uncritical manner, have accepted it as the greatest boon to the church since the conversion of the apostle Paul. I cannot agree.

The Church of the Lord Jesus Christ is not merely a human organization; it was not created by men, nor was it intended to serve purely human needs. Therefore, many of its *objectives* (for example) will not be realized in time but only in eternity. Moreover, objectives of both sorts (eternal, temporal) are not always subject to quantifiable measurement.

How, for instance, can a pastor judge the amount of sanctification of the believer in the pew at any point? Indeed, he has been forbidden to do so. The Scriptures assure him that only God looks on the heart. He has been told that human judgments will prove false: many of the first shall be last, and the last first. Yet, one of the key objectives of the Church is to help the believer to grow by the grace of God ministered to him. The emphasis upon measurable ends (goals and objectives) may encourage the church to develop a pragmatic mentality and may obscure the need for adopting only those goals and using only those means that snugly fit into the biblical principles and presuppositions. Not all ends are acceptable to God, nor is every means that may be used to attain those ends.

Instead of heralding the advent of usable business practices as the salvation of the church, it is time to emphasize the glorious fact that the Church has at its head a divine King who not only rules and guides her by His Spirit through His Word, but that He does this by the means that He has ordained. He leads the Church toward the goals and objectives which He Himself has articulated. The Church is not free to set its own goals and objectives, or to adopt its own means. All legitimate goal-setting and means-using that go beyond the foundational revealed goals and means, at every point must grow out of and depend upon those which are scripturally revealed. Such goals and means, therefore, always will be of a secondary, derived and short-term nature. Any help that may be obtained from Management By Objective, PERT or other business and management schemes must be subjected to strenuous evaluation in the full light of all of the foundational biblical principles. Otherwise (and this is what has happened) the Bible will be by-passed or accommodated to fit the secular scheme.

The pastor must remember that unlike the businessman, he has divine direction available. His situation truly is unique. In this he should rejoice. The organization in which he functions was "built" by the Lord Jesus and was given its commission by Him. Means which may at times seem not too effective (preaching, for instance) may not be abandoned in favor of what may be hoped to be more effective ones. The King of the church has given orders: "preach the Word ... in season and *out of season."* The church has no option about the matter. Her only problem is to improve that preaching; she may not question whether the means is to be continued or not on the basis of whether it is looked upon as foolish. The Lord, through Paul, has already pointed out that in the eyes of unconverted men the preaching of the Word is foolishness. On strictly business principles, preaching probably should be abandoned.

The pastor must recognize that the Scriptures are the basic Management

Guide for the church. Any ways or means, and goals or objectives, that do not accord with that Guide must be abandoned or modified so that they do. The practice of running off after the latest ideas cooked up in the American Management Association think-tanks must give way to more mature evaluation. The greatest danger is for preachers who are discouraged over the growth of their congregations to walk wide-eyed into the conferences held by well-meaning Christian businessmen, and buy the tempting wares that they find displayed on every shelf. These businessmen usually have little regard for the biblical principles of church government, little knowledge of the theology that undergirds the objectives of the church and little ability (or concern) to do the painstaking exegesis that is necessary to acquire criteria by which to evaluate the world's products that they are wholesaling. Pastor, you must beware. You have a Standard of faith and practice, and you should not be surprised to find that this Standard differs radically from the latest pronouncements of the A.M.A. Why should not the church run smoothly if she seriously follows the directions of her Head and King? Should not the A.M.A. take a leaf from the church now and then?

Consider some facts. For one thing, the analogy of the church and a business is not exact. Indeed, while the church is likened to many other organizations in the Scriptures (a flock of sheep, a family, a kingdom), it is not compared to a business organization.[5] Naturally there are similarities, but it is my contention that the differences (which are many) have not been taken seriously. For instance, one would expect to find differences of the sort that exist between a business and a political organization, since the church is God's *kingdom*. In politics not everything is done with profit as the sole objective; there are other considerations as well (international relations, etc.). The differences between a business and a *family* (which like a political government does have a business side) also must be taken into account. For one thing, elements of parental and brotherly love will strongly influence decisions made by the family—an influence that surely would never enter the minds of the hard headed captains of industry, let alone direct their planning conferences. So you can see even from these brief considerations that the uncritical adoption of the business model for applications to the management of the church is unsound and dangerous.

Uncritical Adoption of Business Practices

I say *uncritical* because it is in that aspect of the problem that the danger

---

[5] *Aspects* of business life are appealed to (cf. Matthew 13:45), but while Christians are called sheep, brothers, etc., they are not called *businessmen*.

lies. A Christian is uncritical in adopting an objective, a goal or practice (1) when he has not searched the Scriptures first to see if they speak directly to the matter under consideration, (2) when he fails to test it by the Scriptures from every angle, (3) when he unwittingly brings the branch, trunk, roots and dirt along with the leaf, and (4) when, having assured himself that there is adequate reason for the adoption of a principle or practice, he fails to shape it to fit the Bible but instead allows it to bend the Bible out of shape to make room for it. It is my conviction that this has been done far too often (and far too readily) not only in the area of counseling (about which I have been speaking for some time)[6] but in other crucial areas of church life as well. One of these areas is management and administration. Insofar as the church allows itself to be managed by the world's principles, she can expect to run into problems with God. *He* is running the church and He will have it run *His way!*

Pastors must consider it of prime importance, therefore, not to allow the church to be run strictly according to business principles. Businessmen in the congregation may clamor for more efficiency, etc. (and their pleas must be heeded if the church has become inefficient), but they must not (as a result) be allowed to reshape the church by the principles of business and management. The church must be shaped by her sovereign Lord!

EXERCISE

For the Student and the Pastor

Obtain some business and management materials. Make a casual survey of these materials and list:

1. Practices that are in conflict with the Scriptures.

---

[6]On this subject, see especially my recent book *Your Place in the Counseling Revolution* (Presbyterian & Reformed Pub. Co., Nutley, N. J.:1975), chapters 2 and 3.

2. Practices that, carefully adapted in a critical manner, could serve the church.

CHAPTER III
LEADERSHIP MEANS EQUIPPING OTHERS

Consider the fundamental principle of biblical leadership that is found in Ephesians 4:11,12:

> And he gave some as apostles, and some as prophets, and some as evangelists, and some as pastors and teachers, for the equipping of the saints for the work of service, to the building up of the body of Christ.

Probably there is no more important criterion by which to measure the administration in the modern church than that which is found in this verse. Let us, therefore, take time to open up the verse, together with a few of its implications. This vital passage indicates that the leaders of the church are "given" by the risen, triumphant Christ to His Church. Unfortunately, this is a gift that too often men have set on the shelf and forgotten, failing to recognize its true purpose and importance. This gift does not have an ornamental but rather a practical purpose. The pastor-teacher (in the original these two terms are united in such a way that it is clear that they are used to designate one and the same person[1]) was given for the expressed purpose of equipping the saints[2] for *their* work of ministry. This equipping, in turn, has as its goal enabling the entire body to build itself up in love (v. 16). The fundamental principle to note is that biblical leadership has in view the *challenging and equipping of the whole flock for ministry* (cf. especially Hebrews 13:20,21 where the "Great Shepherd of the sheep" is called upon to *"equip* you in every good thing *to do His will"[3]*).

---

[1]This fact I have indicated by the hyphen: the "shepherd-teacher" or "pastor-teacher."

[2]I.e., the whole body; all of the sheep in the flock. The word *saints* means: "those who have been set apart" by God from sin to righteousness. It is used in the New Testament to designate living persons (all true Christians).

[3]The word *equip* is *katartizo*, the same word that is used in Ephesians 4:12 and, incidentally, in II Timothy 3:17 (in a slightly different form).

The very important corollary to that principle is that neither the pastor nor the elders should attempt to do any of the work for which God holds the whole body responsible. As members of that body, of course, the pastors and the elders must become involved. But, as *officers,* it is not their duty to step in and do for him what Christ has called any member to do himself. Whenever he does so, the shepherd preempts the blessings that belong to the member, deprives the whole body of the benefits that are intended for it, and fails to challenge and train him for his ministry. Instead, in following the principle set forth in Ephesians 4:11,12 he must make every effort to encourage and enable the delinquent member to assume his proper role for Christ.

Let us take a typical example of an area in which this principle speaks to a problem commonly seen in evangelical churches — the evangelistic outreach of the local congregation. Let us assume, as is so often the case, that the members of the congregation do little or no evangelism. They expect the evangelistic work of the church to be planned and executed by the pastor himself. ("After all, what else does he have to do between Sundays?" and "What do you think we pay him for?") In such instances, what does a new pastor (or a pastor who has become newly aware of his biblical responsibilities in regard to this matter) do?

Well, let us answer first by describing what so many pastors do. Frequently, because he is concerned about the unsaved members of the community around him, after failing to get an immediate favorable response to an appeal for help from the flock, the pastor launches out into a personal evangelism program *on his own.* That is to say, he steps squarely into the center of the trap that has been spread before him. I am not condemning either his zeal or his concern; both are commendable. But zeal unbridled by the Scriptures is like a runaway stallion!

What has he done? Let us analyze both the decision itself and its effects in some detail, since together they constitute a formidable problem that illustrates the cause of much of the weakness found in the contemporary church. Not infrequently does this weakness stem from the fundamental error in the conduct of biblical leadership that may be seen in this decision. It is the error of failing to understand and/or to follow the basic principle of shepherdly leadership enjoined in Ephesians 4:11,12.

Again, let me ask, what has he done? The answer is this: the pastor has determined, contrary to his call and ordination (which was primarily to shepherd and teach his flock), to devote to the work of evangelism a significant proportion of the time that he ought to spend as pastor-teacher. Now, please do not misunderstand. I do not think that he should fail to do evangelism both as an individual Christian, *and as a pastor-teacher*.[4] While he should "do the work of an evangelist" (II Timothy 4:5), both as a Christian (i.e., as a member of God's flock) and as an example to the flock (cf. I Timothy 4:12, but especially Titus 2:7, where "in all things" Titus is exhorted to "be an example of good works," one of which is the work of evangelism),[5] and while he might be involved in as much (or even more) evangelism as any other member of the body, that does not mean that he should try to do any of the work of evangelism *that belongs to each member of the flock*. He must remember that it is true not only biologically, but also in evangelism, that it is sheep — not shepherds — who must produce other sheep.[6]

When a pastor on his own tries to do the work of an entire congregation,

1. He fails because he does not have the blessing of Christ upon this program; he has substituted (well-meaningly, perhaps, but none the less highhandedly *substituted)* a human plan for the divine one.[7]

2. He fails because he does not have the many opportunities and contacts that *only* the members of his congregation have.

3. He fails because he spreads himself too thin, trying to do too much as one person. It is nothing less than pride for any one individual to think that he is capable of doing what God has said is the work of an entire congregation.

4. He fails also as a pastor-teacher. In spreading himself so thinly over the works of evangelism as well as that of shepherding and of teaching, he does none of these things well. His sermons suffer, his members are not cared for and even the fruit of the evangelism usually is minimal.

5. He fails — and this is the most significant failure of all — because, wittingly or unwittingly, he has disobeyed and thereby dishonored the Chief Shepherd by whom he had been "given" to the Church in order to shepherd and teach so that the sheep might discover, develop and deploy

---

[4] If he spends time *teaching* evangelism, both formally and by example, that is a needed and legitimate use of time. One of the shepherdly tasks to which he is called is to equip the saints to evangelize.

[5] Cf. also I Peter 5:3 where those who oversee as shepherds are told to lead not by "lording it over" the flock, but by "proving to be examples to the flock." In evangelism, as in all other good works, the shepherd of the sheep should "lead them out" and "go before them." Sheep must be led, not driven.

[6] That is not to say, of course, that he should not evangelize in counseling or even in his pastoral preaching. In the pastoral messages that he preaches, he should relate every passage to the great redemptive theme that is the fundamental and evangelistic message of the Bible. But, while in every sermon he makes the gospel known, that does not mean that he preaches nothing but the gospel. He must remember Hebrews 6:1ff.

[7] Not that God may not use this failure providentially to bring about His own purposes, which *may* include the birth of many lambs into the fold (cf. Philippians 1:15-18).

their own gifts. Thus he fails to equip each member for his own "work of ministry" (including the ministry of evangelism, which, in part, belongs to every believer).[8]

Let us spend a few minutes more considering this all-too-frequent problem that is illustrative of the general failure of shepherds to devote themselves to the work to which they have been called.[9]

The Chief Shepherd knows best; His orders must be obeyed and His plan must be followed. It is not the part of undershepherds to take it upon themselves to determine other goals and methods. To do so is rebellion against the Chief Shepherd who wishes not only the shepherds but also the sheep to be "equipped" to "do His will." How can sheep be expected to follow God's revealed will when the shepherds do not do so? Their bad example (however well-meant) is culpable; it is nothing short of sin. No wonder the Church of Christ suffers so!

But sin is also always foolish. Consider, therefore, how utterly foolish alternate plans appear when they are compared and contrasted with the biblical one. Perhaps the best way to develop this point is to take a hard look at the way in which the Holy Spirit shepherded the evangelistic enterprise in the early Church. Surely, by way of contrast, it is instructive to compare the rapid growth of the New Testament Church (cf. Colossians 1:6: "in all the world"; 1:23: "the gospel . . . which was proclaimed in all creation under heaven"; Acts 12:24; 19:10,20) with the disturbingly slow progress and meagre impact made in so many communities in modern times. While the contrast in the evangelistic approaches used is vivid, of course this difference in itself does not entirely account for the difference in results. Nevertheless, in some large measure, the modern failure may be traced to this difference, since in those instances today where the biblical approach has been followed, similar results frequently have been

---

[8]Cf. Vol. II of this series.

[9]Illustrative, I say, because the problem extends into many areas. For instance, in the work of shepherdly administration many pastors fail to call upon elders and deacons (not to speak of other members of the flock) to help them as they should, either preferring to do it themselves ("the only way to get a job done is to do it yourself") or giving up when an immediate response is not forthcoming after an appeal for help. (The failure in this case actually may be due to dependence upon the scripturally dubious practice of volunteerism; this will be discussed *infra*.) The pastor is *not* directed merely to challenge members to assume their ministries, but rather is required to teach (i.e., to show them biblically both their responsibility to minister, and how to go about discharging this responsibility) and to shepherd the flock (i.e., to lead and guide them by precept and example—an example that provides the living integration of truth in experience). The Chief Shepherd, through His undershepherds, thus "equips" them for "every good work." Apart from this pastor-teaching work, sheep will find it difficult to respond to the challenge (even when put to them properly).

obtained.[10] When you add to this failure the fact that many pastors have abandoned other biblical patterns or substituted their own programs for them (e.g., failure to adopt patterns of administrative delegation, the failure to exercise church discipline, etc.) you can begin to understand the basic reason for the weakness of the modern church.

To continue to etch out the biblical picture in stark contrast to modern substitutes, let me pursue the matter of evangelism a bit more fully.

The early Church moved out of its first stage (preach the gospel in Jerusalem) into the second (and in all Judea and Samaria) not as an evangelistic effort headed by the apostles.[11] Indeed, when in God's providence the persecution under Saul drove the church out of its bottled-up condition in Jerusalem, Luke specifically records the fact that the apostles were not personally involved in that evangelistic thrust ("and they were all scattered throughout the regions of Judea and Samaria, *except the apostles,*" Acts 8:2b). So those who went into those regions were not the leaders but everyday, man-in-the-pew Christians of the Church of Jerusalem.

Note next what they did: "Those who were scattered abroad went about announcing the message of good news" (Acts 8:4, literal translation). They presented the gospel to everyone they met. They did not invite people to church meetings, they did not take surveys in the community; they evangelized (i.e., they announced the good news about Christ). To present the gospel is to announce the good news about what has been *done* by Christ. The good news is not a command or exhortation to do something to save one's self (it is proper to exhort someone to repent and believe the good news, but that is not the good news itself). What, then, is the good news? Paul tells us in I Corinthians 15:1-4. Notice, as you read these verses, how the news itself contains two elements, both of which were prophesied in the Old Testament ("according to the Scriptures"):

> Now I make known to you, brethren, the gospel (good news) which I preached to you...that Christ died for our sins according to the Scriptures, and that He was buried, and that He was raised on the third day according to the Scriptures.

---

[10]Not invariably. It is, of course, God's task to produce the results (I Corinthians 3:6,7). There are times when faithful work does not produce fruit (cf. Isaiah 6:9-13). Yet, it is always the responsibility of the Church, by His grace, to do as He has commanded. Results of some sort then may be expected, for His Word never returns "void." At times the results may be persecution rather than belief.

[11]The Holy Spirit outlined His three-stage evangelistic program in Acts 1:8b. In a vital sense the Book of Acts is based upon this program and amounts to an unfolding of the verse.

Nothing more, nothing less is the gospel. A careful study of every recorded proclamation of the good news in the Book of Acts, whether in personal evangelism or in a public sermon, shows without exception that those two points were always stressed. The same good news must be proclaimed today.

Now, back to the main point concerning organization: in the early church, everyone evangelized everywhere.[12] When this again occurs in the modern church, there will be a return of New Testament power.

Look at the two organizational patterns in contrast.

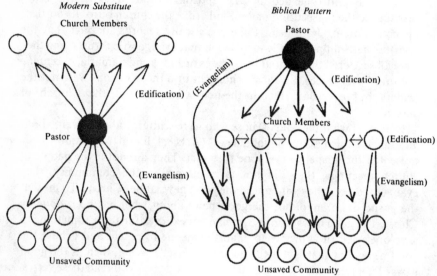

According to this faulty, foolish unbiblical model, the congregation hires a minister to do its work of evangelism. This arrangement is impossible. It is a full-time task to shepherd and teach (edification). One man cannot do that and, in addition, hope to reach the multitudes around him as well. Truly, on this plan, the pastor is in the middle. Nor is the flock taught to engage in edification with the pastor.

According to the biblical model, the pastor and teacher is just that. He instructs, equips, and inspires the congregation to assume its own evangelistic and edificational ministry (note arrows between members). He also evangelizes as a Christian and as the leading example for the members of the local church.

---

[12]The description of a full program entitled *Everyone Evangelizing Everywhere,* based upon this passage, will be found in Appendix A.

EXERCISE

For the Student

1. List the ways and means that you have been equipped by your congregation for ministry.

2. List the ways and means that you have been equipped to evangelize.

For the Pastor
1. How does your church actively equip saints for ministry?

2. What are some ways in which you could improve upon your present program for doing so?

CHAPTER IV
DELEGATION AND SHARING

It is important at this point to look closely at two vital guiding principles of shepherdly leadership and oversight: the scriptural principles of delegation and sharing.

Delegation, in the Scriptures, is inherent in the concepts of scriptural leadership and management. For instance, one who "manages his own household well" may do so to a great extent through the encouragement that he gives to a resourceful Christian wife (like the one mentioned in Proverbs 31 who herself "looks well to the ways of her household," v. 27). To her he may entrust many of those matters for which God will hold *him* responsible as the head of his home. If, indeed, she is a woman who is husband-oriented and will "do him good and not harm all the days of her life" (31:12), he may safely put much authority into her hands. When the "heart of her husband trusts in her" in this way, he is able to rely upon her efforts as a valuable (Proverbs says priceless) asset in carrying out the functions of the home for which God will hold him responsible. Such managerial activity in the church likewise involves delegation of much of the work.

With the delegation of duties, there is, however, the retention of responsibility and accountability. What the husband delegates to his wife, God still holds *him* responsible for. That means that he cannot pass the buck of responsibility to his wife. He must consider himself responsible to God for what she does and for what she does not do. Of course, from her perspective, she is responsible to her husband under God. That means that he must (1) be sure that she is *capable* of doing what he delegates to her before he does so, (2) be certain that she is *willing* to accept the responsibility, (3) continually *keep in touch* with the work that she is doing so that he knows at all times what is happening and (4) *be ready and able to step in* when she needs help, or to do trouble-shooting should the occasion arise.

What is true concerning the possibility of the delegation of duties to others in the home, also holds true in the church. It is interesting to notice how Paul parallels home management with church management in I Timothy 3:4,5. It is not inappropriate, therefore, to ask when considering a man for the position of pastor-teacher, whether (in the home) he tries to do everything himself. How, for instance, does he understand and apply the principles of headship and submission? Does he exercise headship in terms of the principle of delegation demonstrated in Proverbs 31? A man who refuses to use all of the resources that God has provided by giving him a capable wife, and who fails to value her role in the marriage as his helper by happily soliciting her help whenever possible, will not make a good elder. He will find that he has similar problems in delegating work and receiving help from others in the congregation. It is the pastor's duty to put people to work at the tasks that God intended them to do. He must give evidence of willingness and ability to fulfill this duty before he is eligible for ordination as a ruler in Christ's Church. I shall return to the matter of delegation at a later point.

Sharing Work

Paul in I Timothy 5:17 distinguishes between elders who only "preside" or "manage" and elders who also labor at preaching and teaching. The latter are elders to whom has been committed the role of pastor-teacher. The important fact to note is that there are some elders, who, while they do not share in the work of preaching and teaching do act jointly with the pastor-teacher to carry out the work of administration. This concept of *sharing* the managerial work of the local congregation among the elders is of vital importance. God has provided for a plurality of church governors in the local congregation to carry the burden of responsibility and of effort *with* the pastor-teacher. Yet too often church government by elders is minimized in the modern church (1) by pastors who like to make the decisions themselves (many of whom think, "If you want something done right, do it yourself"), and (2) by elders and pastors who look on the ruling elder as someone who attends meetings, debates and votes, but does not actually get involved in the performance of administrative tasks.

Such minimizing of management by elders in large measure accounts for the administrative overload of the minister. Failure to share this administrative load with all of those who preside over a congregation amounts to robbing the elders of the blessings of their call and turns their work into a purely academic task. This failure, moreover, gives them great opportunity to become hypercritical, since they do not have to face the realities of church management themselves. Again, when the pastor endeavors to carry burdens that are too heavy for one man to bear alone, the elders soon will find more than enough to criticize. Much unnecessary dissension arises from this failure to share administration with elders at the level where the rubber meets the road.

From the early days of the organized church of God in the Old Testament, elders helped to bear the load. When Moses attempted to carry the work of ruling his people alone, he soon found that it became too great for him (Exodus 18:18). So, following Jethro's suggestion, he secured others to judge and to become "heads over the people" (Exodus 18:25)[1] together with him. He still handled the most difficult problems personally, while the others judged those cases that were more or less routine (v. 26). Together, they *shared* the work. Thus by this expedient Moses was able to discharge his responsibilities before God.

Moses' willingness to adopt the suggestion of his father-in-law demonstrates that there is a certain amount of proper flexibility about how one may discharge a responsibility. This flexibility, in particular, involves the right to share and to delegate his duties. Yet whenever one shares or delegates, the responsibility always finally rests upon the one whose task it was originally.

Later, we read that God appointed seventy men from among the elders of the people and gave them each a part of the Spirit Who was upon Moses. These men, God said, "shall bear the burden of the people *with you,* so that you shall not bear it *alone"* (Numbers 11:17). The principle of sharing one's task seems prominent in both of these passages.

The continuity of this eldership runs unbroken through the Old Testament (whether there were periods in which prophets, judges or kings also might rule) and right into the book of Acts, where without so much as a word of explanation, of distinction or whatever, Luke moves in one breath from mention of the Jewish eldership to mention of the eldership of the New Testament Church. The transition is so smooth, so natural, so clear that there can be no reasonable doubt that Luke saw the Church's eldership as constituting nothing less than a direct succession from the Old Testament order. Continuity is everywhere apparent: the New Testament assumes much knowledge about church government; there is a decided lack of explicit details, there is a freewheeling use of titles without explanation, etc. One thing is clear, from beginning to end, congregations are described as having a plurality of elders all of whom share in the management of the church.

---

[1]Cf. also Deuteronomy 1:9-15.

Thus, it is vital to understand that delegation and sharing of specific tasks represent two similar, but distinct principles of church management that every pastor must recognize and employ. No minister of the gospel can bear up under the burdens of the governing ministry alone. The picture of a pastor-teacher sharing congregational management with ruling elders, and the delegation of ministry to others within the congregation, gives a much more accurate sketch of biblical church administration than the one commonly seen in the modern church.

Deacons

Yet, not all has been said to complete the biblical picture. Acts 6 describes the origin of the New Testament diaconate, a body of men whose specific calling is to help elders and pastor-teachers by relieving them of numerous administrative details that otherwise might pull them away from the work to which God has called them. When they observed that it was improper for them to serve tables, the apostles were not speaking in a superior attitude, nor were they looking upon such work as "menial" and therefore not appropriate for men engaged in "spiritual" work. No such haughty dichotomy existed either in their thinking or actions.[2] The diaconate was spawned because the apostles recognized that they could not do *everything* and that if they were to remain true to their calling, they would have to place so high a priority upon that work that they could not allow themselves to be diverted from it by a necessary, important, spiritual, but decidedly *different sort of activity* that would be time-consuming. Consequently, they chose to *delegate* the task of the distribution of funds to men of high quality, whose lives were full of the Holy Spirit. They knew what needed to be done, were concerned to see it done well and therefore provided a vehicle that would assure its satisfactory accomplishment.

What is the diaconate? Is it merely a board designed to collect and distribute funds to the needy and poor? Certainly that task was assigned to the original deacons. But the particular issue that occasioned the selection of those deacons called forth a response from the apostles that shows that their function may be conceived of in wider terms. The basic principle behind the diaconate (a "service" or "ministry" board as the word *deacon* indicates) is to give to the pastor-teacher and to the elders whatever help they need to carry on their calling without diversion or distraction. Unfortunately, again and again congregations fail to use their deacons for

---

[2]Indeed the work of the diaconate is spiritual (i.e., Spirit-motivated, directed and empowered) work (cf. Acts 6:3,5 in which there is specific mention of the Holy Spirit's presence in connection with the task).

this vital ministry.[3] Yet, again and again pastors, elders and others can be heard complaining that there is no one to carry out the hundred-and-one small (but important) details that make all of the difference in the smooth functioning of Christ's church. Why should they expect persons to respond to such complaints when they have never been given the authority, the training or the responsibility to do so? Moreover, when general appeals for help are broadcast the responses that are forthcoming may not be the most desirable. Volunteerism is a dangerous practice for which biblical warrant probably cannot be found. Surely when it is substituted for work belonging to deacons it is wrong. Persons who are not fitted for duties may respond so that in the end one might conclude that it would have been better not to solicit help after all. However, in analyzing the situation, it usually turns out that the sense that help was needed was correct; what was wrong was the method by which the help was requested. When a congregation has a vital board of deacons, selected according to the biblical criteria found in Acts 6:3 and in I Timothy 3:8-13, *help of the right sort* is always available.

What, then, is the proper role of the deacon? The diaconate is a board of men chosen by the congregation and ordained by God (and the visible Church through the elders) to serve under the elders (they are fully accountable to the elders who, under God, "preside over" or manage *all* of the activities of the local congregation) as helpers whose task is to relieve the pastor and the elders of any and all administrative details that they assign to them. That means that while the elders are spending their time dealing with a difficult matter of church discipline, let us say, they do not have to take out time to organize the next fellowship supper, or to solve some problem with the ushers or with the florist concerning the flowers for the front of the church, or ... (and, here, you can fill in a hundred small time-consuming tasks necessary to the well-being of the flock). The diaconate is a tremendously important catch-all body that no congregation can afford to do without. The deacon's work is *service:* service to God, to the congregation, to the elders and to the pastor-teacher. The pastor-teacher who does not develop a well-functioning diaconate will find that he has lost one of the essential keys that unlock the secret of good church government.

The Delegation of Delegated Work

Of course, the deacons too may learn to delegate. It is possible that in the

---

[3]One reason for not using deacons adequately is the anomaly of the trustee. Trustees are not a biblical office and should never be assigned the duties of the deacon (except possibly aspects *delegated* by them). Trustees are a legal entity designed to represent the church to the state. Trustees should *always* be elected from the elders and deacons.

discharge of their responsibilities they may delegate portions of these to persons within the congregation who have peculiar gifts for ministry. While retaining their own responsibility to the elders and to the pastor, they may solicit particular persons to engage in specific tasks (e.g., to usher, to cook, to head up a telephone communications system within the congregation, to type and do secretarial work for the pastor, to provide transportation for the young people, etc.). In one sense, they become the ways-and-means committee of the congregation.

Within the principle of sharing, a secondary consideration may be appropriate. It involves the utilization of gifts. While *either* the husband or the wife in the home may have the ability and willingness to keep the financial records for the family, it is neither necessary nor desirable for *both* of them to do so. They must decide, therefore, who will do what. Everything need not be done in duplicate. So, too, within the eldership and within the diaconate, while every member must have all the qualities necessary for doing all of the work required by those offices, it is not necessary for every man to do every job himself. In Christ's organization of the apostles, for instance, Judas (not all of them) carried the bag. Indeed, since everyone does not have every gift in the same proportion,[4] some may *excel* in one or another aspect of the work of congregational management. While it would be unwise to serve only in those areas in which one excels, it might be important to the whole body for an elder or deacon to *focus* his efforts upon those areas.

Moreover, at different periods in his life a man may utilize his gifts in distinct ways. For example, five years ago, when he was a deacon, a man may have developed and utilized certain capacities and particular skills more fully than he does now that he has become an elder. His *emphasis* now may be upon other matters. Before he became a pastor, a man may have spent a much larger proportion of his time doing evangelism, but now since he has been ordained as a pastor-teacher the *emphasis* of his ministry must change to edification. When Moses shared his work with the judges, we noticed, he reserved the more difficult cases for himself and farmed out the more routine ones. The pastor, as a result of his more specialized training, also may wish to do so in some area. On the other hand, an elder with greater financial ability may be able to carry out some of the aspects of financial budgeting better than the pastor or others.

Sharing of work, then, does not necessarily mean exact conformity or duplication of work by those who share it. Sharing means:

---

[4] Cf. Romans 12:6; I Corinthians 12:6.

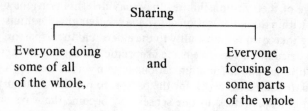

Sharing

Everyone doing   and   Everyone
some of all   focusing on
of the whole,   some parts
                                     of the whole

While certain decisions must be made by all, and certain efforts require the participation of all, various aspects of the work may be apportioned to particular elders or deacons. For example, the details for utilization of the media of communication may be put into the hands of one individual, who also may be peculiarly responsible for publicity since these two areas often converge. He, in turn, may wish to delegate some aspects of the work to others.[5] What he does will be directed by the basic decisions of the whole body, of course, and he will report back to them as he carries out their desires.

Committees

It is tragic when hours of time are consumed by the whole group as everyone attempts to do the work that could be committed to one person. This raises the question of the overuse and misuse of committees. While committees have a valid place, the work of the church has been greatly impeded by too great a dependence upon the committee structure. To lean heavily upon committees rather than upon persons is contrary to the spirit of the New Testament which focuses upon the use of individual gifts for individual ministry to the rest of the body.

Groups, of course, should consult together so that individuals may pool and gather wisdom and thus make better decisions; yet the implementation of those decisions largely must be done by individuals. It is not a wise use of the time of the whole body to decide in a committee meeting how to arrange for transportation to the church picnic when one member of the group is capable of doing this himself. Enough has been accomplished by the whole

---

[5]But one must be sure not to overdelegate; there can be too much of a good thing. Overdelegation breaks down communication and tends to fracture the body. Specialized interests tend to pull a person too far out of the mainstream of the work. Special interests must always contribute to the rest of the body. The eye and the ear must recognize not only their interdependence, but also their purpose in relationship to the whole. Overdelegation has occurred whenever (1) the person first delegating is unfamiliar with the work being done by others to whom his delegatee has delegated it; (2) when someone at, or near, the bottom of a delegation chain is so far removed from the top that he does not recognize the role his work plays in the total picture.

diaconate if the decision to provide transportation has been made, there is an initial input of general ideas, and a trusted individual is appointed to plan and carry out the project.

What is left as a committee's responsibility is really no one's responsibility. That is one reason why it is so easy to proliferate committees; people who do not like to be held accountable know that they may escape that pressure on a committee. Committees tend to shield persons from responsibility. When did you last hear of a committee being reprimanded? It is individuals, therefore, who always should be made accountable for specific tasks even when they must enlist the services of others to help them. As a rule of thumb, committees should be used for communicating information, for general discussion and for study; not for detailed work or for taking concrete action. And, then, the committee structure should be used only when the sort of work committed can be done in no other way. To say it the other way around, a committee should be established only whenever the advantages of group activity clearly outweigh those of individual activity.

There are valid reasons for group activity, of course: pooling of information, coordination of activities, communication, and legitimate compromise. Nevertheless, even when so used, committees quickly should break down and divide distinct aspects of their work, assigning these as areas of responsibility to individuals on the committee. Specific tasks in each area for which he may be held accountable should be committed to each individual. It is also wise to keep committees as small as possible. Since the eldership and the diaconate are, in effect, larger committees, I shall present a sample of how one pastor and his elders break up their tasks. Each task is assigned to a specific elder or deacon (or small group). This sample I have reproduced as I received it (omitting names): I have made no changes. On the original adjoining each responsibility was a name (depicted on the chart by a line). This makes it clear to the pastor who is responsible for what tasks at all times. He is not likely to send people to wrong sources, or to suggest that persons take on tasks that already have been assigned, thus unwittingly crossing lines of responsibility and delegation when they are set forth diagrammatically. Moreover, if problems arise in an area, simple reference to the chart identifies the person responsible. This plan may not necessarily represent the way that you or that I would or even should apportion the efforts of a different congregation, but because the plan is comprehensive, I think that you will find it suggestive.

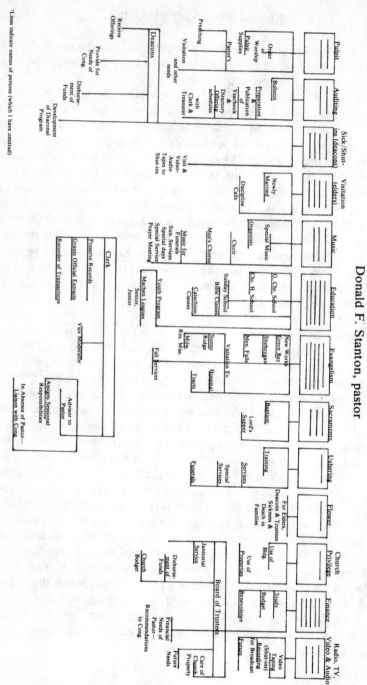

Organizational Chart: Bethel Orthodox Presbyterian Church, Oostburg, Wisconsin, 1973

Donald F. Stanton, pastor

EXERCISE

For the Student and the Pastor

1. Take a careful look at your congregation to see if you can answer the question, "Who is doing what?" about each of the following:

Setting Goals and Priorities _____

Planning the Budget_____

Exercising Control (on paper; in practice) _____

Planning Programs_____

Training Members for Tasks _____

Running the Educational Program _____

Caring for the Buildings and Facilities _____

Working on Publicity_____

Carrying out Evangelism_____

Caring for Guest Speakers _____

Doing Bookkeeping; Keeping Records _____

Regulating Worship _____

Paying Bills _____

Contacting the Florist _____

2. From this survey, suggest ways and means of changing the organizational structure if needed.

For the Pastor

1. Count the number of committees and boards that meet each month to conduct the business of your church:_____

2. Count the number of persons involved in those meetings:_____

3. Count (according to a rough estimate) the number of man-hours spent each month just in committee meetings:_____

4. Count the number of hours that *you* spend in committee meetings:_____

If the figures seem too large, they probably are. Try to work out ways of streamlining committee business, principally utilizing the biblical principle of individual gifts (cf. Romans 12:6,8).

CHAPTER V
WORKING WITH THE ELDERSHIP

Probably the first most significant achievement of any minister who newly assumes the pastorate of any congregation is getting to know his elders well and learning how to function smoothly with them. No time can be invested more wisely during the first year of his pastorate (when, as a matter of fact, much else cannot be done anyway) than the time he spends developing and cultivating a close relationship to his elders. This, he should do, both individually and corporately.[1] He must learn to know these men through and through, and he must be willing to expose himself as fully to them as well. A relationship founded upon truth and mutual trust must be built. All of this is essential so that when he tackles the large tasks and faces the crises that inevitably will come, the pastor will not have to do so alone. In many situations, without the full understanding, confidence and backing of his eldership, a minister will be left in a precarious position. His attempts to exert the authority of Christ will be undercut, his efforts to exercise church discipline for the benefit of an erring and contumacious member may be foiled, and his ability to move quickly and smoothly in emergencies will be seriously impaired.

It is important for the new minister not to discount his elders too quickly. It is my observation that this is a fault of many pastors. When one notes how zealously and patiently Paul labored with Timothy over his timidity, it shows (1) that all was not sweetness and light among the elders of the New Testament Church (it is quite wrong to idealize the situation[2]), and (2) that it is wrong to despair of a man with potential, even when he has some glaring faults. Encouragement, giving him the right kind of task (one in which he is very likely to succeed), or a variety of other such efforts could make a great difference in the release and development of that potential.

---

[1] It is best to start upon assuming the pastorate but at least you can begin correcting matters now if you did not start previously.

[2] The unrealistic way in which some apply the biblical criteria for elders and deacons not only discourages men with potential, but it seems quite foreign to the New Testament approach.

The pastor should attempt to discover (1) whether there is potential (often gifts can be tested only by trying them out) and (2) whether there is a special reason for the elder's weakness (e.g., the former pastor did everything himself, he was afraid of elders growing in power, they received no help or instruction, etc.).

In general, the pastor should expect much from his elders and should let them know so. He should assume that they are (or with proper teaching and encouragement will become) willing and able to accomplish great things. What he expects, he will communicate. What he communicates, he will get. If he gives them the impression that they are hopelessly inadequate, more than likely they will turn out to be just that; and he will be sure his judgment was correct! But also he should be clear about his own willingness to help them to become all that God wants them to be. It is no wonder that so little is done by many elders; when you hear how their ministers speak about them, you understand.

Frequently, elders enter upon their work with great enthusiasm and genuine dedication, only to have both cooled in short order by the fact that they are called upon to do nothing but attend meetings and never become involved in the actual work of ministering to their flock. Moreover, even if they are encouraged to take part in such ministry, they are given virtually no instruction about how to do so. If they are instructed at all, usually it will be in doctrine, possibly also in church government, but rarely ever in the principles and skills of personal ministry to human beings. Rather than excoriating them for failure to enter into such work, instead the pastor might inquire about previous expectations and past training. If he finds that these were inadequate, he would be better advised to set up an elders' training program (either formally or informally).[3] All of the exhortation in the world will not suffice when someone does not know *how* to follow it. Consequently, the pastor would do well to encourage his elders to sit in on counseling sessions *with him,* to learn how to conduct home Bible Studies *with him,* to make visits *with him*, etc. The training that most elders lack is discipleship, or on-the-job training. They need to be taught by example.

At first they must be given the opportunity to work with the pastor to observe and to participate in such activities under supervision. Next, they may be encouraged to minister for a while on their own. After a time, they

---

[3] An excellent manual by George Scipione, designed to train elders (or potential elders), has been published. There is nothing else like it in print. This manual takes elders through all of the biblical passages pertaining to their qualifications and work in a personal and thoroughly practical way. The book is broken into a series of lessons, each culminating in homework assignments. By all means get a copy if you have not seen it. The handbook, entitled *Timothy, Titus, and You,* is available from the Pilgrim Publishing Company, Phillipsburg, N. J.

should gather others from the congregation who show promise, as their disciples, to train them in the same way that they have been trained. Some of these men eventually may develop into deacons or elders.

It is important, I have said, for a pastor to get to know his elders. That takes time but it also takes willingness on the part of the pastor to be warm, friendly, open and truthful to them. Inviting them over to his home, holding elders' retreats for planning, prayer and fellowship in spring and/or fall, and a variety of other elders' activities will be necessary to achieve closeness. Close relationships do not merely happen; they are built.

It is not enough to get to know your elders in the regular elders' meetings. They must come to know you and you must come to know them in a greater variety of contexts. And they need to come to know one another fully as persons too (rather than merely as "that guy who always votes on the other side of an issue"). If the eldership is to become a smoothly functioning body, exerting a powerful force for good in the congregation, its members will have to be molded together into a cohesive entity by effective pastoral leadership. Good leadership means — among other things — creative planning. Do some right away — with reference to your relationship to your elders (see the exercise for the pastor at the end of the chapter).

The openness and honesty that must develop soon between a pastor and his elders is necessary for good communication (cf. Ephesians 4:25). The pastor can foster this by announcing (in his own words, of course) at the very first elders' meeting:

> Gentlemen, I am a sinner, and I shall fail. At times you will be disappointed in me as well as in other members of the congregation. I will need exhortation and help now and then, as indeed you will too. Therefore, you can expect me to be honest and straightforward with you. If I have any complaints or any concerns, you will hear them from me: you won't hear them first on the grapevine. And I expect to hear your concerns and your opinions directly too. I shall not allow your honesty or your frankness with me to separate us. Rather, I shall always encourage it as I consider it *essential* to the adequate communication that is needed to bind us together. I will appreciate you all the more for your truthfulness. So come to me; don't go to anyone else, whenever you have a suggestion or complaint.

It is important for a younger pastor not to allow age to separate him from the older men in the eldership. It is precisely those men who often will have the most valuable counsel for him. Yet, his tendency will be to drift toward those of his own age. The tendency must be overcome. If anything, *special* attention should be given to this matter. Ordinarily, these older men are even more easily approachable than some of the younger ones, and will be deeply appreciative of any efforts along these lines that he may make. Their counsel often will provide just the balance that a young impetuous man may need. As a general rule, a new pastor ought to give careful consideration to what they say and only for reasons of greatest weight disregard their counsel. The older men frequently provide a continuity with the past. By talking to them about things that have been from time to time, a pastor can understand better the things that are. Congregational attitudes, sensitivities, etc., that are otherwise inexplicable, become meaningful as he can place them in context.[4]

The elders of the people (as the Bible often describes them when speaking of their representative character) provide another vital link in the congregational communication chain. Through their eyes, and from their perspective the pastor can take more accurate soundings from time to time. Perhaps there is no more important link to preserve and to strengthen. The congregational chain often is as strong as its weakest elder link.

In short, let this brief reminder of the necessity of establishing a firm relationship with the elders be heeded. There is no more vital relationship for the pastor to develop and maintain on the highest level possible.

Elders' business meetings ought not be held too frequently. Too many meetings is ordinarily indicative of a group that likes to talk, but achieves little. Setting a closing hour[5] as well as an opening hour (a good practice for most meetings) keeps long-winded discussions to a minimum, and tends to make deliberative meetings (as they should be) more decision/action-oriented. The body has met to conduct business; that is what should be done. Other meetings for prayer, general discussion, etc., should be held.[6] An elders' weekly prayer breakfast might be in order. A time for prayer and fellowship before the evening worship service, concurrent with the youth meetings, is another possibility. Typed agendas for business meetings help to keep everyone on track, give an idea of how rapidly work is progressing toward the closing hour, etc. Mail or distribute agendas a week ahead and

---

[4]Cf. *The Christian Counselor's Manual,* pp. 218-221, for an example of this.
[5]And be sure that you stick to it.
[6]Business meetings should be kept to a minimum. Instead, *emphasize* the prayer and fellowship meetings by holding them more frequently. It is possible to get along with regular *monthly* business meetings; other meetings might be held on a *weekly* basis. When times of prayer and fellowship predominate, the character of the business meetings will change too. Also much of the inconsequential small talk will disappear. And a good bit of congregational business will be settled informally by consensus outside of the business meeting (as it should be).

urge members to jot down questions and observations on these, and to gather beforehand data about the matters to be discussed.[7] Too much business time is wasted on informing, asking last-minute questions, and failure to do prior research. All such matters should be attended to as fully as possible before the meeting itself.

EXERCISE

For the Student

Report on the following:

1. Interview several elders to determine what they know about their office, what they do as elders and what their attitudes about their work may be.

---

[7]But be sure to have extra copies on hand for the meeting. You can count on some members forgetting theirs.

2. Ask them what sort of training for the eldership they have had (if any).

3. Ask the elders what lacks they most keenly recognize and what they think may be done about them.

For the Pastor

Design a yearly program for getting to know your elders better. Be sure to schedule each element.

CHAPTER VI
WORKING WITH ANOTHER PASTOR

Closely related to the task of working with the eldership, but significantly different, is the possibility of working jointly with associates and/or assistants in the pastoral-teaching ministry. Some of the principles of sharing mentioned previously should be kept in mind as you read this chapter.

It should go without saying that the "senior" minister must take the lead in establishing and nurturing this relationship, although the responsibilities are, by no means, solely his. For instance, it is usually customary for assistants and associates to give a new "senior" pastor the opportunity to choose his own staff.[1] Yet the new man may be wise to encourage the continuation of the services of previously called associates, at least for a time, for purposes of continuity.

Many observations might be made about such a joint ministry, but let me emphasize only two or three. For one thing, it is a mistake to divide the pastoral labors of the congregation too rigidly. While some division is inevitable, and desirable, a complete dichotomy of labor is unhealthy. Though one principally may preach and another principally may do counseling (for example) it is unwise to make an explicit distinction of this sort. Usually, such sharp distinctions are set forth in titles, such as minister of counseling, minister of youth, etc. Every man who counsels effectively also will want to preach. If he does not, question his ability to counsel, or his real concern for people. He will want to have opportunity to warn against the destructive courses of sin that he sees day after day in the counseling room. If he does not have a preventive ministry as well as a remedial one, on the one hand, he may tend to become unbalanced and warped in his outlook, and, on the other hand, the congregation will suffer from not receiving the benefits of his pulpit ministry. The man who

---

[1]But this implies that associates work for a senior pastor. There is no biblical warrant for this. Both serve God, working side by side with elders to shepherd God's flock. The concept of a "senior" pastor, except as he may *by agreement* take the overall leadership, is not biblical.

preaches exclusively, and does no counseling, may tend to become abstract and pedantic. He must continually apply the principles of the Scriptures to real life problems, if his examples and his applications in the pulpit are to ring true. Both men, while *emphasizing* one phase of the work or another, according to the greater or lesser endowment of gifts that they possess, nevertheless must possess *all* of the gifts for all of the work of the ministry or they should not have been ordained in the first place. It is not as if the qualifications in the Pastoral Epistles could be *divided* between them; each man must qualify with reference to the whole. Each man must *balance* his ministry according to Colossians 1:28 (counseling and teaching) and Ephesians 4:11 (pastor and teacher).

This principle of division of emphasis, not of labor, cuts other ways. Whenever a minister devotes his energies largely to youth work, for instance, he must have complete freedom to work also with any other member of the congregation. He must have the opportunity, whenever necessary, to call in parents together with the young people and counsel all of them *as a family*. Otherwise, his ministry *to youth* will be truncated. While mentioning this point, let me observe that it often is desirable for *both* ministers to counsel jointly as a team under such circumstances, especially whenever there has been counseling previously by one or the other (with one segment of the family) that may have a bearing upon the present problem.

In general, let it be said that where there is more than one minister, care must be taken to see that members of the congregation are not allowed to divide them from one another. They must determine to stand back to back. Close, ongoing communication, including a regular exchange of significant information (at least two weekly information exchange conferences seem desirable), is absolutely essential. Ideas, plans, programs, approaches, solutions to problems, must be hammered out and coordinated. A house divided against itself cannot stand. There is no easier way to divide the household of faith than to provide for a congregation two or more leaders who gather factions about themselves.[2] Frank, frequent, prayerful discussion of this matter, leading to effective preventive and remedial measures, is the only solution to the problem. Failure to acknowledge the existence or the possibility of such a difficulty is extremely dangerous and constitutes a large step in the direction of encouraging divisiveness.

---

[2]Notice Paul's keen awareness of this in his comments in I Corinthians. But also do not fail to notice the use of multiple ministry in that congregation. Everything was not left to one man alone.

From the foregoing discussion, it may seem obvious that while there are advantages (fellowship, the power of specialization, etc.) there are also disadvantages to a multiple-staff ministry. Perhaps the greatest is this: thinking that the addition of specialized staff members itself will serve the needs of a growing large congregation. When "minister of music" (a dubious title), "of youth," and "of visitation," etc. are added, that does not necessarily mean that the congregation will be served better. If it is true that the ordinary pastor-teacher together with his elders cannot adequately minister to a congregation of more than 200 members in a truly shepherdly way (cf. John 10 and comments about knowing the names of the sheep and the voice of the shepherd), then when a congregation reaches the size of 800 or 1000 members, it still does not receive adequate *pastoral* work by the addition of a "minister of music" or a "minister of youth." What is needed is the addition of three or four more "ministers of sheep"! It is a rare congregation that sees this and sufficiently provides for the need. That is one reason why ordinarily it is better to start other congregations nearby rather than to allow a church to become too large (another reason stems from the use of the gifts of members: in a smaller congregation, as a rule, more of the members, in proportion, are called upon to use more of their gifts. Fellowship too, ordinarily, is closer in a smaller congregation). But where the emphasis is upon smaller congregations, provision also must be made for cooperation among these congregations in youth work, senior citizens work, etc. Otherwise, special groups in a congregation that has only a few such members tend to be neglected in the interest of the majority. Careful shepherdly concern is essential, therefore, in larger or smaller congregations, for it focuses not only on the 99, but also the hundredth sheep as well. When God's shepherd does not know each sheep "by name," and when they do not "know his voice," trouble is already on its way, whether the congregation is small or large. A church probably has grown too large when it becomes impossible to pray for those in need by name in the Sunday morning pastoral prayer. It is *adequate* pastoral work by the pastor-teacher and by the ruling elders that is the essential. Other matters, such as size, *per se,* are optional, and sometimes depend largely upon circumstances. There is no option about adequate shepherding. Whatever it takes to obtain it must be done; it is the one essential.

EXERCISE

For the Student or Pastor

Make a list of possible problems that may be encountered in a multiple-staff ministry, together with possible solutions to each. If possible, interview men who hold such a position.

Problems	Solutions

Problems	Solutions

CHAPTER VII
CONGREGATIONAL MEETINGS

Congregational meetings in some churches have become the occasion for the annual church battle. Pent-up resentments, violent assertions of individual authority and rebellious protests against policies of the elders and/or pastor often characterize such gatherings. Sometimes, things said cut deeply into the unity of the congregation and leave lasting scars. Moreover, such meetings have been known to extend into the wee hours of the morning, with colossal amounts of time wasted, with thinning ranks indicating the frustration and disgust of many. All in all, the annual congregational meeting can be the darkest experience of the year.

It is necessary, therefore, by careful preparation, to guard against any such occurrences; not that all ill-will may be dispelled automatically thereby, but that at least it may be kept to a minimum. How may this be done? The basic answer lies in two areas: (1) the meeting should be so prepared and conducted that expressions of bitterness become glaringly inappropriate; (2) if shepherdly care and discipline have been practiced properly during the year preceding, much (if not all) of the difficulty will be eliminated. Often, the existence of an annual protest meeting is dramatic evidence of the lack of such shepherdly concern. I should like to focus on the first of these two factors.

To begin with, much time can be saved by requiring that the reports of all organizations be mailed out to each home at least one week prior to the meeting. These may be compiled in one document together with an agenda, and ought to carry a covering letter explaining that any questions of fact should be asked of the appropriate persons *before* the meeting. (Much time is wasted by members asking endless factual questions that should have been raised beforehand, outside of the meeting itself. It is not fair to the majority to allow this.) The moderator of the meeting should explain at the outset that there will be no time allowed for *such* discussion. This mailing also may include the new Church Directory. Like other meetings, not only an opening hour, but also a closing hour also should be announced.

Members, then, can plan accordingly, and the business will be transacted with much more dispatch.

The meeting should be opened with the singing of a hymn, the Choir's favorite rendition of the year, and a ten-minute message from the Word of God. A congregational fellowship supper preceding allows more to attend and also helps to set a more relaxed tone of fellowship for the meeting. The moderator must exercise a fair but firm hand in conducting the meeting. At the outset, it is good for him to take 2-3 minutes to remind members of the basic rules of parliamentary procedure and to point out that remarks should be confined to issues, and must not be made about people. At the conclusion of the meeting (time should be allotted for this on the published agenda), time should be devoted to prayers of thanksgiving, confession, petition and commitment. Prayer especially may pertain to such matters as congregational losses/gains, projects undertaken at the meeting, etc.

Annual congregational meetings should be held, not in December or January, but in May. Since the Church year begins in September, it is wise to elect officers and initiate programs early enough to allow them to have the summer period for planning.

In preparing the pastor's report, it is helpful to look over the pastor's reports for the last two or three years. In this way, comparisons, trends, contrasts and changes may be noted. Such references may help both the pastor and the congregation to gain better perspective and to assess and gauge progress.[1] The report each year should present some *legitimate* challenge.

---

[1]The check list in Appendix B may prove useful for pastors to review at this point. Perhaps it will provide a rough basis for efforts to be made during the ensuing year.

EXERCISE

For the Student

Interview at least three pastors and a dozen church members to discover what they think about congregational meetings. Focus on problems, possible solutions, improvements, etc. Report your findings to the class.

Notes

For the Pastor

1. In the space below, design a sample covering letter to be sent to the congregation announcing the Annual Congregational Meeting.

Covering Letter

2. Lay out a sample agenda for the congregational meeting.

Agenda

CHAPTER VIII
COMMUNICATION IN THE BODY

Much congregational management fails either from the lack of Christian communication or from its breakdown. A church that makes no attempt to promote Christian communication will discover that communication will take place anyway. To state the problem simply: if the communication that exists is not carefully established and maintained as *Christian* communication, then the sort of communication that develops will tend to be non-Christian; gossip, slander, half-truths will flow quickly along the grapevine. The only effective way to assure against such perversions of truth is to develop and to maintain a vital communication network that, at every point, scoops the grapevine. It must get the truth to each member sooner, more fully, more attractively, and with complete accuracy and honesty. Therefore, it is important for every pastor to understand the principles of Christian communication and to learn how to promote it.

What is Christian communication and how may it be fostered? A fundamental passage concerning Christian communication within the church is found in Ephesians 4:25 (a verse that should be taken in conjunction with Ephesians 4:15):

> Therefore, laying aside falsehood, speak truth each one of you with his neighbor, for we are members of one another (v. 25),

and

> Speaking the truth in love, we are to grow up in all aspects into Him, who is the head, even Christ (v. 15).

These two verses occur in the midst of a discussion of church unity and organization and as a prelude to discussions (in chapters 5,6) of close functional relationships in the Church, the family and at work. These relationships, Paul makes clear, stand or fall on the basis of communication. His efforts to explain how Christian communication may be established and maintained, appearing as they do at this place, are intended to show that such communication is fundamental to any consideration of Christian unity, organization and function. It is of considerable importance, then, to discover what he has in mind.

There are at least four essential factors apparent in these two verses:

Christian Communication is Verbal

1. Communication, to be Christianly significant, to some extent must be verbal. That means that it may not be merely non verbal, or even largely written. When Paul wrote, "Speak truth each one of you with his neighbor" he had face-to-face communication in view. There are great advantages to face-to-face communication, especially when informing others about a change or decision that is likely to be unpopular or that readily may be misunderstood.[1] Written communication is more impersonal; the tone, emphasis and/or attitude of the writer may be missed entirely or misinterpreted. There are large benefits of voice and body in face-to-face communication that are missing from written communication. Moreover, the *reader* has no opportunity to pose questions, to request repetitions, to raise objections or to ask for examples. The *writer* is unable to adapt his presentation of data to such feedback. No wonder, then, in two difficult situations demanding the most of interpersonal contact the apostle John wrote:

> Having many things to write to you, I do not want to do so with paper and ink; but I hope to come to you and speak face to face, that your joy may be made full (II John 12).[2]

Clearly, actions may speak more loudly than words, but usually they do so less distinctly.[3] Frequently, there is a loss of precision when moving from verbal to non-verbal communication. But writing, at times, may be even less informative than some actions. Yet there *are* advantages to written

[1] In beginning a vital new Home Bible Study and Prayer program that would replace a tottering prayer meeting, the pastor of one congregation *personally* instructed six men appointed by the Elders who, in turn, *personally* confronted all of the heads of the households in the congregation about the program, answering all questions and extending an invitation to participate. What had to be accomplished was too important to entrust to impersonal written notices that were not equipped to handle feedback or give needed encouragement. The success of the program largely stemmed from this *personal* implementation.

[2] Cf. also III John 13,14. He is dealing with issues of heresy and of church discipline in these letters. Note Paul's desire for face-to-face communication expressed in Galatians 4:20. He was sure that personal contact would resolve the difficulties that now perplexed him concerning the Galatians.

[3] Actions may speak more loudly than words, but attitudes can outclass both: (1) Hand her a flower (action); (2) say, "I love you" (words); (3) *lethargically* (attitude)! In good communication there is a harmony of the three. Attitudes are sensed or deduced from bodily states, vocal tones and/or word choice.

material just as there are advantages to each of the other modes: more care can be taken to express precisely what one wants to say, diagrams and charts may be included, the material can be used for future reference, etc.

What then should a pastor's communication policy be? In communication with persons in the church, it is better not to rely solely upon impersonal written notices on the bulletin board, or in the monthly calendar, or in the Sunday bulletin. Usually, the best presentation is a combination of the written and spoken word that takes advantage of the values of both (and also, when appropriate, involves non-verbal elements). Often the ideal way to present information is to introduce and explain it personally *from a mimeographed handout* which on that occasion may be distributed to the listeners. Overhead projectors, chalkboards and charts also may be used with profit when communicating with a group. Use of prepared material shows that thought and time have been given to the preparation of the presentation. This will make it clear that what you are saying was not dreamed up on the way to the meeting. People appreciate others taking time and effort to make such preparation.

Often, not only the manner,[4] but even the *context* in which difficult material is presented may be strongly determinative of the result. Difficult changes ought not to be presented in hurried, tense or pressured contexts. It is wise, frequently, to *develop* a proper context for such presentations (e.g., at a fellowship dinner or a men's breakfast called to consider the question).

Timing can be of great importance not only to preserve accuracy but also to assure a proper hearing for the message (presented in correct attitude, context, etc.). If the elders are planning to ask the church organist to allow someone else to share in the accompaniment of the congregational singing, but she learns this *from the newly acquired organist* before the elders get around to inquiring; or if the sunday school teachers hear that there will be a general change of the classrooms *from the grapevine* rather than from the Superintendent of the Church School, needless trouble can develop that otherwise might have been avoided by a proper presentation of the program *in context,[5] in person, in time*. Many of the aspects of proper communication really boil down to three things: (1) showing consideration

---

[4]Such questions are of importance; cf. Colossians 4:3-6.

[5]Suppose the organist discovers the fact by coming to the church to practice on the organ only to find it already in use by the newly considered organist who is already at work practicing! Here is an obvious problem caused by poor communication.

for others, (2) doing what must be done right away and (3) courage to confront others.[6]

Christian Communication Is Truthful

2. Communication, according to Ephesians 4:25, not only must be verbal, but it must be truthful. It is easy to avoid, to shade or to minimize the truth. None of us finds that it is easy to tell the truth under every circumstance. Indeed the concern for truth is a special matter for the Christian because for him even the old saw, "honesty is the best policy," is not true. For him, the sole answer can be that honesty is the only policy. It is not always necessary to tell all of the truth to everyone under every circumstance. Some issues need not be raised ("John, you sure have a big nose"); others may be sidestepped ("How do you like my new hat?" "Oh, it *is* new, isn't it!"). Yet, in all of those matters in which information is necessary for the functioning of the whole body it is important to supply adequate, truthful information.

We have an interesting idea about truth; "the truth hurts," we often say. That saying shows how sinful men fear truth. It also indicates that truth has power. Of course the truth frequently hurts! No one likes to hear that his teaching in the youth group is unsatisfactory; yet he must be told so even though it hurts the teacher's feeling. No one likes to tell an elder that he is failing to serve Christ properly by his unwillingness to assume his responsibilities in the church; yet at times the pastor and the other elders must do so, even though it hurts them all to have to do it. So, it is true that the truth *hurts*.

But, that is not the whole story. The truth helps and the truth heals too. And, what is more, while the truth hurts, it never hurts like a lie. Falsehood among God's people can never help! Until Jane humbly confesses to him, "John, I do not love you: I have never loved you — not when we were first married, nor since. I married you on the rebound and principally for security; I have sinned and I am sorry," nothing can be done about their problem. Of course, it hurt both of them when she said this, but *now*, and only *now*, that the truth is out, can something be done about the matter.[7] Until she spoke the truth, he had known something was wrong but never could decide what. He tried many times to find out, worried about what he

---

[6]One of the last times to opt for written communication over the spoken is when you are afraid to face another, or suspect that he might think you are. It is easy to rationalize turning to the written page at this point by saying, "I can be more precise," etc. Cf. the charge of Paul's opponents and his response in II Corinthians 10:1-11.

[7]Sooner or later, in this life or in the next, the truth about every man will be made public (cf. I Timothy 5:24,25).

could do, blamed himself—all to no avail.[8] Now, she had hurt him by telling him the truth, but it was not like the hurt of not knowing — always sure something was between them, but always guessing about what it might be. Now, she had hurt him like the physician, who hurts in order to heal. This is the hurt of love; indeed, by risking his wrath, his rejection, or whatever response might be forthcoming, she had taken the first step of love toward him.

Not only could something now be done about the problem since at last John had the truth rather than guesses to work with, but the old hurts could vanish. For years the hurts that came from his faulty responses and fears, combined with his ignorance of the true situation and inability to cope with the unknown, continually had plagued them both. Now he could put aside his guesses and wrong responses and together they could move ahead constructively as God would have them, to face the *facts*.

On every level, in the home, in counseling, in the many interpersonal conflicts that arise in the course of the organizational functioning of the body, truth is the vital fluid that oils the machinery to keep it moving freely. Always, it must be applied liberally in order to keep down the heat that arises from friction! This leads us to the third factor.

Christian Communication is Adequate

3. God not only requires personal, truthful communication when He commands, "Speak truth each one of you with his neighbor," but from this verse it is plain that He demands adequate communication as well. It is not enough for *some* to speak the truth; *each one* must do so; and he must communicate to *all* of those who function closely with him (i.e., his neighbors). People must not be taken for granted. One way to be certain not to do so is to be sure that you give everyone all of the data that he needs in order to function properly in coordination with you and with others in the body. That, of course, demands thoughtfulness and concern about the other person. It means pulling *his* socks on and viewing the whole from *his* perspective.

Take an example drawn from the figure that underlies the reason that Paul appends (for we are members one of another): the figure of the body. Elsewhere in the chapter[9] and in I Corinthians[10] the same figure is worked

---

[8]Of course these responses on his part were not proper either and may have made it more difficult for John's wife to tell him the truth.

[9]V. 16. N.B., there Paul clearly observes that it is "speaking the truth in love" (v. 15) that makes such bodily coordination possible.

[10]I Corinthians 12:12ff.

out in more detail. The point is made that all of the parts are necessary; indeed all are necessary to one another and, of course, to manifest the *fullness* of Christ. Here, in v. 25, Paul observes that it is necessary to speak adequate truth in order to establish and maintain good coordination within the body. If the hand and arm have one set of data, and the knees and legs another, the knees may bend and the body may attempt to sit down just as the hand reaches around and pulls the chair out from beneath. Ludicrous! Yes, but no more so than the tragic ways in which members of the same body work at cross purposes, duplicate efforts unnecessarily, and (in general) fail to coordinate activities in the local congregation.

It is the pastor's job, even as Paul considered it his, to see to it that such breakdown of harmony does not result from inadequate communication. For instance, there is *no excuse* for two groups to plan for conflicting meetings on the same dates if an adequate system of communication has been developed.[11] Communication between individuals and between groups must be encouraged and ways and means for assuring it must be devised. It is the pastor's duty to see to it that proper channels are developed, kept clear, and used. He *may* delegate the task (or portions of it — e.g., a telephone pyramid chain),[12] but must never so remove himself from concern with communication that he does not know at all times precisely what sort of communication exists. How can the pastor find out? The very asking of the question by the pastor of a church demonstrates the need for better communication. Were communication what it should be, he would be receiving steady feedback about communication as well as about everything else. If nothing more, he can begin by using the old hat trick. It is very simple: he puts on his hat and goes out and polls a representative group of persons from his congregation (of course, at times, but not always, he could easily delegate *this* task too). He asks questions like, "Did you hear about the last five announcements we made? How did you hear? Do you have any suggestions for getting information to our membership more rapidly? More precisely?" Actually, a good feedback system may be built by appointing sampler reporters. Ten or so persons, in sample situations (a shut-in, a young person, a travelling

---

[11] For such matters, a monthly calendar on which all dates of activities are entered, and which is published or posted and accessible to all members and groups at all times, could forestall such problems. The pastor may readily hand over the task of devising and maintaining such a system to his diaconate.

[12] The chain is simple and effective. The pastor calls deacon Smith who calls three others, who call three others, etc., until all members have been reached. Emergency prayer requests, last minute announcements, cancellation of meetings, births, deaths, causes for congregational rejoicing and thanksgiving, etc., may be phoned down the chain. The setting up and maintenance of the chain may be left to the diaconate.

salesman, etc.), report once each month on how well communication is functioning.

So, to sum up so far, we have seen that spoken, truthful and adequate communication is essential for the coordination and proper functioning of the congregation.

Christian Communication Is Loving

4. But, now notice that the fourth element, prominently mentioned in v. 15, is *love*. Communication not only allows for the movement of data back and forth along the lines,[13] thus providing the proper conditions for coordination, but proper communication also enables the sheep in the flock to develop and to maintain good relations with the Chief Shepherd, His undershepherds, and with one another. Communication provides the setting that fosters brotherly love, and (cyclically) it is brotherly love that fosters good communication. Thus communication is the precondition for the spread and maintenance of Christian love, even as love is also the precondition for speaking the truth. Truth without love becomes a wicked weapon. Love, uncommunicated, is a blunted blessing.

Always, therefore, in endeavoring to further communication, the pastor must be concerned about maintaining good relationships in the body through love. That means that temper and resentment, the two foes of good communication mentioned in Ephesians 4, must be handled. Both temper and resentment close down communication. I do not want to develop this

---

[13]And one must be sure that the communication network in the congregation does operate in *both* directions; otherwise something less than *adequate* communication is taking place.

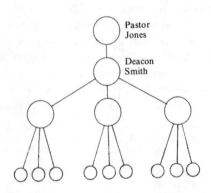

point further since I have said much about it already in other places.[14] Here, let me add only this: in the context of Ephesians 4:25, as Paul continues to discuss communication, he definitively disposes of these twin evils by showing that when held in or ventilated with abandon, anger becomes sin. Only when released under control, and aimed at problems, not persons, may one "be angry yet not sin." The pastor's task is to see to it that sinful manifestations of anger do not block communication within the church.

Because Christians nevertheless are still sinners, rubs will come. Many will be "covered" in love. But some keep throwing the covers off. There is a great necessity for teaching members how to deal with such a situation. Unless the problems that sinners cause by their sinful attitudes and actions are handled in a biblical manner, they will disrupt the orderly work of the congregation.[15] As James put it, "Where jealousy and selfish ambition exist, there is disorder and every evil thing" (James 3:16). This is a matter of vital concern to a leader; whatever causes disorder in the flock must be dealt with quickly and effectively. Moreover, the pastor must see to it not only that members understand, but also put to work these biblical principles for dealing with difficulties.

An example of the need for such a face-to-face confrontation in the case of unresolved anger is recorded in Philippians 4:1,2 where Paul not only exhorts Euodia and Syntyche to "be of one mind in the Lord," but then goes on to urge the pastor[16] to step in to be sure that reconciliation is effected:

> Indeed, true comrade,[17] I ask you to help those women who have shared my struggle in the gospel together with Clement also....

Plainly, Paul determined to put an end to the contention in the church. He was concerned to bring about the reconciliation of persons who formerly had proven to be able to work together with him and with one another courageously in the service of Christ. But because of some difficulty (we are not told what) Euodia and Syntyche (and possibly others with them) had fallen out with one another. Presumably *because in the process*

---

[14]Cf. *Christian Living in the Home,* Chapter Three, *The Christian Counselor's Manual,* pp. 250,322,362ff. I should like also to mention the strong effects of fear in blocking communication.

[15]Cf. *The Christian Counselors Manual,* pp. 52, 359, for a fuller discussion of love covering a multitude of sins.

[16]It is true that the word *suzuge* could be read as a name, Syzygos, but there is no evidence, in the Scriptures or elsewhere, that such a name existed. It is better, therefore, to take the comment to refer to the pastor who was, doubtless, reading the letter to the congregation.

[17]Literally, "fellow yoke-bearer"—a term describing one who worked jointly with him in Christ's ministry.

communication had broken down, Paul not only exhorts them to be reconciled, but also urges the pastor to get involved. He knew that there was only one way to solve the communication dilemma[18]—to enlist the help and counsel of another. The pastor must be ready to trouble shoot whenever he sees a communication breakdown leading to unsettled differences among the members of his congregation. Such help is needed in every circumstance where a brother or sister on his own does not find his way out of his sin (cf. especially Galatians 6:1ff.).

Pastors, then, must be alive both to the possibilities provided by proper Christian communication and to the problems that may arise from its breakdown, nonexistence or the admixture of non-Christian elements. In no case may they ignore the potential of communication (good or bad), for by it the life of the congregation is maintained.

Interpersonal Relations and Differences

Administration in the church bogs down significantly when the pastor himself does not know how to establish and maintain proper relationships with those with whom he must work. And even when he does, the work of the congregation will suffer if he fails to teach others how to do so. Of course all aspects of his ministry are affected adversely when he is incompetent in Christian personal relations.

Good administration requires courage and skill coupled with love and concern in *confronting* people about their differences. I begin by putting the stress here because it should go without saying that the pastor must discover and pursue every legitimate avenue open to him to keep relations on a high Christian plane and to prevent their breakdown at all costs. Many men make good attempts preventively, but utterly fail when they must confront those who have gone astray. No matter how skilled he may become in preventive activities, no matter how well the pastor has been able to avoid innumerable conflicts by wise policy, the inevitable will happen: sinners will differ in sinful and unpleasant ways which, if left unchecked, will destroy not only their own lives, but the witness and productivity of Christ's church. Therefore, it is particularly necessary to encourage pastors to take biblical action when differences arise among the people of God.

I say that it takes courage to confront others at such times. Unfortunately, many pastors lack such courage. Timothy had to be exhorted by the apostle Paul to be more courageous in his ministry (I Timothy 4:12, II Timothy 1:6-8). "Fine," you say, "I wish I *were* more

---

[18]The communication dilemma is this: Communication is necessary to solve problems between persons, including the communication problem!

courageous, but I'm not. How do I become so; is there any hope?" Yes there is. Courage is, as Paul says, *developed;* it does not appear full-grown. Courage comes, not by sitting around praying for it, or waiting for it to come; that is not what the apostle advised Timothy. Rather, courage comes when a pastor recognizes the will of God in the Scriptures, determines that by God's grace he will do whatever he knows that God requires of him, and prayerfully sets out to obey, whether he *feels* courageous or not. If the courage does not come in the doing the first time around, he will find at length, as he continues to follow God's will again and again, that God will develop courage in him. Changes do not ordinarily come instantly between 1:00 A.M. and 1:01 A.M. on Thursday; they take time to develop through the obedient pursuit of biblical practices.

Pastors must not allow personal differences among members of the flock to fester and harden (Ephesians 4:26; Philippians 4:2,3). When they do, these differences will crystallize into bitterness and resentment. Whenever the possibility for this exists the wise pastor will anticipate it and warn against that eventuality. For instance, when he suspects that a heated debate might be likely to occur in a committee meeting, he will take time at the outset to caution against allowing differences of opinion to grow into differences of relationship. He will instruct the committee members to be careful about *how* they differ (choice of words, tone of voice, volume, etc.). He also will pray for a good outcome. He will continually stress the need for members to express their differences regarding their interpretations and applications of the Scriptures, but he will emphasize also that their differences of opinion must not be allowed to become personal differences. By his own behavior, he will endeavor to so set the tone of the meeting. He will see to it that the expression of different viewpoints is never stifled, but also that personal hostilities are minimized. That is part of his job as an officer of the church given to help the members of the church to grow together into the *unity* of the faith in *love* (cf. Ephesians 4:1-16).

The pastor, as a model in all things, must set a good example himself. He must encourage the honest expression of disagreement with his own opinions and must not allow it to get between him and any member of his congregation. Members will best learn how to differ as Christians from observing his own practice. Yet, it is right here that many pastors fail. They become saddened, sit and stew in self-pity and even get depressed because they have been challenged by a member of the congregation. A careful review of the qualities of the overseer in Titus 1:7, 8 makes it clear that he may not follow any such course. Instead, a pastor (who should always be alert for ways to teach the flock) should seize upon the occasion as an opportunity to *demonstrate* the truth he has been teaching verbally. Attitudes, and those actions that grow out of them, often are best conveyed through such informal channels; on the other hand, information usually is best channeled through more formal ones.

The pastor also must learn (by prayerful, committed effort) how to differ, rebuke and encourage in love if he would become an effective leader (cf. especially II Timothy 2:24,25). Some can handle the differences that are expressed against their viewpoint quite well, but they themselves have great difficulty differing with another. And they are the ones who usually find the task of rebuking especially hard. But leadership at times requires doing difficult things such as telling someone he has sinned, and must repent, or that his services no longer are desired in a certain position. Leadership may demand that he confront a church school teacher or a sexton who has been slack in his work. Of course, not every confrontation of this sort should be made by the pastor (too frequently it is assumed that it is solely his job); the elders and the deacons and the other leaders of the congregation also must learn how to handle such situations. But if they have never done so before, or if they have not yet learned to do so well, from time to time the pastor will find it necessary to step in as a trouble shooter and a model, taking the elder or deacon along as he shows him how it is done. The presence of an elder or deacon, besides providing him with the needed experience, can be a plus factor in the confrontation itself. His presence can steady the discussion, keep it from becoming personalized and provide a witness to what was said and done. Indeed, at times the pastor might need one.

One of the most dissatisfying and disheartening things that can happen in a church is for members to sense that there is an underlying tension between the participants in meetings as they try to work together. It throws a wet blanket over everyone's spirit. This tension is due almost always to unresolved difficulties. It is important, therefore, for the pastor not only to preach about such matters, but periodically to give talks and lectures to the members of each organization in the congregation about the proper means of working together for the honor of Christ. And there are times when he must take various members aside and talk to them about their relationship to one another and how it is affecting the ministry of the congregation. He may never allow anything that he sees to be hindering the effective working of the body to continue to hamper the work of Christ. Probably more churches are split (or go limping along) because of interpersonal differences that were not dealt with biblically than because of doctrinal disagreements. Much power is drained off and enormous amounts of energy are wasted in unnecessary tension and misery arising from mishandled conflicts. The pastor must be vigilant to follow the directions given in Matthew 5, Matthew 18, Luke 17, Ephesians 4 and the principles of other key passages that insist upon the speedy and full resolution of all personal differences between God's people.[19] As he does so, he will become the prime example and living embodiment of the reconciliation/discipline dynamic (cf., especially, the Chapter of that name in *The Christian Counselor's Manual* for details on how to do this).

EXERCISE

For the Student and the Pastor

Diagram the lines of communication that actually exist in your (another) congregation.

---

[19]Cf. *Competent to Counsel* and *The Christian Counselor's Manual* for detailed discussions of these passages.

CHAPTER IX
COMMUNICATION LINKS

Let us now consider some of the varieties of communication links that might be formed to move information back and forth from the pastor (and other officers of the church) and from the members of the congregation.

1. *Weekly announcements* may be given from the pulpit and in the church bulletin. Not every announcement in the bulletin should also be announced from the pulpit. However, whenever there are announcements not made audibly, it is wise to indicate the fact by saying, "For further announcements consult the bulletin," or words to that effect.[1] Bulletins should be prepared under the guidance of the deacons, who may act, in most publicity and informational capacities, as a liaison between the pastor and the members of the congregation.[2]

2. *A monthly newspaper* (including a monthly calendar of events) is an extremely valuable asset to any congregation. As in the case of the bulletin, it should be edited by a responsible person (usually one of the ordained office bearers is desirable) who will be able to make wise judgments about what should (or should not) be included, when to alter wording, etc. Here, in this paper, budding young (or old) writers have an opportunity to serve Christ by means of their pens. Always, there should be a shut-ins section, *written by* and distributed to them. Older members, who may be making

---

[1]Some think that announcements of church affairs do not constitute a worthy part of the worship service. I disagree. If it is worthy to be done by the church, it is worthy to be announced. No artificial, unbiblical dichotomy between doing the Lord's work and the worship of God ought to be held. A study of the New Testament terms *latreia* and *leitourgia* provides an interesting commentary on the question. They show that worship and service are inextricably bound up in one another.

[2]Much more may be said about bulletins. Later, in a subsequent volume, I plan to discuss some liturgical matters concerning the order of worship but here I refer only to the second page of the bulletin. In discussing written communication, it is of importance to note that the pastor should *never* get involved in the mechanical affairs of production. Too many pastors busy themselves with repairing mimeograph machines when they ought to be repairing marriages. The pastor should keep a file of bulletins for his own future reference. He will be surprised how often this reference source will provide needed information. A second file, bound, should be placed in the church library.

the transition from the first phase of their lives to a second,[3] may wish to take the opportunity to write. This monthly paper should be mailed to those not present on the day of its distribution,[4] to servicemen, students at college, and persons who have visited previously. An extra supply, for guests and for members who wish to distribute them to friends and neighbors, ought to be made available.[5] This should be encouraged through the various channels of communication.

A standard printed cover, in color (I suggest warm colors: oranges, reds, yellows), will give added attractiveness to the paper. There ought to be sections devoted to calendar and general news, to children, to youth, to the infirm and shut-ins, to the family, to a daily prayer calendar (for members, missionaries, needs), to Christian fiction, etc., each of which may be mimeographed on different colored paper stock to easily distinguish them. In general, color attracts more than white and black. These papers should be bound and filed in the church library for future reference. You will be surprised at how often you too will turn to your own bound set for various reasons.

3. *Bulletin boards, charts, graphs, posters* provide a useful means for announcing events, posting missionary letters (which when taken from the board may be bound in the congregational missionary scrapbook and placed in the library),[6] reminding members of the church library (announcing new acquisitions, etc.), and dozens of other purposes.[7] It is vital to have several boards, placed in strategic locations where those who are concerned about the information that they contain may easily see them. One general board causes crowding, allows for little creativity in terms of posters and other art work, and discourages use. It is essential for each board to be reviewed and updated *weekly*. Torn or soiled notices containing dated materials communicate too, but what they say to guests is not

---

[3]Cf. Vol. II, pp. 262-271.

[4]This implies that a careful record of attendance is kept. Attendance records are vital as well for good pastoral care. Several methods are in use: (1) Passing an attendance record sign-up sheet or book, (2) Depositing a card in the offering plate (or a box at the rear of the church building), or (3) The plain old usher count (the ushers have lists of families and simply look over the congregation and mark off those present and those absent).

[5]Mailing lists should be checked by a person assigned to weed out dead addresses at least quarterly, but especially to be sure that all new ones have been added.

[6]These will be found useful for later missionary programs, studies, talks, etc.

[7]A photograph report of last year's summer camping experience on the Young People's board will probably encourage more to attend this year than bland announcements in writing, or even the full-color brochure published by the camp. Yet, in all such good things, someone must be made responsible to take the pictures *with this in mind* (other shots by participants also could be included) and then someone also must be responsible for arranging these in a display, or it will not come off well.

what we should want to communicate. The only way to be sure that each board is properly cared for is to make someone associated with it responsible for it, and to make someone responsible for checking on his work (not in a censorious, but in a helpful and encouraging manner).

4. *Tapes (audio and video),* and sometimes mimeographed or printed transcriptions of these, become a useful adjunct to the other teaching ministries of a congregation. Shut-ins, and others at a distance, may profit from a weekly diaconal tape ministry faithfully carried out.[8] However, the Christian Church has only *begun* to utilize tapes. Cheap, portable and dependable, these recorders can be employed in Christ's service in many ways.[9] For instance, one member of the congregational teaching staff may be sent to an important conference or lecture with the expressed purpose of taping and then playing the tape(s) at discussion groups planned for this purpose. Missionaries and congregations, through cassette, can draw nearer. Youth groups can plan and produce programs to be exchanged with other youth groups. A tape library should be built up by each congregation. A tape deck (that plays, but does not record, i.e., does not erase tapes) should be provided by the library to assure the safety of the tapes. It is possible to tape planning meetings (or those portions of them that would be valuable to the members of the planning group or to others later on). These then may be circulated among the participants for further reflection. Reports of individuals or of committees may be prepared ahead of time on tape and brought (or even sent) to members of the larger body. Vast vistas of creative use of the cassette yet lie immediately ahead.

5. *Telephone and telephone chains*[10] quickly deliver emergency, crucial or last-minute information.[11] By use of the telephone, one may reach out beyond the congregation and even extend a contact as far as the mission field. A personal phone conversation with a home or foreign missionary (taped, or amplified and played live) at a prayer meeting or missionary conference will add a vital dimension.[12] Prayer, for someone rushed to the hospital in critical condition on Thursday, should not wait for Sunday or

[8]Cf. Vol. I, pp. 126,127.

[9]Cassettes are now universal. The time may be coming when video cassettes will be almost as accessible to us. Creativity is needed to exploit the full range of possibilities that cassette tapes provide for communication.

[10]Cf. p. 385.

[11]Including, as Mick Knierim, one of my students rightly pointed out, matters of *praise* as well as other matters. But do not *overuse* the chain or (1) it will soon break down; (2) it will lose its power to give special significance to a message.

[12]Rather than chase furloughed missionaries all over the map (especially during those years when their teen age children need them at home) congregations with profit could arrange for two or three amplified phone calls from the missionary and his family on prayer meeting nights. Gasoline, food and lodging are far more expensive than phone calls!

for next week's Wednesday night prayer meeting. The request for prayer may be sent down the telephone chain so that, frequently, the entire congregation can be alerted to pray within a few hours.[13] The telephone is an invaluable timesaver when used wisely and considerately. Much business, that otherwise would take people from their homes to attend meetings, can be carried on by way of a conference call. Use of the conference call, in the long run, is more economical and certainly less time-consuming. It best may be used for urgent or last-minute decision-making, providing new information, matters requiring only brief discussion, and brief reporting. Many pastors do not use their phones often enough.

6. *Face-to-face contacts of all sorts,* nevertheless, must remain the fundamental and bread-and-butter means for conveying information. Regular meetings are essential for this purpose. But most meetings last too long because they are conducted poorly (irrelevant discussion may preponderate),[14] because insufficient individual tasks have been assigned previously (people come unprepared to report and to discuss), and because a closing hour has not been set. Some of the other five suggestions mentioned previously may help to slim down regular meetings.[15] Pastors must not forget that much of the best communication takes place informally between persons invited to regular meetings. Therefore, the basic rule should be: keep the meeting itself brief and schedule a fellowship time in conjunction with it (a meal or a snack often provides the necessary context for informal discussion). It is especially important to provide for such informal fellowship among persons who must meet and work together regularly, even if little or no task-oriented communication takes place, since it provides further opportunities for them to develop the good personal relationships that are essential to clear channels of communication.

---

[13]One congregation has no regular prayer meeting, but members meet at the church (as they are able) upon request. They may meet any time of day according to needs. The pastor of the church reports more vital prayer and greater attendance than before. Prayer for regular needs is encouraged in various groups and in the family.

[14]This sort of discussion should be postponed to the informal coffee-and-doughnut period that follows (or interrupts; the interrupting fellowship time assures full participation. The one that follows the meeting allows some to slip off more quickly for home).

[15]Slimmed-down meetings are desirable whenever possible. Communication is not improved by more words; it is productive words alone that count.

EXERCISE

For the Student

Together with a group of four or five other students, produce a simulated monthly newspaper. Try to think through creative and interesting ways of presenting the material.

For the Pastor

Check out the congregational communication links mentioned in this chapter (together with others you may have developed) to determine how well they are functioning.

CHAPTER X
ENLISTING AND TRAINING

A full discussion of the individual gifts of members cannot be carried on here with any sort of adequacy. Yet there are some fundamental factors that are relevant to the matter of enlisting and training members of the flock for their work of ministry that should be considered.

First, notice that these gifts of the Spirit are *that,* and exactly that—gifts. They are not rewards given to those Christians who earn or deserve them by the so-called "spirituality"[1] of their lives. No congregation of Christians mentioned in the New Testament was more unsanctified in doctrine and life than the Corinthian Church, yet gifts were given to that congregation in *fullness.* (Paul wrote: "You are not lacking in any gift," I Corinthians 1:7.) It is clear, then, that the gifts of the Spirit are *gifts* graciously dispensed— nothing more, nothing less. They are distributed sovereignly by the Spirit, as He wills, according to the measure determined by Him, for His own inscrutable purposes (cf. Ephesians 4:7; I Corinthians 12:4-7; 11b). They are neither earned nor merited.

We are not told explicitly *when* God imparts gifts to His children, but since they are said to be spiritual gifts, they are to be thought of not as natural talents, but as abilities given (probably at the new birth, concurrent with the Spirit's coming into each life)[2] in addition to those natural capacities given at the first, or physical, birth. Of course these gifts might include a heightening of natural talents.

The extraordinary, or apostolic gifts, however, were given later, by the laying on of the hands of the apostles, to *confirm* their apostolic witness and word (cf. II Corinthians 12:12; I Corinthians 1:6; Hebrews 2:2-4; Acts 8:14-20; 19:6). If the miraculous gifts could come to any and to all believers

---

[1]Such use of the term spirituality is inaccurate and disturbing. It stresses human merit when all that is spiritual is the work (fruit) of the Spirit.

[2]However, the special, extraordinary gifts clearly are marked out as given at a later point (cf. Rom. 1:11; I Corinthians 14:13; II Timothy 1:6, etc.).

in any other way,[3] they would not be the "signs of an apostle" (II Corinthians 12:12), nor would they "confirm" (Hebrews 2:3,4) God's revelatory words spoken and written by the apostles or under their supervision. If every Christian could obtain the miraculous sign-gifts from a source other than from the apostles, then such gifts would be the signs of a *Christian,* and not as Paul claimed, the signs of an *apostle.*

The officers of the church, listed in Ephesians 4, plainly are divided into two groups: (1) *apostles and prophets,* whose temporary functions, in the same book, are called "foundational" (cf. Ephesians 2:20; 3:3-5); (2) *evangelists (missionaries) and pastor-teachers* whose work continues perpetually in the church. As these two kinds of offices (special and ordinary) existed in the early church,[4] so too there were two distinct sorts of gifts: (1) *special,* "confirmation" or "sign" gifts, that came to believers through the apostles; (2) *ordinary,* "service" gifts, that came to believers directly from the Spirit. We shall speak in this section, then, only of those ordinary gifts given by God to enable His Church in any age to function and to carry on its many ministries.

Next, let us recognize that *every* Christian has gifts (cf. Ephesians 4:7, "to each one of us..." and I Peter 4:10, "as each one has received a gift..." and I Corinthians 12:11, ". . .distributing to each one individually"). All Christians, therefore, must be encouraged to find a place of usefulness in ministering to others. It is the pastor's task not only to preach and teach this fact, but (in addition) to help each individual to discover, develop and deploy his gift. The pastor must remember that, according to Ephesians 4:12, it is the object of his shepherding ministry to equip each sheep to minister. Recruiting and enlisting Christians for those ministries that accord with their gifts, then, is a fundamental and first task of pastoral leadership. In a course of study for new converts (and/or for others who need the instruction) one of the prime concerns of the pastor or elder who teaches it is to instruct those who attend about gifts. At the conclusion of the course, hopefully, most of those who have attended should know at least in what possible areas their gifts may lie and should be prepared to test

---

[3]Of course, in the two great outpourings of Pentecost (Acts 2) and the gentile pentecost (Acts 10) the confirmation, or sign-gifts, were given directly, signifying the *immediate* coming of the Spirit. But in the two spill-overs from each of these outpourings (Acts 8; Acts 19), the apostles gave the Spirit (with His gifts) by the laying on of hands *mediately.*

[4]Also called "gifts" (Ephesians 4:8,11). The officers were men gifted for their work as well as Christ's gift to His Church. Both ideas seem to be in the apostle's mind as he writes in Ephesians 4. They were gifted gifts.

their gifts by being directed into tasks in the congregation that belong to those areas.[5]

The teacher of such a course may wish to develop a program based upon Romans 12:3-8 in which the framework for such a discussion may be found:

Evaluation

1. Every member must be taught to evaluate his life soberly in order to discover God's gifts (v. 3). And in doing so, he must not think more highly of himself than he ought to think. On the other hand, sober judgment demands no by-passing or underestimating of the gifts of God. One is to evaluate the "measure of faith" allotted to himself. The phrase "measure of faith" is peculiar. Instead one might expect to read words like "varieties of gifts" or "particular tasks." Clearly, that is what Paul is referring to, the allotment of distinct gifts for particular ministries. But why, then, does he use this expression instead? To what does he refer when he speaks of "a measure, or portion, of faith"? Murray thinks that the distinct endowments variously distributed to believers, each receiving his own measure, are called measures of faith in order to "emphasize the cardinal place which faith occupies...in the specific functions performed."[6]

Coordination

2. He must recognize the place and the function of his individual gift in the body (vv. 4,5). He, together with other believers, must function as part of a whole. Recognizing his place, its relation to the whole and the place and function of others will help him to think more highly of himself but also to see the essential contribution that the exercise of his gift makes to all. He will recognize both his dependence upon others and their dependence upon him. Paul, in his great Declaration of Interdependence, puts it this way:

> Just as we have many members in one body and all the members do not have the same function, so we, who are many, are one body in Christ, and individually members one of another (Romans 12:4,5).

So then, first, the pastor must help each member to make a sober judgment

---

[5]In examining possible gifts, the lists given by Paul may be used with profit as suggestive of what spiritual gifts are like, but should not be thought to be exhaustive any more than the other lists that Paul gives elsewhere in his letters.

[6]John Murray, *The Epistle to the Romans*, Vol. II (Wm. B. Eerdmans Pub. Co., Grand Rapids: 1965), p. 119. Cf. also the use of the word "measure" in II Corinthians 10:13.

about his gifts; after that it is important for him to help each one to gain a recognition of the place and purpose of that gift in the work of the whole congregation. This will steer a course around any temptations to develop lone-wolf attitudes, or (on the other extreme) to think one's ministry is irrelevant. But there is one more step necessary.

Participation

3. Each member, having soberly taken stock of his gifts, and having recognized where he fits into the big picture, must in fact begin to take on tasks in the area or areas of his gifts and begin to function as a contributing part of the body. This is what Paul has in mind in verse 6:

> And since we have gifts that differ according to the grace given to us, let us exercise them accordingly....

The pastor will be concerned about helping every Christian in the congregation to discover, to develop and to *deploy* his gifts.

Not everything can be done at once. Gifts may become growingly useful, or may atrophy through disuse; they may be used properly for scriptural ends, or may be misused for sinful ends.[7] They may be used selfishly or, as intended, for the benefit of all. Therefore, the development of the gifts of the members of the body through instruction, putting them to use, encouragement and critique, are all matters that should be of great concern to the pastor. The pastor will see to it that he introduces a new Christian into ministry slowly; he will be sure that he does not subject him to unnecessary temptations toward pride, by recognizing his novice status. With reference to elders Paul writes, "Not a new convert, lest he become conceited and fall into the condemnation of the devil" (I Timothy 3:6). He will be zealous to follow Paul's directions in I Timothy 5:22: "Do not lay hands on anyone too hastily." If he seems to possess qualities that may be used in the eldership or diaconate, the pastor will wait to be sure before encouraging ordination and, instead, will insist first that he be tested (I Timothy 3:10; II Corinthians 8:22). The same principles apply, of course, to any member of the congregation using any gifts. No one can at first accomplish what he can produce only by subsequent study and experience.

How does this turn out in practice? Perhaps Fred possesses gifts that would seem to point toward the diaconate. Paul says, "Let him be tested first" (I Timothy 3:10). Since gifts are not the only factor to consider (such matters as one's faithfulness in using them, not to speak of his attitude or the ends for which he uses his gifts, are relevant factors too), the pastor will

---

[7] Cf. the misuse of spiritual gifts in Corinth.

be interested in putting Fred into circumstances that will test out not only his gifts, but also his faithfulness, his fervency, his humility, his willingness, his capacity for working with others, etc. He may be asked to usher, to do auditing of the church books, etc. If he performs well in these tasks, others may be given, until it is clear to all that he is ready, able and willing to serve God in the larger capacity as a deacon.

Volunteers

How does one ask another to take on a task? There is no indication in the New Testament that persons were asked to volunteer. Asking for volunteer Church School teachers, for instance, is one sure way to destroy the teaching quality of the school. Moreover, it brings on all sorts of unwanted problems arising from the willingness of persons to serve who have neither the gifts nor other essential qualities for serving well. Instead, after testing several likely persons in other or in similar tasks (have them teach for a period every now and then as a substitute, etc.), and after agreement by the members of the board of elders, the person chosen should be appointed to the task, then told so by the pastor and/or another elder. He should not be *asked* if he will serve, but should rather be told that he is the man (woman) that they want for this task. While reasonable causes for declination should be honored (the man truly does not have the time *now* to do this because of certain previously unknown family matters),[8] if less weighty reasons are adduced, the pastor should press the appointment by challenging him to enter into the opportunity (which should be spelled out specifically along with the obligations and duties involved) and stress the need of the whole body for his ministry. Unless truly weighty reasons are forthcoming, the pastor should refuse to take no for an answer.

It is important too to offer adequate help, resources, guidance and training, and the offer should be genuine and concrete. ("Bill, I've already arranged for Tom to spend the next six weeks taking you along with him as he distributes the tapes to the shut-ins and ministers to them. Then, he promises to remain on call at any time to be of help in difficult situations, and to counsel with you about any aspect of the work.") At some point, every member of the congregation, who is not already serving, should be approached in this manner about a ministry in which he or she may engage, whether it is teaching or ushering, providing transportation for a poor widow to attend church or taking on some aspect of the youth work.[9]

---

[8] But, before appointing him, it is important to take all such matters into consideration so far as they *are* known.

[9] But shun that all too frequently given (but totally unsavory) advice to offer jobs to unbelievers "in order to get them interested in the church."

The person enlisted should be given a clear picture of the purpose for which he has been enlisted. I did not say a job description, because that (as necessary as it may be) puts the emphasis in the wrong place. You do not enlist someone "to teach" or "to take the young people's group." The stress of the appointment should be upon some purpose or purposes that are in view: "to get the young people interested in serving Christ" or "to teach the nursery class that they come to church to find out about Jesus" or "to help the young couples to have happier marriages." It is not a job description only, but also a job *accomplishment* that you want to convey by your remarks. Your stress should not be upon function but upon purpose—not so much how (that must come later) but rather upon what.

In approaching persons with gifts that seem to be directed toward service in a particular area, the pastor must remember that not *every* task in that area may be pursued as well by every person who has gifts that are appropriate to the area. That is to say, gifts differ not only in kind, but also in purpose *and* results. Listen to the following:

> Now there are varieties of gifts... varieties of ministries, and... varieties of effects (I Corinthians 12:4-6). These gifts differ also "according to the measure of Christ's gift" (Ephesians 4:7).

It is wrong to place persons in positions that demand more than they have the capabilities to deliver, or on the other hand, to cramp them with jobs too small to fit them. Nor is it right to allow persons to remain in tasks whose skins they have burst.[10] In the latter case, either they must be moved on to a larger work since they have outgrown the previous task, or the job in which they have been laboring must be enlarged to fit them.

Differing measures of the same gift will result in somewhat differing results. Comparisons with others are particularly odious in the light of this fact. Therefore, it is important for the pastor to help each man to find a task (1) in the area of his gifts, (2) that fits the measure of his capacities, and (3) that challenges him to work in it to *his* fullest capacity.[11]

Finally, notice the basic short-term purpose (on the long term, the purpose always is to honor God: I Peter 4:11b) of these gifts:

> ...to each one is given...for the common good (I Corinthians 12:7; cf. also vv. 14-31).

and,

---

[10] Tasks should be reviewed regularly. What satisfied a person a year ago, today may be bad stewardship of his labors and thus no longer may bring a sense of achievement.

[11] That will not be the same as the capacity of another.

As each one has received a gift, employ it in serving one another, as good stewards of the manifold grace of God (I Peter 4:10).

Gifts are given in order to bring about the mutual ministry of each believer to all of the others in the body. No Christian, therefore, can be happy in his Christian experience until he knows that in some way he is doing something with his gifts, and that what he is doing is bringing blessing and help to other Christians. No pastor may allow any Christian in the congregation to miss such blessing by failing to challenge him to use his gifts for Christ, nor may he allow the body to suffer from the disuse of gifts that the sovereign Spirit thought necessary for the health and welfare of the entire body. All the gifts in a congregation are important and are needed by all (I Corinthians 12:14-31). As Peter says, it is a matter of stewardship:

As each one has received a gift, employ it in serving one another, *as good stewards* of the variegated grace of God (I Peter 4:10).

What is stewardship? It is the proper recognition and assumption of the duties that correspond to the abilities and opportunities that one has to perform them. From the other side of the picture: stewardship is simply being yourself; i.e., becoming all that God has given you the gifts to be. It is required of stewards that they be faithful (I Corinthians 4:2).

Training for Service

Training is an essential part of enlisting persons to use their gifts. Many persons fear to attempt what they could achieve because they know that they are not ready to do so, and they do not know how to get ready. Pastors must plan, enlist, and teach (and teach others to teach) every person who is asked to take on a new task. In ministry, training is of essence. The "discipling" of all nations (Matthew 28) speaks not merely of conversion, but goes far beyond that when it refers to keeping "all" that Christ commanded. Just as everywhere in the Scriptures, the new life of the believer is said to be both *taught* (by formal preaching, teaching, etc.) and also *caught* (by learning from models how to live and apply the teaching), so too one learns to serve Christ in *both* ways. Christ frequently instructed the disciples formally, but he also taught them by example. For a full discussion of this important matter, it might be well to consider again some of the scriptural data that I have brought together elsewhere.[12]

Paul frequently stressed the importance of modeling, or a good example,

---

[12]What follows in the next few pages is an attempt to do just that.

in learning how to structure living. The importance of showing others how to obey God's commandments through example cannot be stressed too strongly. Role play or rehearsal may also be one valid means of extending the principle that scriptural discipline may be taught by example. Thus Paul called his readers not only to remember the words that he spoke, but also to recall the kind of life that he and his associates lived among them. Often principles can be impressed upon others most permanently and most vividly by means of example. Reference to example was not something unusual for Paul. Paul frequently used his own behavior as an example for others. This is apparent in passages like the fourth chapter of Philippians. There Paul directed his readers not only to pray and concentrate upon the things that were honorable, right, pure, lovely, and of good repute, but he continued:

> The things you have learned and received and heard and seen in me, practice these things: and the God of peace shall be with you (Philippians 4:9).

In the previous chapter of the same letter, he had already said,

> Brethren, join in following my example, and observe those who walk according to the pattern that you have in us (Philippians 3:17).

Paul considered his own life a model for new Christians. This emphasis is not limited to Philippians; Paul expressed the same thought in several other places. For instance, in I Corinthians 4:16 he wrote, "I exhort you therefore, be imitators of me."

Paul also mentioned modeling when he said, "You also became imitators" (I Thessalonians 1:6). The Greek term "imitator" is the same word from which the English word "mimic" comes. He wrote, "You became imitators of us and of the Lord." They learned, it seems, how to imitate the Lord by imitating what Paul was doing in imitation of his Lord. Again, Paul commended *them* for *becoming* models. After they learned how to imitate Paul in imitating the Lord, they themselves became examples for others: "You became an example to all the believers in Macedonia and Achaia" (I Thessalonians 1:7).

But it is not only Paul who stressed modeling. Peter similarly advised the elders of the church to which he was writing not only to "shepherd the flock of God," but without lording it over those allotted to their charge, to prove themselves to be "examples to the flock" (I Peter 5:3). The word used by Peter was *tupoi* ("types"). Elders are to be types or patterns for their flocks.

The idea of the model runs throughout the New Testament.[13]

This idea of modeling also occurs in John's writings, as well as in Peter's and Paul's. In III John 11, John's words show that he assumed that imitation will take place. He says, "Beloved, do not imitate what is evil, but what is good." He said, in effect:

> You're going to imitate. You can't help imitating. As a child you learned to imitate, and throughout life you are going to continue to imitate others. So make your imitation consciously purposeful by imitating that which is good.

The influence of older children in a home clearly demonstrates the importance of example. Younger children pick up their ways of speaking, their words, their actions and their attitudes. The influence of parents is even more striking. The influence which a counselor exerts in counseling is an important matter, as well. Counselors in all that they do, model, implicitly. At some times they model explicitly as well. And so the idea of modeling as a means of bringing about discipleship is something which must receive adequate attention.

Modeling was a principal teaching method of Jesus. At the beginning, it is of importance to notice that the Lord Jesus *appointed* the disciples as His students. The teacher sought out His pupils and accepted into His school only those whom He, Himself, had selected. Perhaps this principle of selectivity has too frequently been lost sight of, particularly in theological education. At their appointment, the purpose and methods that Jesus had in view, what He planned to do with these twelve disciples over the next few years and how He intended to do it, were explained. He appointed (or chose) twelve that they might be "with him." That is the key word: *"with him."* You may say, "I thought He was going to teach them; I thought He was going to *instruct them."* And isn't that what He did? Don't we see Jesus Christ subsequently sitting privately with His disciples explaining to them in detail what He taught the crowd in general? Do we not read of His instructing them in important truths? Don't we see Him teaching, teaching, teaching His disciples? Yes, we do. But teaching, as many people in modern times conceive of it, is thought of very narrowly. It is often considered to be merely that contact which takes place between a teacher and his students in which the teacher imparts factual information. Certainly, that is a large portion of teaching, and *nothing* I say here should

---

[13]Cf. I Thessalonians 1:6; Philippians 4:9; 3:17; I Corinthians 4:16; II Timothy 3:10; II Thessalonians 3:9; I Timothy 4:12; Titus 2:7; Hebrews 13:7; I Thessalonians 1:7; III John 11, etc.

be construed to mean that I do not believe in the teaching of *content*. We *must* teach subject matter; indeed, much more than is taught elsewhere. But there is also much more to teaching than the teaching of content. That is why the Bible does not say that Jesus appointed twelve that He might *instruct* them. He does not say that He appointed twelve that He might send them to class. Nor does He say that He appointed twelve that they might crack the books and take His course. That was all a part of it, but, note, only a *part*. There is a much larger concept in these words: "He appointed twelve that they might be with Him." "With Him!" Think of all that meant. Those two words describe the fulness of Jesus' teaching. Such teaching is full; it is rounded, balanced and complete. For the length of His ministry, the disciples were to be with Him to learn not only what He taught them by word of mouth, but much more.

"How do you know?" you ask. "Aren't you possibly reading a lot into that phrase?" No, I don't think so, and I'll tell you why. The reason why I say that I'm not just reading my own ideas into this phrase is that in a definitive passage, Jesus Himself gave a description of teaching that accords exactly with this interpretation. In the sixth chapter of Luke, verse 40, He defines the pupil-teacher relationship, what goes on in that relationship and its results. Jesus says, "A pupil is not above his teacher, but everyone after he has been fully taught will be like his teacher." Now, did you get the full import of those words? He says, "everyone" who is fully taught "will be like his teacher." Jesus did not say, "will *think* like his teacher." That is part of it, but, again, it is only part of it. Jesus said that a pupil who has been properly (fully) taught "will *be* like his teacher." He will be like him, not just *think* like him. This passage helps us to understand the principles of education underlying Jesus' appointment of the twelve to be "with Him" in order to send them forth to teach. He was calling them to become His disciples (pupils) that they might be *with* Him in order to become *like* Him so that they might teach like Him.

"But, did these principles work? Did their education really make them 'like Him'?" The evidence provides a clear answer to that question. After Jesus had risen from the dead and ascended into heaven, He sent His Spirit back to continue His work through the Church. In Acts 4:13, Luke gives us a view of how the enemies of the Church looked upon the disciples (now called apostles) who were the leaders in this work:

> As they observed the confidence of Peter and John and understood that they were uneducated and untrained men (that is, formally so), they were marveling and began to recognize them as having been with Jesus.

The evidence is now complete. Look at it: He appointed twelve that they might be *with* Him. He said that a pupil, properly taught, will be like his teacher. And in the course of time others recognized that the disciples had become, in large measure, *like Him*.

Thus, in enlisting for evangelism, for teaching, for ushering, or for any number of other tasks in the church, it is important to provide discipleship (or apprenticeship) opportunities for instruction. Someone has said that in any organization, the key is persons, not systems. In one sense that is very true, but in another, it is dangerously deceptive. This is so because some systems, in emphasizing only content, delivered in formal contexts, tend to *keep persons away from persons*. The discipleship system in contrast *emphasizes* learning from the whole person. So persons are the key, but the system must allow for the personal element to surface meaningfully.

EXERCISE

For the Student

Using Romans 12:3-8 as a basis, develop a program for helping new Christians to discover their gifts.

For the Pastor

Determine how you best can help not only new converts, but also long-standing members of your congregation to discover, develop and deploy their gifts.

CHAPTER XI
SETTING UP A PROGRAM

We shall turn at this time to a consideration of the church program. The pastor *leads,* through the dark valleys and the barren wastes to the green pastures and the still waters. But by what route? How does he help the members of his flock to walk in the paths of righteousness for the sake of God's Name? This he does by setting before himself and the flock three goals under one. To the honor of God, he seeks to achieve three, and only three purposes: (1) to lead the flock into the proper worship of the living God, (2) to lead the flock into edifying ways (i.e., the building up of itself in love, Ephesians 4:16), (3) to lead the flock into evangelistic outreaches. To accomplish these three goals the pastor must devise and follow a congregational blueprint, for it is only by a program, well planned and executed, that these ends may be attained. Jesus Christ followed a carefully laid out program in doing the will of God. It was a program planned and scheduled from "the foundation of the world."

Although the principle behind a biblical program is simple enough in concept, often it is difficult to apply. The principle is this: anything that does not enable the flock to worship God better, to be edified and to edify one another, and to evangelize the lost, must be eliminated; it has no place in the program of the church. On the other side of the page, however, is this: anything that would facilitate and foster these three biblical ends that is not already a part of the program must be added as soon as possible. In short, any church program must honor God; and God is honored when His own revealed purposes are adopted and pursued.

A pastor, coming to a congregation, will bring new ideas about the ways and means of reaching these three scriptural goals. That, of course, is one value of a change of pastors. However, he must be careful not to expect everything in the pastorate to change, or to change right away. And, it is important for him to be ready to experience change himself. There are very few situations in which he will not learn from the new congregation, if he allows his own ideas and his own methods to be challenged.

He must be cautious about the way that he seeks to bring about change; otherwise he may become divisive. The only way to effect change solidly is by a thorough persuasion of the leadership of the congregation from the Word of God. Usually, this takes time. But if he is willing to work and wait, as a by-product he will learn patience, and when the change comes he will know that it is *solid* because it will be based upon conviction. Change by conviction is better than change by coercion. Every pastor must spend time winning the confidence of the leaders of the flock and of the members of the church by wise actions and teaching. During the period in which he is building confidence, he also should be making an analysis of the congregational situation. Using the three goals mentioned previously as his criteria, he should measure, compare and contrast every aspect of the current program. As a result, by the end of his first year, he ought to have a set of written objectives, listed in the order of priority, and built into a comprehensive five-year plan.[1]

This five-year plan should consist of general objectives and specific ways and means for reaching them. It should cover every aspect of congregational activity, stating what should be continued, what may be enhanced (and how), and what must be changed or eliminated. Hopefully, the period of building of confidence and the period of production of the plan will correspond roughly to one another, so that during the spring of the year (an ideal time; but any other will do), following his installation, he may begin to speak to the elders about his plan, and, hopefully too, may see the first stage of the new program develop and get under way during the fall that follows. (Fall, remember, is the *beginning* of the church year.)

The five-year plan may be explained in part or in whole to the elders, as the pastor deems best at the time. Like Jesus, the pastor will find that he cannot unload everything upon others all at once because they are "not yet able to bear it." Often, more instruction, the encouragement from the success of the first phase of the five-year plan, etc., will be needed before he can do so. Sometimes, the whole plan may be spelled out to the elders at once. The congregation, because it will contain people of every sort of spiritual growth, ordinarily would be shown the plan in stages. But, at any rate, whether the entire plan is presented to the elders from the outset or only the first stage, it is essential that the *pastor himself* have the overall plan. Otherwise, what he does this year he may find it necessary to tear down the next. That is not to say that there can be no revisions. Certainly there can. Every pastor, like his people, should grow; growth (not to speak

---

[1]Cf. Appendix C for help in formulating a five-year plan.

of God's own providential revisions) alters perspective. Yet, if there is no plan and no framework, all will be in flux and the pastor will not know where he is going. At all times, therefore, he should be operating toward something, not merely operating. He is a shepherd who ever seeks clearer waters and greener pastures for the flock. Leadership is always toward objectives. If he does not know what those objectives should be, how to attain them and persuade others to become enthusiastically committed to reaching them too, he can not be considered a *leader*. He himself will be like one of the sheep without a shepherd, wandering aimlessly.

A Covenantal Program

One basic principle for setting up a congregational program is to be sure that it is covenantal. That is to say, the pastor must be certain that the program in every way possible coordinates, rather than competes, with the family and home life of the members of the congregation. Far too often, the very meetings in which families are exhorted to preserve and develop deeper Christian values compete with the avowed purposes for which they were called. The calling of special meetings of the congregation must always be considered in respect to number (how many per month?), size (are crowds necessary; desirable?), content (is it truly additional to what can be given during the regular meetings?), time (flexibility? geared to family? could it be done on Sunday?), frequency (why not once per month rather than every week?) and persons invited (could the whole family come instead of a part only?). All special meetings should strengthen and encourage family life, not tend to tear it apart by placing demands upon it. Many things can be done *without* holding meetings. Decisions may be made by using the telephone, making conference calls or even using the mails (Why take six or eight men away from their families another night unless absolutely necessary?). And, why must the pastor exhort the congregation to turn out in crowds for weekday meetings? Our great concern for crowds often is sinfully motivated. Even when it is not, and there is a true desire to *help many,* the zeal is often "without knowledge." That is to say, on balance, the pastor would find that more good might be achieved by urging many of those who were inclined to come only out of a sense of duty to stay home instead. The persons who truly *need* to be at the meeting and *only* they are the ones who should attend. And, the pastor might *say so* when making the weekly announcements ("Now on Monday there is...Tuesday...Wednesday...Thursday...Friday...Saturday... and, of course, the regular services next Sunday. Please *do not attend* any of the meetings apart from the regular services of the church unless you have a good reason for doing so.[2] We want only those who especially need them to be present. Be sure to spend adequate time with your family this week, and you must see to it that church meetings do not keep you from doing so").

A Family Program

However, it is not *enough* to discourage running to meetings; at the same time the pastor must encourage a family program of worship, edification and evangelism. The need for this — all week long — has been felt by those who seek to provide it in urging attendance at a plethora of weekday meetings. Yet that solution is not viable, we have seen. But the need for more remains. That is why *a family program,* complementing the church program and coordinating with it, should be developed. Instead of spending time at meetings away from the home, the pastor may encourage members of each family to spend time *in their homes, as families* in similar activities. These programs may be keyed into the regular services and meetings of the congregation. Rather than planning *meetings,* the pastor might more profitably plan and publish *materials* (family study, worship and activity guides) for weekday family use. The work accomplished may feed into the Sunday sermons (e.g., a guide for family Bible readings, complete with questions for study and discussion and outside reading materials, may be published each month in the congregational newsletter. Then Bible portions for each week may cover the passages upon which the sermon will be preached on the following Sunday evening. Ideas, suggestions, questions, examples, etc., may be phoned in to the church secretary or to a member appointed for that purpose by the Friday preceding the sermon. The pastor may then incorporate some of these in the message itself). Families may be encouraged to visit one another in order to foster Christian fellowship and hospitality. Participating members may have their family names drawn from a hat and published in the newsletter one month in advance ("The Harry Smiths will entertain the Wm. Joneses"). In this way families that otherwise might be reluctant to entertain one another will be encouraged to come to know each other better. There is no end to the possible ways and means for families to be encouraged to do things together.

Time and Planning

I have said a good bit already about time at an earlier point.[3] I wish to

---

[2] Five persons vitally involved are better than seventy-five who are not. If too few attend, then perhaps the meeting is ill-conceived.

[3] Vol. I, "Repossessing Time," Chapter 7, pp. 39-50.

make only one further observation: to get the time he needs, a pastor must *plan* for it. In the earlier discussion not only did I mention planning, but I provided basic worksheets for enabling the pastor to do so. Yet the discussion there focused more upon the pastor's individual planning. Here I wish to stress that all such planning must be fully coordinated with the corporate planning of the church. If the pastor does not consciously make every effort to coordinate his personal planning with congregational planning, continually he will find that his own plans will become subordinated to it.

That is to say that he must see to it that he always takes congregational planning into consideration when he makes personal plans. His datebook *cannot merely contain personal or even individual pastoral engagements;* it must also encompass all church activities which in any way bear upon his own time and scheduling.[4] Next, he must so insist upon the good stewardship of everyone's time that he influences the number as well as the date and time of meetings which are held. Rather than a matter of least significance, the pastor should work zealously at the question of setting the *proper* time and place for the next meeting of any group that he attends. Some organizations meet too frequently; he should say so, if he thinks that they could do with fewer meetings (if it is fellowship that is needed then that should be acknowledged and provided for in a better way). If the date means another day away from home, when a meeting could be held concurrently with the Church School or the Evening Youth Group, he should make that point. If the Women's Auxiliary could meet during the day, rather than spend another evening away from husbands and children, he may find it of importance to raise the question of the time of the meeting. In general, since time is so vital to him, the pastor should become increasingly alert to ways and means of saving time for himself and for others; he has none to waste.

One or two additional observations regarding time may be of help. It is of prime importance for every pastor to plan his work in such a way that he rarely ever does only one thing at a time. That is to say, whenever he puts out time and effort to do one thing, *if possible* he should be preparing (thereby) for several other things as well. For example, as he studies for a series of sermons, he decides to use some of the material developed in that preparation in an article that he has been asked to write for the

---

[4]Not that he has to attend all church meetings (as some pastors wrongly believe they should). The average conservative pastor probably could cut the number of meetings that he attends by at least half. Some he could attend *less frequently.* At times, when forced to make the choice, he should wisely make appointments that overlap church meetings rather than those that overlap his family activities.

denominational magazine. At the same time, he determines to use some of it for a talk that he is scheduled to give at the Evangelical Ministerium next month. Continually, he insists (to himself *and to others*) that by this practice he will not allow himself to be spread too thinly. When he is requested to speak, *he* specifies the topic, and rarely allows others to do so for him, thereby allowing for time-saving through overlapping study and multifocused preparation.

Let me issue a warning about schedules. The schedule belongs to the pastor; he does not belong to it. He must make it, shape it, revise it. But, like a good friend, once he has it, he must stick to it (or revise it); he must *never ignore it*. Schedules must provide unscheduled cushion time for flexibility. This too is important.

Lastly, in all of his congregational planning, the pastor repeatedly should ask himself, "Is there someone else who could do this job?" and "Can someone else help me do this (or a part of it)?" Too few pastors know how to delegate. Those who have problems with learning to delegate, and who want to do something about it, might write out the two questions just mentioned on a card, place it on the desk (or under the glass on the desk) as a reminder to help them plan properly. But whatever they do, the key factor to keep in mind is that they will achieve the desired changes sooner and most dramatically if they combine delegation with planning. It is too difficult to delegate well *on impulse*. Delegation itself must be *planned* or (1) it will not happen, or (2) should not happen in the shoddy way in which it has been handled.

EXERCISE

For the Student

Using a format similar to the one found in Appendix C, draw up a five-year plan for a congregation with which you are (or become) familiar. If you can secure the cooperation of the pastor of the congregation, work with him in the preparation of this program. Give him a copy and distribute a duplicate to each member of the class (include only the Program Planner and not the Worksheet).

For the Pastor

Using the Worksheet and Program Planner (Appendix C), draw up a five-year program for your church. Take your time, and write in pencil so that changes may be made later. But set yourself a deadline of no less than one month for setting up the objectives of the five-year program of change.

CHAPTER XII
ORGANIZATIONS IN THE CONGREGATION

It is vital for the pastor (and through him for everyone in the congregation) to understand that all of the activities of a congregation, including those carried on by organizations like the Youth Groups, the Church School, the Women's Society and the Choir are *a part of the congregational program*.[1] These organizations are not separate entities answerable only to God and themselves, but a portion of the congregational effort subject to the oversight and discipline of the elders of the congregation. Often this fact is neither known nor is the proper relationship of such organizations to the board of elders a reality.

The fact must be communicated and the reality must come into being. Otherwise, as the result of independent attitudes and practices foreign to the New Testament, growing disunity, conflict, inability to check heresy, inefficiency and ineffectiveness will result, all to the dishonor of God and the destruction of the flock.

More often than not, the difficulties in a congregation grow out of the failure to conform to biblical principles of church government. In the Scriptures, it is a plurality of elders to whom is given the rule in a congregation; all that happens is subject to their approval and oversight. If there is no one central, coordinating center of authority in the congregation, no shepherdly leadership, the flock will be scattered. Members will begin to wander off. Factions will grow and the flock will be divided. Remember, flocking is a significant task of shepherdly leadership; sheep do not flock *on their own*. Shepherdly leadership helps each organization to see itself as *a part of the whole,* not as a separate entity.[2]

---

[1]On no other basis can such organizations be justified biblically. This justification rests upon viewing organizations as congregational ways and means developed for carrying out Christ's mandates for worship, edification and evangelism.

[2]It is important for the various organizations to communicate with each other. Rarely is this done. Leaders in each group should meet at least quarterly (in addition to one yearly joint planning session in the spring) to discuss matters of cooperation, coordination and united efforts. Otherwise, organizations will find themselves working *against* one another and the family. The pastor and other elders should attend these joint sessions (perhaps held on Sunday evenings at the time of the Youth Meeting).

How can such a unified system be taught and effectuated? There is only one sure way: *authority is demonstrated when the responsibility that accompanies it is assumed*. Nothing can cause more difficulty than for a pastor or his elders to begin to assert their authority, rightful as it may be, by issuing directives and leveling criticisms *without shouldering the burdens of authority* that are involved in oversight.

What are those burdens? Well, responsibilities differ from organization to organization, but such questions as showing interest in and acquaintance with the organization and its members, helping out as a trouble shooter when there are problems and difficulties, sharing in the decisions made at business meetings, expressions of appreciation for accomplishments, willingness to attend meetings, prompt, fair responses from the elders to questions or suggestions stemming from the organization, and regular prayerful concern for the projects it undertakes are fundamental. When pastors, themselves, take the lead in such matters they are in a position to encourage their elders to do so too.

It is possible, of course, for designated elders to exercise special oversight toward particular congregational organizations. This is often a good way to assure responsible concern and rule. When such a plan is adopted, it is wise to have reports on each organization from its overseeing elder at every regular elders' meeting.[3] This keeps the need for oversight constantly before the board of elders and lays the responsibility of concern for at least one organization heavily upon each elder. If he continually reports "no report," the board (or perhaps first the pastor quietly behind the scenes) asks: "Is there some reason why you are unable to give adequate oversight to this organization, John? Is there anything we can do to help?" His answer may lead to the discovery of difficulties in John's life (disorganization, overloaded schedule, priority problems, growing lack of interest, laziness) or perhaps in the organization itself ("They keep changing the dates of their business meetings" or "They told me that they didn't want the elders shoving their oars in" or "Really, there's nothing to report; nothing significant ever happens").

Let us consider a couple of typical problem areas in two specific organizations to discover concretely how problems may be prevented or remedied by proper oversight. We shall take a look first at the Choir, then at the Church School.

The Choir

To begin with, several issues seem to be perennial Choir problems. Since

---

[3]Probably held on a monthly basis.

they are, there is every reason to take steps *beforehand* to avoid the difficulties.[4] Good oversight is first preventive. Here are three such problems: (1) Who may become members of the Choir? Believers only? Church members only? Trained singers only? (2) Who determines the type of hymns sung? Is the emphasis to be placed upon words or upon music? (3) How can the Choir be deactivated as a gossip network that so often crackles with information (and *mis*information)?

Proper oversight will require that each organization of the congregation shall have a set of by-laws drawn up and approved by the session in consultation with the leadership of that organization. These should be duplicated and made available to all who are involved. These by-laws will contain such information as (for the Church School) qualifications for teachers or (for the Choir) qualifications for membership. All by-laws will state prominently that the organization is an extension of the congregation, holds to its particular objectives, and what its place and functions are in relationship to the whole. Its relationship to the elders should be made crystal clear. Obviously the by-laws themselves, when properly constructed and used, will help to keep problems such as (1) and (2) from arising. The by-laws are preventive and must attempt to *anticipate* as many difficulties as possible.

But by-laws, good and useful as they may be, cannot do everything. Indeed, they are only as useful as the *persons* who operate within them. And, moreover, it is only the right *persons* who finally can deal with such problems as (3), the gossip network. It is important, then, not only for the board of elders to exercise keen oversight toward the Choir, but also for them to select the choir director with great care. It is essential, for instance, to find a person of sound Christian conviction who (1) will be concerned not only about the quality of the music, but also about the quality of its message, (2) will be able to work with people and who (3) will be able to set the proper tone for each choir practice by explaining the import of the message of the music and its purpose in the service, and who (4) will be alert to and able to deal with such matters as gossip when he sees them arise.[5]

Usually the pastor will find it necessary to draw up sample by-laws

---

[4]Always a good policy—much better than the usual policy of doing nothing until something tragic happens.

[5]Sometimes it is better to have no choir than to have one that is poorly directed (and by directed I mean ability to direct in all four of the above areas). If choices must be made, it is probably more important to sacrifice first-rate music for the other qualities. It is not wrong to pay a choir director, but better still is to discern gifted persons and appoint them to the directorship and to membership in the choir. Sometimes it is better to pay to send a trusted member of the congregation to school for further instruction in directing than to hire someone

himself (or at least one such) in order to present the matter to the board of elders. The pastor may have to show them how the by-laws are designed to prevent problems from developing. When introducing these to the organization in question, he must do the same for the members, but only after already having taken the time to explain these facts to the leadership of the organization and after enlisting their help (indeed, if the Choir leader or Sunday School superintendent himself can enthusiastically and clearly give the explanation, so much the better).[6]

The Church School

Let us now take up a typical Church School problem (one that we have considered already, the qualification of teachers). We saw how by-laws can help to forestall difficulties in this area. But in what ways can persons having the qualifications set forth in those by-laws be found? Surely, they do not usually walk in the church door, fully prepared, and announce their availability. Usually, these persons must be discovered, appointed, trained and provided with adequate resources. One way to provide training is in a yearly Teacher Training Course for prospective and appointed teachers. The course may be taught by the pastor in conjunction with the revolving Adult Church School Curriculum at the tertiary level during one of the four quarters.[7] But a teacher training course, devoted to the general principles of teaching, is not, in itself, adequate. Instead there must be an apprenticeship or discipling program available too. It is even possible for the pastor to develop a teacher or two to teach the Teacher Training Course also. In doing so he would use the same basic apprenticeship model that he uses in training men to teach the other courses in the curriculum. That is to say, the first time through, the pastor himself teaches the course, developing a syllabus, assignments, lectures, etc. He then appoints someone who sat in on the course and who, by his participation, gives evidence of understanding and gifts to do so, to teach it the next time, while the pastor sits in (behind the scenes, the pastor coaches, gives helpful criticism, encourages, trouble shoots and, in general, gives strong backing). Thereafter, the teacher teaches the course by himself. Since it is a teacher training course, in most instances the pastor would be wise to select

---

from outside the body. Volunteer directors and volunteer choirs bring problems. Oversight involves work by the pastor and elders in discovering, developing and deploying the gifts God has provided within the body.

[6]Remember, if the pastor and/or elders drew up the by-laws *in conjunction with* the organization's leadership (as suggested above), support and fuller understanding are more likely to be obtained from the leadership.

[7]See the next chapter for a description of this program and an explanation of these terms.

someone ahead of time to sit in for this purpose, someone who already has demonstrated ability to teach.

So, just as it is not enough to adopt by-laws for governing the Choir (we have seen that proper leadership is also required), so too it is not sufficient merely to set forth by-laws for a Church School (determining among other things the qualifications for teachers). In addition, various ways and means for discovering persons with adequate gifts and for developing those gifts also must be worked out. Most failures in attaining well-thought-through, doctrinally sound results come from two omissions: (1) failure to secure the proper persons by appointment; (2) failure to train them by both formal and apprenticeship methods. What has been said here about the Church School, and earlier about the Choir, holds for every other organization as well, simply because organizations are organizations of *people*. People have different capabilities, maturity of doctrine and life, concerns and commitments. The personal factor, in the end, often is what really makes the difference.

But while this is true, let us not forget that the right person, *without* adequate training, with an inadequate task description, with no authority or without the proper resources cannot be expected to do the job either. The pastor, for instance, may not sit back with a sigh of relief, thinking that all will be well now that the church has hired a theological seminary student to work with the youth. That student may or may not be the right one to work with youth. He may or may not need much instruction. All of these matters must be considered and the pastor or some elder alerted by him to do so must stand closely by to be sure that the work is done properly. The youth worker may need heavy backing at first to help him see needs and even to decide how best to meet them. If he becomes so bogged down with his studies that the youth work suffers, he may need encouragement and help in drawing up a personal priority list leading to a new and more realistic study/work schedule. Usually we forget that able people with strong convictions often need help too.

Appreciation

And, in speaking of getting the best service of God from those who work in the church, the pastor (and he by example and suggestion should teach others to do so too) should take a leaf from the Chief Shepherd's notebook. He must learn to express appreciation for work well done ("well done, you good and faithful servant" is what Christ will say). Even in some of those seven Churches where there was little to approve, Jesus (nevertheless) found something that He honestly could commend ("this you have") and stated that first. Appreciation is an oil that it is essential for him to apply freely if the pastor wishes to keep the complex machinery of congregational activity running smoothly.[8]

EXERCISE

For the Student or the Pastor

In the space below jot down elements you would like to have in a set of by-laws for the Choir. Students, in groups of four or five, then should together draw up an actual set of by-laws. A pastor, in conjunction with some neighboring pastors, may do the same.

---

[8]For further examples of the expression of appreciation, study the New Testament epistles (especially those by Paul). Begin with a study of Romans 16.

CHAPTER XIII
A CHURCH SCHOOL FOR ADULTS

The Adult Department of the Church School, apart from those exceptional situations in which the presence of an unusual teacher has made the difference, has a dissatisfying record of mediocrity. The sad level of half-hearted participation and performance, so frequently exhibited in such classes, usually parallels rather closely a low level of weekday Christian living that is part and parcel of the same failure. This failure stems largely from an inability to study and apply the Scriptures practically and in depth.[1] Existing programs, for the most part, fail to satisfy this need. As a consequence, neither businessmen nor housewives know how to get the help that they need from the Scriptures when they need it — when they have decisions to make and problems to solve on Thursday and Saturday. If this need to enable Christians to use their Bibles more effectively and practically is to be met, *adults must be taught how to do so.*

Retracing the missionary journeys of Paul for the umpteenth time in their Sunday School careers, useful and important as that may be for its purpose, will not meet that need. Something far more ambitious, far more comprehensive, far more well-rounded must be done. The proposal in this section, successfully followed in various forms in three congregations, endeavors to point the way (many modifications and improvements are necessary) to a solution to the problem.

To begin with, consider the odds against which the average Church School[2] teacher labors:

---

[1] I am convinced that while there are a great number of exceptions to this rule, the lethargy in the church, and the low level of living evidenced, derives more frequently than we may realize from ineptness than from lack of desire. Of course, the two are not mutually exclusive: failure to achieve often leads to resignation, which (in turn) may lead to lethargy. Discussions with hundreds of laymen concerning this matter, however, lead to the conclusion that great changes for good could be effected quickly by introducing a plan of teaching that would overcome the difficulties I have mentioned. That is why this program was envisioned and is articulated here.

[2] I prefer not to use the title "Sunday School" because of the unfortunate connotations that this word has for so many adults. To each of them it may mean many things, but rarely do the words convey the idea of a genuine school where significant learning takes place. Pastors would be wise when introducing the new plan to give the school a different title.

1. Usually he has had no training in teaching.
2. He has had no special training in his subject matter.
3. His class labors under no stated obligation to learn.
4. He has no feedback (examinations, reports, papers, etc.) to help him determine whether what he attempts to teach is in fact being learned.
5. He must work in truly abysmal learning conditions.
   a. There are no desks, no textbooks, etc.
   b. There is no homework required.
   c. No one is expected to take notes.
   d. Classes meet only every seventh day.
   e. Levels of understanding are ignored.
6. He must teach new material each week, never repeating material taught before.
7. He must become a generalist, equally able to teach Old Testament or New Testament, Bible geography, or Doctrine or anything else.
8. He teaches in an open-ended context — on and on — with no semesters or other terms (etc.) marked out.
9. He has no "time off."
10. He has no opportunity to learn and grow under another's teaching since all teaching is coterminous.

These considerations are only a few of the more obvious ones that might be mentioned. Clearly, pastors ought to be concerned about them. If, as shepherds, their task is to equip the saints for their works of ministry, pastors must make every effort to sharpen this dull but important tool. Millions of members waste countless hours of time every year in adult classes, that could be thoroughly productive.

The average Adult Church School either ought to be abandoned or revitalized; it should not be permitted to go on as it has. The lives of many persons are affected adversely because they think that the mediocrity that they experience is the best that Christianity has to offer. It is not, and pastors must not allow them to think so. The Adult School, instead, can be turned into a challenging and exciting learning experience.

"I'm willing to try almost anything," you may respond. "I know what you are talking about!" Fine, if you are willing to work at making the school in your church a genuine *school,* capable of *teaching* and thus influencing the lives of many adults positively for Jesus Christ, I assure you that it can be done. But, let me warn you, not only will you run into resistance from various quarters, you also will discover that the transformation will call for work on your part. You must be ready and able to devote yourself to the task for a period of time to get it under way. If you are game, read on. If not, skip the rest of this section of the book, and turn again to it only after you have spent another month observing the futility of what so often is labeled (wrongly) "teaching" in the adult class(es).

If you are prepared to go ahead (out of eagerness, despair or both), let us begin by asking the question: What are the prime goals of the church? The answer is amply supplied by what is called The Great Commission (Matthew 28:19,20). The passage should not be allocated solely to missionaries; it is *your* overall directive for church life and activity. After all, when you think about it, you *and* your congregation are converts on a foreign mission field. Jerusalem was the home base; you live in one of the "uttermost parts" of the world (cf. Acts 1:8).

The so-called Great Commission describes the church and her work in *educational* terms. Her task is to "make disciples"; that is, to gather in *students* (as the word disciple means). Every Christian is a student, who when he becomes a part of Christ's church (thereby) becomes a student of Christ in Christ's school (the church). The call to baptism is a call to matriculation and to admission into the institution. But *once* they become a part of the church (the school), they are to be *taught* (v. 20). Adults, therefore, should be encouraged to learn, should understand that learning is a large part of what their membership and participation in church life is all about, and should be given genuine opportunities to learn not only in preaching contexts but also in the Church School.

The teaching that is in view (v. 20) is not casual or limited to certain areas, but both extensive and intensive. It is to extend to the whole corpus of information and skills that were given to the church by Christ: "*all* that I commanded." And, notice especially, it does not extend merely to the acquisition of information, but *beyond,* to the application of truth to life ("teaching to *observe*"). Thus the teaching must be so intensive that it aims at influencing life, and is conducted in such a way that, in truth, it does bring about such changes as were commanded by Jesus.

Now, of course, that is a large order. Yet, it is what Christ requires, and it accords exactly with the task of the pastor-teacher in Ephesians 4:11,12. Your efforts are to build up your sheep by *teaching* them to *observe* all that Christ commanded so that they may serve Him well in ministry through the use of their gifts.[3] The time and effort, therefore, that you expend in efforts

---

[3]The task-oriented titles "pastor" and "teacher" correspond nicely to the two tasks *teaching* (teacher) to *observe* (pastor).

to improve the teaching program in your congregation, is well spent.[4] You must see that it is at the heart of your responsibility and not simply ancillary to it.

Let us then take those three factors mentioned earlier and examine them more fully. Jesus requires:

1. *Complete, comprehensive teaching:* "teach them to observe *all* things that I commanded" (what Paul called the "whole counsel of God" — Acts 20:27).
2. *Effective teaching:* "teach them to *observe* all things that I commanded."
3. *Correct teaching:* "teach them to observe all *things that I commanded.*"

It is those three elements that continually must guide the pastor as he sets up and evaluates any program of teaching in the church. They too are the criteria by which he may test the present teaching program. He may (must) ask such questions as "How much of the body of Christian truth is being taught?," "How clearly is this truth being made known?" "How well are the lives of those taught being affected by it?" and "How accurately is it being presented?" Whatever in a program that hinders students from receiving comprehensive and accurate teaching that edifies must be eliminated; whatever enables it must be added.

Let us ask, "Can the average layman learn more, considerably more than he usually does?" The answer is yes. Not only has Jesus required *all* of the students in his school to learn *all* that he commands, but there are institutions that have demonstrated that when the effort to do so is made, man-in-the-pew Christians can be taught great amounts of truth effectively and in ways that influence their lives significantly. Take, for instance, the work of the Bible School movement. I refer not only to the day schools but to the night-school programs carried on in many cities throughout the country. Far more teaching is offered there than is usually taught in the average Church School. But why is this so? Does it need to be? Why must members of your congregation take out another night away from their families and spend extra funds to get from some other source what your church failed to teach? Moreover, can you be sure that what is taught there is altogether accurate? Will not the doctrine often be of a least-common-denominator variety since persons from such a variety of backgrounds must be served? Will not many important biblical truths, therefore, be bypassed or distorted? Could you not develop a better program in your

---

[4]Well spent because it is spent doing what the Lord commands.

congregation, one that retains all of the strengths of the Bible School (which only a limited number of your adults would/could attend anyway) but eliminates all of its weaknesses? Yes, you could!

How? Well, having convinced your elders (and that may mean such things as at first running an experimental pilot program for a part of the adult members who agree to participate), you must then carve out the time for such a program. That will be your first real hurdle. You cannot either teach or learn when you do not have sufficient time to do the job well. The half-hour teaching time that some adult classes allot to themselves is not only insufficient, it is preposterous. Who can learn anything worthwhile in a half-hour-one-day-per-week setting? Do not try to make the change, therefore, unless you can allocate sufficient time in which to effect it. Otherwise, your efforts will be set for failure before you have begun.

One way to recapture valuable time is to eliminate the "worship service" or the "opening exercises" or other preliminaries that usually take up to half of the time devoted to the Church School. The adults do not need this anyway. Anyone who is old enough to worship in the regular worship service will find this duplication unnecessary and time-consuming. Worship at home and in the regular worship services of the congregation is sufficient if carried out well. By dropping this opening period, and beginning to teach immediately after prayer, a full hour for teaching can be obtained.

Yet, a better arrangement is possible. If the Church School can begin at 9:30 A.M. instead of 10:00 A.M., that additional half hour provides for much more opportunity to do *many more* things. Look at some of the possibilities:

1. There can be two teaching periods each Sunday:
   9:30 - 10:10 (40 minutes)
   10:15 - 10:55 (40 minutes)[5]
2. Two periods each morning allow for opportunity for teachers (adult and otherwise) to sit in on one of these so that they too may receive instruction.
3. Two periods allow for other Bible-related courses, such as those taught in Bible Schools, to be offered *along with* (instead of *replacing*) regular courses in the direct study of the Bible. Courses in cults, evangelism, Bible Geography, etc., can be taught.
4. Opportunities to do more significant things in the children's and youth departments are opened up.

---

[5]Forty-minute periods are not as adequate as single hour-long periods, but they are quite sufficient when doubling up on periods. The five-minute breaks at 10:10 and 10:55 allow for time to change classes and to get to morning worship (11:00).

    5. Other special courses (teacher training, new converts, courses, etc.)
       may be offered at one of the two hours without replacing a Bible
       Study course and rather than taking time during the week to do so.
    6. The change of teachers and subjects that two periods allow is
       refreshing, especially if one of the two teachers is not too apt.

These suggestions are only a few of the many possibilities that the two-period system provides. The flexibility it builds into the program is what both pastors and members alike will find most desirable.

The next concept to visualize is the need to break down the Sunday School *class* concept in favor of the *course* concept. The *class* is a group of persons of varying levels of spiritual maturity and understanding who are trying to learn together. Frequently visitors and unbelievers also appear in such classes. This does not provide for optimum learning conditions. The idea that you will destroy the fellowship of the class is fallacious. If the Church School exists primarily for fellowship, then let us acknowledge this openly and call it the *fellowship* hour. Then, in all honesty, the period can be designed to promote fellowship (I am not saying that this could not be done, nor that it should not be done periodically, say, once every two months). There are many other better ways to promote fellowship (not that learning together will not do so too). But, if the primary purpose of the Church School is to promote learning, then that purpose must not be sacrificed for a secondary one.

The course concept develops from and, indeed, is suggested by the idea of complete or comprehensive teaching ("teach them to observe *all things*"). There is much to learn, and it is not all the same. Therefore, in order to teach more systematically and thoroughly, and in order to be sure that the full range of biblical concern is covered, a curriculum consisting of various courses to be pursued over a period of time should be developed. Of course, no curriculum will be perfect or complete, but without one, teaching becomes hit-or-miss.

The courses may be developed as 10 or 12-week periods offered on a quarter system (with Fall, Winter, Spring and Summer quarters). If courses are 12 weeks in length, they will require 48 of the 52 weeks in the year. That permits the Church School to have four *special* programs each year (Christmas, Easter, Rally Day?, Reformation Day?). If the 10-week concept is adopted, more flexibility is built in: (1) More special programs are possible, (2) Field-trip days can be developed, (3) Fellowship hours can be inserted periodically, etc.

The concept of courses allows individual teachers to specialize; the idea of a curriculum allows them to teach courses again and again, thus becoming more proficient in doing so. Courses *build* over the years as one teaches them over again. The most experienced college professor would refuse to teach only new material, on any and all subjects, to a motley group of students, yet we expect inexperienced and untrained teachers to do just that! Teachers (especially if there is a large Church School) may belong to departments (Bible, Doctrine, Christian Living, Bible History and Geography, etc.). These departments may wish to plan their offerings together with the aid and direction of the pastor.

The concept of courses allows a teacher to think of his teaching more systematically, in terms of 10 to 12-week packages, rather than in an open-ended, who-knows-when-we'll-change-or-stop manner. And, if he is allowed to teach no more than one course per half year, and only every other quarter (2 courses per year), this means that (1) he can on each Sunday sit in on a class taught by someone else (he can learn about methodology in teaching thereby as well as benefit from the instruction);[6] (2) he can have two one-quarter breaks during which he can prepare ahead of time for his next quarter's course. While not every Church School will have enough teaching personnel at the outset to effect this, it should be an aim. Since the curriculum envisions offering a teacher training unit, the possibility of developing teachers is good. Since this sort of instruction *builds* members more quickly, teaching potential is realized more rapidly than one may realize.

Now, let us look at curriculum possibilities. I have suggested a basic division between the two periods:

Period One (9:30 - 10:10) Bible-Related Courses
Period Two (10:15 - 10:55) Bible Study Courses

Bible-related courses focus on Bible study too, but they are not designed as direct Bible Study courses. Hence, the distinction. A one-year sample curriculum may look something like this:

---

[6]Too many teachers dry up from failure to participate in a course themselves. It is not good always to give and never to receive.

1976

		FALL	WINTER	SPRING	SUMMER
Level I	Period One	Bible Doctrine #1 (Scripture)	Bible Interpretation	Bible Doctrine #2 (God)	Personal Evangelism
	Period Two	N. T. Introduction	Bible #1 (John)	Bible #2 (Judges)	Bible #3 (Acts)
Level II	Period One	Christian Living in the Home	Bible Doctrine #3 (sin/salvation)	Christian Living at Work	Cults
	Period Two	O. T. Introduction	Bible #4 (Romans)	Bible #5 (Proverbs)	Bible #6 (1 Corinthians)
Specials	Period One	Teacher Training		Prospective Elders' Course	
	Period Two	New Converts' Course			

The pattern above does not necessarily represent what you and your congregation would do. But it does visualize the possibilities. According to this sample, in the fall at the 9:30 hour (Period One) three courses would be taught to three different groups of people. Those taking Bible Doctrine #1, the Doctrine of Scripture, would be starting out on the first year of the curriculum (designated as Level I). Those taking the Christian Living in the Home course would have already taken the eight Level I courses offered during the year 1975. Those taking Teacher Training are a special group who wish to teach, but who need preparation in order to do so. Presumably, the sample would represent a program that has been in operation for only two years. Several more levels are possible (up to as many as you want, though probably not more than six or seven in all). Some of the titles of additional courses that might be offered are:

Period One Courses	Period Two Courses	Specials
Bible Doctrine #4 (Sanctification)	Bible # (any number of Bible books may be studied)	Greek
Bible Doctrine #5 (Church)	Life & Work of Christ	Visitors' Class
Bible Doctrine #6 (Future)	The Parables	Teacher Training
Christian Living in the Community	The Miracles	
Church History	Prophecy	
Defense of the Faith	etc.	
Bible Geography, Manners & Customs		
Bible Archeology		
Cults		
Personal Evangelism		

Naturally, you may add, subtract or alter this program in any number of ways. It is designed for maximum flexibility. I have used it in small congregations and large, with few initial teachers and courses, and with many.

Resources

One more matter must be mentioned before closing this chapter. There should be a true teaching situation. Chairs should not be positioned in a circle. They should either have an arm tablet for writing, or be placed at tables or desks. Note-taking should be encouraged. Loose-leaf notebooks may be purchased by the Church School with dividers labeled to correspond to the various courses offered. Not only notes, but coordinated course-outlines, handouts, syllabi, workbooks, etc., could be kept in the binder.

Adequate visual aids should be purchased — overhead projectors, chalk boards, maps, pictures, etc. A cassette videotape recorder might be utilized with great profit since lectures for some courses could be prerecorded for use at later points. (This could save on personnel.) The cost today is no longer prohibitive.

Students in the courses should be given homework, should do research, give reports and take examinations (which they may grade themselves).

Textbooks (and syllabi developed by teachers or by the pastor) are valuable assets. These materials begin to build personal libraries for Christian families. Moreover, with a program like this, a good church library is an essential (and it will be *used*).

All in all, the concerned pastor will discover (I think) that this suggested approach will point toward the solution to some of the most serious problems of stimulating interest and personal growth that he may be pondering. Much prayerful time and effort have been expended in developing and effectuating this program. It is not untried! It works. One 80-year-old woman told me that after one year in this program she had learned more from Church School than in the 75 or so years previous. While not everyone responds in the same fashion, the overall response has always been similar. Teachers especially profit from it. And they begin to enjoy their teaching in a new way. Many soon develop a new competence and a new ability to teach. Persons qualified for the eldership emerge more rapidly, and in general the whole church is affected for good. Try it, but not half-heartedly. Either determine to throw your fullest effort into it or wait until you are ready to do so. It cannot be undertaken successfully unless you do.

CHAPTER XIV
LEADING CHILDREN AND YOUTH

The pastor, as a good shepherd, cares not only for the sheep, but also for the lambs. God, as Shepherd, describes His concern for those little ones in the flock in these tender terms:

> Like a shepherd He will tend His flock. In His arms He will gather the lambs, And carry them in His bosom; He will gently lead the nursing ewes (Isaiah 40:11).

Surely, the risen Savior's reinstatement of Peter also placed a strong emphasis upon pastoral ministry to children when He commanded: "Tend my lambs" (John 21:15).

Pastors today can do no less. Their concern for the youth of the congregation must in every way exemplify and be guided by the Lord's own deep concern.

While it is not possible to develop a program for the leadership and pastoral care of children and youth in this volume (perhaps something fuller can be done at a later point in another volume devoted solely to this subject), I do wish to say at least something to pastors about each of these areas of pastoral leadership that may prove of significance to them and through them to their congregations by arousing them to take action. Because of their place of leadership, pastors are able to exercise great influence upon the work carried on with children and youth. There are a few large concerns that I wish to share, therefore, for whatever benefit they may have in stirring the thinking of pastors who lead.

Junior Church — A Live Option?

There are two diametrically opposed viewpoints among conservative, Bible-believing pastors (and their people) about the place of the child in the worship service. Should all of the children once they are able to waddle from the nursery be lined up for an hour (or hours) on the pew alongside of their parents? Does this demonstrate the covenant relationship of God to the family, and does it train children in the ways of worship for a lifetime to come? Or, as others aver, does it rather train them to sleep in church, to endure a sermon that they cannot understand, and thereby teach them how not to hear it? Does this train them not to worship at all, but to fidget around with hymn books, bulletins, etc.?

Clearly the prejudicial wording of the sentences in the previous paragraph makes it abundantly plain that I adhere to the second position. While surely children should appear on the pews as early as it is possible for them to participate meaningfully in the morning worship service, I do not think that it does them or anyone else (neither parents nor others nearby can worship well with the interruptions they cause) any good to be hauled into place every Sunday for an hour's worth of who knows what. Anything but optimal learning/worshipping conditions exist. But, what does the Bible say about this? Well, the answer to that question is: "Nothing directly." But there is a principle that is articulated in the Book of Nehemiah that does carry great significance; this principle is set forth in Chapter 8, verses 2 and 3:

> Then Ezra the priest brought the law before the assembly of men, women and *all who could listen with understanding....* And he read ... in the presence of men and women and *those who could understand;* and all the people were attentive to the book of the law.

Here, the children who were too young to understand the public reading, and explanation of the Scriptures (cf. also vv. 8,9), were excluded from the assembly. This did not break the covenant unity of the family. Rather than to show this unity artificially, there was a deeper concern expressed: to assure the attentive listening of those who were present. The purpose of worship is not to demonstrate the unity of the family. Those who assembled as a result neither were disturbed by the restlessness of the children, nor were the children disturbed by the restrictions placed upon them to sit and stand quietly during a meeting in which they could not participate meaningfully. Thus, this wise measure was taken to assure the attentiveness of all assembled. That this particular meeting was longer in duration than the average worship service is granted, but notice that the text says nothing about the exclusion of the children because of the time factor. Rather, the operative factor was simply their *inability to understand.*[1] That factor seems to be the determinative one, therefore, in deciding (1) whether

---

[1]Since the meeting was of extraordinary length, one would expect that this fact would be stressed if it was the determinative one. That it is never coupled with the exclusion of the children clearly shows that it was not the significant factor involved in that decision.

children should be admitted to the church service, and (2) when any particular child should be. Note too that no specific age level was mentioned. Understanding of the reading and of the preaching of the Scriptures, therefore, is the only element involved in the decision to admit or exclude. Since young children differ so radically in their readiness, they would not all be able to move into the adult worship service at the same age. Parental judgment, or possibly some simple tests of the ability to understand, might determine when that time would come for any given child.

The concept of "Junior Church" is one way to go. However, I hold no brief for that particular name. Perhaps a term that more clearly indicates the preparatory nature of the period would be preferable. I have no desire to nail down one title over another, so I will not even venture a suggestion; it is the content of the period that is of significance. During this time there is an ideal opportunity for the assistant pastor, a seminary intern, elders in rotation, deacons, or others from the congregation who have the competence to do so, to give instruction about the elements of worship that make up the adult worship service from which the children have been excluded. This instruction, of course, will be on their level, with variety conforming to the attention span of the children (including lots of singing), and with at least minimal participation on their part (taking up the collection, etc.). The Lord's Prayer and the Apostle's Creed can be explained. The place and use of the offering may be discussed. The purpose of singing and preaching may be explored. Information on such simple matters as how to use a bulletin or such crucial ones as how to listen to a sermon may be given. Sometimes, when there is to be a baptism, when the Lord's Supper is celebrated, when new members are admitted, or when elders or deacons are to be ordained, the children may be instructed about these features of the service in their own meeting and then (either prior to or after that instruction, according to the order of the event in the order of worship) they may visit the worship service during the specific time when that event occurs. There should be plenty of opportunity for the children to ask questions and to make observations about what they see. When children have been thoroughly instructed about what is going on in the other worship service, while also conducting worship on their own level, they will begin their attendance at the regular services with much more understanding and at an age where they can enter into the worship in a meaningful way. And you will find that they look forward with anticipation rather than boredom to becoming participants in the worship service. Moreover, rather than having to learn better habits of worship, after having learned bad ones for so long (some adults have never unlearned the bad patterns that they developed as children!), they are more likely to start out on a better footing. This will be so not only because of prior instruction, but also (and, remember, this is the *prime* emphasis of Nehemiah) because of their greater maturity.

The church that does not provide some such help for its younger children will regret it. Pastors may find it necessary to exercise courageous leadership in introducing a program of this type, since there are many laymen who (out of pride, or quite sincerely) will object. Yet the biblical principle must prevail. And for the sake of the church — both adults who wish to worship with less interference, but especially for the sake of the children who are learning all the wrong things on the pews — the pastor must take the initiative and fly straight through the objections.

Work With Youth

While it is not desirable to mix Junior Highs and Senior Highs, it is essential to view them together in planning and in coordinating the Youth Work in the church. To think of their several programs in airtight compartments is a serious error. Because so often we have done so, in many ways we create problems that emerge in working with High School Youth Groups. Yet we fail to realize that these problems are of our own making. Pastors must come to see that the Senior High product is manufactured in the Junior High period, and that if it does not suit our standards at a later point, that is because too little early concern was given about the kind of product that we wished. The *key* to building a good Senior High Work is to mold it when it is still in Junior High. Junior Highs are plastic; many of the ways of Senior Highs (more often than not) already are set. While God can surely change Senior Highs (often in spectacular ways), it is unwise to wait till then to ask Him to do so. Especially can we see that this is so when we realize that we are responsible for not having done more at the earlier period.

The Junior-Senior High programs should be viewed as two parts of a whole. Each segment bears a meaningful relation to the other. In the Junior High period the product is *manufactured* for *use* in the Senior High period. If a faulty product is handed down, then it becomes difficult to make the proper use of the energy and power of the High Schoolers. Indeed, precisely what we find is that their strength often is used destructively. I am firmly convinced that the secret to a significant youth work, therefore, is found in the successful pursuit of such a sequential pattern. The Junior High work should (self-consciously) be aimed at *preparing* these students for what they will be doing as Seniors in the church.

But, what should Seniors do? Many things, concretely speaking, might be mentioned. But, more generally (I suggest), they should be *using* their faith. Individually and corporately, within and without, they should be putting into practice those many truths that they should have been *learning* for so many years, and that they more recently should have been *learning* how to use in the Junior High period. The Junior High stress on *how to* should culminate in a Senior stress on *doing*.

But, if truth merely has been stored for quick retrieval for the next Bible quiz up to and even during the Junior High period, and there has been little or no instruction or opportunity to use that truth, when young people enter the High School period they cannot be expected to do so automatically. And, since so often they have not been prepared previously as they should have, they do not. It is not enough then to scold them for not doing so; instead what must be done is to give the needed instruction (1) belatedly, (2) against hardened, wrong patterns developed during the more flexible Junior High period, and (3) in spite of the discontent and rebellion that such failure often encourages. This is difficult, not necessary, and frequently unrewarding. It is therefore time to reconsider the Junior High period.

What, more specifically, should Junior/Senior Highs be learning/doing? For one thing, they should be discovering how to use their Bibles in the practical manner in which they were intended to be used (cf. II Timothy 3:16—the "scriptures ... are *useful*"). It is one thing to know the catechism answers, to be able to recite favorite Bible portions, or even to know how to turn to key Scriptures to prove doctrinal positions. It is *quite* another to know how to find the scriptural answer to a practical problem encountered at school on Tuesday. Not only do very few Juniors and all-too-few Seniors know how to use the Bible in this way, but many of their parents have never learned to do so either. This skill, above all others, is the crucial one to be taught and learned (in the Junior years) for use in the critical Senior years (when so many vital issues and decisions face them) and beyond. Unless these skills are taught and used, the Bible will become little more than a book of history and impractical pious platitudes to Senior Highs. No wonder many Seniors see no value in the Scriptures — they have been taught to do so.

The other principal area for basic instruction (in Junior years) and for service (in Senior years) involves the discovery, development and deployment of gifts.[2] It is during Junior years that leaders should begin to

---

[2] For more on this see *supra*, Chapter 10.

emerge and leadership skills should be developed. Persons with musical abilities (both singing and instrumental) should be encouraged to use these for the Lord. The testing of gifts for preaching should begin by providing opportunities for young men to speak and teach. Regular ministry to others both within and without the congregation should take place. What Juniors stumblingly learn to do during those tadpole days, Senior frogs can accomplish with aplomb. And the skills encouraged and learned during both periods will go far toward developing strong church leadership potential of the proper sort for the next generation. Congregations with no such vision sow the seeds of their future destruction. Pastors themselves must promote a vital youth program based (at least) upon these crucial understandings. They cannot sit by idly while wave upon wave of young people move through these periods with their lives unaffected by those things that will count (individually and corporately) for Jesus Christ.

Just a final word must be spoken to emphasize the need during both of these periods for active meaningful youth programs that influence the young people, not only on Sunday, but that also provide weekday Christian fun and fellowship. There are few things more tragic than to discover that so little is happening among the covenant youth during these years when friendship and peer pressure are so important, that many of them make friends and subject themselves to detrimental influences outside of the church. Every pastor must be vigilant to guard and work against any such deficiency. Parents of teen-agers desperately need the help that can be provided only by full, vital training in Christian living. Whatever it takes in any congregation to achieve this goal, the pastor must do. He cannot merely deplore a bad state of affairs; he must take action to rectify it.

Finally, a vital growing youth program involves a strong evangelistic effort by the youth of the church. Young people grow most when they serve both one another and the unsaved world around them. A youth group composed only of covenant youth will lack in zeal and reality. It continually must be fed by a life-giving stream of converted unbelievers if it would not become crusty. The faith comes alive to covenant youth growing up in the church where their views and ways are regularly challenged by new converts. The latter keep the former honest; the former help the latter to understand. A good mix of the two is essential for a healthy youth work. Thus, as a significant emphasis of the youth work teaching and programs for doing evangelism must be developed at the Junior High age and continued through the Senior period. Nothing helps youth come to know their Bibles and their faith better than the need to use both in evangelism.

EXERCISE

For the Student

Make a list of the topics that you might wish to teach children who have been excluded from the worship service in order to prepare them for participation at a later point when they become more mature.

For the Pastor

Take a hard look at your Junior High program. If it is deficient, develop a truly significant program as soon as possible. Give this *high priority*.

CHAPTER XV
MAKING THE CHURCH LIBRARY WORK

Let me say it at the outset! When beginning a church library, do not ask for books in general, unless you want to get hundreds of worthless volumes to waste space on your shelves, along with dozens of heretical works to boot. And, don't forget the potential for hurt feelings that this procedure involves, since you will find it necessary to reject the worthless books offered. No, in making the appeal for funds and for gift books, see to it that those who are in charge take the trouble to decide and to mimeograph and distribute a list of the books desired. "Volunteerism" in donating furniture, books, etc., is always as bad a policy as when one requests volunteers for jobs around the church. Instead always determine what or who is wanted and go after that.

The library should be located prominently and should be accessible to all. Posters and/or announcements of new accessions should be made regularly in the congregational newsletter. Posting of book jackets on the library bulletin board under the heading "New Books In Your Library" is one way to announce their arrival. If the jackets become torn and dirty before they are replaced by new ones, that is one possible indication that the library is not acquiring new titles rapidly enough. The library should be financed by the regular church budget, from time to time should make special appeals for large sets (of commentaries, etc.) and should regularly make requests for presentations of specific titles that are out of print. The selection of books placed in the library should be under the direct review of the pastor and the elders. Of course, they may entrust the matter to some doctrinally sound member, perhaps a deacon. Arrangements for other matters pertaining to the functioning of the library should be handed over to the deacons. Older persons, chosen by them, who do not have the gifts for other tasks may make fine librarians.

Probably, in setting up a church library, the pastor will have to make the initial effort to determine the basic content of the library. To him also will fall the task of suggesting books all along to the deacon in charge. Reviews and reports of the health of the library should be made regularly by the deacons to the elders.

The library may promote special programs from time to time in the Church School and in the Youth Groups. These programs may be helpful for alerting members of the congregation to new materials, and for giving instruction and encouragement to the youth of the congregation to read good Christian literature. The library should acquire and feature as many of the *best* children's books as it can afford. Sunday School books, papers and leaflets (which may be bound) ought also to be placed in the Church library. The library may wish to develop and sponsor a Book Club, which might meet monthly to review and to discuss current books.

Cassette tapes and audio-visual equipment for use at home or in the church may be assigned to the library to keep tabs on and to promote their use. It is better to assign this equipment to a central unit, like the library, that is already concerned with the problems of record-keeping and checking out and checking in, than to assign the task to the Church School. Equipment is less likely to get lost, and to be abused thereby. What is the whole Church's responsibility is no one's responsibility. The library should be open at definite, posted hours. The personnel should be chosen for faithfulness and regularity. Assistants and other back-up workers also should be appointed.

EXERCISE

For the Student

1. Make a list of topical headings for use in the beginning of a small church library.

2. Under each topic, list at least five basic books.

For the Pastor

1. Review your church library for worthless books, for glaring omissions, and for doctrinally unsound materials. Analyze library use, policies and procedures.

2. Bring a report to the Board of Elders about the state of the library, together with your suggestions for improvement.

CHAPTER XVI
CHURCH BUILDINGS

Gatherings of the early church were held in private houses,[1] in school buildings[2] or (it seems) wherever it was possible to find a suitable place in which to meet and worship. The Jews had built synagogues (the word means literally "gathering places") all over the Mediterranean world. Jesus and the early missionaries attended services and preached in these buildings in order to proclaim the gospel to those in attendance. While no scriptural directions to build meeting places of any sort exist, it is perfectly clear that (in principle) the New Testament does not oppose the construction and use of church buildings. Nor, it should be observed, does it require them. Buildings, therefore, are viewed solely in a functional manner in the new age. In contrast to the symbolism of the Old Testament Temple, in which the various features, furnishings and functions typified the coming Messiah and His redemption, the New Testament considers both the form of worship,[3] and the building in which it is carried on, something indifferent. A house, a school, a special building constructed specifically for the purpose of worship—all will do. Attempts by Protestants to design church buildings symbolically in order to express Christian truth, are therefore bound to fail. There simply is no philosophy of Christian symbolism in architecture, because the New Testament gives us none. Apart from the most general principles like (1) the importance of good stewardship in construction, (2) doing all things well to the glory of God, and (3) bearing a witness to others by all that we do, there is little more that can be said about the biblical principles concerning church buildings.

It would seem that balance, witness to the community, and function constitute the three prime implications growing out of them. A balance between overexpenditures leading to mismanagement of the Lord's money in poor stewardship (on the one hand), and (on the other) drab, shabby or

---

[1]Romans 16:5; Colossians 4:15; Acts 18:7.
[2]Acts 19:9,10.
[3]We shall discuss liturgical matters in a later volume, D.V. Of course, specific directions, in accord with the general principle of order, were given (cf. I Corinthians 14).

uninviting barrenness that turns off the public ought to be struck. Moreover, a combination of the principles of stewardship and function (which points to the principal reason for the investment of funds) demands that the property be designed for use on more than one day per week. Designers should take into consideration the possible weekday use of the building for a Christian School, as furloughed missionary quarters, as office space for Christian organizations, for a Christian bookstore, for daily youth activity, etc. In this way, and in this way alone, can large expenditures for buildings be justified.

Witness too is important. Probably there is no more sad commentary on many Protestant congregations than the shabbiness and unkempt condition of their church buildings. Of course, there are many marvelous exceptions as well. But, no church ought to engage in building unless there are both the will and the resources to keep the building and its environs attractive and in good repair at all times. The condition of the church property is all the witness that some in the community will ever see. I am not referring to ornateness or to any extraordinary expenditure of funds for special features, but simply to the matters of neatness and appearance. Uncut grass (or lawns with bare spots), blistering and peeling paint, poor landscaping, inadequate off-street parking, or a hundred-and-one other factors that lead to the run-down condition of a church say something to the community; but not what the church intended, surely. Gingerbread, like garish signs, illuminated glass brick crosses, and other tasteless touches also say much that was not intended. The elegance of neat simplicity combined with good upkeep tells the community that the congregation cares about God, and about the neighborhood. When the church property is the eyesore of the vicinity, the community gets the opposite message. The love of God and the love of one's neighbor demand concern.

In addition to the church auditorium, the pastor's study and the nursery are two critical areas for special care. The study is a place where many people (members and others) come for counsel. Here is one place where the pastor himself has the opportunity (and obligation) to set and to maintain high standards of excellence for the rest of the congregation. If the study is neat (though not unused), clean, pleasant, etc., it will serve as a model for the congregation in their care of the rest of the building. I mention the nursery because mothers are concerned about finding cleanliness, safety features, and adequate facilities (toilet, sink, cribs) in this room for their infants. When you remember that the church-going habits of many young married couples are formed at this point in their lives, you can recognize the importance of not allowing nursery failures to put unnecessary obstacles in their way. Evident concern for their children is a message that the church nursery *must* convey.[4]

Thus, the church building will bear a good or a bad witness to the honor or dishonor of Christ. There is no neutrality here; the building helps or hinders. It is the task of every pastor to help his elders and deacons to see that the church property is a sharp and effective tool for worship and for witness. While it is not his job to design buildings himself and to do the upkeep that is necessary, it is his duty to stress the principles of stewardship, function and witness that apply. The minister cannot ignore gross failures to show concern about such matters. It is his obligation to alert, educate, encourage and (when necessary) to rebuke those who are responsible for the failure.

The youth room(s) should be decorated by them — not by the church. While certain limits may need to be set, a large amount of freedom should be given to them (to paint, put down multicolored carpet samples on the floor, etc.). They need a place to call their own, and in which they can conduct their meetings and hold their activities with comfort. If they have worked on the room themselves, they will take pride in it, be more likely to spend time in it, and treat it with care.

The Sexton

Most American pastors will not experience either of the extremes for good or ill that some of us have. In my ministry, for instance, I have worked with a slimmed-down version of the Scottish Beadle, who turns out to be far more than the church sexton. Indeed, he conceived of himself as my right-hand man. He brought cookies and tea every morning during my study period and, in general, tried to serve not only by caring for the building, but also for its occupants. The only thing that can be said about such a sexton is that if you ever get one, do not take advantage of him!

On the other hand, at another church, I had a sexton who conceived of himself as the owner and sole proprietor of the premises. This I discovered (to my chagrin) when he sharply took me to task for rearranging the location of some bookshelves in the pastor's study. His words (most of which thankfully I have forgotten) were to the effect that I had rearranged *his building*. To this day those last possessives vividly stand out in my memory.

But, as I say, most will not face either of these extremes. Instead, most

---

[4]Not only by the physical facilities, but also by the personnel who man the nursery. (Instruction should be given to every worker in the nursery so that a consistent level of care is maintained.)

sextons will be persons, often hard up for work for one reason or another (the reasons *can* be vital), who normally (but not always) do a reasonably good job of keeping the church neat and clean. A wise pastor will cultivate, not ignore, the church sexton. First, since many others will tend to look down on him, it is the pastor's duty to set a proper example for the rest of the congregation in accordance with James 2:1-9. He must not show favoritism for the rich, well-educated, etc. Secondly, since the upkeep and appearance of the church are of such vital concern to the witness of the church, it is important for the pastor to be on such terms with the sexton that he can encourage him to see to it that this witness does not suffer.

The concern of the pastor for a good relationship with the sexton should not only be direct; it also should be indirect. That is, it should be expressed concretely in personal ways (taking time to sit down and chat — perhaps the pastor himself might start the tea-and-cookie routine) in showing interest in projects in which the sexton is engaged around the church building, etc., and in other ways as well (urging the congregation to increase his wages, reminding those who are married in the church of the extra time and effort that weddings mean for the sexton, and suggesting that they express their appreciation to him for it in some substantial way, etc.).

A good relationship with the church sexton is of genuine importance to the effective use of the church facilities. Every pastor therefore should work hard to establish and maintain such a relationship.

EXERCISE

For the Student

Drive around and look at the outer community witness of the church buildings of at least 25 evangelical congregations. Note, below, the condition of each, and basic improvements that might be made.

For the Pastor

Who is in charge of the buildings and grounds of your congregation? When did you last consult with him? Could you profitably hold a meeting or two with him to discuss improvements ("You know, Frank, I was thinking that if. . .)?

Ideas for Improvement

CHAPTER XVII
FINANCES IN THE LOCAL CHURCH

If you expected a long and detailed study of finances in the local church and a thorough discussion of the pastor's prime role in handling them, you will be sadly disappointed. I see no biblical warrant for the pastor to busy himself with the details of church finances. Notice, I said *details*. Instruction in giving and in good stewardship is indeed a vital part of his teaching ministry (a fact that too many pastors forget or conveniently neglect). So crucial is this type of pastoral activity that Paul exhorts Timothy to set up a special rich men's Bible study in order to instruct wealthy persons how to use their money for the honor of Christ (cf. I Timothy 6:6-10; 17-19)! It is tragic to realize how many churches and other Christian organizations suffer precisely because the pastors of wealthy Christians have never taken seriously the charge given to them in verses 17-19.

Yes, the pastor must develop courage to speak generally and to specific individuals about money. It is his job, with Paul, to see that special offerings are taken for worthwhile causes among the people of God. Also like Paul, he will find it necessary to instruct, to exhort, to rebuke and to encourage. When it comes to giving, many Christians show little evidence of sanctification. About his duties in this regard, there can be no question. But it is *not* his duty to determine all of the details of the church budget, to distribute the church's funds personally, to make financial arrangements with visiting speakers and a score of other details. This he and the elders need to leave safely in the hands of the diaconate.

His own giving, again, should set the example for the entire congregation. And, if at times his salary is meager, like the widow, he can give his mite. But, he should also be an example to the flock in the way in which he insists upon an adequate salary for his family.[1] Congregations are notorious for giving insufficient funds to pastors, yet all the while expecting them to keep their homes and their clothes in the best style, and wondering

---

[1]Cf. Vol. I, pp. 65,68,69.

why they do not run all over the map in a large, respectable car that carries lots of Sunday School children and drinks gasoline. It is time for pastors to summon the courage to tell their boards that all that it takes to support a pastor is ten families giving a tenth. Simple math makes it plain that they easily can give him a salary equal to the average salary of the ten. Monies given by all other families are gravy for the maintenance of the property, missions, etc. Galatians 6:6 makes it clear that the pastor-teacher is to live on a level equal to that of the members of the congregation: The one who is taught is to "share *all good things*" with his teacher. No, it takes no more than simple math *and* the grace of God for the members of a congregation to see this! The church should never be in need of money — especially for the pastor's salary — there ought always to be an excess. The church's problem constantly should take this form: "Where would God have us use these excess funds?" It is not many people who are needed to support the ministry of a local congregation financially; it just takes a few *dedicated* families to do so.[2]

EXERCISE

For the Student

1. Determine how much money it will take for you to live and take care of your family (if not yet married, postulate a wife and one child) in your first pastorate. Interview several pastors for help in this matter.

2. Call up the local I.R.S. office and ask about the best way of breaking down a minister's salary (e.g., is it better to ask for a manse allowance, car allowance, book allowance, utilities allowance, etc., than to receive the same amount as straight salary?).

3. Be prepared to report on your findings.

---

[2]New congregations should be declared to be *congregations* only (1) when they are self-supporting (ten families giving a tenth) or the equivalent thereof. . . but, the stress should be upon proper giving by *all* from the outset, and (2) when they have adequate elder material to form a board of elders. Prior to this, the pastor (to be) and the congregation are in a missionary relationship.

For the Pastor

1. What have you done in general to give financial instruction to your members?

2. To those who are rich? (Or have you been afraid to approach them about the use of their wealth for Christ?)

3. What should you do about each?

CHAPTER XVIII
PUBLICITY

It is sad to scan the columns of a newspaper searching for the location of the congregation of God's people that you wish to visit, only to find that this church does not advertise. Yet, there on the religious news page is the ad for every liberal church and every cult in town. Far too many Bible-believing pastors, who ought to be the first to recognize the value of promoting the work of Christ through the media, seem never to have given serious thought to the variety of legitimate ways and means that are available. For instance, in inquiring about information from the local Chamber of Commerce of a city to which you intend to move, you may receive a letter from three or four congregations in that city. Why didn't the one in which you especially were interested also write? The answer again: because that congregation has missed the publicity opportunity.

Publicity is not sub-Christian. Some of those who piously decry the use of publicity do so, I fear, in order to excuse their lethargy. Yet, God sent John the Baptist "before" Jesus to *prepare* a people for him. That preparation involved much more, of course, but in it was the element of publicity: John announced, "The Kingdom is at hand." He spoke of the One who would come after him, and gathered together a people who were expectant (Luke 3:15). Here is an example of the highest-level publicity: it prepares people to expectantly meet Christ. It did so by announcing the facts about the coming of the Messiah. The work of the Seventy was a kind of publicity effort too, whatever else it may have had in view. Publicity, then, when accurate, honest, appropriate and Christ-centered is scriptural. Publicity, in general, must not be equated with the sensationalism, the exaggeration, and the fraudulent misrepresentations that have characterized much American religious publicity. It is because of this abuse of publicity that a seemingly reasonable case against publicity has been made. But all good things (sex, preaching, etc.) may be abused. That is no argument against them, when *properly* used.

Publicity has characterized some of the more effective ministries that truly honor God and His Son. We must not throw away the package with its torn wrapper.

There are many ways in which to publicize the work of a local congregation, and I shall not attempt to list or categorize all of them. Rather, I wish to stimulate the pastor to think through the ways in which he can promote the use of good publicity both within and without his congregation.

To begin with, it is important to encourage every organization within the church to appoint someone (with the gifts to do so) to publicize the work of that organization. These are the church Reporters. The elders should see to it that the deacons handle all of the general publicity for the church, and that they supervise the publicity of the other organizations of the church. Whoever is appointed by the deacons to the position of Head Reporter for the church should be capable of offering helpful suggestions to the other organizational Reporters. These suggestions may include help about what to publicize, ways and means to do so, how to get better circulation of publicity, and how to coordinate it with other publicity that is going into or coming out of the church. He should instruct these Reporters in the use of news releases and provide them with a supply of News Release forms. The pastor, in turn, may from time to time make suggestions to the Head Reporter, who acts as general coordinator, and may encourage him to see that others responsible for publication produce acceptable publicity and do not fail to seize opportunities.

Public Media

A key factor in publicity is the local newspaper. This, along with radio and TV stations, should be used as fully as possible and that does not mean merely to rent space and time for paid advertisements. Particularly in small towns and cities (but not only there) it is possible to obtain *much* more space for the local church than the average church has any idea. Free time on local radio stations, opportunities for interviews (especially of visiting speakers) on TV shows, and many other public media possibilities exist. Yet, only a few pastors enter into these in an adequate way.

Upon beginning a new pastorate, one of the first things any pastor should do is to make appointments with the public media representatives that he will be working with in his new community in order to get acquainted and to discuss the best ways and means to assure the best cooperation. For this appointment the pastor should offer to take the representative to lunch (funds for such luncheons should be paid out of the pastor's yearly contingency fund, provided by the church for all such occasions[1]). In this interview, the pastor should be ready to make some promises that he is willing to keep. In many communities, the Religious Editor is paid by the word. He (or she) *wants news* and is more interested, therefore, in feature articles and basic newsworthy material than in the announcements that appear in the paid-for columns. The pastor must assure this editor that, unlike many of the pastors with whom he or she has worked in the past (and they will tell you that pastors have bad records) who promise, but fail to deliver, he will keep the news coming in a steady flow. There is nothing that could make the editor happier than this; it is his (her) bread-and-butter. Moreover, he should make it clear that he will do all that he can to inform the editor of conventions or other special features of the programs of his church that may merit special coverage (such as a reporter and photographer on hand), far enough in advance to make plans for it. Furthermore, he will see to it that a *written description* of each week's meetings (not merely an announcement of each) will be sent for the newspaper's Church News column, together with glossy pictures of any noteworthy persons that the church may bring to town. In order to impress upon the editor that he means business, he may hand to him a copy of the mimeographed News Release that he intends to use. This may be discussed so that (1) any modifications necessary may be made; (2) both understand its full purpose. A copy of this follows:

---

[1] If there is no such fund, here (at the outset) is an occasion for requesting it.

8½"

NEWS RELEASE

_____ Church

Address_____

Phone _____

1. For immediate release _____ .
2. For release on

_____ .

3. For release at any time _____ .

11"

Subject:

Released by _____

The Reporters from each organization also must be encouraged to be faithful in sending information. Probably such information should be sent to the church-appointed Head Reporter, who in turn (perhaps in consultation with the pastor from time to time) will edit and revise and send in compound news releases containing all of the significant facts about each organization in a blended form.

Printing is expensive, mimeographing is less so. The local church will find that a used multilith machine and an IBM typewriter with paper masters will produce fine-looking materials at a cost only slightly higher than the cost of mimeographing. Church bulletins, brochures of all sorts, tracts, pamphlets, cards, announcements, etc., all can be produced by the use of a multilith. However, it is essential to find someone (or a couple of persons) within the congregation who will be willing to spend the time and the effort to learn how to operate the machine well and who will view their continued work in printing as a ministry. It can become an enormous asset to the local church. This printing press will, in time, not only pay for itself many times over, but will provide attractive materials for use in every phase of the congregational activities.

EXERCISE

For the Student and the Pastor

Together with no more than five other pastors[2] (students) brainstorm new ways of publicizing the work of the church. Procedures:

1. Brainstorm for one hour.
2. A secretary should record ideas *during* the one hour session.
3. Build on each other's ideas.
4. Following the session jointly and/or individually evaluate each idea scripturally and practically (if scriptural, is it feasible or workable for my congregation?).
5. Record all acceptable ideas below.

---

[2]Perhaps in a presbyterial gathering with several small groups.

CHAPTER XIX
CONCLUSION

I do not wish to make this chapter any longer than necessary. Therefore, rather than sum up in some other way, I have determined to challenge you with one final summary exercise. It is a test. There are only twenty-five questions; that means that normally you would grade each question with a weight of 4 on a scale of 100. But, your Lord does not settle for 50's and 60's, or even 80's. He says "be perfect." Therefore, grade each question with a weight of 100! Until you can answer each His way, you have changes to make. I think you will find the Check List provocative.

A Pastoral Leadership Check List
1. Do I run a one-man show?
2. Do I allow my decisions to be influenced by pressure?
3. Do I exercise biblical leadership, or do I sense the direction of the prevailing winds and go in that direction?
4. Have I concentrated on discovering, developing and deploying the gifts of others?
5. Do I tend to shirk responsibility whenever possible?
6. Do I run or compromise when the going gets tough?
7. Am I complacent? Discouraged? Weary from well-doing?
8. Do I have a desire for self-glory?
9. Do I love my people? If not, what am I doing to cultivate that love?
10. Do I know the problems and the needs among the flock? Do I know what to do about these? Am I doing something?
11. Is there adequate communication in the congregation? Do I know? If not, what does that indicate?
12. Is my time properly organized? By priorities? By whom?
13. Is my life a vital example to my flock?
14. Do I know how to lead rather than drive my flock?
15. Am I using/misusing/not using the authority that Christ gave to me?
16. Do I set goals and plan my work to meet them?

17. Am I trapped by formality, custom and tradition?
18. Am I personally growing in my relationship to God?
19. Do I faithfully work at administration in my congregation?
20. Do I believe in doing administrative work?
21. How do I need to improve as an administrator?
22. Do the members of my congregation look to me as a leader? If not, why not?
23. How many hours per month do I spend in committee meetings?
24. What do I do when I run into problems with members of the congregation?
25. How do I encourage the expression of differences of opinion while discouraging personal differences?

APPENDIX A
EVANGELISM AND THE PASTOR

While, strictly speaking, evangelism might not be considered an element essential to this volume because it involves the outreach of a congregation (and individual members from it) to the unconverted community in which God has placed it; nevertheless, there are so many pastoral leadership functions connected with congregational evangelism (planning, guiding, teaching, etc.) that it would be a mistake to avoid the subject. This is true, especially because of the dominant part that evangelism plays in the life of a Christian and of the Church. Moreover, the pastoral effects of evangelism are substantial. A healthy church requires a continual mix of covenantally raised converts with those converted from raw paganism. The former bring a background and heritage to that mix while the latter "keep them honest" by their questions, observations, etc.

It is also important to note that *as the Shepherd* Jesus came to "seek and to save" those who were lost.[1] He has "other sheep" than those from the "house of Israel" (John 10:16). Thus, pastors, as Christ's undershepherds who care for the flock, should be vitally concerned to increase the flock, and in particular, to encourage the evangelistic fervor of every member of the congregation. The pastor must be in the vanguard of every such effort, constantly doing all that he can to bring about a congregational concern and capability for the work.

In order to enable the pastor to lead his flock into an evangelistic outreach into the community, I shall sketch out (in *some* detail) a congregational visitation–evangelism/Bible study plan that I have used successfully and that other congregations also have found useful.

The fundamental biblical presuppositions behind this plan are three:

1. Evangelism is the work of the *whole* congregation; it is not the task of the pastor only.

---

[1]Luke 19:10; Ezekiel 34:6 ("there was no one to seek them"), 8 (they "did not search"), 11 ("I myself will search for my sheep and seek them out"), 16 ("I will seek the lost, bring back the scattered"). Cf. Zechariah 11:16 in which the worthless shepherd is contrasted as one who "will not seek the scattered or heal the wounded." Cf. also Jeremiah 23:3,4: "I . . . shall bring them back to their pasture" and "nor will any be missing."

2. Evangelism, like other Christian tasks, must be taught by the discipleship (or modeling) method,[2] and the pastor is the principal (though not sole) teacher/model.
3. Evangelism involves a full presentation of the gospel (and nothing less) that may require time and continued contact, and is not done properly by hit-and-run methods.

Let us then see how these three elements may direct a combined visitation-evangelism and Bible study approach. This program may be used in a small congregation, in a very large one or when attempting to begin a new congregation.

The program is entitled:

Everyone Evangelizing Everywhere[3]

It is based upon Acts 8:4: "Therefore, those who were scattered abroad, went everywhere announcing the message of good news" (a literal translation). The following materials have been developed for use in training participants in the program. Other materials (referred to in them) are for use in the evangelistic enterprise itself.

The Instructional Materials

Leader's Manual

You are the key to this Visitation Evangelism Program. It is a program that involves the spiritual welfare of many persons. In your particular congregation it can mean the beginnings of a revival and new spiritual growth for your people. And of equal importance — its great purpose is the salvation of souls.

This plan has been tested in a number of communities and shown to be effective in reaching men for Christ. But will this approach succeed in your community? This may depend largely upon the faithful preparation and presentation that you are willing to give it. If it is to be effective, you must be willing to spend the necessary time in study and preparation. Work hard! Only then can you fully understand the way it works and direct others in carrying it out. Don't even think of starting unless you are willing to face this task with enthusiasm and dedication. Your vigorous leadership is necessary for stirring enthusiasm in others. Anything less will fail.

[2]Cf. *Competent to Counsel*, Chapter 11; *The Big Umbrella*, Chapter 12; and *The Christian Counselor's Manual*, pp. 332ff.

[3]The materials for this Visitation Evangelism program are available from the publisher of this volume. A *V.E. Packet*, containing a *Leader's Manual*, 200 *How To Do* Manuals, 25 *Teacher's Guides*, 1000 *Inserts*, 1000 *V-Cards* and 100 *Student's Workbooks* (H.B.S. Workbooks) is available at a special price.

The pastor or an elder in an established congregation ordinarily will be the leader of the Visitation Evangelism Program. If the church has not yet been established, and has no pastor or elders, the leader should be the most enthusiastic and well-versed member of the nucleus of interested people. The materials, however, have been written in such a way that each person who participates may readily understand the work to be done at his level. Every effort has been made to be clear and simple.

The plan also calls for completeness. This means that, without becoming complicated, the materials are comprehensive. The leader will find, therefore, that he will be greatly aided by following the *entire* program *exactly* as it is presented. This is necessary because it hangs together as a *whole*. It cannot be used as successfully in part. If you find the program too "ambitious" or "rigorous," it might be better not to use it at all. A half-hearted effort is almost certain to fail and bring unnecessary discouragement to you and your people. You will find, though, that the program is really worth all the time and effort that you can invest.

THE CONCEPT OF CONCENTRATION is central to the whole plan. The idea is to work in a concentrated way with a few people for a number of weeks. This also means that your work would be confined to a relatively small territory. In contrast to the shallow hop-skip-and-jump methods of survey campaigns and the hit-and-run nature of some Visitation Evangelism programs, this one sets up the goal of at least eight successive visits in one home: the initial call, the return call, and the six-week Home Bible Study Course.

Though the key concept of concentration must be maintained at all times, the plan is extremely flexible in application. The leader must organize the campaign along lines that fit his own situation. The number of teams and the choice of the area to be covered will depend upon local factors. Any number of visitors, from one up, may engage in this program. Naturally, the elaborateness of the planning will depend upon the number of workers participating. In organized churches, the program may be set up with the pastor as leader. Under him the Board of Elders will head teams composed of members of the congregation. Usually the number of teams will correspond to the number of session members. In unorganized groups, the approach should be similar, but in such circumstances it is likely that there will be only one team and one captain.

THE JOB of the leader is sixfold. He must:

1. Inspire the group (especially the Board of Elders) to adopt and support the plan.

2. Mark out the territories and fields, designing and mimeographing maps for all participants.
3. Confer with team captains, instructing them in their duties and apportioning to them the membership of their teams and the territories to be covered.
4. Instruct the visitors and teachers how to do visitation, using the *How To Do* manual as the basic textbook.
5. Supervise and guide the entire program while in process, assisting wherever his help is required.
6. Receive, file, and study all V-cards after each campaign is completed.

The team captains should be elders or other capable persons who are able to assume and carry out responsibilities. Each captain should first survey the "Territory" apportioned to his team, noting the relative lengths of various streets and the number of houses involved. The captain should then divide his team into equal "Fields" and assign each member of his team to a particular Field. Note: This preliminary survey work should be complete *before* the opening day of the campaign. Maps of the whole area should be made and displayed. Maps are also valuable aids for working in the Territory and the Field.

In larger groups, the elders, or whoever the captains may be, will teach the six-week Home Bible Study Courses while the rest of the members make initial visits and return calls. This arrangement is adaptable to local conditions, and it is even possible for the same person to visit as well as teach. The *Teacher's Guide* explains how to use *The Student's Workbook* most effectively. Each teacher should have one.

The team captains, therefore, are expected to teach the six-week Bible course in the home. Teaching, however, must be done by the leader as well as by the team captains. It is the leader's job to teach each captain and team *how* to carry out the program. This initial teaching of those doing the calling is crucial. In cases where there is more than one team, a separate teaching session for each captain and his team should be conducted. This also enables people who may not be able to come one night to attend another evening. As much as possible, of course, team members should try to attend the evening allotted to their own team. This keeps the instruction period small and informal and initiates team spirit. Incidentally, new members, brought into the church by the program, may well want to be assigned to the team which contacted them.

THIS TEACHING CLASS for the teams should be two hours long. The first hour should be pure *instruction* without discussion. The next half hour, *illustration*. Following this, there should be a five-minute *intermission*. And finally, the closing twenty-five minutes (or less) may be thrown open for *inquiry* and discussion. Adhere firmly to this schedule.

I. *Instruction* (by the Leader)

Begin the instruction with theory. The visitor's *How To Do* manual will be the basis for this instruction. You may want to begin by writing the four main stages on the blackboard (Instruction, Illustration, Intermission, Inquiry), and by explaining the reasons for this procedure. Immediately assure the class that ample time will be provided at the close for any questions that remain unanswered. But insist that they be withheld until then. Suggest that they jot them down in their notebooks so that they won't forget them. Explain that there is much to cover under theory and that most questions will be answered there and in the illustrative period.

By way of general instruction, explain the principles found in the Introduction to the *Leader's Manual*. And more specifically, present and interpret the material found in the *How To Do* manual. (Distribute copies of the *How To Do* manual to the students at the beginning of the instruction period and use it as an outline. Since repetition is helpful in teaching, it won't hurt for them to hear it from the leader and later to read it from the manual. The leader, certainly, has the liberty to expand and explain in his own words, but in order to avoid confusion, he should be careful to preserve the uniform terminology employed in all the literature (e.g., "Return Call," "Field," "Householder," etc.).

In teaching, a blackboard, charts, maps, and sample copies of the materials should be employed as visual aids.

II. *Illustration*

"At the door" problems, and how to handle them. (This is a study in visiting principles and techniques.)

Introduction

The following situations have been exaggerated somewhat in order to make the principles stand out. They should be acted out to demonstrate proper and improper techniques. The effect may be heightened by the construction of a frame doorway. Supports, purporting to be railings, are an attractive means of holding the door and its frame upright. Of course, a normal doorway may be used.

The characters in this dialogue are: *Narrator* (part taken by the leader), *Householder* (woman), *Visitor* (man), and *Sound Effects Man.*

Props: Frame doorway, wet spaghetti mop, bucket full of water, briefcase containing Visitation Evangelism literature, and Bible.

Nothing is more important than the initial contact. First impressions are lasting. Failure here often destroys all opportunity to witness later. That is why this section of the training program is so necessary. You will find that it stimulates real interest and is a great help to your visitors. *Don't fail to use it.* Be sure your actors rehearse and learn their parts thoroughly. If the actors ham it up a bit, that's good so long as the point of each skit is not obscured thereby.

The leader (narrator) begins by announcing:

Three fundamental principles to be remembered are:
   1. Establish and maintain rapport.
   2. Consider every objection a challenge to be overcome.
   3. Be flexible.

Situation No. 1

   A. Wrong:

Narrator: You are about to observe the acting out of the first situation. Initially, it will be handled incorrectly, then repeated in a proper way. Watch carefully, and try to determine what main principle the visitor has forgotten. It would be advisable to take notes.

   (Visitor appears on the scene carrying briefcase and Bible. Knocks on door. After a moment's pause, disheveled lady appears with spaghetti mop in one hand and bucket of water in other. She is obviously in the midst of housework, and appears quite disturbed by the interruption.)

Householder: Yeah? Whadda *you* want?

Visitor: How do you do? My name is Cuthbert Cobblestone. I'm from the new church that ...

Householder: (Who hasn't heard a word he said, since she has been looking over her shoulder) Say, Joe, Will you pin those diapers on the baby?

Sound Effects Man: (Answers from offstage) Oh, all right.

Householder: (Looking at visitor at last) What didja say?

Visitor: How do you do? My name is Cuthbert Cobblestone. I'm from the new church that is being built on Baker Street. I'm visiting in this neighborhood today to ...

Sound Effects Man: (Baby lets out shriek and continues to cry from off-stage while exasperated householder continues)

Householder: I'm sorry mister, I gotta' go. He's pinned the diaper to the baby again! (She slams door)

Narrator: Horrors! Wasn't that terrible? What important *principle* did the visitor forget? (Here entertain responses) Yes, the visitor was guilty of a common fault — INFLEXIBILITY. Just as no two doors look exactly alike, so no two doors will present the same situation. Visitors must be flexible, ready to meet any situation. Let's do it again; only this time, the right way.

B. Right:

(Visitor knocks on door, and a woman opens with same props as first time)

Visitor: Oh! It looks like you're really busy today!

Householder: You can say *that* again!

Visitor: I can appreciate your being busy, and I won't disturb you. I have something important to discuss with you. When will you be free to talk? Would four o'clock this afternoon be a better time?

Householder: Important? Well ... I guess you could come back about four o'clock this afternoon.

Visitor: Fine, I'll see you then. Good-bye.

Householder: (Remains in doorway, leans on mop and muses) Important? I wonder what that could be.

Narrator: Well, that's more like it! Now let's look at a different problem. See if you can detect the forgotten principle here. First, let's look at it incorrectly handled.

Situation No. 2

A. Wrong:

(Visitor approaches door as before and knocks. Woman householder appears)

Householder: Yes?

Visitor: How do you do? My name is Cuthbert Cobblestone. I'm from the new church that is being built on Baker Street. I'm visiting in this community today to get acquainted with our future neighbors, tell them something about our church, and what we believe.[4] May I come in?

Householder: Thanks anyway, but I've got my religion.

Visitor: Oh ... I see ... Uh ... Ah ... Well ... Good-bye.

---

[4]The words "and what we believe" are important; they make what you do later on ethically justifiable.

(Visitor walks off; woman closes door)

Narrator: Pretty sad! What was wrong here? What principle was forgotten? (Here entertain responses) Right, the principle here is: CONSIDER EVERY OBJECTION A CHALLENGE TO BE OVERCOME! He gave up far too easily. No salesman would do that. Let's see how we might overcome that argument.

B. Right:

Householder: Yes?

Visitor: (Here he repeats exact speech as above)

Householder: Thanks anyway, but I've got my religion.

Visitor: Oh, I see. Well, I'm certainly glad to meet you. It's good to meet someone who is really interested in religion. You'd be surprised how many people I've talked to who don't seem interested at all.

Householder: (In a tone already softened) Is that so?

Visitor: Definitely! I know *you especially* will be interested in hearing something about our new church. May I have a few minutes of your time?

Householder: (Somewhat hesitantly at first) Why yes, won't you come in?

(Visitor enters; door closes)

Narrator: Very nicely done! But what made the difference? The first visitor allowed the objection to become a barrier and gave up; the second one considered it a challenge, and *turned the objection itself into a stepping stone* by which he gained entrance. How did he convert a liability into an asset? Note this: write it down—and never forget it: *HE FOUND SOMETHING IN THE OBJECTION THAT HE COULD HONESTLY COMMEND.* This is very important. Now, let's consider one final situation.

Situation No. 3

A. Wrong:

(Visitor knocks at door as previously; a woman answers)

Householder: Yes?

Visitor: (Here he repeats exact speech as above)

Householder: I'm not interested. I go to the Catholic Church.

Visitor: That's a shame!

Householder: What do you mean, *Sir?*

Visitor: Just this. (Pointing and shaking finger at woman) The trouble with you Romanists is that you worship Mary and the saints instead of God. And that's not all ...

Householder: (Breaks in indignantly) Well! I've heard just about enough! (Slams door in his face)

Narrator: Well, he certainly deserved it! I don't have to point out to you that he lost *rapport* immediately by launching into an argument. His language, manner, and approach were all antagonistic. The Bible speaks of the "offense of the cross," but that is quite different from the offense of the visitor. Let's see one way that he could have dealt with this common problem.

B. Right:

(Visitor knocks at door; woman answers)

Householder: Yes?

Visitor: (Here he repeats same opening speech)

Householder: I'm not interested. I go to the Catholic Church.

Visitor: I see! I am certainly happy to meet someone with religious convictions. There are so *few* people who have any convictions today.

Householder: (With noticeably renewed interest) That's right.

Visitor: We are glad that the Vatican Council encouraged discussion between persons of all religions. I'd like to hear *your opinion* on one or two questions and *explain some of our beliefs.* May I come in for a moment?

Householder: Well ... I suppose it *would* be interesting. Come on in.

Visitor: Thank you. (He enters)

END

III. *Intermission*

Following the Illustration period there should be a brief five-minute intermission for the people to move about and talk—cookies and coffee might help. Call the group to order promptly at the end of the five minutes.

IV. *Inquiry*

The final twenty-five minutes should be reserved for questions and discussion as promised. Here the Leader should be prepared to answer any reasonable question about the program that may be asked. It is essential for him to have a thorough familiarization with all aspects of the program, and all of the materials.

HOW TO DO VISITATION EVANGELISM
(An Instruction Manual for Field Workers)

The How To Manual (Every visitor gets a copy)

Introduction

The need for evangelism is plain. Christ said "go"; few if any come seeking. Therefore, the gospel must be *taken* to them. Evangelism can be done *occasionally* (as the occasions arise or as individual Christians make them) or it may be done according to a *program*, by the members of a congregation. Either way we must go: Acts 8:4 says that "those who were scattered abroad *went* ...." The duty is also clear: Evangelism is not a special work for special persons to do at special times. It is not an *extra*, but a basic task of the whole church. The evangelism in Acts 8:4 was carried on by everyday, man-in-the-pew Christians (driven out of Jerusalem in the providence of God on an evangelistic mission). This is clear because Acts 8:1 indicates that all were scattered abroad *"except the apostles."* The leadership was not included in that first congregation-wide evangelism effort. Presenting the gospel is one thing that every Christian is capable of doing. Anyone who knows enough to be saved, knows enough to evangelize another. That is why this program carries the word *Everyone* in its title.

Purpose

This program has two goals (the same two set forth in Matthew 28:19, 20:

1. *Evangelism:* Witnessing to lost men and women for the purpose of discipling them to Christ through faith in Him. They must repent of their sin and believe the gospel (the gospel is summarized in I Corinthians 15:3, 4: "... that Christ died for our sins according to the Scriptures, that he was buried, and that he rose again on the third day according to the Scriptures"). The word *gospel* means "good news." Evangelizing is "announcing the message of good news" (Acts 8:4).
2. *Edification:* These disciples are to be brought into fellowship with the church, signifying and sealing their membership in that body by water baptism. In this fellowship they must be taught "to observe" (not merely to know) all the things that Christ "commanded." Some evangelistic programs neglect one of these two goals for the sake of the other. This should not be. The effort here is to emphasize both

properly. The visitor first goes to explain the gospel; afterwards, he confronts every convert with his obligation and need to unite with the church.

Preparation

Before each visitation check out these items:

1. Have I studied the Bible, marking key passages for use and memorizing the substance of the passages and the book and chapter in which they are located (do not bother to memorize verses or verse numbers)?
2. Have I prayed for the salvation of those to whom I shall go?
3. Is my own relationship to God what it should be?
4. Do I have my pen, Bible, tracts, publicity literature and V-cards?
5. Do I know exactly where I am going and what I intend to say?

Theory Of The Visit

Each visitor is assigned one *Field* consisting of a given number of houses for which he is responsible. Each house should be visited at the convenience of the visitor. Visits may be made at night or during the daytime. They may be made by one concentrated effort in one week, or throughout the seven-week period of the campaign. They should be completed by the expiration date. *But,* it is more important to do a thorough job than to visit the entire field. The idea is to cover a limited number of homes intensively. That is, we want to continue working in each home as long as possible. The emphasis is upon depth rather than breadth. One may visit alone, or with another, as he chooses.[5] In the latter case, where persons may wish to assist one another, such arrangements should be made informally, but one visitor must assume responsibility for a particular field. NH (not home) listings should be revisited until contact is made. If the field work must be abandoned before completion, contact and inform the elder or district supervisor immediately. V-cards should be filled in fully with special care. Unless the evaluation is clear and concise, the V-cards are of no help for the follow-up program.

Return calls are a very essential part of the program. Every effort must be made to arrange for them. If possible, set the date for sometime during the following week. Make certain to agree upon A DEFINITE

---

[5]There are certain advantages to solo visitation: More territory can be covered in less time, the householder does not feel "ganged up" upon, in a 1-to-1 encounter he is more likely to speak frankly (a third person always becomes an audience). There is, of course, an advantage to duet visitation: an inexperienced worker can be trained in this manner. This is the basic method for training new visitors: they should be discipled by experienced visitors. But visitors, when working together, must learn not to interrupt one another or divert any line of thought which is being pursued.

TIME AND DATE. On the Return Call, the gospel should be discussed more fully and if possible an endeavor may be made to help the householder to come to faith in Christ.

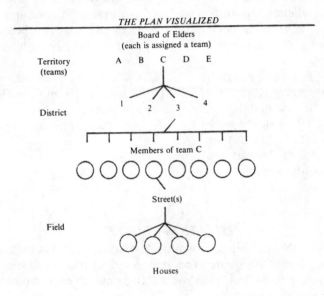

THE PLAN VISUALIZED

Board of Elders
(each is assigned a team)

Territory
(teams)

District

Members of team C

Street(s)

Field

Houses

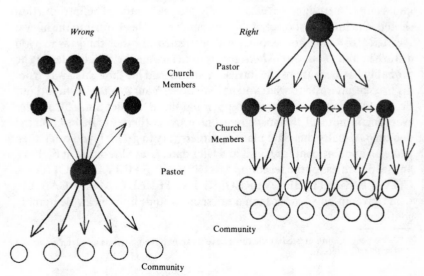

TWO PLANS OF EVANGELISM

Wrong

Right

Church
Members

Pastor

Church
Members

Pastor

Church
Members

Community

Community

According to the usual plan, the local church hires a minister to do its work of evangelism and edification. This is impossible. It is a full-time task to be pastor and teacher of the flock, and no one man can possibly hope to reach the multitudes himself. It is simply a mathematical absurdity. Truly, the pastor is "in the middle." In taking upon himself the work his congregation should do, a minister spreads himself too thinly and does neither his work nor theirs well.

According to the biblical plan, the pastor and teacher is just that. He instructs and inspires the congregation to assume its own evangelistic responsibility. In this way, the task becomes a mathematical possibility. This does not mean that as a Christian the pastor refuses to evangelize. He must be a leader and an example, but he is not a substitute for his congregation.

VISITATION PROPER

VISITATION itself is not very difficult. Getting started is the hardest part. If you prayerfully desire to assume your Christian responsibility to carry the gospel to the lost, soon you will find yourself enjoying the work and becoming adept at it.

Introducing yourself at the door. The first 30 seconds are most important. "Introduce" means literally "to lead into." The introduction should lead into the subject of your discussion and lead you into the house! REMEMBER: the householder was interested in other things when you disturbed him. Your *immediate goal* is to overcome the negative feeling he probably has because of the intrusion and to lead his thoughts away from his present interests to what you have to offer. Your *attitude* is important. Be positive; consider everyone a potential sheep. Smile! Smile! Consider everyone in need of the gospel until he proves otherwise. Be brief on the doorstep. Usually this is no place to witness. Try to get in. If you can't, then make an appointment for a visit at a later date. Leave literature at EVERY house, regardless of the reception.[6] CONSIDER EVERY OBJECTION A CHALLENGE TO BE OVERCOME TACTFULLY. MOST CAN BE. Don't give up any sooner than a salesman would. Look neat. Be humbly confident.

---

[6]Often people, uninterested at the time, have picked up the materials at a later point and read with real interest.

When the householder responds, introduce yourself (and any companion) by name. Say something like this, "How do you do? My name is John Jones. I am from Smithville Church, the NEW church that is being built on Baker Street. (Advertising studies prove that the word *new* is the most important word in selling appeal. People like to hear about something new. If you can do so honestly, work the word into the initial introduction.) I'm visiting in your community today to get acquainted with our future neighbors and to tell you something about our church *and what we believe* (be sure to add this phrase; it is the ethical justification for presenting the gospel). May I come in for a few moments? (At this point move toward the door expectantly.) If the campaign is conducted in an entirely new area, where there is no church yet established, the opening words might be: "How ... I represent the _____ Church. We are going to begin a NEW church in this community. I'm visiting . . . ," etc.

If the householder is busy, or circumstances indicate that a visit at this time would be inappropriate, say something like this: "I appreciate the fact that you are busy. So I don't want to disturb you. When may I return to talk to you?" Then, set a definite time and date, perhaps later on in the same day. Remember, NO TWO DOORS WILL BE THE SAME. Be flexible. (Here typical situations may be acted out.)[7]

NOW THAT YOU ARE IN,[8] what comes next? Upon entering, stand still until invited to take a seat. Be friendly. Relax! Tension causes barriers. Expect to have a good time and you probably will. Take a brief interest in the children or exchange some pleasantry. But do so sincerely, not hypocritically. If TV sound annoys, get it turned off diplomatically. Speak softly, so that the householder has difficulty hearing you and becomes aware that the TV is a hindrance. Don't waste time on small talk. Get down to business. Here is one way to begin:

"Our church is the _____ Church. (The name of your church may sound like an off-brand. Since you will have to tell him sooner or later that you are from this church, it is best to emphasize your liabilities from the beginning so that you may turn them to advantage. Otherwise the householder may use them to your disadvantage.) The reason that we use this name is not that there is anything strange about our church, but that unlike many churches today, we still believe the Bible to be the Word of God.

[7]See the brief skit describing ways of handling objections at the door in the *Leader's Manual.*

[8]In this section a fairly full presentation of the gospel is given. This presentation may be adapted to given situations. Scripture verses that teach each point are included; not all may (or should) be used in every presentation.

(That's enough on Liberalism for now; you'll have a much better occasion to deal with it in detail in the H.B.S.[9] course under the doctrine of the church.)

"For instance, we believe the Bible when it says that 'all have sinned and come short of the glory of God' (Romans 3:23—you can probably quote this from memory—but don't! Read it from your Bible, so that the householder may see that it actually comes from God's Word). That includes you and me, as well as everyone else. It also tells us that heaven is an absolutely holy place from which all sin is excluded. Sin is breaking God's laws. Therefore, it is an offense against God himself. We have all sinned and this puts us in a difficult position with God. Sin would 'defile' heaven, and God says He will not allow this (read Revelation 21:27a). This means, that, because of our sin, none of us can go to heaven. Furthermore the Bible says that He will punish sinners in hell (Matthew 25:46). I am sure that you don't want to go to hell and that you want to go to heaven, don't you? (Often it is helpful to ask questions which you suspect the hearer will answer affirmatively. This tends to create a more favorable atmosphere for conversation.) Well, that's one reason why God gave us the Bible—to explain how people can get to heaven in spite of their sin (II Timothy 3:15). The Bible is a record about Christ. It tells how He came into the world to solve the problem of sin. (Here you may read Matthew 1:21 to confirm your statement.) Christ solves the problem of sin by taking man's guilt and punishment upon Himself. When He died on the cross, He was dying in the place of sinners. He became their substitute (I Corinthians 15:3 is one among many texts that prove this). The Bible says that every one who believes that Christ died for his sins and rose from the dead will be saved from hell and go to heaven. His sins will be forgiven, and his faith will be counted for righteousness (Romans 10:9 and other verses in Romans are good here).

"It is not doing good works, joining a church or going through ceremonies that makes a person fit for heaven. Only the death and resurrection of Christ can do that. When I became a Christian, all that I could or needed to do was to trust in what He did for me. (Here, you give your own witness to what Christ has done for you. At this point Ephesians 2:8,9 may be useful.) In the Gospel of John (Saint John, if you are speaking to a Roman Catholic) the word *believe* occurs over 90 times. Faith is the one thing that God requires. To believe (or have faith) means to *depend* upon what Christ has done. I wonder if *you* have ever understood and

---

[9]H.B.S. = Home Bible Study.

believed this message before?" (Be sure to end on a question of this sort which will lead the householder to express himself in such a way that you may determine what he thinks and thus what to say next.)

From this point on, the discussion (which, by the way, *YOU should be directing* to the goals that *you* have in view) may take almost any turn.[10] Ask enough questions that you may find out exactly what the person believes will get him to heaven, so that you may dispel all false notions and show how this comes through dependence upon the work of Christ alone. Don't overtalk. Ask questions until you think you know enough to see clearly what the householder's problems are. Do not turn off the householder by your questions or remarks. Try to avoid unnecessary argumentation; instead *discuss* points. Stick closely to the main questions of sin, hell, heaven, and salvation through the gospel of Christ. Close the discussion with prayer when appropriate. If the householder seems open, lead him to trust Christ as Savior by praying a simple prayer that you may word for him. Do not push too hard on this initial visit. Especially do not try to push anyone into a decision to believe; let others indicate to you when they are ready to do so. It is important to maintain good relations so that you may return a second time.

Most persons are not ready to believe on the first visit. Go as far as you can in the discussion but no further. Become sensitive to people. Flexibility means that you may not be able to say and do all that is suggested here. Learn how to adapt to each situation.

Arranging for the return call. Regardless of the response to the initial visit, your major goal at this point is to arrange for the Return Call. Future contacts will depend upon success or failure here.

You will have with you three distinct pieces of visitation literature: Several copies of "The _____ Church Invites You ...,"[11] the "Inserts,"[12] and one sample copy of the H.B.S. Workbook.[13] This literature is designed as an aid to assist you in arranging for Return Calls. Learn to use it skillfully.

---

[10]Sometimes the householder will raise a large question. It is often advantageous to withhold an immediate reply and say instead, "I'd like to discuss that with you next time." If you have been asked a question you honestly cannot answer, be glad. Admit you do not know the answer (this creates respect) *and then* promise: "I'll find out and let you know." Either way you have paved a second path to the householder's door for the RETURN CALL.

[11]Each congregation should produce a pamphlet for this purpose describing its location, phone number, services, beliefs, etc., and on the back containing a gospel presentation. The title of this may be "The_____ Church Invites You. . . ." The pamphlet should be slightly smaller than the colored insert that protrudes from it.

[12]See *infra.*

[13]See *infra.*

Throughout the visit, you have had in your hand the brochure "The _____ Church Invites" (hereafter designated "Tract"), with a "Can You Answer These Questions?" insert (hereafter designated "Insert") inside. You have *not* yet handed it to the householder. Now is the time to do so— but only after an explanation something like that which follows:

I've enjoyed our visit, but I promised not to take much of your time, so I should be going now. Before I do, however, I'd like to leave a couple of pieces of literature with you. This one (holding up the Tract) tells a little bit more about our Church. On the back it has some of the Bible verses about which I have been speaking in case you should care to look them up for yourself. This other piece (removing the colorful Insert for the first time— the surprise element creates new interest) explains about a free 6-week Home Bible Study course that we offer without obligation. (Here hand them both to the householder. Immediately reach into your briefcase, large handbag, etc., and for the first time produce the attractive H.B.S. *Workbook*.) As the insert says, the course includes private instruction in your own home and free workbooks like this. (Hold it up, but do *not* pass it over to the householder to look at closely. Put it away quickly and proceed.) I am sure you'll want to take time to read this material and talk it over with your husband/wife (or together) before you decide. Would this same hour next Tuesday be the best time for me to drop in and find out what you've decided? (*Assume* that you are coming back. Put the stress on *WHEN* you may do so. Be sure to settle upon a definite day and hour. With a very brief pleasantry of some sort leave as soon as possible. When you get into your car be sure to record the exact time arranged for the Return Call in the appropriate place on the V-card, with an initial evaluation. Pray silently for God's continued blessing upon your visit. Do not be discouraged if you are not always able to arrange for a Return Call. But be sure that you have made every legitimate effort to do so. Commit the household to God in prayer. Do not give up easily. *The Return Call is crucial for future contact.*)

Making the return call. Entering this time should be easy. You already know the householder and an appointment has been made. However, you may find that sometimes the householder has forgotten about it. Don't let this disturb you. If he is not home, leave a note and cheerfully call again as soon as possible. (Do all that you can to relieve him of any embarrassment this may have caused.) Other exigencies may be handled by the principles set forth earlier.

The twofold purpose of the Return Call is: (1) to talk further about salvation in Christ — but again only as fully as you sense would be appropriate; (2) to arrange for an H.B.S. Make this your fundamental aim, for whenever an H.B.S. is set up it provides at least six additional opportunities to speak about Christ. Discussion of the H.B.S. flows naturally from a question about the literature that you left on the first visit: "What did you think of the pamphlets I left? There were some rather interesting questions on this insert, weren't there?" It would be wise to carry additional copies in case your householder has lost or misplaced or thrown his away. Assume that he has read it, but keep him from the embarrassment of having to admit that he didn't. You may do this by immediately reading some of the questions on the Insert to "refresh" his mind, *before* you allow him to answer your question.

If it appears that it will be possible to establish an H.B.S., it is probably wise to do so immediately (again by arranging for a definite time and date) and depart as soon as possible.

Where the householder appears hesitant, encourage him by stressing additional advantages of such a study and by disclosing new facts. It may even be advisable at this point to take out the Workbook once more and point out a section or two in the first or second lesson that you think may arouse interest. Think positively: assume that he will agree to an H.B.S. After additional discussion, make what the salesman calls a second "close." Ask *when* (not whether) he would like to have the H.B.S. Successful salesmen know that objections are not always real and that people often like to be "sold" and sometimes need help in making good decisions. Offer all the genuine help and encouragement you can without employing questionable or unethical "hard sell" techniques.

If it appears that you are likely to receive a definite "no," try two more approaches: (1) Attempt to forestall that kind of a "no" by suggesting that perhaps the householder is not yet fully prepared to make a decision and should take another week or so to decide (and possibly to talk it over with another person). You may even suggest leaving the H.B.S. Workbook for a week so that the family may glance over it. (Indicate, of course, that you will return to pick it up. This will give you—like the Fuller Brush man— another reason for coming again at a time when it is possible that the householder will be in a different frame of mind.) (2) If that approach and all others fail, stay as long as is polite and present the gospel again as fully as possible with an exhortation to believe.

Once an H.B.S. date and time is arranged, *immediately* contact your team captain and/or H.B.S. teacher and give him (them) all pertinent information. The teacher should immediately send a personal letter (or phone the householder) confirming the time and place and introducing himself by name. The letter is often more effective, because it does not give as ready an opportunity as the phone for a change of mind. The first day of the study, the visitor who arranged the study should accompany and introduce the teacher.

Note: This manual should be used in conjunction with the rest of the materials in the Visitation Evangelism Packet. This method depends upon the functioning of the entire program as a unit. The manual should be given out at the time of instruction and demonstration of techniques, as provided for in the *Leader's Manual*. Discussion of questions and problems is necessary as well.

The Teacher's Guide

The Teacher's Guide to the *Workbook* and teaching of the Home Bible Study Course, *Cardinal Doctrines*.

Preparation

A. The teacher should read the ENTIRE course through, looking up all references, studying and understanding their relationship to the doctrine under discussion and underlining them in his Bible.

B. The teacher should fill in all correct answers to study assignments in his copy of the *Workbook*.

C. The teacher should make any necessary notes on his copy of the *Workbook*.

D. The teacher should pray for his students daily.

Teaching

A. The teaching period ordinarily should be one hour long. Make this a rule of thumb. With a peculiarly responsive group, perhaps 1½ hours will be better.

B. This hour should be divided into three parts:

1. Fifteen minutes for reading and discussing the answers to last week's assignment. The first week this time may be used to explain the *Workbook* and its use.

2. Twenty minutes teaching this week's lesson.

3. Twenty-five minutes for discussion of the lesson. (The last two
items may vary according to the circumstances, but ample time
should be given to both teaching and discussion.)

Particular Points to Stress

A. SALVATION. Every lesson has within it opportunities to stress
salvation. Note these and use them. Thus there are a number of built-
in opportunities to lead the student to faith in Christ somewhere
during the series of studies. The answers to the third question in the
third lesson and the concluding questions in the sixth lesson are
designed to help you determine whether the student has yet come to
faith in Christ. The length of the discussion period (among other
things) is arranged to give opportunity to engage the student in
personal discussion about his salvation.

B. BAPTISM. While one must take care to emphasize that baptism
does not save, upbaptized persons who become converts should be
urged to obey the scriptural injunctions to be baptized.

C. CHURCH MEMBERSHIP. The series of studies should begin
without mention of this matter. As it progresses, however, and the
teacher begins to win confidence, the *Workbook* raises the question
in the fifth (the next to last) week. At this point, and not before, the
matter of Liberalism and the challenge of biblical Christianity
should be presented. The questions to be answered on the sixth
week also raise the discussion. During the last two weeks your
students may be invited to attend your church services, if they have
not done so previously.

D. SPECIAL PROBLEMS. Matters of special concern to the
householder that lie within the scope of the *Cardinal Doctrines*
course, should be discussed if the student raises them. Matters
beyond this scope should be deferred to a later time, when they can
be considered in a second course. The teacher can help create lasting
interest if he confines his discussion to the *Cardinal Doctrines,*
always indicating that there will be opportunity to discuss these
other matters after the course is completed. The doctrinal material
given is minimal and looks forward to much more in greater depth
at a later point.

Miscellaneous

If questions are asked that the teacher cannot answer, he should admit it honestly, and promise to find out the answer for next week. If he cannot obtain the answer on his own, he should contact his elder or his pastor about it. It is always wrong to try to "cover up" by giving some conjecture for an answer. The student will have more respect for the honest teacher. In teaching, explain everything; assume nothing. But do not move too rapidly in seeking to convert students; no one can believe until God has made him ready. Your responsibility is to present the gospel plainly and persuasively; it is God's part to work faith in him.

H.B.S. literature, left on the first visit, should be discussed, and during the return call a time and place for the beginning of an H.B.S. should be scheduled. This should be attempted whether the householder has professed faith in Christ or not. The visitor should be prepared to commit the H.B.S. teacher to a definite date and time for the beginning of the class. This calls for prearrangement and subsequent contact with the teacher. If a H.B.S. is refused, try to arrange for another Return Call. Where it is possible, H.B.S. courses may be given for several families in a neighborhood at the same time in a conveniently located home.

The Program in Brief

1. INITIAL VISIT — Short gospel explanation (unless obvious opportunity for witness in depth is available); arrange definite time and place for return call; leave publicity and H.B.S. literature ("I shall return to discuss this with you when you have had an opportunity to read it").
2. RETURN CALL — Longer visit; discuss need for and way of salvation in depth. Mention H.B.S. literature; arrange definite time and date for H.B.S.
3. HOME BIBLE STUDY — A six-week course in the *Cardinal Doctrines of Christianity*. They are: The Doctrine of Scripture, God, Man, Salvation, Church, Future.

N.B. You can see that this program does not call for surveys or a mere invitation to attend the _____ Church. Nor does it seek to win souls to Christ, then leave them. It endeavors to fulfill both of Christ's commands in Matthew 28 and thus avoid the pitfalls of many systems. APART FROM A DETERMINED EFFORT TO FOLLOW *BOTH*

PARTS OF THE PLAN, IT WILL BE FOUND INEFFECTIVE. A fundamental thesis is that it takes time and instruction to win men to Christ and to establish them firmly in the faith. Workers must count the cost.

SECONDARY APPROACHES

It was said earlier that the Visitation Evangelism campaign was a unit. No parts were to be dropped from it. Yet, this does not mean that other Home Bible study programs cannot be effective. One simple, straightforward method that has proved successful in actual experience is for members to invite friends and neighbors to a projected Bible study at their home. This can often be conducted in a very congenial atmosphere over coffee and doughnuts. Sometimes it is wise to relax the one-hour rule under these circumstances.

Unchurched parents of Sunday School or Vacation Bible School pupils (or Pioneer Girls or Boys' Brigade) also may be invited to a Home Bible Study. In the course of extending the invitation to participate you may suggest: "We know your child is learning a good bit about the Bible at Sunday School (V.B.S.). Undoubtedly he will have questions. He may have asked you some real stumpers already. Some of these questions will be along these lines (hand the *Insert* to the parent). We think that it is important to help parents to know the answers to these questions so that home and church together can influence Johnnie in the right direction. So our church is offering a Home Bible Study Course for parents ...."

If fall and spring V.E. - H.B.S. campaigns are scheduled, it may be well to use the secondary approaches during the winter when it is difficult to visit door-to-door. And members of the congregation or the minister may also use the Home Bible Study program for a wide variety of particular needs and opportunities available to your congregation. Be creative.

The Student's Workbook

First Week: THE DOCTRINE OF THE SCRIPTURES

A. Revelation ("uncovering")

1. For men to know God, He must reveal Himself.

2. He has done so in two ways:

a. *General Revelation*—through creation (Psalm 19:1-6). Creation reveals to all men that there is a Creator, and that we are sinners against Him without excuse (Romans 1:20), but does not tell us how to be freed from sin. Sin blinds men to the message of general revelation (I Cor.22), so we need—

b. *Special Revelation*—through the Bible (Psalm 19:7-11). The "law." (Scripture) imparts truth that can "convert the soul" (v. 7). See also II Timothy 3:15. It contains "all things that pertain to life and godliness" (II Peter 1:3), so that Christians may be "thoroughly furnished unto every good work" (II Timothy 3:17). General revelation may be understood only through special revelation.

B. The Bible (this word means "book").

1. Is inspired in the original Hebrew and Greek languages (Old and New Testaments respectively).

a. "Inspired" means "God-breathed" (II Timothy 3:17). This means its words are as truly God's as if He actually breathed them out in audible speech.

b. Note: the writers were "moved" (II Peter 1:21) and their writings "inspired."

c. The Bible is the inspired words of God given through men.

d. Inspiration assures us that the Bible is true and inerrant (cf. Psalm 119:140).

2. The Bible is the standard of faith and practice. That means it is the rule by which we determine what to believe and do.

3. Scores of prophecies, given hundreds of years before an event, concerning minute details, and fulfilled exactly, confirm the truth that the Bible is from God. Here are three examples: cf. Micah 5:2 with Matthew 2:1; Zechariah 9:9 with Matthew 21:1-5; Psalm 22:16 with Luke 23:33, John 20:25, Zechariah 12:10.[1]

---

[1] Other passages for study might include Genesis 49:10; Psalm 2; 22:7, 8, 18, 27; 110:1-4; Daniel 9:24-27.

STUDY ASSIGNMENT *This Week:* Study II Timothy 3:15-17 and list four ways in which Scripture is profitable
1........................ 2........................ 3........................ 4........................
Consider: Have YOU been made "wise unto salvation"? Yes..... No.....
Next Week: List any questions you wish to ask. Make it a rule to study part of the Bible every day, beginning with the gospel of John, then Romans, then Acts, then Galatians, then Luke, then the rest of the New Testament.

Second Week: THE DOCTRINE OF GOD

A. The Existence of God and Atheism.
    1. An atheist is literally "one without God," but popularly it means "one who says there is no God."
    2. God's estimate of an atheist: Psalm 14:1.
        a. God never makes charges lightly, without reasons.
        b. A fool speaks beyond his knowledge. No one knows enough to say there is no God. To say there is no God, one must be capable of being everywhere at the same time. Otherwise God may be where he is not. To do this one would have to *be* God. A fool speaks against all the evidence (fulfilled prophecy, abundant testimony, the Bible, etc.).
 B. The Knowledge of God and Agnosticism (literally, "ignorance").
    1. Two kinds of doubters: honest and dishonest.
    2. Dishonest men enjoy their doubts; honest men are pained by them. The latter are really seekers to whom God will give the truth (John 7:17).
C. The Nature of God and Theism (belief in God).
    1. It is not enough to "believe in God" (James 2:19). It must be the true God.
    2. Kinds of theism people believe in:
        a. Polytheism ("many gods")—Greeks, Romans, Mormons.
        b. Pantheism ("God is all")—Buddhism, Christian Science.
        c. Unitarianism ("one God")—Jews, Mohammedans.
        d. Trinitarianism ("one God Who is three Persons: Father, Son and Holy Spirit")—Christians.
    3. As Father God planned salvation; as Son He came to earth to effect it; as Spirit He applies it to individuals.
D. The Attributes of God.
    1. God is a Spirit (John 4:24)—A spirit is a person without a body.

2. God is infinite ("no bounds")—Psalm 147:5.

 a. As to presence—omnipresent ("present everywhere at once").

 b. As to knowledge—omniscient ("all-knowing").

 c. As to power—omnipotent ("all-powerful"—God can do anything He wants to do).

3. God is eternal—always has been and always will exist (Psalm 90:2).

4. God is immutable ("unchangeable")—James 1:17.

 a. As to person—love, mercy, justice, holiness, wrath.

 b. As to purpose—promises and commands remain the same.

5. God is sovereign—everything is under His control and happens according to His purpose.

STUDY ASSIGNMENT *This Week:* Study Matthew 28:19; II Corinthians 13:14 and Titus 1:4. It would be blasphemous for the names of any persons less than equals thus to be linked with God, the Father. How do Acts 5:3,4 prove the Holy Spirit is God?
....

Next Week: Study Genesis 2:7. Of what two elements was man made?........ and.........According to Genesis 3:1-21, what happened to man?........ .... How does this affect us?...............

Third Week: THE DOCTRINE OF MAN

A. Man Before the Fall.

 1. Creation of: created "very good"' (Genesis 1:31) in God's "image" (Genesis 1:26)—this image is not physical, because God has no body, but spiritual, intellectual and moral (cf. Colossians 3:10; Ephesians 4:24).

 2. Nature of: Man has a physical and non-physical element (Genesis 2:7; James 2:26); Man IS a soul and HAS a body.

 3. Duties of: To glorify God (Revelation 4:11); rule over the earth (Genesis 1:26); beget children (Genesis 1:28); work (Genesis 2:15—but not *labor* until fall).

B. Man After the Fall.

 1. Consequences — shame (Genesis 3:7, 10); separation (Genesis 3:8); sentence of death (Genesis 2:17).

 2. Life and death summarized:

	LIFE (union)	DEATH (separation)
Physical	Body + Soul	Body — Soul
Spiritual	Soul + God (1 John 5:20; Romans 6:11)	Soul — God (Genesis 2:17; Ephesians 2:1)
Eternal	Body + Soul + God (John 5:24,25; 1 Thessalonians 4:13-17)	Body + Soul — God (Revelation 20:14; 2 Thessalonians 1:9)

All have physical life; all who have spiritual life will have eternal life too. Do you have spiritual life? eternal life?

C. Sin is fundamentally "lawlessness" (I John 3:4).

1. Two aspects: (a) original sin. All are born with a sinful nature (Psalm 51:5; Romans 5:12). Adam's representative act brought guilt and corruption upon all. (b) actual sin (Romans 3:23).

2. Two ways of sinning: doing what the law prohibits; not doing what the law commands.

3. Forgiveness of sin.

a. Sin is rebellion against God (Psalm 51:4), and therefore forgiveness must come from Him.

b. Forgiveness is through Christ alone (Ephesians 1:7).

c. This forgiveness comes when a sinner puts faith in Christ as Savior (Acts 26:18).

STUDY ASSIGNMENT *This Week:* Do you consider yourself a sinner? ....Study Revelation 21:27. Do you think your sins would defile heaven, and keep you from going there unless forgiven? Yes........ No........ Are they forgiven? Yes........ No........ *Next Week:* Read Matthew 27:24-54. Why did Christ die?...

Fourth Week: THE DOCTRINE OF SALVATION

A. Need for Salvation. Last week's study showed how sin keeps men from heaven, and sends them to eternal death in hell. This is man's dilemma: How to be saved ("rescued") from hell to go to heaven. Salvation is from sin and its consequences.

B. False Ways of Salvation (Proverbs 14:12):

1. Good works (trying to do the best you can, or attempting to keep the Ten Commandments, etc.)—Ephesians 2:8,9.

2. Water baptism (or other outward ceremonies): I Peter 3:21 makes it clear that it is the internal reality and not the external ritual that saves.

C. Salvation from Sin by Christ Alone:

1. Christ came to save sinners (I Timothy 1:15): God takes the initiative in salvation.

2. Salvation by faith in Christ—in His substitutionary and penal death for our sins (I Peter 2:24) and His bodily resurrection from the dead (I Cor. 15:4).

D. Salvation has three phases (whoever has been justified is now being sanctified and at death will be glorified).

JUSTIFICATION (a past act)	SANCTIFICATION (a present process)	GLORIFICATION (a prospective act)
We have been saved	are being saved	will be saved
from the penalty of sin	the power of sin	the presence of sin

E. Assurance of Salvation. God would be a heartless Father, if He failed to let His children know they are His. He wants us to know it when we are saved (I John 5:11). We know, because He has gone on record in the Bible. It is not arrogant to say you *know* you will go to heaven, because this salvation is Christ's work, not yours.

F. Permanence of Salvation. There are only two places where anything could go wrong with salvation: with the inheritance or the heir. But God has protected both (I Peter 1:3-5). See also Romans 8:35-39; John 10:28, 29; 17:12. Once saved, one can never be lost. God sees to it that all who are saved persevere to the end.

STUDY ASSIGNMENT *This Week:* Have you been saved? Yes...... No.... Uncertain..... Do good works have anything at all to do with getting to heaven? Do they help? Yes..... No..... Why?..... .... Why is it not presumptuous for a Christian to say he knows he is saved?...................... .... If when once saved, we can never be lost, can we then sin as we please? ....
Next Week: Read Matthew 16:18. What church is this?

Fifth Week: THE DOCTRINE OF THE CHURCH

A. Meaning of the word "church" (in the Bible this word never refers to a building).

   1. The Greek word means "assembly of called-out ones."

   2. The church is God's people whom He has called out from the world to transact His business.

B. The Church has two aspects: Invisibility and Visibility.

   1. Invisible Church—is the body of Christ; composed of all who have been saved. There is no salvation outside of it (cf. Ephesians 5:23-27).

   2. Visible Church—mirrors the invisible; though membership is not necessary for salvation, God commands membership in it (Hebrews 10:25; 13:7). Composed of all who make a profession of faith and their children.

C. The Organization of the Church.

   1. Christ is Head. He exercises His lordship through men whom the Bible terms "elders." "Elder" occurs over 100 times in the Old Testament (see Numbers 11:16; I Samuel 8:4,5; Ezra 10:8). In the New Testament: Luke 22:66; I Timothy 3:1-7; 5:17; Titus 1:5-7; and Acts 20:17,28. "Elder" and "bishop" are used synonymously in the last two references. "Elder" speaks of his qualifications—maturity in the faith. "Bishop" speaks of his work (it means "overseer").

   2. Congregations were not independent. They were bound together, and elders from the churches made decisions that affected the whole church (Acts 15:6; 16:4,5).

D. Not all churches teach the truth (II Peter 2:1,2).

   1. Christ and the apostles predicted false teachers would come into the visible church (Matthew 24:11; Acts 20:29,30).

   2. Christians should separate from them (II Corinthians 6:14-7:1; I Timothy 6:3-5), as the apostles separated from paganism and the apostate Jewish church of their day.

E. Sacraments.

   1. Water baptism—commanded by Christ (Matthew 28:19,20). By sprinkling or pouring (cf. Acts 1:5 with Acts 2:3,17,18,33—where the mode that the word expresses is shown: "poured"); never by immersion. Water baptism pictures the inward baptism of the Holy Spirit who is poured upon those who are regenerated (Romans 8:9, I Cor. 12:13). It depicts union with Christ and all that this entails (Romans 6:3-5).

   2. The Lord's Supper—I Corinthians 11:23-27; a remembrance and a witness; not a sacrifice. Christ is present spiritually (not physically) to bless those who partake in faith.

STUDY ASSIGNMENT *This Week:* Are you a member of the invisible Church? Yes........ No........ Are you a member of a Biblical church? Yes........ No........ If not, what should you do?...
Next Week: Read Luke 16:19-31, and consider what happens when we die. Are you prepared to die? Yes........ No........

Sixth Week: THE DOCTRINE OF THE FUTURE

A. The Intermediate State (between death and resurrection of the body).

1. Death—the separation of the spirit from the body (James 2:26).
2. After death—conscious existence in joy or suffering (Luke 16:19-31).
3. Believers go to be "with Christ" (Philippians 1:23), Who is in heaven (Colossians 3:1). This is gain (Philippians 1:21).

B. Christ will return (Acts 1:11). This is called the "Second Coming of Christ."

1. His return is yet future.
2. He is coming personally (Acts 1:11).
3. At His return living Christians will be "changed" — their bodies will become immortal and incorruptible (I Corinthians 15:52)—and "caught up together" with dead Christians whose bodies will be raised (I Thessalonians 4:16, 17).
4. The time of this return is unknown (I Thessalonians 5:1).
5. Unbelievers will receive the wrath of God (I Thessalonians 5:3-9; II Thessalonians 1:6-10).

C. The Eternal State.

1. Christ will send some into everlasting punishment, and others into everlasting life (Matthew 25:46).
2. Compare also the following: John 14:2,3; Revelation 20:15; 21:4,5.
3. Remember: Christ is the only way to heaven (John 14:6).

WHAT NEXT? It has been a privilege to meet and study God's Word with you these six weeks. By this time you should be able to answer the following questions. If you can't or if you are not sure about any of them, ask your instructor. 1. Have you been saved? This is the primary question. 2. Have you been baptized? 3. Do you belong to a Biblical church?

This booklet was presented to:

_____

By the _____ church

_____

The Visitation Materials

1. The Insert

CAN YOU ANSWER THESE QUESTIONS?

What happens when we die?

What is the purpose of life?

Is the Bible full of mistakes?

Will the world be destroyed by missile warfare?

What is God like?

Why did Jesus Christ die?

Is there a heaven or hell?

IF YOU CANNOT, YOU NEED TO STUDY YOUR BIBLE.

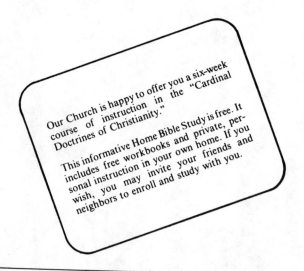

Our Church is happy to offer you a six-week course of instruction in the "Cardinal Doctrines of Christianity."

This informative Home Bible Study is free. It includes free workbooks and private, personal instruction in your own home. If you wish, you may invite your friends and neighbors to enroll and study with you.

2. Visitation Record Card (V-Card)

Front

V-CARD

FAMILY NAME_____ PHONE_____

ADDRESS _____

Husband's first name_____Wife's_____

	Children's names	ages
Church affil._____		
Territory_____		
District_____		

Date of INITIAL visit_____ Response (NH, G, P[1])_____

RETURN CALL arranged for: Date_____Time_____

H. B. S. arranged for: Date_____Time_____

EVALUATION:

Visitor's Name_____

Reverse

H. B. S. REPORT

Week	Attend.	Assgmnt.	Salv.	Other
1				
2				
3				
4				
5				
6				

BAPT.?_____ CH. MBRSHP.?_____

COMMENTS:

Teacher_____

[1]NH = Not Home, G = Good, P = Poor.

APPENDIX B

CHECK LIST

TEN PROBLEMS PREVALENT IN CONSERVATIVE CHURCHES

1. Families torn apart by too many meetings, emphasis upon crowds.

2. Lack of biblical priorities; wrong view of church, what constitutes "God's work," etc.

3. Pastors trying to do work that the people should do, contrary to Ephesians 4:11,12.

4. Abstract and impractical use of the Scriptures in preaching, counseling, teaching and administration; people bored, frustrated in attempts to effect change.

5. Fear of the world (science, etc.); result: a professionalism that sells the Scriptures short.

6. Failure to emphasize discipline, structure and scheduling; sloppiness.

7. Failure to exercise Church discipline; weakness.

8. Resistance to biblically-induced change; rebellion spreading.

9. Lack of fellowship among members; hunger and dissatisfaction.

10. Unresolved personal difficulties in families and among members; loss of joy.

Procedure:

a. Rate your Church on each problem. (Good, fair, poor)

b. Then ask, "What are we doing about these problems?" (answer: significant effort being made, little being done, nothing)

c. Determine what should be done about each.

d. Be sure to do all of this on paper. Check your results with your elders. You might first ask them to rate the church as you have before comparing results.

APPENDIX C
THE FIVE-YEAR PLAN

In the following pages adequate space has been left to draw up five five-year plans. For each there is a Worksheet and a year-by-year Program Planner. Programs, for different churches, kept in this same place will prove valuable for future references when drawing up new ones.

Plan One

Worksheet

I. Items in the present church program that do not foster worship, edification or evangelism:

Item	Eliminate altogether (state reason why)	Alter or revise (state how)

II. Items missing from
the present church
program that would
foster worship, edifica-
tion or evangelism:

Item	How to introduce it (describe place in program and process for bringing about the change)	Difficulties likely to be encountered in making the change and how to overcome them

Program Planner

Five-Year Plan

Years:_____ to _____	Eliminate	Introduce	Record of actual out-come (yes, no, date)
Changes			
First Year			
Second Year			
Third Year			
Fourth Year			
Fifth Year			

Plan Two

Worksheet

I. Items in the present church program that do not foster worship, edification or evangelism:

Item	Eliminate altogether (state reason why)	Alter or revise (state how)

II. Items missing from
the present church
program that would
foster worship, edifica-
tion or evangelism:

Item	How to introduce it (describe place in program and process for bringing about the change)	Difficulties likely to be encountered in making the change and how to overcome them

Program Planner

Five-Year Plan

Years:____ to ____	Eliminate	Introduce	Record of actual outcome (yes, no, date)
Changes			
First Year			
Second Year			
Third Year			
Fourth Year			
Fifth Year			

Plan Three

Worksheet

I. Items in the present church program that do not foster worship, edification or evangelism:

Item	Eliminate altogether (state reason why)	Alter or revise (state how)

II. Items missing from the present church program that would foster worship, edification or evangelism:

Item	How to introduce it (describe place in program and process for bringing about the change)	Difficulties likely to be encountered in making the change and how to overcome them

Program Planner

Five-Year Plan

			Record of actual outcome (yes, no, date)
Years:_____ to _____	Eliminate	Introduce	
Changes			
First Year			
Second Year			
Third Year			
Fourth Year			
Fifth Year			

Plan Four

Worksheet

I. Items in the present church program that do not foster worship, edification or evangelism:

Item	Eliminate altogether (state reason why)	Alter or revise (state how)

II. Items missing from
the present church
program that would
foster worship, edifica-
tion or evangelism:

Item	How to introduce it (describe place in program and process for bringing about the change)	Difficulties likely to be encountered in making the change and how to overcome them

Program Planner

Five-Year Plan

Years:____ to ____	Eliminate	Introduce	Record of actual outcome (yes, no, date)
Changes			
First Year			
Second Year			
Third Year			
Fourth Year			
Fifth Year			

Plan Five

Worksheet

I. Items in the present church program that do not foster worship, edification or evangelism:

Item	Eliminate altogether (state reason why)	Alter or revise (state how)

II. Items missing from the present church program that would foster worship, edification or evangelism:

Item	How to introduce it (describe place in program and process for bringing about the change)	Difficulties likely to be encountered in making the change and how to overcome them

Program Planner

Five-Year Plan

			Record of actual outcome (yes, no, date)
Years:____ to ____	Eliminate	Introduce	
Changes			
First Year			
Second Year			
Third Year			
Fourth Year			
Fifth Year			

SCRIPTURE INDEX

INDEX

Ability to tasks, matching, 403
About Behaviorism (Skinner), 170
Adequacy in communication, importance of, 384-386
Adjustments in old age, 267-270
Administration. *See* Management of the church
Age as barrier between pastor and elders, 363-364
Agnosticism, 491
Alteration in schedule, 46-47, 53
American Management Association, 335
Analysis, Freudian, 162-163
Anger, 387
Announcements, 393
Anticipation response, 144
Apostolic gifts, 398-399
Appearance, physical: of minister, 21; of church building, 448, 450
Application of Bible to daily life, need for, 89, 108, 237, 280, 282, 370, 424, 426, 438
Appreciation for good work, 421-422
Apprenticeship program, 420
Approach to counselees, proper, 227-230, 292-293
Architecture, church, 447-448
Arteriosclerosis, 258 n. 10
Art in the Bible, 18-19 n. 1
Atheism, 491
Attendance records, 394 n. 4
Attitude: toward death, 137-138; in communication, 381 n. 3
Attitude (Visitation Evangelism), 480
Attributes of God, 491-492
Audio-visual equipment, 395, 443
Authority, minister's, 263-264
Authority of God versus authority of men, 122 n. 7, 133

Authority structure of the church, 328-332, 417-418

Baldinger, A. H., 91
Baptism, 274-275, 477, 487, 494; water, 495
Barnabas, 108
Behaviorism, 163-165
Believer and unbeliever, question of marrying, 236, 240 n. 11, 242
Believers for marriage, qualifying, 242-243
Beyond Freedom and Dignity (Skinner), 170
Bible, doctrine of the, 490
Bible as counseling textbook and standard, 185, 215-216, 220-223
Bible reading: during house calls, 89-90; in visiting the sick, 118-119
Bible School movement, 427-428
Birth control, 250
Bishop, 8, 495
Body, care of the, 18, 20-21, 51-52, 150, 185 n. 2
Book Club, 443
Books, the minister's interest in, 26, 304
Brainerd, David, 52
Breakdowns in communication, the pastor's task to reconcile, 387-388
Brooks, Hal, 167
Buildings, church, 447-450
Bulletin, 393
Bulletin board, 394-395, 442
Burdens of authority, 418
Business models for church government, adopting, 333-336
By-laws of organizations, 419

Calendar, monthly, 385 n. 11, 393
Call, unmade, 47-48, 90, 112